APPROACHES TO COGNITION:
Contrasts and Controversies

APPROACHES TO COGNITION:
Contrasts and Controversies

Edited by

TERRY J. KNAPP

University of Nevada, Las Vegas

LYNN C. ROBERTSON

Veterans Administration Medical Center, Martinez, California
and
University of California, Davis, School of Medicine

LEA LAWRENCE ERLBAUM ASSOCIATES, PUBLISHERS
1986   Hillsdale, New Jersey   London

153
Ap6

Lawrence Erlbaum Associates, Inc., Publishers
365 Broadway
Hillsdale, New Jersey 07642

Library of Congress Cataloging in Publication Data
Main entry under title:

Approaches to cognition.

Includes bibliographies and indexes.
1. Cognition—Addresses, essays, lectures. I. Knapp,
Terry J. II. Robertson, Lynn C.
BF311.A64 1986   153   85-20551
ISBN 0-89859-623-8

Printed in the United States of America
10 9 8 7 6 5 4 3 2 1

Contents

141305

Preface

Albert Gilgen in 1982 asked historians of psychology to rate what they felt were the major events and influences in the discipline since World War II. "Skinner's contributions" and "the increasing influence of cognitive theory" tied for second place, and the "general growth of psychology" ranked number one.

It is perhaps due to the general growth of psychology that few cognitive psychologists are aware of the continuing impact of Skinner's work. This may also be the reason that most psychologists who ascribe to Skinner's views are unlikely to know much about recent developments in cognitive psychology.

To the vast majority of academic psychologists the study of cognition refers to that area of psychology known as "cognitive psychology." The major basis of this area has been the computer metaphor with its accompanying notion of the individual as an information-processing system. Yet within the field the study of cognition is much broader and has a history that reaches into antiquity, whereas "cognitive psychology" as information-processing psychology has only recently become the standard bearer of cognitive studies.

One of the purposes of this volume is to articulate some of the fundamental distinctions between and concordances among different orientations concerning the study of cognition. The collection includes chapters on information processing, ecological, Gestalt, physiological, and operant psychology.

We begin with Daniel Robinson's prefatory essay on the philosophical roots of cognition. This survey leads him to argue for a logical distinction between perception and cognition that he believes is not observed by most contemporary cognitive psychologists. This is followed by Terry Knapp's chapter that traces the development of cognitive psychology through the decades after World War

II. This is done by chronicling the influential works in the area with a systematic analysis of these works within the context of the times in which they emerged.

There is little doubt that the information-processing approach to cognition has had the most influence on the study of cognition in recent years, and Stephen Palmer and Ruth Kimchi capture its ingredients with a discussion of the assumptions and limitations of the approach. This is the first time to our knowledge that such an enterprise has been undertaken by psychologists who work within the framework of the information-processing approach.

Contrary to common opinion, one of the people interested in what others call cognition is B. F. Skinner. Although he attacks the present mainstream approach to cognition, it is not because he believes such things as thinking, imagery, and problem solving are uninteresting, but because he believes contemporary orientations are misguided in invoking the notion of cognitive *explanations* for these phenomena. Continuing in this same vein, Robert Epstein presents a synopsis of his own work and discusses its implications for behaviors that have been labeled *cognitive*. He argues that such things as ''insight'' and ''self-awareness'' can be produced in pigeons and can be explained through an examination of the history of the animal. No reference to cognitive processes or representations need be applied. In direct contrast, Donald Riley, Michael Brown, and Sonja Yoerg argue that behavior in animals cannot be adequately explained without utilizing cognitive constructs. They discuss data from studies in their laboratory to support this notion.

A very different, but complementary, sentiment to Skinner's and Epstein's thesis is expressed by William Mace. He argues for an ecological cognitive psychology in which structure in the environment is central, and the idea of cognitive representations is a salient exclusion. The ecological approach was derived from J. J. Gibson who was highly influenced by the Gestalt school of psychology and its emphasis on systems and direct perception (i.e., perception that is not indirectly computed).

Within the information-processing approach to cognition, perception has enjoyed renewed significance. It is in perception that the first stages of information transformation take place. In line with this interest, Gestalt psychology, with its emphasis on perceptual organization, has been increasingly influential. Lynn Robertson captures this renewed interest in her chapter and compares the Gestaltists original ideas to some theoretical notions of her contemporaries. This is followed by Irvin Rock's chapter in which he argues that the study of perception is rightfully placed under the banner of cognition (in direct contrast to some of Daniel Robinson's arguments). Rock was a student of the Gestalt school, and his chapter reflects the thorough and thoughtful way that the experience of the perceiver can be used to support theoretical claims.

The notion of a cognitive construct caught full wind when the computer gave psychology a new way of talking about different ''levels'' of analysis. The computer has both a hardware and a software level of operation, which makes it possible to discuss, develop, and understand software independent of the hardware on which it runs. Under the umbrella of this metaphor one could study cognition (or the software of the brain) without much consideration of the brain itself. Stephen Kosslyn, who holds very strongly to an information-processing view of cognition, argues that this notion has been misplaced. The hardware for cognition in individuals is *always* the brain and not some other system. Kosslyn makes the case that the way in which the brain breaks down can be useful in discovering the components that comprise cognition. The subsequent chapter by Dean Delis and Beth Ober complements Kosslyn's arguments by discussing several areas of perception, memory, and language that have been augmented by data from brain-damaged patients. They also demonstrate that cognitive psychology fares quite well when applied in a medical environment.

The success of a cognitive orientation does not express itself equally well in all applied areas. Louis Gomez and Susan Dumais discuss the limitations that psychologists may encounter when attempting to apply cognitive theories and methods to the complicated task of designing a computer system. They argue that questions that motivate the study of cognition must be molded by ''real'' world problems.

A concern with applied problems has been one of the defining features of the success of operant psychology, and one of the sharpest schisms in contemporary psychology is that between ''cognitive'' and ''behaviorist'' commitments. We end the collection with Roger Schnaitter's arguments that cognitive psychology and Skinner's brand of behaviorism (normally referred to as radical behaviorism) are not opposites on a continuum, and that researchers in each area should be able to work together without violating their own conceptual convictions.

The chapters in this book should be of interest to anyone in the field who has ever wondered what happened to experimental psychology in the twentieth century, how it happened, why it happened, and what will be the possible results. The answers are not glib, and the scope of the book is for those who have made a career in psychology or who are thinking about doing so. How cognition is conceptualized from various viewpoints reflects not only the history of our science but also points the way to its future.

Lynn C. Robertson
Terry J. Knapp

1 Cognitive Psychology and Philosophy of Mind

Daniel N. Robinson
Georgetown University

Discourse on the nature of thought has been an integral feature of the history of philosophy since the time of Socrates and his anthropocentric dialogues. And, although experimental modes of inquiry do not appear until the nineteenth century, this older philosophical tradition turns up any number of important leads and insights. It is not these, however, that will most repay the attention of contemporary psychologists who have, after all, committed themselves to the scientific study of thought or "cognitive processes." The modern investigator may be impressed but generally not informed by the conclusions and overall perspectives arising from philosophical reflections on the subject. Instead, what most recommend the latter are the larger implications philosophers have drawn from their assessments of human cognition; implications of metaphysical, moral, social, and political consequence.

The present essay does no more than review the highlights of philosophical approaches, noting where appropriate how a given discovery or argument bears upon the concerns or practices of contemporary psychologists. The author's assignment here is to provide an introduction to essays of a more focused and technical nature; to provide a broad philosophical context within which such focused and technical treatments may be located and organized.

COGNITION AND THE PROBLEM OF KNOWLEDGE

Metaphysics is concerned chiefly with the interdependent studies of ontology and epistemology. Ontology is the disciplined inquiry into the nature of real existence or "being" and with an exhaustive determination of what constitutes "being." Whether or not there are mental events, for example, is an ontological question. Epistemology is the disciplined inquiry into the nature of knowledge itself, and the critical examination of the methods by which we acquire (claimed) knowledge. Whether or not introspective reports provide valid evidence of mental events, for example, is an epistemological question.

Among the pre-Socratics, it was perhaps Heraclitus who most fully appreciated the difficulty of developing a coherent and valid conception of reality. The famous maxim, *Nemo descensit bis in idem fluminem,* is popularly understood as referring to the river's endless changes; to the constant flux of nature that is never the same on successive occasions. But there is a deeper claim contained in the expression. The claim is not simply that the *river* does not remain constant, but that *no one enters* the same river twice. The observer, too, is a changing creature whose dynamics mingle with that of nature itself. Even if the river were constant, the observer is not.[1]

In the more psychological of the *Dialogues* (e.g., *Meno, Protagoras, Theaetetus, Republic*) Socrates draws a number of important inferences from the fact that, although the material world is indeed constantly changing, human rationality is able to grasp utterly immutable and necessary truths. This fact poses both ontological and psychological problems and, although much progress toward solving the former would be made by later philosophers, the psychological dimension still remains incompletely charted. It is instructive to note the difference between the ontological and the psychological sides of the issue. The former may be illustrated by the Pythagorean theorem, $a^2 + b^2 = c^2$, true for any and every right-angle triangle. The drawn ("empirical") triangle never perfectly honors this equation and thus we could not develop such a relationship out of mere observation. Moreover, a perceptually based theorem could rise no higher than the level of probable truth, whereas the Pythagorean theorem is a necessary and certain truth. The ontological question arising from this is whether in fact there are such ideal or true figures; the perfected archetypes of which material (e.g., drawn) right-angle triangles are but defective and transient approximations.

Aristotle insisted[2] that Socrates never granted ontological status to such "true forms," though it is clear that Socrates' theory of truth requires just these properties of immateriality, abstract relationship, and immutability. It remained for later empiricistic philosophers (e.g., Hume) to argue that the truth and certainty of such propositions are entirely verbal. Thus, the Pythagorean theorem does no more than rediscover the definition of a right-angle triangle such that its

---

[1]The generalization that would have anthropocentric philosophy begin with the Socratics probably underestimates the interest of pre-Socratic thinkers of whose teaching we have only fragmentary knowledge. Historians of psychology have neglected this question.

[2]Aristotle. *Metaphysics* (XIII, 4, 30–33). "Socrates did not make the universals or the definitions exist apart . . . ," etc. In *Basic works,* Richard McKeon (Ed.). New York: Random House, 1941.

"truth" is analytic. It is true in just the way that *All unmarried men are bachelors* is true.

Note, however, that although this addresses the ontological claim as to the alleged existence of perfect or true forms, it is utterly aloof to the psychological question as to how we come by conceptions of necessity, certainty, and immutable truths. When Piaget depicted the empiricist as one who believes we discovered the series of positive integers *one-at-a-time*[3] he may have been too dismissive, but he did underscore the difficulty of explaining universal concepts experientially. In any case, it is important to recognize that the ontological fate of universals does not determine or explain their psychological standing. To know that $a^2 + b^2 = c^2$ necessarily and universally cannot simply reflect a peculiar habit of speech or an elaborate form of synonymy. The adverbs are, after all, referential, even if all that is referred to is a definitional truth. The *concept* of necessity or of certainty is the psychological fact needing explanation. To invoke the rules of logic or the law of contradiction is not to explain but to rediscover the fact.

In his treatise on the soul or mind (*De Anima*) Aristotle[4] directly addressed the psychological aspect of such concepts and accorded to human beings a special faculty for them. He called this *epistemonikon* that, despite convention to the contrary, should not be translated "reason" (*nous*) or "wisdom" (*phronesis*). There is, as it happens, no suitable English word. Indeed, even in the Fourth Century B.C. *epistemonikon* was a philosopher's term. It is most accurately rendered by the phrase, "that by which we comprehend *universal* propositions." Interestingly, Aristotle notes that this faculty " . . . does not move," a qualification intended, I should think, to draw attention to its nonmaterial nature. It is not Aristotle's purpose in *De Anima* to examine the ontological status of universals but to provide a gross classificatory scheme that respects the major differences displayed by living things. Though all are animated by "soul"—defined simply as the first principle (*arche*) of all that lives or is alive (*zoön*)—this principle expresses itself variously in a number of distinct powers or faculties. Except for *epistemonikon,* all such powers are treated by Aristotle as resulting from natural, biological processes. A good case can be made for taking *De Anima* as occasioning the birth of the so-called MIND/BODY problem. In light of the history of the problem, it is to Aristotle's credit perhaps that, having recognized it, he chose not to "solve" it!

In the Hellenistic period of Greek philosophy, both Epicurean and Stoic systems would address the nature of concepts and would depart in one or another way from Plato and Aristotle. Epicurus was decidedly empiricistic in his cog-

---

[3]A similar charge was brought against J. S. Mill whose radically inductive epistemology would reduce even pure mathematics to a congeries of empirical inference.

[4]Aristotle. *On the soul.* In *Basic works,* Richard McKeon (Ed.). New York: Random House, 1941.

nitive psychology; something of a pre-Humean in arguing that general concepts (universals) arise from the compounding of simple sensations and are embraced linguistically by general terms.[5] A concept (*prolepsis*) is formed by such Humean principles as repetition and resemblance by which a mental image becomes installed in memory. New experiences are then compared with the stored *prolepsis* to determine if they are to be included in an established category or, as we now would say, *schema*. The Stoics, too,—at least in the School's early period (Zeno, Antipater, Chrysippus, Cleanthes)—were reductionistic in their cognitive psychology that was, after all, answerable to their essentially atomistic ontology. Convinced that all real existence was but the various orderings of elementary constituents, the early Stoics treated concepts as associational notions grounded in experience. But they went further and deeper into the functions of language than did the Epicureans and anchored all conceptual knowledge to linguistic competence.

From the early Christian (Patristic) period until the Seventeenth Century, the subject of Cognitive Psychology was tied to the larger mission of Christian teaching and scriptural exegesis. Patristic and Scholastic philosophers, nearly all of whom were theologians first, attempted to discover the most apt way of comprehending the truths of that faith that regarded man as made in the image and likeness of God. Recall that even Socrates found in human rationality the means by which we might actually resist Olympian forces. And so we find St. Augustine in the Fifth Century and St. Thomas Aquinas in the Thirteenth devoting long passages to human cognition, its reach, and its implications. An illustration from each of these writers is sufficient to convey how cognitive theory fit into the larger context of religious philosophy.

Augustine[6] in one place makes the important distinction between *percepts* and *concepts* by noting that, although we can *conceive* of a thousand-sided figure, we cannot *perceive* it. (This, of course, is one way Augustine established that we can have true knowledge of that which is otherwise unavailable to experience.) The relevant psychological point is that concepts are abstractions that, even if arising from experience, are not possessed *as* experiences. It is not sufficient, therefore, to show that a given concept might be reducible to elementary perceptions, e.g., that we move from triangle to square to pentagon, etc. on the way toward conceiving of a chiliagon. The latter is not conceived of as a mental image or picture, for such a figure cannot even be perceived as what it is. Rather, conceptual knowledge corrects or improves or completes the sensory record. I return to this later.

---

[5]A most accessible treatment of Stoic and Epicurean philosophies is A. A. Long, *Hellenistic philosophy*. New York: Scribners, 1974.

[6]This is central to Augustine's distinction between (perceptual) *knowledge*, "a rational cognizance of temporal things" and (cognitive) *wisdom*, "an intellectual cognizance of eternal things." St. Augustine, *De Trinitate (Book XII, Ch. 15)*. In *Basic writings of St. Augustine* (2 vols.), Whitney Oates (Ed.). New York: Random House, 1948.

In Thomistic psychology a similar thesis is advanced in connection with the problem of "universals." We perceive objects, though a given object is but the instantiation of a universe of kindred objects. Perception can never be of universals, only particulars. But cognition is able to abstract the universal from perceptually provided single instances. Moreoever, *abstrahentium non est mendacium.* *The abstraction is no lie* for the universal is, as it were, there to be uncovered.

DESCARTES AND NATIVE COGNITIONS

Modern philosophy is often said to begin with Descartes, though there is nothing in the records of thought to warrant so sharp a break. As with Bacon earlier in his century and Locke at the end of it, Descartes wrestled with problems bequeathed by Scholastic philosophy, often arriving at essentially Scholastic solutions. There was great originality in the works of Bacon, Hobbes, Descartes, and Locke but originality is "modern" whenever it appears, and it has appeared in all but a few of the past twenty centuries.

Descartes, however, can be said to have erected *philosophy of mind* on a new foundation, a distinctly psychological foundation. He was interested in mind *qua* mind and not as an entry point into cosmology or theology or ethics. His famous "method of doubt"[7] is but the introspective method seeking the ancient *prolepsis.* Can anything be known *beyond doubt?* It was only because Descartes could not find a perceptual basis for a number of fundamental concepts that he took recourse to nativistic considerations. That he never subscribed to a trivial theory of "innate ideas" is established by his own explicit disclaimer.[8] Nativism with Descartes is reached by default, not by design. This can be shown through the example of our concept of matter or, more psychologically, our belief that perceptions are caused by external material bodies. Descartes' epistemology was of the phenomenalistic variety, akin to that proposed by Aristotle, by any number of Epicurean and Stoic authorities, and by the major writers in the Scholastic period. According to this thesis, the external world physically alters the organs of sensation such that the mind is furnished with perceptual *effects* of stimuli and not with stimuli themselves. These effects are *phenomena,* not physical objects. Phenomenalism is just the doctrine that confines human knowledge to the realm of such phenomena.

But it was precisely because of Descartes' commitment to phenomenalism that the concept of "matter" or an external material world seemed queer. Let us assume that from the moment of birth—or even during intrauterine life—all we

---

[7]Rene Descartes, *Discourse on method.* In *The method, meditations and philosophy of Descartes* (J. Veitch, Trans.). New York: Tudor, 1901.

[8]Descartes' disavowal is given in his reply to a pamphlet by Regius and appears in Vol. 1 (p. 44.2), *The philosophical works of Descartes* (E. S. Haldane & G. R. T. Ross, Trans.). Cambridge: Cambridge University Press, 1911.

ever experience directly are our own sensations. These can amount to no more than *phenomena* and as such can never be parlayed into something *material*. How, then, would we ever arrive at the notion that the phenomena are caused by (nonphenomenal) *material* objects? Descartes could find only one coherent answer, viz., that the mind *natively* fabricates the concept out of the facts of experience. The concept is "innate" in the sense of being nonempirical.

On the same grounds Descartes concluded that the mind was also predisposed to fashion abstract mathematical concepts and, alas, the concept of God. Such abstractions could not arise from sensory commerce with a world of objects but were, nonetheless, part of the mental equipment of all civilized persons. So too with respect to the creative use of language; the nature of language, its variety and lawfulness, its transcendent range simply could not be explained in terms of mere experience.

Descartes, as is well known, was the father of Analytical Geometry and was especially interested in the nonempirical dimensions of mental life. His MIND/BODY dualism is to be understood as answering to just these dimensions. Descartes was not out to preserve the soul for Christendom; only to provide a consistent and noncontradictory account of human nature. Like Aristotle, he was satisfied that much of this nature was explicable in biological terms, even hydromechanically. This was surely the case with perception, trial-and-error learning, pain-avoiding behavior, and the like. But human psychology consisted of more than these; more than is ever found among actual animals or conceivable automatons. Human psychology includes abstract rationality for which there is no corresponding material entity. Accordingly, this rational faculty cannot be the effect of any such entity. Hence *dualism.*[9]

John Locke's celebrated critique of the theory of innate ideas—a critique that never mentions Descartes—is not to be regarded as a defense of radical empiricism. Locke, after all, attributed mind with a number of "original acts"[10] (e.g., the Law of Contradiction) and added to perceptual modes of knowing both an *intuitive* and a *demonstrative* mode. Nevertheless, Locke's credentials as an empiricistic psychologist are sound. His aim was to lay a Newtonian foundation on which a natural science of the mind could be constructed. Thus he corpuscularized cognition into elementary ideas arising from still more elementary sensations. David Hartley and David Hume would develop the associationistic principles even further and to the point where J. S. Mill could assemble a systematic psychology of nearly contemporary proportions. But all the luminaries—Locke, Hartley, Hume, Bain, James Mill, J. S. Mill—would plunge into what William James would later call *the psychologist's fallacy;* the fallacy of assuming that, just because one can analyze thought into components, thought

---

[9]*Ibid.,* p. 443.

[10]John Locke, *An essay concerning human understanding* (Book IV, Ch. 1). Chicago: Henry Regnery, 1956.

itself is no more than a congeries of the same. To this *psychologist's fallacy* might be added the *linguistic fallacy* by which I refer to the view that an explanation of a concept is provided once we have discovered the linguistic conventions by which it is expressed. Locke and especially Hume and Mill were prone to this line of reasoning and were surprisingly indifferent to the fact that our conceptual language must be answerable to bona fide mental constructs. As I argue, a concept is nothing but a proposition of logical form, but it is not "explained" by our examination of the linguistic conventions adopted by a given cognizer. It is not the choice of a term or the frequency of its employment that creates the mental (cognitive) construct. It is the latter that confers meaning on the terms themselves. Thus, when J. S. Mill chose to define matter (phenomenalistically) as "the permanent possibilities of sensation,"[11] he could only be offering an ontological or metaphysical criterion and not a psychological account of the concept of matter. Similarly, Hume's famous analysis of causation, which would reduce causation to nothing more than "constant conjunction," will have its metaphysical standing determined by metaphysicians, but as an account of our *mental concept* of a "cause" it is unarguably defective. It is surely not by a "constant conjunction" that I know myself to be the cause of the words on this page, nor is such a conjunction able to convince me that day is the cause of night. Much work needs to be done on the concept of causation: work addressed to the psychological (cognitive) conditions that constitute the concept itself. Hume began ambitiously but, it seems, obliquely. At this date we cannot say that even the Piagetians have progressed much further. Although their non-Humean premises would appear to be sounder, I raise reservations regarding them later in this chapter.

KANT AND THE CATEGORIES

It was Kant perhaps more than any earlier philosopher who elaborated a veritable cognitive psychology in the process of developing his own massive system of Philosophy. I should note right at the outset, however, that this elaboration was not a form of "psychologism" by which the peculiarities of human thought would stand as the arbiters of philosophical claims. Thus, we are never to think that Kant regarded either the metaphysical or the moral branches of his teaching as being merely relative to the nuances of cognition. The inviolability of the Law of Contradiction is mandated by an ultimate logic against which the claims of human cognition are to be weighed, and not vice versa.

---

[11]This is discussed in Ch. 2 of J. S. Mill's *An examination of Sir William Hamilton's philosophy* . . . provided in Vol. 9 of Mill's *Collected works*, J. M. Robson (Ed.). Toronto: University of Toronto Press, 1979.

In the central matter of epistemology, Kant was at pains to show that, although Hume and other empiricists were correct in claiming that our knowledge arises out of experience, it is not grounded in experience. Indeed, experience that *can* ever rise to the level of coherence and intelligibility must itself be grounded in nonempirical ("pure") principles of mind. The mind must furnish the epistemic context within which experiences occur and are ordered. The objects of experience are but physical ones, none of them conveying either *time* or *space* that are nonetheless ubiquitous features of any and all experience. Thus, the *pure* (nonempirical) *intuitions* of time and space are a priori; they are *logically* antecedent to experience in that they constitute necessary conditions for there to be experience of any kind. Their a priori status is not something to be verified or studied by developmental psychologists, for it is not something that depends on the biological oddities of human maturation. The *pure intuitions* are formally a priori in the same sense that the rules of chess are formally a priori with respect to any possible game of chess. There is room, of course, for enlightening research on the ontogenesis of rationality or moral judgment: research that is concerned with the purely psychological rather than epistemological dimensions. But the latter are not beholden to the former for their validity. Time and space are necessary aspects of all possible experience—even if there had yet to be a percipient anywhere in the universe!

As all experience is grounded in the *pure intuitions* of time and space, all rationality is grounded in the *pure categories of the understanding*. The categories are the regulative maxims of thought per se. They are *necessary* for there to be understanding and are thus not "relative" to a particular culture or to the merely contingent facts of human physiology. If A is greater than B and if B is greater than C, then A is *necessarily* greater than C. But the modal category of *necessity* is not a property of objects or perceptions of objects. The necessity contained in such propositions must be supplied by the understanding itself, for it could not be conveyed by any possible experience or constellation of experiences. J. S. Mill's attempt to reduce necessity to exceptionless correlations is notoriously defective as a psychological account of the concept. Only the child is likely to conflate "very high probability" and "necessity," and it is to the extent that there is a tendency thus to conflate that we say the child lacks the *concept* of necessity.

It was chiefly in the works of Fichte and Hegel that the dialectical interplay of the categories was developed but Kant had surely anticipated much of this. Each act of affirmation is also an act of negation; for every "this" there is the entire balance of reality that is "not this." Similarly, *necessarily p* entails that *not p* is necessarily false. If *p* is *probable*, it is not *necessary*, etc. There are now stirrings of interest in these dialectical processes of thought but it is too early to tell whether a richer appreciation of cognition is thereby to be gained. In light of the systematic confusions Psychology has brought to the Kantian Categories, one may be at most cautiously hopeful. Today's literature is bountiful in studies of the child's "concept" of necessity or universals or conservation and the like—all quite "Kantian" on the surface—but all quite beside the point. The child who examines beakers of liquid or urns of beads or in any way grounds his claims on perceptual data may be said to have no *concept* at all!

I have argued elsewhere[12] that *concepts* are propositional and not empirical and this is what distinguishes them from *percepts*. Transitivity, commutativity, associativity, necessity, conservation, and the like are *formal* relationships never perfectly instantiated empirically. (Some liquid poured from A to B remains on the sides of A and some evaporates in transit. Thus, the quantity is "conserved" *propositionally,* not empirically.) With this distinction respected, the psychological study of concepts becomes the study of propositional performances and is thus inextricably tied to linguistic development. This is not so because language is the way of expressing concepts, but because the latter *are* linguistic from beginning to end, or so I have proposed.

COGNITION AND CONVENTIONALISM

Perhaps the most suggestive implication to be drawn from these proposals is that our concepts are not private mental constructs but conventional modes of representing propositional truths abstractly by way of language. The implication would seek support from a Wittgensteinian critique of "private language" and would be enlarged to defend what is finally a conventionalist epistemology or a so-called "sociology of knowledge."

There are good reasons for resisting this implication, however. First, it is not at all clear that Wittgenstein's well-known critique of "private language" deserves the nearly protected status it has come to enjoy in some philosophical circles.[13] More to the point, however, there is a difference between claiming that linguistic forms are conventional and claiming that logical forms are conventional, even though the latter are expressed in an otherwise conventional language. The fictions addressed by Wittgenstein were dubbed *grammatical fictions* and are not to be taken as challenges to our formal (logical) modes of analysis. In arguing that concepts are propositional I do not assert that they are ipso facto true or valid, only that they are formal representations or abstractions and as such are empirically contentless. Obviously the prevailing conventions of a given linguistic community will determine what might be called the literal character of such propositions, but their internal logic remains tied nonetheless to categories of the Kantian sort. Just as external objects allow the realization of the pure

---

[12]Daniel N. Robinson. *Systems of modern psychology: A critical sketch* (Ch. 4). New York: Columbia University Press, 1979.

[13]This is discussed in Daniel N. Robinson, *Philosophical psychology.* New York: Columbia University Press, 1985.

intuitions of time and space, so also do externalized linguistic conventions allow the realization—in propositional form—of conceptual modes of knowing. Whether the latter are conceived of as "categories" or "faculties" or "schemata" is not of theoretical consequence, but *how* they are thus conceived is.[14] Psychologists have tended to regard conceptual modes of knowing as rather complex perceptual processes made richer by learning and memory. As a result, the very logic of thought has been neglected in favor of such nonconceptual processes as "mental rotation," short-term memory, semantic coding, etc., i.e., processes that are either merely perceptual or perceptual once removed. It is not surprising that three decades of research on "information processing" have not elucidated *any* of the cognitive functions associated with logical reasoning. During the same period, the more "Piagetian" paradigm has, it would appear, merely rediscovered the essential identity of "concepts" and propositions of a given type. At the risk of being controversial, I am inclined to summarize the Piagetian findings as reflecting no more than the ontogeny of *linguistic* representational thought. A study of the child's sentences might well have been sufficient!

It is consistent with the thesis I have been developing that concepts are idealized in addition to being abstract so that even when they are empirically referential they include not actual but idealized perceptual content. The observer who maintains that the volume of a fluid remains constant (is "conserved") regardless of the shape of the container is overruling or disregarding the bald facts of experience. The fact that some of the volume remains on the inner sides of the container and that some has surely evaporated in transit is ignored. The empirical phenomenon has now been conceptually idealized in a way not radically different from those idealized accounts common to the laws of science. The laws of motion as applied, for example, to balls rolling down an inclined plane assume perfect sphericity of the moving object and a completely frictionless medium. These are not the *empirical* facts of the matter and thus the predictions contained in the laws are never perfectly confirmed by the carefully measured behavior of the moving objects.

Note, then, that to have a *concept* is to possess a representation that, far from being a species of *percept,* replaces percepts and renders them unnecessary. To have the concept of conservation is to have an idealized representation that makes looking unnecessary. We no longer inspect the beakers or wonder if a few drops were lost in passage, for we know that volume qua volume is not determined by the shape of the vessel. Nor is the process to be regarded as a version of generalization or induction. The *concept* of conservation is not a weighted average of some number of previous perceptions. All these not only contradict the proposition that volume is conserved but could never yield more than a probability estimate. Again, to have the concept of conservation is to know that

[14]See, for example, a sophisticated revival of "faculty Psychology" by Jerry Fodor, *The modularity of mind.* Cambridge: M.I.T. Press, 1984.

volume is always and necessarily independent of the shape of the container. This universalized proposition is evidence enough that the process is not at base perceptual. At base it is *syllogistic*. On this construal, faulty concepts are the product of false premises or of invalid arguments.[15] Ordinary discourse respects this. When we seek to make our concept of something clear to another, we do not draw a picture; we develop an argument in which the initial assumptions (major premises) and relevant facts (minor premises) support a given conclusion.

We see, therefore, that concepts as understood here are no more "conventional" than is propositional logic even though linguistic conventions are and must be honored by those who would frame and express their conceptual understandings. Concepts are not "relative" in the cultural sense, or at least this would be a misleading way of putting the case. All human communities are sufficiently equipped with the rudiments of propositional logic to mint any number of bona fide concepts. How a particular enclave actually does idealize the facts of perception and abstractly represent them is of course a reflection of cultural or tribal traditions and beliefs. By virtue of these there will be often striking differences in the major premises, uttered or not, that make up the prevailing concepts or "revealed truths." The concepts are, then, *relative to these premises* but the regulative maxims of logical argument are not. Indeed, they must be invoked even as a condition of challenging them.

BACK TO THE ARMCHAIR?

Needless to say, a major obstacle to the adoption of this concept of concepts is the apparent lack of *experimental* implications. But the lack is only apparent, for research has already proceeded in this vein even without the benefit of the foregoing analysis.[16] The problem is not so much that possibilities for research are hard to see but that the research may be entirely gratuitous. The discipline of Logic is well developed and has disclosed just those laws of thought that a mature Cognitive Psychology would be required to incorporate. Studies of the commoner forms of faulty logic and of the resulting defective concepts are much needed, but there is the danger that such studies would lapse into arid tabulations of semantic nuances.

Whatever the experimental prospects may be, however, there is a very great need for a reconceptualization of cognition: a reconceptualization that distinguishes between perception and cognition and that respects the purely formal attributes of the latter. This kind of work is probably best conducted, if not in an armchair, then in some similarly undistracting location.

---

[15]See the excellent article by Mary Henle, "On the relation between logic and thinking." *Psychological Review*, 1962, *69*, 366–378.

[16]Mary Henle, *op. cit.* Years earlier, a nearly unpursued start on these problems was initiated by R. S. Woodworth and S. B. Sells, "An atmospheric effect in formal syllogistic reasoning." *Journal of Experimental Psychology*, 1935, *18*, 451–460.

2 The Emergence of Cognitive Psychology in the Latter Half of the Twentieth Century

Terry J. Knapp
University of Nevada, Las Vegas

A history demands specification of its object. There are problems in this regard when considering a history of contemporary cognitive psychology. One cannot proceed except by reference to a great number of persons, concepts, methods, tasks, and a few findings. This is not as true of the history of alternative psychologies. An adequate if not complete account of behaviorism can be given by consulting the relevant works of only two persons: John B. Watson and B. F. Skinner. A similar claim, with the necessary qualifications concerning nuances and "neoisms," may be made about the history of psychoanalysis. Cognitive psychology, because it has no locus in the work of a single or even a few persons, seems a more elusive content and its boundaries more difficult to specify. There appears to be no lessening of its current appeal and consequently much of its history is in progress. In fact, it seems a safe forecast to assert that future historians will characterize twentieth-century psychology as a half century of behaviorism followed by a half century of cognitivism.

The story of cognitivism is told in professional (Haber, 1974; Posner & Shulman, 1979), and still more recently, in lay circles (Hunt, 1982; Miller, 1983). Such histories contain accepted beliefs about the history of cognitive psychology, and these are also a source of problems. For example, Lovie (1983) has examined "the modern truism that cognition was almost completely suppressed by Watsonian behaviorism" (p. 301). He cites many sources in which this belief is asserted, yet when he tabulated the percentage of publications concerned with one category of cognition (attention) in the *Psychological Index* and the *Psychological Abstracts* from 1910 to 1960, he found that research on attention was published continuously during the period and not an inconsiderable amount (654 papers). Although Lovie has not examined the rate of publication associated with other categories of cognition, his conclusion is worth reflection and suggests the limited state of our current historical appraisal of cognitive studies. He (Lovie, 1983) says: "Those who consider the history of cognitive psychology should read what actually happened, instead of copying each others opinions about what they think happened" (p. 308).

Despite the diversity of activity that developed into present-day cognitive psychology and the problems associated with understanding its history, there are several pivotal figures in the field, and their work can be analyzed over the decades from World War II, at which time cognitive psychology really began to take shape (Gilgen, 1982), and the changes in their speaking and writing can give some indication of the stages by which the "cognitive revolution" took place.[1] As we see later, the conditions so often regarded as necessary before cognitive psychology could develop were present years earlier.

The availability of the modern digital computer and its associated languages is often given credit for the advent of cognitive psychology as we know it today. An electronic system could be made to simulate human behavior. It was possible to speak of a hardware and software level, a very appealing metaphor for many psychologists long perplexed by brain-behavior relationships. Ever since, the prevailing notion has been that the computer for the first time gave psychology the concepts needed in order to develop a science of cognition, one that could stand independently from the science of physiology.

If the computer metaphor proves successful, then the general program undertaken by psychologists during the first half of the twentieth century has been resolved, resulting in a psychology freed of physiological explanations but without denying the ultimate physiological basis of behavior, a goal shared by Freud (1917), Skinner, (1938), and Tolman (1932), among others. Freud had traced the origins of behavior (not merely conscious experience) to early life events and to

---

[1]A variety of earlier histories are available (Haber, 1974; Lachman, Lachman, & Butterfield, 1979; Posner & Shulman, 1979). Recent accounts (e.g., Leahey, 1980; Wasserman, 1983) portray cognitive psychology more as an evolutionary descendant of behaviorism than as a revolutionary movement that overcame it. Leahey's is perhaps the strongest position in this regard. He (1980) asserts, "If Tolman was correct in calling himself a behaviorist . . . then information processing is also a form of behaviorism" (p. 375). An interesting "quantitative" history of cognitive psychology is White (1983), who calculated mean citation rates in cognitive textbooks for the 50 most frequently cited publications. Gilgen (1974) presents a qualitative description of the period. Other relevant histories are those on mechanical computing machinery (Chase, 1952), automatic computation (Campbell, 1952), feedback control (Mayr, 1970), and the history of information theory (Cherry, 1952). Though dated, the chapter in Allport (1955, pp. 467–530) is perhaps the best early summary on perception and cybernetics. Biographical works of the period are just beginning to appear; see especially Broadbent (1980), Bruner (1983), Norman (1976), Simon (1980), also works on Wiener (Heims, 1980) and Turing (Hodges, 1983). McCorduck (1979) has written a popular account on the history of artificial intelligence, and Shurkin (1984) has done a similar volume on the history of computers. Brief historical accounts on information theory may be found in Machlup and Mansfield (1983).

the conflict between a person's instinctual makeup and the demands of civilization. Whatever gap existed between the past environmental influences and current behavior was bridged with an elaborate mental apparatus that often became an object of study in its own right. Skinner had restricted explanations of behavior to the genetic endowment of the individual organism and the history of the organism's contact with the environment (both public and private). Tolman bridged Skinner's environmental antecedents and consequences to current behavior by proposing a system of intervening variables. Cognitive psychology has developed what is finally for many psychologists a credible language in which to characterize the intervening states.

There is an omission in this history of "gap filling." Mechanical and other metaphors are common stock in psychological theories, and it is curious that a radio metaphor was not employed in analyzing "cognitive" phenomenon, nor in conceptualizing the relationship of psychology to the field of physiology. There is some distance after all between the development of telephone switchboards and digital computer circuits. Radio technology expanded rapidly during World War I with the superheterodyne receiver, an important advancement that remains today as the basis of any radio found in the home. The circuits it contains do more than tune a particular frequency and detect a modulated radio wave (recover the audio component referred to on occasion as the "intelligence" of the signal). They "process" the incoming signals by stages. Most block diagrams specify five.

The one stage that most clearly defines the superheterodyne circuit mixed (heterodyned) the incoming tuned signal with an internally generated one (a variable high frequency permanently stored) to produce a third constant (intermediate) frequency that can be more consistently amplified, detected, audio amplified, and converted into sound waves. The accompanying figure is typical of those appearing in the 1930s. Signals were transformed, but at a speed and

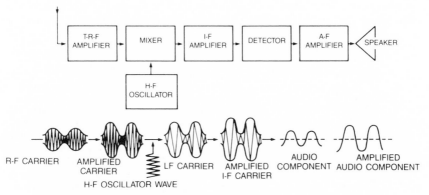

FIG. 2.1.   Block diagram of superheterodyne receiver, showing signal passing through receiver.

capacity that did not invoke the necessity of buffers or short-term memory. Broadbent, who is often given credit for introducing block or flow diagrams to psychology, did employ a radio analogue in his 1958 book on *Perception and Communication* (pp. 41–42), though only in passing. When he presented a "mechanical model for human attention and immediate memory" in 1957 it was in fact mechanical: a ball placed in a Y tube. It would be some time before the block diagram employed by psychologists to describe the arrangement of their experimental apparatus became a tool to represent the alleged arrangement of processes in the experimental subject's head.

Thus one could argue that much of the conceptual equipment that resulted in psychological processes being analyzed as a series of stages, which in turn were comprised of more elementary processes that operated on "intelligence," was available with the advent of sophisticated radio circuitry in the 1920s and 1930s.[2] The elementary units (e.g., inductance, capacitance, resistance, transformation, rectification, etc.) performed certain well-defined functions; each could be characterized independently of any particular hardware substantiation and were combinable in a large variety of ways to produce higher level processes (tuned circuits, voltage dividers and multipliers, detectors, power supplies, and with the advent of vacuum tubes, amplifiers, modulators, oscillators, etc.). These in turn could be hierarchically arranged to perform still higher level functions such as transmission and reception. Even the concept of self-regulation was available in the form of the automatic gain control developed in the 1920s.

Despite such possibilites, people were not conceptualized as radio receivers that in a teleological fashion detected stimuli in the environment, decoded the "intelligence" in them, and transformed them to another form. Only in telepathy was the radio metaphor invoked. Perhaps the computer with its expicitly "cognitive" behavior was required to elicit the analysis of electronic machine and human ability as conceptually parallel, or perhaps it was the development of programming languages that seemed to give life to processes independent of the machine.

Whereas sophisticated radio receivers were ignored during the 1920s and 1930s, cognitive psychology was not. In 1939 T. V. Moore, a Benedictine Monk and Professor of Psychology at Catholic University of America, authored the first book in the English language entitled *Cognitive Psychology*. Twenty-five

---

[2]Broadbent (1971) has observed that "in the 1950's the preferred analogy for the workings of the nervous system was the radio or telephone channel; while now the analogy is the general-purpose computer" (p. 2). A delay also occurred in connection with the introduction of information theory. Its concepts were available in the 1920s and 1930s as Garner has noted (1962, pp. 11–12). One could find during the 1920s, however, an analysis of complex activities ("recognition of an object," "thought of another object"), which included "processes intervening between stimulus and movement . . . schematically repesented as a series of stages," and each with a "latency or reaction-time." All were analyzed by Woodworth (1927) in terms of stimulus and response sequence.

years later the appearance of Neisser's similarly titled volume marks for many commentators the full emergence of the discipline. Moore's interests were not far from those of contemporary cognitive psychologists. It was his intention (Moore, 1939) to "throw light on the problem of how knowledge gets into the mind" (p. v.) by describing "that branch of general psychology which studies the way in which the human mind receives impressions from the external world and interprets the impressions thus received" (p. v.).

In one of his earliest research efforts, he sought to differentiate and determine the temporal order of images and meaning by measurement of reaction time (1915). He presented names of easily visualized objects tachistoscopically (e.g., tree, lamp, knife, etc.) to subjects who were instructed to react by releasing a telegraph key either "just as soon as" they knew the meaning of the word, or in another condition, "just as soon as" they had formed an image of the object named by the word. Reaction time was shorter under the "meaning" condition than under the "imagery" condition. The introspective reports agreed with the reaction-time data. Moore concluded, "meaning . . . appears to be a conscious process," one that is "distinct from imagery" (p. 201).

Tolman (1917) in his first published research paper challenged Moore's findings, even though introspectively they appeared to hold true for himself. He was able to locate among a large group of subjects a number who failed to replicate Moore's results. In reply to Tolman, Moore (1917) allowed as how individual differences in the latency of meaning versus imagery might be expected without negating his general views. Despite whatever approximations in methods and concepts Moore's work may bear to more recent efforts (Knapp, 1985), it initiated no revolution and remains obscure.

The 1940s: Information, Communication, Cybernetics

An observer in the latter part of the 1940s would not likely foresee the dramatic changes that lay ahead for academic psychology during the next 40-year period. There is no evidence that changes were anticipated in the academic products of that decade. *The Handbook of Experimental Psychology* edited by S. S. Stevens, although bearing the copyright date of 1951, was completed in manuscript form by the fall of 1949 and thus serves nicely as a status report on psychology at the close of the 1940s. Little of what could be regarded as contemporary cognitive psychology is in evidence. The best approximation is Leeper's chapter on "Cognitive Processes," which is devoted to inductive and deductive concept formation. Miller's contribution on speech and language introduces information theory, primarily as related to the problem of syntactical analysis. Only in Fitt's chapter on engineering psychology and equipment design does one find a description of the individual as a system, one involving servo control mechanisms. To be sure a tenet of later cognitive psychology is acknowledged when Leeper

Leeper (1951) defines "cognitive process [to] include all the means whereby the individual represents anything to himself or uses these representations as a means of guiding behavior" (p. 736). We are told that "after virtually disappearing from the vocabulary of psychology," cognition in this sense "has been reappearing in the writings of psychologists" of the 1930 and 1940s (e.g., Tolman). Bruner (1983) has summarized the point well as regards the Stevens' volume. "The mind was not doing well in psychology," he said, "the eye, ear, nose, and throat fared far better" (p. 106).

No change is foreseen either in the memorable textbooks of the decade. They concerned conditioning and learning (Hilgard & Marquis, 1940), or the theories thereof (Hilgard, 1948). The principal impression was that people were behaving organisms, and the fundamental problem was the identification of the necessary and sufficient conditions for learning to occur. The Laws of Behavior were thought discoverable in animal laboratories, although they seemed to differ depending on whether the laboratory was located in Berkeley, New Haven, Cambridge, or Iowa City. The classic learning volumes reached their peak of sales near the end of the decade, *The Behavior of Organisms* (Skinner, 1938) in 1947 and the *Principles of Behavior* (Hull, 1943) 2 years later. The major researchers and theoreticians were self-acknowledged behaviorists, and whatever their differences, they shared an affinity for the biological nature of the organism and for explanations of behavior that need not await the advancement of physiology.

Something approximating a contemporary cognitive conceptualization is found within psychology, however, just at the close of the decade. Though published in 1951, Postman in 1949 describes a theory of cognition in which hypotheses or "expectancies or predispositions of the organism . . . serve to select, organize, and transform the stimulus information that comes from the environment" (p. 249).[3] The notion of hypothesis-guiding behavior is not new with this account, but the identification of processes or mechanisms that operate on information has an exceedingly contemporary ring, particularly if one compares it to the opening sentence of *A Study of Thinking*, where Bruner (1956) and his colleagues discuss "the means whereby organisms achieve, retain, and transform information" (p. vii), or to Neisser's (1967) language of 10-years later, in which "sensory input is transformed, reduced, elaborated, stored, recovered, and used" (p. 4).

---

[3]The Postman paper deserves more attention than afforded here. The theory it advocates was developed in collaboration with Jerome Bruner and relies upon the earlier work of Bartlett, Brunswik, Krech, Tolman, and Woodworth. Many concepts later subsumed under contemporary cognitive psychology are discussed: sensory input, information, perceptual process as a cycle, transformation of information, reaction-time relative to number of alternative stimuli, schemata, organization of information, gestalt principles, memory as reconstruction, converging operations.

Although only a few psychologists were beginning to speak the language of "information" and "processes" that operate on it, such talk during the 1940s was common among persons outside the profession. Fragments can be found in Weaver's prefatory essay to the book version of Shannon's *The Mathematical Theory of Communication* (1949), but it is to Wiener's *Cybernetics* (1948), subtitled "control and communication in the animal and the machine," that one must look for any strong approximations to the content of contemporary cognitive psychology. The individual chapters of *Cybernetics* do not cohere well and this may explain the tendency of textbook and other secondary account writers to dismiss the book once the concept of feedback control has been explained. One could easily gather the impression that little else is discussed by Wiener. But even a cursory reading will reveal many contemporary topics. Among them are mathematical transformations of information (p. 50), working memory (p. 121), imagery (p. 142), recognition by template matching (p. 136), visual processing (p. 138), subassemblies performing a particular cognitive function (p. 136), form perception (p. 133), and executive functons (p. 42). All these topics are subsumed, however, under "one of the lessons of the . . . book," namely, "that any organism is held together in this action by the possession of means for the acquisition, use, retention, and transmission of information" (p. 161). Action in this context refers to homeostasis of societies and the "means" refers to communication systems, but Wiener held the description equally applicable to any "organism" because that term is best understood as "any system."

Little of what is now regarded as cognitive psychology appeared during the 1940s within the field itself. There was the concept of representations and operations upon them, but they had not yet become central notions, and there was also the emerging talk of information, communication, and cybernetics but this occurred mainly outside of the field. Within there was only a mild dissatisfaction with the then prevailing S–R formulations. A hint of what was to come is found in the closing pages of Hilgard's *Theories of Learning* (1948). He notes, "it may be that the stimulus–response language has outlived its usefulness, now that molar psychologists have freed themselves from the necessity of explanation according to physiological mechanisms" (p. 349).

But if physiology was no longer a source of exploratory hypotheses, from where would explanations originate? And, if explanations were not tied directly to physiology, what level would they occupy? As the 1940s come to a close, these become the central issues (in some manner they always had been) that separated theorists. It was the basis of Skinner's objections to certain kinds of theories (Skinner, 1950); it was perhaps the most significant difference between Tolman and Skinner (Skinner, 1966, p. xi); it was the source of similarity between Tolman and contemporary cognitive psychology (Riley, this volume); it was the issue on which philosophers came to focus in criticizing cognitive psychology, and it was part of the reason why commentators in the 1950s were calling for a new language for psychological discourse.

The 1950s: Information Theory, Information Flow, Information Processing

Most observers have placed the origins of contemporary cognitive psychology in the decade of the 1950s.[4] The variety of particular events during the decade are not easily partitioned, but talk dealing with "information" can be placed in at least three rough categories: information theory, information flow, and information processing.

Information theory was introduced in 1949 by Shannon and Weaver. In its original form it described a model of a communication system and raised particular questions that were of interest about the system. The model had five basic parts, an information source, transmitter, channel, receiver, and destination. A sixth component was noise that may or may not be present in the channel. The particular questions Shannon and Weaver addressed were about the relationships among the variables of channel capacity, rate of transmission, redundancy of encoding, and noise. The answer they proposed (really Shannon) was a very general statistical formulation describing these relationships. Redundancy of encoding was later selected by psychologists as the salient aspect of information theory and they began applying the statistical procedures developed by Shannon.

Information flow refers to encoding processes and the path by which information travels though a system. In terms of the individual organism information is encoded and makes its way through the nervous system eventuating often in some motor output. In a flow chart arrows represent the path by which information gets passed. This view says nothing about symbolic manipulation of information. The language of information flow was introduced to psychology (in any influential way) by Broadbent (1958). Anyone who used similar language can be placed in the category of ascribing to information flow. The category is without explicit boundaries, but it does identify talk that brings to mind the tracing of a signal through a radio, but without the radio technician having a preformed notion of the general processes he will encounter. Processes are described on an ad hoc basis and may be given a variety of descriptions.

Information processing is generally identified in psychological discussions with the formulations of Newell and Simon (1972). Their system consists of a limited set of elementary information processes that operate on a set of symbols. Although a variety of computer programs can implement such a system, Newell and Simon also developed a specific programming language (called Information-Processing Language) for this purpose. The use of the phrase "information processing" is further complicated because it is also taken to refer to how information gets processed within the individual (see Palmer & Kimchi, this volume). In fact, one can find talk of "information processing" in the psycho-

---

[4]It is unclear just when the talk of a cognitive revival or revolution first appeared because statements to that effect can be found in each decade since World War II.

logical literature before Newell and Simon published a single paper on the subject, and one of the yet unanalyzed issues in the history of cognitive psychology is the earliest source of an "information-processing" description of the individual. For the purposes of the present explication, information processing refers to the specific contributions of Newell and Simon.

The precise historical relationship among the vocabularies within each of the three frameworks is also a matter awaiting analysis. The first step, however, is to understand the possible distinctions that have been too often blended in general expository works. In the section that follows, these distinctions are discussed from an historical perspective.

Information Theory.   The credit for introducing psychology to the statistical formulations developed by Shannon is often given to Miller in light of a series of publications beginning in the late 1940s (Frick & Miller, 1951; Miller, 1951, 1953, Miller & Frick, 1949, among others). *Language and Communication* (1951) is the most interesting of these because Shannon's theory is given more attention than a mere explication, and because the book is often seen as a bridge between the old psychology of behaviorism and the new cognitive psychology of the postwar years. Miller gives many illustrations of how information theory can be applied to problems in psychology. Despite these innovative contributions and their occassional citation in histories of cognitive psychology (Haber, 1974, p. 318) it is the general stance of the book that is of interest. Miller (1951) holds that "the use of mentalistic concepts is a lapse from scientific standards and little more than plausible fiction at best" (pp. 8–9). The author has a self-confessed bias, "not fanatically behavioristic, but certainly tainted by a preference" (p. v). The book is after all one of the early sources for Skinner's views on verbal behavior (pp. 159–173).

Information theory may not initially have resulted in any changes in Miller's thinking because it was viewed as fundamentally neutral in so far as one's approach to psychology.[5] This is reflected in its varied applications, one of the earliest of which is Miller and Frick's (1949) analysis of response sequences and their later "statistical description of operant conditioning" (Frick & Miller, 1951). The neutrality was still being proclaimed as late as 1959. Fred Attneave's book *Applications of Information Theory*, once described as required reading for any psychology student (Marx & Hillix, 1963, p. 372), opens the concluding chapter with a caution: "Information theory is not psychological theory. . . . informational analysis is as completely neutral with respect to psychological schools and controversies as is analysis of variance or x^2" (p. 81).

---

[5]Whether information theory was to make its contribution as a "statistical tool" or "new language" for psychology was debated at the 15th International Congress of Psychology in 1957 (Garner, 1959).

The demise of information theory as independent of any particular approach to psychology was at hand. Psychologists ceased talking about information theory as a statistical theory applicable to any psychological data, rather it become a source of ideas and vocabulary. Attneave (1959) reveals this in the following way: "it would be quite unrealistic to deny that certain broad concepts of information theory, which have little or nothing to do with the specific statistical techniques, are also having their effect on psychological thinking" (p. 81). The closing sentence of the book is indicative of what was to arrive with the 1960s and points toward the transition from the specific and statistical concepts of communication theory to less defined and more metaphorical concepts of information (Attneave, 1959): "The value of the concept of information theory in leading us into new areas of investigation is not lessened, however, if in the pursuit of these investigations we find it possible to abandon information measures in favor of others more informative" (p. 88).

This is precisely what happened. The line of effort from Shannon and Weaver's original work, to Miller's explications, to the early conferences and symposia (Brussels, Illinois), to Attneave's book, and others like it culminated in what might be regarded as the final work of this tradition: Garner's *Uncertainty and Structure as Psychological Concepts* (1962). Information (now multivariate analysis of uncertainty) is brought to bear on characterizing the structural aspects of stimuli.

However, Garner is careful to emphasize that he is not advocating a general theory of behavior nor a specific mathematical model of some psychological phenomenon, nor a total theory of any sort. Whereas there is no evidence of metaphorically extended information-theory concepts in Garner, in reaction to Cherry's declaration that some persons uses of information concepts went beyond established use, Garner (1962) replied: "if going beyond or even disturbing established usage helps solve our behavioral problems, then we should feel free to do so" (p. 15).

When first introduced to psychologists, information theory had a well-specified meaning, was mathematical in nature, without theoretical commitment, and constrained in its applicability. By the late 1950s and early 1960s it had lost its conceptual specificity and soon became a metaphor for a wide range of claims and views. The attempt to give an interpretation to "information" beyond the notion of reduction in uncertainty failed, whereas the broadening of the applicability of communication theory continued at an ever rapid pace. Such generalizations probably reached their broadest stroke in the theories of speaking and writing begun with Berlo's book, *The Processes of Communication* (1960).

If one sought a conceptual link between information theory and discussions of persons as information processors, it could be partially found in the notion of persons as communication systems and in the concept of stimulus coding. The former was derived from a straightforward application of the parts of Shannon and Weaver's model to the psychological abilities of a person. Hence, one could ask the same questions about humans that might be asked about communication systems (e.g., What is the channel capacity? How redundant is the encoding?). It is not far from talking about people as channels of information to talking about them as processors of information.[6] Similarly, as psychologists became focused on the stimulus as encoded rather than its structural properties per se, its path through the organism could be traced with due attention to any processing along the way.

Information Flow.   From a historical perspective Broadbent's book, *Perception and Communication* (1958) represents the first in a series of attempts to make use of communication-theory language in conceptualizing traditional psychological subject matter, primarily auditory attention. Haber (1974) refers to Broadbent as the contemporary father of information-processing psychology (p. 317), and Anderson (1980) has described him as "probably the most influential in integrating ideas . . . and developing the information processing approach" (p. 9). The new formulation was a "fresh language" (p. 35), "the language of information flow" (p. 304), borrowed from "telephone engineering" (p. 36), with the hope of avoiding "the emotional reactions which are sometimes aroused by the phrases of cognitive theorists" (p. 267). The new "cybernetic language" (p. 304) had advantages over S–R talk (see pp. 304–307), but the "main reasons for departing from stimulus–response language are the need for considering the coding of input into output, the need to consider the whole ensemble of possible stimuli rather than simply the presence or absence of each one, and the need to distinguish between the arrival of the stimulus at the sense-organ and use of the information it conveys" (p. 59). According to Broadbent (1963), the new language was said to fill the "large gap between the study of behavior and that of neurophysiology" (p. 34).

Others were also contributing to the new language. MacKay (1956) in "Towards an information-flow model of human behavior" suggested that:

> a research model of the human organism considered as an information flow system might provide a common . . . language in which hypotheses might be framed and tested. . . . it is sufficient if it can develop and grow on paper as a hypothetical information-flow map of the human organism. (p. 31)

Some years later in reflection, Broadbent would add (Cohen, 1977): "We had a language to talk about what happened inside a man which was not a mentalistic introspective language, which was not hypothetical neurophysiology and which wasn't simply a description of the visible behavior" (p. 63).

---

[6]For example, McCormick (1964) has a chapter titled "Human Information Processes," which in content is largely concerned with applications of information theory, but in which "the ability of human beings to process information" (p. 95) is discussed. Newell and Simon are not mentioned, nor is their conceptualization of information processing intended by McCormick's use of the phrase.

To what language was he referring? Perhaps the same language as used by other experimental psychologists in the early 1950s. A student of Postman who said in (Mathews) 1954: "psychologists are interested in the organism's processing of information—how it is received or selected, organized, stored, made available when needed" (p. 241). Or the somewhat similar language Fitts (Fitts & Deininger, 1954) used when identifying the objective of his study of S–R compatibility as discovering the: "conditions under which these effects occur, and to establish principles that will permit specification of the nature and difficulty of perceptual-motor tasks in terms of [hypothetical intervening] information transformation processes" (p. 483). Psychologists had always had an interest in how organisms behave and frequently had relied upon hypothetical constructs in seeking explanations of behavior. Now some psychologists were turning their attention from behavior (performance in their view) to "information flow," or "information processing" and to the explanations of processing in a language of "information."

Information Processing.   The third "language" to emerge during the 1950s was the information-processing system offered by Newell and Simon. It first appeared in the psychology literature in 1958 (Newell, Shaw, & Simon) though was available through conferences sometime earlier.

Newell and Simon (Newell et al., 1958) maintained:

> that the appropriate way to explain a piece of problem-solving behavior is in terms of a program: a specification of what the organism will do under varying environmental circumstances in terms of certain elementary information processing it is capable of performing. This assertion . . . has nothing to do—directly—with computers. Such programs could be written [now that we have discovered how to do it] if computers had never existed. (p. 153).

Newell and Simon proceeded (see their own account, 1972, pp. 873–889, and that of a sympathetic general history, McCorduck, 1979) to develop programs for theorem proving, chess playing, and later with Feigenbaum, the Elementary Perceiver and Memorizer Program that for the first time moved the effort into the traditional psychological field of paired-associate learning.

The general strategy of Newell and Simon may be the most valuable aspect of their work, but the origin of their vocabulary is the most interesting from a historical viewpoint. They (1972) provide a brief account:

> The term "information processing" originated in the late fifties in the computer field as a general descriptive term that seemed somewhat less contingent and parochial than "computer science," which also came into use during the same period. Thus, it was the name of choice for two of the encompassing professional organizations formed at the time: the *International Federation of Information Processing Societies* and the *American Federation of Information Processing So-*

cieties. Although the transfer of the phrase from activities of computers to parallel activities of human beings undoubtedly occurred independently in a number of heads, the term was originally identified pretty closely with computer simulation of cognitive processes (see, e.g., Hilgard and Bower, 1966); that is, with the kind of effort from which arose the theory in this book. (p. 888)

Much the same view (that information processing when first introduced to psychology referred to computer simulation) was maintained when Simon (1979) introduced his collected papers on cognitive psychology:

It [the information processing revolution] has introduced computer programming languages as formal ['mathematical'] languages for expressing theories of human mental processes; and it has introduced the computers themselves as a device to simulate these processes and thereby make behavioral predictions for testing of the theories. (p. ix)

The Newell and Simon approach was strongly reflected in two works published during the early and mid 1960s: Hunt's *Concept Learning: An Information Processing Problem* (1962), and Reitman's *Cognition and Thought: An Information-processing Approach* (1965). "Information processing" in the subtitles of both works indicates the commitment of each author to explain problem solving in terms of IPL language. In fact, it was presumed that learning an information-processing approach to psychology entailed learning to program in IPL language, and Reitman (1965) included in his book an appendix titled "Introduction to the Programming of Psychological Models in IPL-V" (pp. 263–290), to that end. This "concrete," as opposed to metaphorical, formulation of the information-processing approach did not get carried forward as a mainstay component of cognitive psychology, although it did find a home in the field of artificial intelligence.

Although Newell and Simon's work of the mid and later 1950s is the most precise definition of information processing, and though it found its way into significant works of the period as well as undergraduate textbooks, the analysis of problem solving or memory by the writing of programs in IPL-V did not become the dominant content of the early, or even later, cognitive psychology courses and manuals. In fact, many aspects of their approach (individual subject data, use of verbal protocols, nonreliance upon statistical analysis, theories as programs, Newell & Simon, 1972, pp. 10–13) are not well integrated into cognitive psychology. The contribution of Newell and Simon to some degree stands in isolation from cognitive psychology much in the same way that Skinner's behaviorism stood in isolation from mainstream behaviorism. Instead, attention, auditory and visual perception, and short-term memory came to dominate the early textbooks, along with the traditional group designs and analysis of variance. The slight tensions between these two formulations of "information processing'' may be seen in contrast if one compares Haber's and Reitman's respective chapters in a volume edited by Voss (1969).

Plans and the Structure of Behavior, (Miller, Galanter, & Pribram, 1960) once described as the first classic in the recent tradition of cognitive psychology (Leahey, 1980, p. 369), appeared in 1960 and on that account provides a convenient summary of the state of the field as the 1950s came to a close and also supplies a bridge between the decades of the 1950s and 1960s. What often remains of this work in contemporary textbooks and classroom lectures is the concept of a TOTE (Test-Operate-Test-Exit) as the unit of behavior analysis, one intended to replace the reflex. Whereas the new unit may be found in many textbooks and even some experimental work, its ultimate fate was similar to that of the earlier unit of analysis (the bit) derived from information theory. Both are only of historical interest.

Newell and Simon's information-processing formulation is the major influence on the work itself, and the derivative treatment accorded that formulation constitutes the historical significance of the book. The authors ''are reasonably confident that program could be substituted everywhere for plan in the following pages.'' They tell us, ''however, the reduction of plans to nothing but programs is still a scientific hypothesis and is still in need of further validation'' (p. 16). The significance of this quotation lies in the move that it reflects away from a concrete interpretation of ''our understanding of man viewed as a system for processing information'' (Miller, Galanter, Pribram, 1960, p. 57) toward a more abstract conception in which a computer program is now a hypothesis about a ''plan.'' Programs are only one among many possible kinds of hypotheses.

When future historians examine the psychology of the mid-twentieth century, they are likely to look broadly and abstractly for the origins of the concept of persons conceived as information processors. The contest will be between the early, fragmentary, loosely specified talk, and the somewhat later, but more concretized, language of Newell and Simon. The divergent and clearly independent origins of these two ''personkind as information processor'' views is probably most evident in their treatment of S–R behavioral psychology.[7] The early work of Postman, Bruner, Broadbent, and others includes doubts about the

---

[7]In searching *Administrative Behavior* (1947) by Simon one may seek precursors of his later development of information processing, any such items would genuinely be of interest because programs for computers were some years off when the manuscript was drafted in the 1938 to 1946 period. The only explicit reference to psychology is to Tolman, because of his emphasis on purpose and choice in behavior. One might force a generalization on Simon's book to the effect that organizations in their operation bear some resemblance to information processing (a flow of directives, decisions made at critical choice points, hierarchical structures, memos as memory stores), but a feature identified by Simon as most significant would be missing: a conceptualization that is at a level of description free of its physical embodiment. Of course, in a general sense, that is what *Administrative Behavior* offered because it sought to characterize the behavioral activities of managers at a level of abstraction applicable to any organization.

adequacy of "stimulus–response" language; whereas the work of Newell and Simon evolved outside the framework of mainstream academic psychology and had little to say about S–R psychology. Thus, Hilgard and Bower (1966) could rightly claim in their exposition of the view: "that it is historical accident that most theories realized in this way [as computer programs] have in fact a distinctly 'cognitive' bias" (p. 384). Simon could be uninterested in the argument among psychologists about S–R psychology for the same reasons (see Voss, 1969, p. 112).

The 1960s: Information Processing or Cognitive Psychology

If cognitive psychology had its origins in the 1950s, its solidification as a separate, distinct, and new paradigm only came in the latter 1960s, and the central event in these matters was the publication of Neisser's textbook in 1967. This book gave a label to the field, and one that probably served it better than *information processing,* if only because of the generic nature of the latter. Nothing in the opening years of the decade (e.g., the self-acknowledged "subjective behaviorists" of *Plans and the Structure of Behavior*) suggested what might emerge as the key term for the field, though from early on there were two contenders.

The significance often attributed to Neisser's book is probably well placed precisely because he chose to call it cognitive psychology, though "information processing" could by present-day usage equally describe its contents. In retrospect, the rhetorical advantages were with *cognitive psychology.* It was a label appropriate for *psychologists* because it did not require them to change professions (as in having to become "information processors," a title in fact used by some and easily confused with aspects of the subject matter under their investigation). "Cognitive Psychology" offered a wide latitude as to the precise nature of one's interests and to the exact nature of one's theoretical commitment. Moritz (1972) has observed more than a dozen uses to which psychologists had put the terms *cognitive, cognition, cognitive processes* during the period.

The first chapter in Neisser's *Cognitive Psychology* provides an opportunity to identify the end product of the historical processes that occurred during the interval since T. V. Moore's 1938 work. The chapter is entitled "The Cognitive Approach" and begins with the notion that our access to the world is a mediated one. The viewpoint implied (Neisser, 1967) is to be contrasted with the psychodynamic, behavioristic, and the physiological approaches: "The task of a [cognitive] psychologist trying to understand human cognition is analogous to that of a man trying to discover how a computer has been programmed" (p. 6) or to an economist discussing capital formation and flow. Neither transistors for the psychologist nor paper money for the economist is directly relevant to the sought-after explanation, because of the level at which the phenomenon of interest is described, a level best typified by the "information sciences."

The efforts of a cognitive psychologist are directed toward a particular level of description. Moreover, the cognitive psychologist seeks a particular kind of account at this level of description. According to Neisser (1967), a computer program is "a recipe for selecting, storing, recovering, combining, outputting, and generally manipulating" (p. 8) information. "The cognitive psychologist would like to give a similar account of the way information is processed by men" (p. 7). Making use of the "program analogy" does not entail a commitment to computer simulation of psychological processes; in fact, the "book can be construed as an extensive argument against models of that kind "(p. 9).

By the 1960s most of the behaviorists had died or ceased professional activity (Hull in 1952; Guthrie in 1959; Tolman in 1959; Spence in 1967), and it remained for their students to defend the S–R position against the intrusion of the new cognitive approach. Collected readers of the period (Anderson & Ausbel, 1965; Harper, 1964) remain as artifacts that give evidence of the unresolved conflict between the cognitivists and neobehaviorists. However, when the "death rattle of behaviorism" was proclaimed, the announced successor was not cognitive psychology or information processing but "experientialism" (Koch, 1964, p. 34). Paradoxically, radical behaviorism under the banner of the "experimental analysis of behavior" grew dramatically and forcefully during the period, and in isolation from the new cognitive paradigm and mainstream psychology (Krantz, 1972). Although occasional note was taken of the cognitivist (Salzinger, 1973; Skinner, 1938 [66]), only during the last several years have any direct exchanges taken place in print between cognitive psychologists and radical behaviorists (Wessells, 1981, 1982, also see Schnaitter this volume).

Though too early to assert with great confidence, it seems likely that the 1960s will be best remembered as the decade in which the term *cognitive psychology* emerged to identify a loosely conceptualized perspective, and to a lesser degree as the decade in which (though not discussed here) reaction time as a method for differentiating mental stages or processes found a renaissance 100 years after its first introduction to psychology (Posner & Shulman, 1979).

The 1970s: Cognitive Psychology Institutionalized

During the decade of the 1970s, cognitive psychology became institutionalized as mainstream academic psychology. The 1960s closed with the founding of *Cognitive Psychology* as a quarterly journal. *Cognition* began publishing in 1972 and was followed a year later by the reorganization of the journals of the Psychonomic Society, resulting in the appearance of *Memory and Cognition*. The first Loyola Symposium on Cognition was held in 1972 and was followed by subsequent conferences in 1973 and 1974. Sometime in the early 1970s or even late 1960s professors of cognitive psychology were sought to fill positions previously advertised as human learning, verbal learning, perception, or simply experimental psychologists. Students seeking graduate instruction could now turn to training programs that did not merely identify themselves as devoted to experimental psychology but rather were concered with the new information-processing psychology or, at other institutions, with cognitive psychology. Nearly 10 years elapsed between the appearance of Neisser's *Cognitive Psychology* and similarly titled textbooks, but by the mid 1970s sufficient undergraduate courses in cognitive psychology were offered to prompt the early appearance of new textbooks devoted to the area. The trend still continues, and more than a dozen are currently in print (see reviews by Lewandowsky & Dunbar, 1983). Though often overlooked, such institutional factors are significant in the developmental history of the social sciences. They give a coherence to the endeavor termed cognitive psychology that may only weakly be in evidence at the conceptual level.

Once institutionalized, its history became "the cognitive revolution," though a revolution in which there appear few who could be called reactionaries. The radical behaviorists paid no mind; the neobehaviorists were no longer active. What evidence one can find of resistance to the new cognitive psychology appears in the late 1960s and early 1970s; it stemmed largely from psychologists and philosophers influenced by ordinary language philosophy, particularly of the Austin and later Wittgenstein variety. Malcolm's (1971) "The myth of cognitive processes and structures" is perhaps the most widely referenced of this literature. The essence of the argument was roughly that talk about cognitive performances such as recognizing and remembering does not necessitate the positing of cognitive processes (recognition and memory, respectively) to carry out these activities. Cognitive processes are not another level of organization, structure, or mechanism; they are rather parameters of behavior or ways of carrying out activities.

The best place to directly examine the resistance to the cognitive revolution is in the papers and verbatim dialogues of several conferences. Two samples may suffice to give a general impression of the criticism. The late William Battig (1975) asserted:

> What makes the current high popularity of cognition especially astounding is that even its most dedicated advocates seem unable to provide us with a clear or consistent definition of exactly what is meant by or encompassed under the cognitive label, or how it is to be distinguished from the allegedly noncognitive character of whatever is (or was) not described as cognitive psychology. (p. 195).

The views of Bourne (1973) seem more specifically derived from the earlier mentioned ordinary language philosophy:

> Cognitions and competences are behavioral concepts. They *do not* characterize anything nonpsychological, neurophysiological, electronic, hypothetical, or the like. They are aspects or attributes of behavior. No behavior is noncognitive. No behavior is without competence. Behavior, itself . . . and please notice I do not say performance or overt action . . . is characterizable in terms of a set of param-

eters or attributes which fall into the categories cognition, competence, intention, and performance—all psychological, all behavioral, *nothing less*. (p. 315)

Even Neisser in a surprise to many, and perhaps a disappointment to some, concluded in 1976 that "the very notion of information processing deserves closer examination" (p. xii). He was followed some years later by Haber, (1983) long a chief advocate and spokesperson for information processing, in wondering "is the whole model wrong" (p. 10).

By the late 1970s the rhetorical if not conceptual victory was at hand. According to Kreitler and Kreitler (1976): "The term 'cognitive' [was] being used so widely that one might wonder whether there is anything in psychology that is not cognitive" (p. 4). A similar thought was echoed almost a decade later by Hilgard (Fisher, 1983), who lamented that cognition "might be defined as 'something you put in front of a book title that wouldn't have been there a couple of years ago'" (p. 18).

Cognitive Psychology and Learning Textbooks

Historians have few instruments by which to assess the impact of new influences on a discipline. Textbooks are one possible device. During the period of interest, *Theories of Learning*, first authored by Hilgard (1948, 1956) and later by Hilgard and Bower (1966, 1975, 1981), has undergone five editions. The first issue (1948) reviews the classic learning theories and a few now forgotten approaches (e.g., Wheeler's organismic psychology). A reader consulting the index would find that the only entry related to information leads to a discussion of Thorndike's distinction between the confirming influence of a reward versus one that is informative. The only entries under "cognition" refer either to a discussion of the distinctions between a "reaction psychology" of movements versus a "cognitive psychology" of "perception-like and idea-like processes," or to Tolman's views on intervening variables, among which he includes cognition and purpose. "Cognitive structure" indexes a discussion of certain notions of Kurt Lewin who was attempting to develop a spatial model in which psychological phenomena could be understood (see Robertson, this volume).

With the 1956 edition a noticeable change has occurred, though not one that would likely strike the attention of a contemporary student of cognitive psychology. The Wheeler chapter is dropped, a new one in Freud's psychodynamic approach is added, and the Gestalt Psychology chapter is now termed *classical*. The independent treatment of Lewin continues. More importantly, however, within a chapter entitled "The emergence of mathematical models," a section is devoted to "some models from other fields potentially useful for learning theory." Shannon and Weaver's mathematical theory of communication is briefly described in a section on "The Information-Theory model," and a separate but equally brief treatment is given to "The Feedback Model" consisting of the cybernetic approach of Wiener. Most of the chapter is reserved for a presentation of Estes' stimulus sampling theory and Bush and Mosteller's stochastic analysis of learning. Cognitive psychology in any contemporary sense was still a long way from the mainstream textbooks on which undergraduates rely. However, the suggestion that sciences other than biology and physiology might contribute to the analysis of behavior was now clearly acknowledged, if only in passing.

The third edition of *Theories of Learning* (1966) is a significant departure from the first two versions. The most significant changes are the deletion of the chapter on Lewin's theory and the inclusion of an entirely new chapter entitled "Information Processing Models," authored by Bower who clearly conceptualized information processing within the Newell and Simon definition of the term. Most of the pages of the chapter are devoted to the possibilities of developing computer programs that will serve as models or theories of cognitive accomplishments. No longer is there any discussion of or reference to Shannon and Weaver. Information processing has replaced information theory. The mathematical–statistical sections of the book are moved to a separate chapter and substantially revised. A contemporary student would feel at home with the material added to the third edition under the rubric information processing.

The subsequent editions of Hilgard and Bower make few substantial changes from the 1966 version. A contemporary or future reader of any one of these three editions would still conclude that information processing is the construction of computer programs as models of psychological processes and that the work of Newell and Simon is relevant in identifying both the origin and essential nature of information-processing accounts.

Summary

Contemporary cognitive psychology emerged in the twentieth century, and the significant concepts associated with its perspective were in place by the late 1950s. Only rhetorical and institutional components appeared later. As an object it is likely to occupy historians for some time because how its history is best conceptualized remains problematical: as more renaissance than revolution or as Skinner suggests a retreat; as an analysis of psychological phenomenon that trades upon a particular piece of electronic machinery; as a return to the original concerns of nineteenth-century psychology: the science of mind; as the problem of representationalism replacing prediction and control of behavior as the fundamental issue; as a contemporary substitue for Tolman's older psychology of intervening variables; as an evolutionary product of the neobehaviorism that preceded it; or as a shift to the abstract and artificial where the systems and processes under study need not be embedded in a biological entity.

Whatever judgments future historians may make, this much is clear: The issues that concern contemporary cognitive psychology have a long history within the discipline, the forces that have shaped its current form lie outside the science of psychology, and currently more than at any other time in its history, contemporary psychology has more of a commitment to the engineering and mathematical sciences than to any parentage in biological or philosophical analysis. The wisdom of this commitment must await the passage of time for a complete assessment.

ACKNOWLEDGMENTS

My appreciation is extended to Maureen Moen, Joseph Raney, Lynn Robertson, and Mark Small for assistance on the manuscript.

REFERENCES

Allport, F. H. (1955). *Theories of perception and the concept of structure.* New York: Wiley.
Anderson, J. (1980). *Cognitive psychology and its implications.* San Francisco: Freeman.
Anderson, R. C., & Ausbel, D. P. (1965). *Readings in the psychology of cognition.* New York: Holt, Rinehart, & Winston.
Attneave, F. (1959). *Applications of information theory to psychology.* New York: Holt, Rinehart, & Winston.
Battig, W. F. (1975). Within-individual differences in "cognitive" processes. In R. L. Solso (Ed.), *Information processing and cognition.* Hillsdale, NJ: Lawrence Erlbaum Associates.
Berlo, D. K. (1960). *The process of communication.* New York: Holt, Rinehart, & Winston.
Bourne, L. E. (1973). Some forms of cognition: A critical analysis of several papers. In R. Solso (Ed.), *Contemporary issues in cognitive psychology.* Washington, DC: Winston.
Broadbent, D. E. (1957). A mechanical model for human attention and immediate memory. *Psychological Review, 64,* 205–215.
Broadbent, D. E. (1958). *Perception and communication.* New York: Pergamon.
Broadbent, D. E. (1963). Flow of information within the organism. *Journal of Verbal Learning and Verbal Behavior, 2,* 34–39.
Broadbent, D. E. (1971). *Decision and stress.* New York: Academic Press.
Broadbent, D. E. (1980). Biography. In G. Lindzey (Ed.), *A history of psychology in autobiography* (Vol. VII). San Francisco: Freeman.
Bruner, J. (1983). *In search of mind: Essays in autobiography.* New York: Harper & Row.
Bruner, J. S., Goodnow, J. J., & Austin, G. A. (1956). *A study of thinking.* New York: Wiley.
Campbell, R. V. D. (1952). Evolution of autonomatic computation. In *Proceedings of the Association for Computing Machinery* (pp. 29–32). Pittsburgh, PA: Richard Rimbach.
Chase, G. C. (1952). History of mechanical computing machinery. In *Proceedings of the Association for Computing Machinery* (pp. 1–28). Pittsburgh, PA: Richard Rimbach.
Cherry, E. C. (1952). A history of the theory of information. In *Proceedings of the Association for Computing Machinery* (pp. 22–43). Pittsburgh, PA: Richard Rimbach.
Cohen, D. (1977). *Psychologists on psychology.* New York: Taplinger.
Fisher, K. (1983). 'Mind' slowly returns to legitimate inquiry. *APA Monitor, 14* (10), 18.
Fitts, P., & Deininger, R. L. (1954). S–R compatibility: Correspondence among paired elements within stimulus and response codes. *Journal of Experimental Psychology, 48,* 483–492.
Freud, S. (1917). *Introductory lectures on psycho-analysis* (Vol. XV–XVI). In the standard edition of the complete psychological works of Sigmund Freud. London: Hogarth.
Frick, F. C., & Miller, G. A. (1951). A statistical description of operant conditioning. *American Journal of Psychology, 64,* 20–36.

Garner, W. R. (1962). *Uncertainty and structure as psychological concepts.* New York: Wiley.

Garner, W. R. (1959). Information theory and its applications in psychology, a symposium. In *Proceedings of the 15th International Congress of Psychology.* Amsterdam: North–Holland.

Gilgen, A. R. (1974). *Converging trends in psychology.* Paper presented at the meeting of American Psychological Association. New Orleans.

Gilgen, A. R. (1982). *American Psychology since World War II: A profile of the discipline.* Westport, CT: Greenwood.

Haber, R. N. (1974). Information processing. In E. C. Carterette & M. P. Friedman (Eds.), *Handbook of perception* (Vol. I). *Historical and philosophical roots of perception.* New York: Academic Press.

Haber, R. N. (1983). The impending demise of the icon: A critique of the concept of iconic storage in visual information processing. *The Behavioral and Brain Sciences, 6,* 1–54 (includes commentaries and author's response).

Harper, R. J. C. (1964). *The cognitive processes: Readings.* Englewood Cliffs, NJ: Prentice–Hall.

Heims, S. J. (1980). *Jon von Neuman and Norbert Weiner: From mathematics to the technologies of life and death.* Cambridge: MIT press.

Hilgard, E. R. (1948). *Theories of learning.* New York: Appleton–Century–Crofts.

Hilgard, E. R., & Bower, G. (1966). *Theories of learning* (3rd ed.). New York: Appleton–Century–Crofts.

Hilgard, E. R., & Bower, G. (1975). *Theories of learning* (4th ed). New York: Prentice–Hall.

Hilgard, E. R., & Bower, G. (1981). *Theories of learning* (5th ed.). New York: Prentice–Hall.

Hilgard, E. R., & Marquis, D. G. (1940). *Conditioning and learning.* New York: Appleton–Century–Crofts.

Hodges, A. (1983). *Alan Turing: The enigma.* New York: Simon & Schuster.

Hull, C. L. (1943). *Principles of behavior.* New York: Appleton–Century–Crofts.

Hunt, E. B. (1962). *Concept learning: An information processing problem.* New York: Wiley.

Hunt, M. (1982). *The universe within: A new science explores the human mind.* New York: Simon & Schuster.

Koch, S. (1964). Psychology and emerging conceptions of knowledge as unity. In T. W. Wann (Ed.), *Behaviorism and phenomenology.* Chicago: University of Chicago Press.

Knapp, T. J. (1985). A note concerning T. V. Moore and his *Cognitive Psychology* of 1939. (Manuscript under review)

Krantz, D. L. (1972). Schools and systems: The mutual isolation of operant and non-operant psychology as a case study. *Journal of the history of the behavioral sciences, 8,* 86–102.

Kreitler, H., & Kreitler, S. (1976). *Cognitive orientation and behavior.* New York: Springer.

Lachman, R., Lachman, J., & Butterfield, E. C. (1979). *Cognitive psychology and information processing.* Hillsdale, NJ: Lawrence Erlbaum Associates.

Leahey, T. H. (1980). *A history of psychology.* Englewood Cliffs, NJ: Prentice–Hall.

Leeper, R. (1951). Cognitive processes. In S. S. Stevens (Ed.), *Handbook of experimental psychology.* New York: Wiley.

Lewandowsky, S., & Dunbar, K. (1983). Cognitive psychology: A comparative review of textbooks. *American Journal of Psychology, 96,* 391–403.

Lovie, A. D. (1983). Attention and behaviorism—fact and fiction. *British Journal of Psychology, 74,* 301–310.

Machlup, F., & Mansfield, U. (Eds.). (1983). *The study of information.* New York: Wiley.

MacKay, D. (1956). Towards an information-flow model of human behavior. *British Journal of Psychology, 47,* 30–43.

Malcolm, N. (1971). The myth of cognitive processes and structures. In T. Mischel (Ed.), *Cognitive development and epistemology.* New York: Academic Press.

Marx, M., & Hillix, W. A. (1963). *Systems and theories in psychology.* New York: McGraw–Hill.

Mathews, R. (1954). Recall as a function of number of classificatory categories. *Journal of Experimental Psychology, 47,* 241–247.

Mayr, O. (1970). *The origins of feedback control.* Cambridge: MIT Press.

McCorduck, P. (1979). *Machines who think: A personal inquiry into the history and prospects of artificial intelligence.* San Francisco: Freeman.

McCormick, E. J. (1964). *Human factors engineering.* New York: McGraw–Hill.

Miller, G. A. (1951). *Language and communication.* New York: McGraw–Hill.

Miller, G. A. (1953). What is information meansurment? *American Psychologist, 8,* 3–11.

Miller, G. A., & Frick, F. C. (1949). Statistical behavioristics and sequences of responses. *Psychological Review, 56,* 311–324.

Miller, G. A., Galanter, E., & Pribram, K. H. (1960). *Plans and the structure of behavior.* New York: Holt, Rinehart, & Winston.

Miller, J. (1983). *States of mind.* New York: Pantheon.

Moore, T. V. (1915). The temporal relations of meaning and imagery. *Psychological Review, 22,* 177–225.

Moore, T. V. (1917). Meaning and imagery. *Psychological Review, 24,* 318–322.

Moore, T. V. (1938). *Cognitive psychology.* Philadelphia: Lippincott.

Moritz, M. (1972). The concept of cognition in contemporary psychology. In J. R. Royce & W. W. Rozeboom (Eds.), *The psychology of knowing.* New York: Gordon & Breach.

Neisser, U. (1967). *Cognitive psychology.* New York: Appleton–Century–Crofts.

Neisser, U. (1976). *Cognition and realty.* San Francisco: Freeman.

Newell, A., Shaw, J. C., & Simon, H. A. (1958). Elements of a theory of human problem solving. *Psychological Review, 65,* 151–166.

Newell, A., & Simon, H. A. (1972). *Human problem solving.* Englewood Cliffs, NJ: Prentice–Hall.

Norman, D. (1976). Biography. In R. I. Evans (Ed.), *The making of psychology.* New York: Knopf.

Posner, M. I., & Shulman, G. L. (1979). Cognitive science. In E. Hearst (Ed.), *The first century of experimental psychology.* Hillsdale, NJ: Lawrence Erlbaum Associates.

Postman, L. (1951). Toward a general theory of cognition. In J. H. Rohn & M. Scherif (Eds.), *Social psychology at the crossroads.* New York: Harper & Row.

Reitman, W. R. (1965). *Cognition and thought: An information-processing approach.* New York: Wiley.

Salzinger, K. (1973). Inside the black box, with apologies to Pandora. *Journal of the Experimental Analysis of Behavior, 19,* 369–378.

Shannon, C. E., & Weaver, W. (1949). *The mathematical theory of communication.* Urbana: University of Illinois.

Shurkin, J. (1984). *Engines of the mind: A history of the computer.* New York: Norton.

Simon, H. A. (1947). *Administrative behavior.* New York: Macmillan.

Simon, H. A. (1979). *Models of thought.* New Haven: Yale University Press.

Simon, H. A. (1980). Biography. In G. Lindzey (Ed.), *A history of psychology in autobiography* (Vol. VII). San Francisco: Freeman.

Skinner, B. F. (1938). *The behavior of organisms.* New York: Appleton–Century–Crofts. (Reprinted with a new introduction, 1966).

Skinner, B. F. (1950). Are theories of learning necessary? *Psychological Review, 57,* 193–216.

Stevens, S. S. (Ed.), (1951). *Handbook of experimental psychology.* New York: Wiley.

Tolman, E. C. (1917). More concerning the temporal relations of meaning and imagery. *Psychological Review, 24,* 114–138.

Tolman, E. C. (1932). *Purposive behavior in animals and men.* New York: Appleton–Century.

Voss, J. F. (Ed.). (1969). *Aspects of thought.* Columbus, OH: Merrill.

Wasserman, E. A. (1983). Is cognitive psychology behavioral? *Psychological Record, 33,* 6–11.

Wiener, N. (1948). *Cybernetics: Or Control and communication in the animal and the machine.* Cambridge: MIT Press.

Wessells, M. G. (1981). A critique of Skinner's views on the explanatory inadequacy of cognition theories. *Behaviorism, 9,* 153–170.

Wessells, M. G. (1982). A critique of Skinner's views on the obstructive character of cognitive theories. *Behaviorism, 10,* 65–84.

White, M. J. (1983). Prominent publications in cognitive psychology. *Memory & Cognition, 11,* 423–427.

Woodworth, R. S. (1927). Gestalt psychology and the concept of reaction stages. *American Journal of Psychology, 39,* 62–69.

3 The Information Processing Approach to Cognition

Stephen E. Palmer
University of California, Berkeley

Ruth Kimchi
University of California, San Diego

Of the many alternative approaches available for understanding cognition, the one that has dominated psychological investigation for the last decade or two is information processing (IP). For better or worse, the IP approach has had an enormous impact on modern cognitive research, leaving its distinctive imprint on both the kinds of theories that have been proposed and the kinds of experiments that have been performed to test them. Its influence has been so pervasive, in fact, that some writers have argued that IP has achieved the exalted status of a "Kuhnian paradigm" for cognitive psychology (Lachman, Lachman, & Butterfield, 1979). It is unclear whether or not this claim is really justified, but the fact that it has even been suggested documents the preeminence of IP in modern cognitive psychology.

Whenever an approach so dominates a scientific field, it is important to understand—or at least to try to understand—its foundations: the nature of the assumptions that underlie its use. These must be scrutinized for their consistency, plausibility, empirical support, utility, and potential limitations. Only then can one begin to see how the approach is related to others, how firmly it is rooted, why it has taken the field to its present state, and where it is likely to lead in the future. The goal of such an enterprise is essentially to provide a theory of a particular scientific approach to capture the activities and intuitions of its practitioners accurately and succinctly. If the practitioners agree that the analysis succeeds in capturing the nature of their beliefs and their work, it can eventually replace vague intuitions with well-defined constructs as the basis for further research.

We believe that the time has come to examine the foundations of information processing in psychology. There has been some work along these lines, but it has come primarily from philosophers and computer scientists rather than from IP psychologists themselves. From IP-oriented philosophers have come formulations of a new philosophical doctrine—called *functionalism*—offered as a possible solution to the age-old mind/body problem (e.g., Dennett, 1978; Fodor, 1968; Putnam, 1960). From computer scientists have come related proposals that the operation of the human mind can be simulated, or perhaps even duplicated, on modern digital computers (e.g., Newell, 1980; Newell & Simon, 1972, 1976). The trouble is that many cognitive psychologists who consider themselves IP practitioners, ourselves included, find that some of the assumptions made in these arguments are too strong or of the wrong type (or both) to accurately reflect the nature of IP in psychology.

The present chapter represents our attempt to present a principled description of the IP approach as it is practiced within psychology. We try to formulate the assumptions underlying IP in terms that are based as explicitly as possible on how IP theories are constructed and tested by most IP psychologists. The accounts given by philosophers and computer scientists are just too far removed from what psychologists actually do to be certain that their views accurately reflect our own. Perhaps it will turn out that they do—although we argue otherwise—but this certainly is a matter that requires and deserves more serious attention than it has yet received. We must not *assume* that their views are the same as ours but rather *determine* whether they are or not. One of our principle aims, then, is to analyze the nature of IP with an eye toward clarifying its relation to these other proposals.

In the first half of this chapter we attempt to give a fairly broad characterization of the information-processing approach to cognition and the assumptions on which it is based. In the second half we consider the relation of IP psychology to other approaches to cognition, discussing how they agree and how they conflict.

FIVE ASSUMPTIONS OF INFORMATION PROCESSING

We take as our starting point the proposition that the intuitive basis of the IP approach is a theoretical analogy between mental activity and a program running on a computer. Whatever deeper roots IP psychology might have in communication theory, mathematical logic, or formal linguistics, the idea that the mind works like some sort of computer program is certainly the principal reason for IP's current popularity. The analogy runs roughly as follows. Certain information from the environment (the "input") is available to the mind through sensory systems, much as input information is available to a computer program through peripheral devices such as terminals, card readers, and the like. Some of this information is then manipulated in more or less complex ways by mental operations, much as a computer program manipulates information according to the rules it embodies. Among these mental operations are ones that select, transform, store, and match information arising from the present situation, from memories of past situations, from plans for future situations, or (usually) some combination of these. As a result of such operations, the mind produces information in a different form (the "output") that is expressed as overt behavior, in much the same way that a computer program outputs information through the activity of its peripheral output devices such as terminals, line printers, and so forth. Interestingly, this general proposal about mental operations was made as early as 1943 by Kenneth Craik, long before modern digital computers were generally available.

Is there anything more to IP theory than this loose analogy? We believe that there is and try to specify what it is in the remainder of this section. We have structured our discussion around five assumptions that are almost universally held by IP psychologists and are fundamental to their beliefs about how to construct theories of cognition. We list them here without background or discussion as a preview of the analysis we are about to present:

1. *Informational Description:* Mental events can be functionally described as "informational events," each of which consists of three parts: the *input information* (what it starts with), the *operation* performed on the input (what gets done to the input), and the *output information* (what it ends up with).

2. *Recursive Decomposition:* Any complex (i.e., nonprimitive) informational event at one level of description can be specified more fully at a lower level by *decomposing* it into (1) a number of components, each of which is itself an informational event, and (2) the temporal ordering relations among them that specify how the information "flows" through the system of components.

3. *Flow Continuity:* All input information required to perform each operation must be available in the output of the operations that flow into it.

4. *Flow Dynamics:* No output can be produced by an operation until its input information is available and sufficient additional time has elapsed for it to process that input.

5. *Physical Embodiment:* In the dynamic physical system whose behavior is being described as an informational event, information is embodied in states of the system (here called *representations*) and operations that use this information are embodied in changes of state (here called *processes*).

We do not pretend that this list exhausts the assumptions underlying IP psychology, but they are certainly among the most important ones and form a widely held set of "core beliefs." In the following discussion we try to justify these assumptions, elaborate on their significance, and analyze at least some of their implications. Unfortunately, space does not permit any corresponding discussion of the equally important methodological and empirical aspects of IP psychology.

Assumption 1: Informational Description

Saying that the mind is like a computer program really just means that we can describe both of them in essentially the same way. We don't want to restrict our formulation of the analogy to modern digital computers because many mental processes—especially ones at the sensory and motor ends—seem to operate a lot more like "analog" machines than digital ones. Furthermore, we want to avoid using the term *computational* altogether because of its technical meaning in the theory of computability (cf. Johnson–Laird, 1983; Newell, 1980), which we do not want to presuppose. Therefore, we state the first assumption in terms of describing mental processes as something we call *informational events,* which we define as follows:

(1) Mental events can be functionally described as "informational events," each of which consists of three parts: the *input information* (what it starts with), the *operation* performed on the input (what gets done to the input), and the *output information* (what it ends up with).

By "mental events" we mean to include not only conscious experiences but all internal happenings that influence behavior, many of which will not produce any conscious experiences at all. For instance, native speakers seem to be able to parse sentences quite well without any conscious experience of the corresponding mental processes, and yet one will almost certainly need to suppose that there are some internal events of this sort to explain how people understand language. Naturally, we do not mean to *exclude* events of which people are conscious either. The phrase "mental events" in our first assumption is really just a placeholder for whatever events turn out to be necessary to account for what things people are able to do and how they do them. The concepts of "information" and "operations" also need to be defined, of course, but we postpone this lengthier discussion to a later section.

The sort of description proposed in the first assumption can be represented by a "black box" diagram like the one shown in Fig. 3.1A. It is assumed that the output is *determined* by the input together with the operation performed on it, and so one really needs just the first two of the three parts—input plus operation—to specify what is going on. If the operation is complicated enough that one cannot describe it directly, the operation can be expressed implicitly by specifying the mapping from input to output. When the operation so defined is ascribed to the human mind, we call this specification a "mental mapping."

Functional Description.   Another aspect of the first assumption that needs to be discussed is the notion of a "functional" description. The intent here is to single out a domain of discourse for IP theories of mind that appropriately reflects the kind of accounts they offer. In this context, *functional* descriptions are to be distinguished from both *physical* and *phenomenological* descriptions.

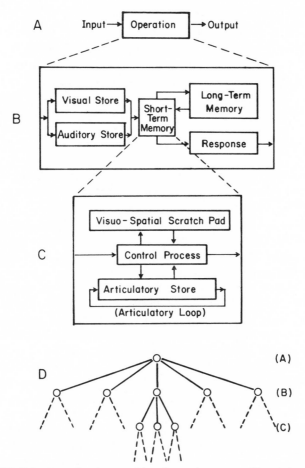

FIG. 3.1.   Recursive decomposition of mental processes. The mind can be described as a single, complex informational operation that maps input stimulation to output behavior (A). This operation can be decomposed into an information flow diagram of several simpler component operations (B), each of which can be further decomposed into still simpler operations. The resulting recursive structure of theoretical decomposition can be represented by a hierarchical graph (D) in which the nodes at a given level correspond to the component operations of the flow diagram at that level and the links (arcs) connecting them represent the decomposition relations between different levels of description.

We claim that it is possible to construct theories relevant to psychology at any of these levels and that there are important relationships among them. However, IP psychology is identified primarily with the "middle" level of functional descriptions, and secondarily with how this level relates to the other two levels.

Theories at the physical level are concerned with the nature of material substances and events that take place within brains. Descriptions at this level are given in terms of causal sequences of biochemical events involved in neural firings and interactions. Such descriptions are ultimately reducible, at least in theory, to quantal happenings among countless quarks, or whatever the most microscopic level of physical reality happens to be. Very few, if any, theories in psychology are proposed solely within the physical domain.

Theories at the phenomenological level are concerned with systematic and principled descriptions of conscious experiences in terms of other conscious experiences. Such experiential descriptions are different in kind from any sort of physical description, a fact that has led philosophers to debate issues about the relation between mind and body for centuries. Phenomenological accounts of mental events were once the primary theoretical goal within psychology, when the "introspective method" reigned supreme. Because the subjective experiences on which they are based are not publicly observable entities, however, true phenomenological theories fell from favor with the advent of behaviorism (Watson, 1913). Since then phenomenological description has played an important, but decidely supporting, role in psychology. This is true despite the fact that many psychological theories—particularly in the field of perception—still have as their goal an account of phenomenal experience. The crucial difference is that, since Watson, psychological theories have seldom been advanced in which the account is given *solely* in introspective terms. Outside of psychology proper, however, important phenomenological theories have been offered by philosophers such as Heidegger (1962) and Merleau–Ponty (1962).

At this point it is appropriate to give a clear definition of the functional level. Unfortunately, we do not know of a good one—other than the one implied by the information-processing approach—and so we can only appeal to intuitive notions here. Theories at the functional level are concerned directly with neither material substances nor subjective experiences, but rather with how the brain or mind *works* or *behaves* within the context of the environment. The presumption is that this functional level of description is considerably more abstract and general than the physical level (in the sense that many physically quite different objects can have the same function), and yet this functional description is still tied to physical reality in principled ways. Most psychological theories have at least one foot firmly in this functional level. Even physiological theories, which might seem to be exclusively physical, are usually about the relation between some physical structure and its function, as when researchers attempt to say what a given cell "signals" in the environment (e.g., Hubel & Wiesel's (1968) "edge detectors" and "bar detectors"). Prominent examples of psychological theories couched exclusively or primarily within the functional domain include Skinner's (1953) theory of organismic behavior, Piaget's (1950) theory of cognitive development, Freud's (1933) theory of personality, and the many theories that came out of the "functionalist" school, as well as all modern IP theories.

Information and Operations.   What distinguishes IP theories from most other functional theories in psychology is its further claim that the appropriate type of functional description is *informational;* that is, mental events are to be characterized in terms of information and operations that relate information.[1] We cannot here present rigorous yet uncontroversial definitions of information and operations because they are among the least understood and most problematic aspects of the whole IP enterprise. This may seem surprising given how heavily the entire theoretical approach seems to rest on them, but the most basic concepts in science often prove to be the most difficult to analyze explicitly.

The situation is especially peculiar with respect to "information" in that, at first glance, it might seem as though there is a readily available formalization in Shannon's (1948) mathematical theory of information. But Shannon's conception of information is not what we meant when we talked about information in the first assumption and not, we suspect, what any other IP theorist means by it either. To see why, one needs only to consider the general nature of Shannon's formulation of information: It is a unidimensional quantity (measured in "bits") that expresses the reduction in uncertainty by a receiver about a source via a message transmitted through a noisy communication channel. Even without the mathematical details it is easy to see that this is not what the first assumption is about. As many commentators on the mathematical theory of information have also noted (e.g., Dretske, 1979; Garner, 1962), Shannon's conception of "information" refers only to the *amount* of something as measured in bits, whereas "information itself" is about the *something* that gets measured in these bits. What IP psychologists mean by information is far more closely related to the content of the "messages" and the whole communication context that surrounds them than it is to the "amount of reduction in uncertainty." Shannon's theory is really about the *informativeness* or *surprise value* of messages rather than about their actual *information content*. This means that we are almost back to where we started: We know that information is not the same as Shannon's measure of informativeness, but we still don't know what it is or how it is related to his formulation. This is a rather embarassing situation, but one that accurately reflects the present state of affairs in IP psychology.

As we are using the terms, information is an abstract construct in theoretical descriptions of mental events. We have used it in this way to reflect the pervasive belief among IP psychologists that IP theories are *abstract, functional* entities that do not depend on at least certain physical characteristics of the events being described. But we still need to define this level of abstraction and to say how it arises in the IP paradigm.

The key to understanding the abstractness of the IP level lies in the abstract nature of information itself. This abstraction can be intuitively demonstrated by examples in which two physically very different signals can carry the same

---

[1]We say "most" because there are some examples of functional theories based on informational descriptions that are, nevertheless, not instances of IP theories. The most notable example is James J. Gibson's (1966, 1979) theory of ecological optics in which informational descriptions play the central role, but which does not conform to the additional assumptions of IP.

information about some referent state of affairs. For example, Paul Revere and his coconspirator agreed that information about the arrival of British troops was to be carried by the number of lights hung in the church window ("one if by land and two if by sea"). However, the *same information* could have been equally well transmitted by the opposite arrangement ("one if by sea and two if by land"), or by the color of a single light ("red if by land and blue if by sea"), or by the number of cannon shots fired, or, indeed, by any other pair of signals that Revere could have distinguished from his vantage point on the opposite shore, provided that he and the signal-sender had agreed on the signals and their corresponding interpretations in advance.[2] There is an important sense in which all these alternative signals—one light, two lights, red light, blue light—would have been *informationally equivalent* under the corresponding scenarios, despite their wide variety as different physical events. The reason is that they all "stand for" or "represent" the same referent event. This informational equivalence is, by definition, more abstract and general than mere physical equivalence. It is a form of *functional equivalence* because it is concerned with the extent to which different events could be substituted for each other and still "work in the same way" or "cause the same outcome." It is in precisely this sense that IP descriptions are more abstract than the physical events they describe. The abstract functional nature of IP descriptions thus lies in the nature of information itself, specifically in the abstract equivalence relation defined by substitution.

Mapping Theories.   At this point in our development of IP theory the whole operation performed by the human mind is conceived as a single, complex function that maps input information to output information. Informational theories of mind can be and have been proposed at this highly abstract level. We call such theories "informational mapping theories" or simply "mapping theories."[3] They specify *what the mapping is* in a systematic and well-defined way

---

[2]Whereas in this example Revere and his partner had to agree explicitly on the informational correspondence between events and signals (and hence the interpretation of the signals by Revere), the same cannot literally be true for informational theories of mind, because there are no parties to do the agreeing. Instead, the role of agreement in this example must be played by some other method of arriving at a conventional interpretation: namely, some *process of selection,* such as evolution in cases of innately given interpretations (e.g., simple unlearned reflexes) or learning in cases of organism-acquired interpretations. In informational theories of mind, interpretations of signals carrying information about the world must be *achieved* through some process that provides feedback about the appropriateness of the chosen interpretation. Thus the informational correspondence is "agreed" upon by what *works:* which interpretation is evolutionarily successful or which one leads to desired outcomes in the learning situation. The end result is the same as if an agreement had been made between the environment and the organism: The signals carry information about the environmental events that is largely independent of the specific physical nature of those signals.

[3]Mapping theories are very similar to what Marr (1982) has called *computational theories.* We find his label unfortunate because it strongly suggests that the mapping is accomplished by some sort of computation. If the mapping theory really makes no claim about *how* the mapping is accom-

without claiming to specify *how this mapping is accomplished*. In other words, mapping theories make no psychological claims about what goes on "inside the mental black box"; they merely describe the result of the mapping performed from inputs to outputs.

Despite this limited goal, mapping theories of large domains can be notoriously difficult to construct and are correspondingly rare. In part this is because precise specification of the mapping often requires extensive use of formal mathematical tools such as algebra, geometry, formal grammars, predicate calculus, computer programming, and the like. Another difficulty lies in the vast scope of a mapping theory for the entire range of human performance. Therefore, it is not surprising that the available examples attempt to define the input–output mapping only for some modest subdomain of human mental abilities: e.g., Chomsky's (1965) transformational grammar theory of linguistic syntax, Horn's (1975, 1977) differential geometric theory of perceiving shape from shading, Johnson–Laird's (1983) predicate calculus theory of syllogistic reasoning, Leeuwenberg's (1971, 1978) symbolic coding theory of shape perception, Longuet–Higgins and Prazdny's (1980) theory of optical flow, Marr and Poggio's (1979) "computational theory" of stereoscopic vision, and Ullman's (1979) theory of motion perception, to name some of the most prominent examples. If the scope of the mapping theory is sufficiently narrow, of course, then it can be defined simply by enumerating the input–output correspondence, e.g., the mapping theory of naming the capital letters of the alphabet in a particular type font can be specified completely by a list of 26 ordered pairs. Such simple mapping theories are seldom stated explicitly because they are so intuitively obvious.

Because mapping theories do not attempt to specify *how* the mapping from inputs to outputs is accomplished, scientific interest in them centers on their formal rigor, predictive accuracy, and ecological validity. Unfortunately, it is often unclear just how accurately the specified mapping predicts the mental mapping because the theorist makes some form of the "competence assumption": an assumption that the theory specifies the mapping independently of any "performance" or "resource" limitations (cf. Chomsky, 1965). This strategy can be justified on the grounds that if one does not care *how* the mapping gets done, the theory need not—indeed, should not—take such considerations into account. However, the fact that such limitations usually do affect the observed mapping weakens the empirical implications of the mapping theory and, therefore, makes it hard to test. The problem is that it is difficult to discriminate cases in which the inaccuracies arise simply because the competence assumption is inappropriate versus cases in which they arise because of fundamental inadequacies in the mapping theory itself.

---

plished, calling it "computational" seems to prejudge an important issue that lies outside the mapping theory itself. We discuss these issues in more depth in the later section on "Computationalism."

Mapping theories are also often judged by criteria of ecological validity as well. The reason is that if a theory concerns only *what* mapping is performed, it is important that the mapping be one that applies, at least in principle, to a wide range of realistic stimulus situations. If not, it is unclear what the importance of the theory is for understanding human behavior. Unfortunately, the criteria for deciding how valid a theory is ecologically are seldom well defined, and judgments usually rest on vague intuitions about the superficial similarity between the conditions to which the theory applies and the naturally occurring conditions in the ecology of the organism. Ecological criteria are usually taken to be less critical in evaluating theories that attempt to specify *how* the mapping occurs. Such theories are taken to be primarily about the internal mechanisms they postulate, and so application to simple (and seemingly ecologically invalid) situations are valued for the additional scientific rigor they often permit in empirical tests.

To the preceding list of mapping theories one might wish to append some important related theoretical efforts that are similar in kind but miss one of the critical attributes of rigor, accuracy, and ecological validity. James J. Gibson's (1950, 1966, 1979) "ecological optics" theory of spatial perception was clearly in the spirit of a mapping theory by our definition—i.e., he tried to specify the mapping from proximal stimuli to perceptual responses—and had strong claims to ecological validity, but only infrequently did it achieve the requisite level of rigor to specify the actual mapping (e.g., Gibson, Olum, & Rosenblatt, 1955). Naturally, when a mapping theory is not well enough defined to determine the mapping unambiguously, its accuracy is correspondingly difficult to evaluate, and this has been a problem with many of Gibson's proposals. Other possible candidates for mapping theories come from "normative" theories, often adopted wholesale from other disciplines. They are usually rigorous but often turn out not to give a very good account of human performance, even taking the competence assumption into account. Examples of this type include mathematical logic as a theory of human reasoning (e.g., Henle, 1978; Inhelder & Piaget, 1958; see Johnson–Laird, 1983, for a critique), mathematical information theory as a theory of human performance (e.g., Fitts & Posner, 1967; Garner, 1962), and Bayesian probability theory as a theory of human inference (e.g., Edwards, 1965, 1968; see Kahneman & Tversky, 1973, for a critique).[4]

---

[4]Given the indeterminacy mentioned previously in determining whether inaccuracies in the mappings are due to errors introduced by the competence assumption or more fundamental errors in the theory, there is a certain unavoidable element of personal judgment in deciding whether a given theory is an instance of a "good" mapping theory or belongs in this category of "inadequate" normative theories. There seems to be a correlation with the theory's age: Older mapping theories are more likely to be thought inadequate, probably just because they have been more thoroughly tested. Chomsky's (1965) transformational grammar theory, for instance, would now be thought by many to be an inadequate "normative" theory rather than a psychologically interesting mapping theory.

The relatively small number of currently viable mapping theories should not be taken as evidence that they are unimportant. Indeed, their advocates have argued that they are absolutely critical to the enterprise of understanding the mind and that the lack of such theories is largely responsible for psychology's slow progress (cf. Chomsky, 1965; Gibson, 1966, 1979; Marr, 1982). IP psychologists are interested in them—or should be—because, even though they do not *propose* internal mechanisms, they strongly *constrain* possible mechanisms, and they are testable. The constraints arise from the fact that knowledge about the mapping eliminates or makes implausible an enormous set of possible mechanisms. Their testability derives from the fact that they are directly tied to empirical reality at both the input and output ends and so can be compared directly to human behavior. The importance of mapping theories in psychology is confirmed by inspecting the foregoing list. Even in cases where they have clearly failed as psychological theories, testing them to find out when and how they go wrong has produced important results that have strongly affected further theorizing. For example, the ways in which formal logic (cf. Johnson–Laird, 1983) and Bayesian probability theory (cf. Kahneman & Tversky, 1973) have failed as theories of human performance have led theorists to more accurate formulations.

Notice that there is nothing about mapping theories that is unique to the IP approach. They are certainly *consistent* with it (cf. Marr, 1982), but the relationship is a weak one. Gibson, for example, was a strong advocate of what we are calling mapping theories, yet he was openly opposed to and critical of the IP approach. Some of his followers in ecological psychology are even more adamant about their opposition (e.g., Shaw & Bransford, 1977; Turvey, 1977). What these theorists primarily object to is IP's further assumption that a psychological theorist should *decompose* the mental mapping by postulating a structure of internal events that purport to describe *how* it is achieved. We now turn our attention to this second critical assumption of the IP approach.

Assumption 2: Recursive Decomposition

Perhaps the most central assumption of IP theories is that any unitary informational event can be described more fully at a more specific (or "lower") level by decomposing it into simpler informational events. We state this conjecture as the assumption of *recursive decomposition:*

> (2) Any complex (nonprimitive) informational event at one level of description can be specified more fully at a lower level by *decomposing* it into (1) a number of components, each of which is itself an informational event, and (2) the temporal ordering relations among them that specify how the information "flows" through the system of components.

Informational theories that make use of this assumption are true *IP theories* (or "process models") because they make claims about what is inside the "black box" of the mind. This level of theory corresponds to what Marr (1982) has called the "algorithmic" level. Unlike mapping theories, which only specify *what* the mental mapping is, IP theories try to specify something about *how* that mapping is accomplished. Such IP theories are usually represented graphically by drawings such as those shown in Fig. 3.1B and 1C. We call these *IP flow diagrams*.[5] For instance, Fig. 3.1B shows a possible flow diagram for the unitary operation depicted in Fig. 3.1A. It is typical of first-level IP flow diagrams proposed as theories of mental structures involved in cognitive tasks (e.g., Atkinson & Shiffrin, 1968). Each of the components at this level has its own "primitive" description in terms of the three functional parts of an informational event: (1) its input information, (2) the operation that gets performed, and (3) the output information that results.

A flow diagram is only an *incomplete* representation of an IP theory, however, because it does not show precisely what input-to-output mapping is accomplished by the operations depicted in the flow diagram. What is needed to complete the theory is a "mini-mapping theory" for each of the internal informational events postulated in the diagram or, equivalently, a direct description of the operation. In some cases the mapping theory of the components is so trivial that it does not really need to be spelled out. However, in many other cases the mapping claimed for the hypothesized components is very complex and does need to be explicitly defined, although theorists often fail to do so. The primary difference between these "mini" mapping theories for components within an IP theory and "pure" mapping theories that stand alone at the highest (undecomposed) level is that the former are only indirectly tied to empirical reality, whereas the latter are directly tied to it. For this reason the IP theorist has substantially more freedom in postulating "internal inputs" and "internal outputs" for hypothetical informational events inside the head than the pure mapping theorist has for defining the nature of "external inputs" and "external outputs."

The decomposition assumption states that operations can be broken down into a flow diagram. Because this does not exclude operations that resulted from previously decomposing a higher level operation, it implies that the decomposition of operations into flow diagrams can be performed *recursively*. For instance, Fig. 3.1C shows how one operation in the structure shown in Fig. 3.1B, short-term memory, might be further decomposed into a flow diagram of still simpler

---

[5]We purposely avoid calling them "flowcharts" because of the more restricted, technical meaning this term has in computer science as a device for specifying "transfer of control" in a serial computer. The IP flow diagrams we use here are intended to be a more general representation of how information flows over time through a system of processing components, more or less like a "time-lapse photograph" of the dynamic IP system in action. There are many difficult and technical issues involved in specifying just what these diagrams mean, but we ignore them here and rely on an intuitive understanding of them, fully realizing that this will need to be specified further at some later time.

operations (Baddeley, 1976). Naturally, any of the other operations shown in Fig. 3.1B could be similarly decomposed, although we have not shown this in our diagram.

The recursive nature of decomposition implies that a tree graph can be constructed to represent the hierarchical embedding of flow diagram components, as shown in Fig. 3.1D. The vertical dimension reflects what we have been referring to as "height" ("high level" versus "low level" operations) or "specificity" ("general" versus "specific" descriptions), and the horizontal dimension simply enumerates the components that belong to each level of flow diagram. Later we use this conception to clarify the relation between IP theories and computer programs that simulate them.

The Role of Primitives.   It is clear that without some stopping rule the decomposition assumption could, in principle, be applied recursively ad infinitum. We have included an implicit stopping rule in our second assumption through the concept of a "complex (nonprimitive) informational event," because only these can be further decomposed. By implication, then, a *primitive* informational event *cannot* be further decomposed. We have intentionally left this stopping condition vague because there are at least two plausible and well-used strategies for defining such primitives, one based on "software" considerations and the other on "hardware" considerations. They broadly characterize two styles of theorizing that coexist relatively happily within the IP approach, a "computational" or "software" one based on choosing primitives for computational plausibility and a "physiological" or "hardware" one based on choosing primitives for their neurological plausibility.[6] There is, in addition, a third strategy for dealing with the conditions under which to stop decomposing, and that is simply not to worry about it. Many IP psychologists, perhaps even most of them, are quite satisfied to work at a level that is well above any ultimate "primitives" and leave theorizing at such a "low" level to other theorists.

The computational strategy is to base the stopping rule on "software primitives": choose some set of simple, well understood, primitive IP operations *a priori* and stop when these are reached. For instance, Newell and Simon (1972) define a plausible set of primitive IP operations which are equivalent in power to a universal Turing machine (Newell, 1980), and IP theories have been proposed in terms of just such primitives (e.g., J. R. Anderson, 1976, 1983; Just &

---

[6]The distinction between "computational" and "physiological" approaches is *not* precisely aligned with the disciplines of computer science and psychology, respectively. Some computer scientists have proposed theories that are essentially "physiological" in our sense (e.g., Feldman, 1981; Hinton & Anderson, 1981; Marr & Poggio, 1976, 1979). Conversely, some psychologists have proposed theories that are "computational" in our sense (e.g., J. R. Anderson, 1976, 1983). Still, there does seem to be a tendency for psychologists to favor the physiological strategy and computer scientists to favor the computational one.

Carpenter, 1977; Newell & Simon, 1972). This approach has the logical advantage of definiteness: one does indeed know just what the conditions for stopping are. However, it has the disadvantage of potential inapplicability: one does not know beforehand whether these conditions will ever be reached. In choosing a given set of primitive operations it is important to know, for example, that they are logically *sufficient* to capture the full range of mental capabilities one wishes to describe. Using a set that has the same computational power as a universal Turing machine is obviously a good place to start, but as we will discuss later (see the section "On Computationalism"), there is no way of knowing *a priori* that even this will turn out to be sufficient.[7] If the primitives chosen are insufficient, any theory based on them will necessarily fail. Even assuming that the primitives are logically sufficient, they should also be the psychologically correct primitives. Different sets of primitives can yield quite different IP analyses of the same behavior, so choosing the wrong set in advance will produce the wrong theory.

The physiological strategy is based on "hardware primitives": stop when the hypothesized IP operations are functional descriptions of known physical components in the device being described. This approach can be illustrated by analogy to "black box" problems in physics. The student presented with the box knows beforehand that the electrical components inside the mysterious container are things like resistors, capacitors, transistors, and the like, each of whose functional descriptions he or she supposedly knows well. When a "theory" of the contents of the box is specified as a circuit in which each hypothetical component has the functional description of a resistor, capacitor, transistor, or whatever, then the "bottom" has been reached. Naturally, the student cannot really *know* until the box is opened that it does not contain some far more complex circuit— such as a microcomputer that simulates the hypothetical simple circuit—but as long as the functional characteristics of the physical components are known in advance, there must be at least one correct answer in terms of the functional descriptions of these hardware primitives.

---

[7]Many theorists believe that a set of primitives equal in power to a universal Turing machine *must* be sufficient to capture the nature of mental events (e.g., Johnson–Laird, 1983; Newell, 1980). Their belief rests on the intuition that "Turing's thesis" is correct. Turing (1936) proposed that any scientifically well-defined procedure (usually called an "effective procedure") could be carried out by some Turing machine. If so, one can conclude that if the nature of mind can be captured by an effective procedure, then any set of primitives equal in power to those of a universal Turing machine will be sufficient to capture the nature of mind. Turing's thesis remains a conjecture, however. The fact that no one has yet discovered a well-defined procedure that is beyond the capabilities of a universal Turing machine does not mean that no one ever will. We may currently be in much the same position that geometers were for many centuries when Euclid's geometry was thought to be the only one. In the last two centuries, however, many non-Euclidean geometries have been discovered. Perhaps there is an enormous class of as-yet-undiscovered effective procedures that are beyond the scope of Turing machines. The fact that none have yet been encountered is only weak evidence that Turing's thesis is correct.

The strategy of hardware primitives has much to recommend it. It is necessarily applicable because the functional description of the hardware *must,* by definition, be applicable to describing its behavior. By the same token, it must also be logically sufficient to account for the capabilities of the device, because that is how the device actually does it. There are several potential problems, however. One is that the level of hardware primitives may be considerably "lower" (more specific and detailed) than that of software primitives. For example, the hardware primitives in modern digital computers are much lower level than the software primitives found in the languages that people typically use to program them. If this is also true of the mind/brain, using hardware primitives will unnecessarily increase the complexity of the "bottom level" IP description.

A potentially more serious problem is that cognitive psychologists probably are not yet in the same position as a physics student with a "black box problem" in that we do not really know what the brain's critical physical units are with respect to mental function. The most obvious candidate is, of course, the neuron. However, the important structures might ultimately turn out to be much smaller, such as molecular processes at synaptic membranes, or much larger, such as complex Hebbian cell assemblies (Hebb, 1949). There are at least a few cases in which there is currently good agreement between an IP description and a known physiological structure, all of which do currently point to the neuron as the basic physical unit of processing. However, most of these examples come from fairly peripheral sensory systems—such as color vision (De Valois & De Valois, 1975) and spatial vision (De Valois & De Valois, 1980)—and the relevant unit of processing might conceivably be quite different for more complex cognitive operations.

Still, many IP theorists do seem to use a "hardware primitives" rule, at least implicitly, in that they couch their theories in terms of excitation and inhibition among processing elements more or less like individual neurons or neural pathways (e.g., Feldman, 1981; Hinton, 1981; Marr, 1982; McClelland & Rumelhart, 1981; Palmer, 1983; Palmer & Bucher, 1981; Posner, 1978; Rumelhart & McClelland, 1982). It is perhaps not too surprising that these physiologically oriented theories tend to be of relatively peripheral mental operations such as sensation and perception, processes about which at least something is known of the corresponding neural hardware. Computationally oriented theories tend to be of more complex, central processes like memory, language understanding, and problem solving, processes about which relatively little of importance is yet known with respect to the hardware involved. The principle exception to this generalization comes from recent attempts by some physiologically oriented theorists to explore the potential capabilities of quasineural devices for higher level cognitive processes like memory and categorization (see Hinton & Anderson, 1981, for a good sample).

Complexity Reduction.   The rationale for decomposing mental operations into well-formed flow diagrams is to specify the nature of a single *complex* operation in terms of information flow among a number of *simpler* operations. In principle, at least, the decomposition should "factor out" some portion of the complexity *implicit* in a mental operation when it is considered as a unitary informational event by making it *explicit* in the flow relations among a number of simpler operations. This is what we mean by "complexity reduction": With each lower level of description the internal complexity of the component operations should decrease. Generally speaking, this reduction comes at the cost of more components and more complex flow relations among them. However, the goal is to make complexity explicit, so the net effect of decomposition is to reduce the unwanted commodity: implicit complexity. In effect, as one proceeds down the decomposition tree (see Fig. 3.1D), more and more of the complexity is accounted for by additional arrows and boxes (the part made *explicit* in the flow diagram) and less and less by the "mini" mapping theories of the boxes themselves (the part still *implicit* within the operations).

The assumption that decomposition reduces implicit complexity probably *should* have the same status within IP as the previous two, but it does not for several reasons. The primary problem is that being rigorous about it would require well-defined measures of IP complexity both for mapping theories (i.e., the internal nature of the unitary operations) and for IP flow diagrams (i.e., the ordering relations among these unitary operations). No such measures of either kind are currently in use or, to our knowledge, have ever been suggested. Most IP practitioners probably do believe, at least implicitly, that something like this complexity reduction assumption applies to IP theories because they feel that they understand more about what is going on after an operation has been decomposed than they did when it was a unitary, unarticulated event. This intuition depends heavily on the initial unitary operation being more complex than the several operations into which it is decomposed. Without any well-defined measures of informational complexity, however, it is difficult to tell for any given IP theory whether such beliefs are really justified.

Emergent Properties.   One effect of decomposition not captured by the notion of complexity reduction is that the resulting component operations are not only quantitatively simpler than the initial one, but *qualitatively different* from it. For instance, what would be described as a unitary operation at a high level as a memory search operation ("look for a target, T, in list L") is radically recast in terms of the information flow among its component operations: data retrieval ("get the next element, E, from list L"), pairwise comparison ("compute the similarity, S, of E to T"), decision ("is S greater than some critical value, C?"), and conditional control ("if so, return positive; otherwise, go to start"). Notice that although each lower level operation does something quite specific that is easily described on its own, none of them does anything like "search sequentially through a list." Only when they are configured into an appropriate flow diagram do they, *together,* perform a search operation. "Search" does not really exist in any of the lower level components individually; it *emerges* only when they are put together in the proper flow relations. Strictly speaking, then, it is appropriate to speak of a "search" taking place only at the higher level of description where what is happening is conceived as a unitary event.

Thus we see that higher level IP descriptions sometimes contain *emergent properties* that lower level descriptions do not. It is the *organization* of the system specified by the flow relations among the lower level components that gives rise to these properties. There is nothing mysterious in this. It is equally true in physical systems where systemic "macro" properties arise only in large systems of elements with different "micro" properties. As a simple example, the gaseous, liquid, and solid states of matter arise only in aggregations of many molecules, because no single molecule, by itself, has the properties of being gaseous, liquid, or solid (cf. Putnam, 1975; Searle, 1983); such properties depend on the relations among many molecules. Even better physical analogies can be found in complex human artifacts like stereos, automobile engines, and telephones: The properties of the object as a whole are qualitatively different from those of its smaller physical components. It seems entirely appropriate to conceive of emergent properties in IP systems in essentially the same way; there is no magic involved, just the configural interaction of different subsystems in ways that produce different properties at the systemic level.

Assumption 3: Flow Continuity

Information-processing theories postulate decompositions of mapping theories into psychologically meaningful components. Not just any decomposition will do, of course, because the ordering or "flow" of information among components imposes certain important constraints. These constitute the third assumption of IP, concerning the syntax of IP flow diagrams:

(3) All input information required to perform each operation must be available in the output of the operations that flow into it.

This assumption is perhaps so obvious that it almost goes without saying; it is really just a corollary to the decomposition assumption. In terms of flow diagrams, it states that the input for each "box" consists of the output of all the other "boxes" that lead directly to it by forward-going arrows. If this information is not sufficient for the operation to occur, then the flow diagram is not "well formed," and the theory it represents is logically deficient in the sense that it could not actually carry out the operation it purports to describe. To determine whether such flow constraints have actually been met, the IP flow diagram of an IP theory must be supplemented with a "mini" mapping theory (in the sense described earlier) of each hypothesized operation. In reality, most IP theorists give, at best, a rather vague, verbal description of the input–output characteristics of the components, and it is often hard to determine whether the flow-continuity constraint has been met from such verbal statements. As Newell and Simon (1963) have argued forcefully, this problem can be solved by supporting the theory with a computer simulation, because the program necessarily specifies a "mini" mapping theory for each operation in the flow diagram. Unfortunately, simulations are seldom actually done, and some residual amount of "handwaving" invariably remains in any verbally stated theory. (Later we discuss the relation between simulation programs and IP theories in greater depth.) Flow diagrams that meet the flow-continuity requirement, insofar as this can be determined, constitute IP theories of the unitary informational event at some lower level of description.

Assumption 4: Flow Dynamics

Some additional assumption is needed to specify the temporal properties of information flow within the system. Here we try to specify some of the most general constraints in terms of the assumption of *flow dynamics:*

> (4) No output can be produced by an operation until its input information is available to it and sufficient time has elapsed for it to process this input.

The dynamics of information flow are particularly important in psychology because they often play a central role in empirical tests of the theory. We have attempted to capture only the constraints that (1) processing cannot begin until at least some input information is available and (2) that every operation takes some amount of time, no matter how small.[8] Beyond these two notions, flow dynamics are pretty much up to the theorist and the constraints imposed by the proposed flow diagram.

The most frequently made additional assumption about the time course of processing is that each operation in the flow diagram constitutes a discrete *stage* (Sternberg, 1969a). In stage theories, each operation has a specific duration (plus or minus random variability) that depends on parameters determined by the input information. Before the end of this time interval the operation has no output, and at the end its output is assumed to be fully available as input to the next operation. This notion of discrete stage theories gained immense popularity with the

---

[8]Some mathematical models have been proposed that assume an exponential distribution of completion times (e.g., Townsend & Ashby, 1983). Taken literally, this implies that stages can take no time at all. Because this distributional assumption is generally made for reasons of mathematical convenience rather than psychological validity, we do not see such models as real contradictions of the assumption that all operations take some finite amount of time: If an otherwise equally attractive alternative were available that did *not* allow for the possibility of "instantaneous" processing, we presume that it would be used in preference to exponential models.

success of Sternberg's (1966, 1969b) work on memory scanning and his formulation of the additive factors method (Sternberg, 1969a). In one form or another, stage models have dominated IP theories of flow dynamics ever since.

Other conceptions of flow dynamics are not ruled out, of course; they just make things more complicated. Norman and Bobrow (1975) suggested that a more flexible and realistic conception of information flow was needed than stage theories provided and proposed the hypothesis of "continuously available output" as an alternative. McClelland (1979) developed a specific mathematical theory of this type that he aptly called "cascade processing." In cascade theory, each operation begins to produce some output almost as soon as it gets some input, and certainty in the result increases over time as more and more input is received from preceding operations. Whether this more complex conception of information flow actually provides a more accurate model of IP dynamics than does stage theory is currently unclear, but the formulation of alternatives to stage conceptions of flow dynamics has been an important theoretical development. Even if stage processing does turn out to be correct, the crucial evidence will undoubtedly come from explicitly testing its assumptions against those of well-defined alternatives (e.g., Meyer, Yantis, Osman, & Smith 1984; Miller, 1982).

Among the most important issues related to flow dynamics is whether a given pair of operations are executed sequentially (serial processing) or simultaneously (parallel processing). This is specified in the information flow diagram by the obvious conventions: a "chain" of arrows from each operation to the next (serial) or several arrows diverging from a point and leading to several operations at once (parallel). Although this distinction is quite clear theoretically, it turns out to be much harder to pin down experimentally than was initially suspected (see Townsend, 1971, 1972; Townsend & Ashby, 1983). The problem is that many different versions of serial and parallel process models can be constructed and, depending on which additional assumptions are made, some serial models make predictions that are not empirically distinguishable from some parallel models, and vice versa.

This points out a problem in testing IP models, a problem that we suspect may be far more general than this particular example. It may be quite difficult to produce rigorous tests of large classes of alternative IP models (e.g., serial versus parallel) because pairs of models in the different classes make the same or insufficiently different predictions when they are examined in detail. The moral may well be that rigorous tests require comparisons between much more detailed classes of models than are usually considered.

Assumption 5: Physical Embodiment

Earlier we argued that information and operations are abstract, functional entities that exist in the domain of IP descriptions. Now it is time to acknowledge fully that information processing actually takes place in the concrete physical world of mechanical, electronic, optical, and biochemical devices and to say something about how abstract information and operations relate to the physical reality of this material world. Clearly they need some physical "vehicles" in the dynamic real-world event that is being described in terms of information and operations. We make explicit the intuitions that information and operations are carried by some physical "medium" or "substrate" in the fifth assumption of the IP approach, that of *physical embodiment* (or "implementation").

(5) In the dynamic physical system whose behavior is being described as an informational event, information is carried by states of the system (here called *representations*) and operations that use this information are carried out by changes in state (here called *processes*).

Notice that as we are using the terms, *representation* refers to the physical system that "carries" (or "contains" or "embodies" or "instantiates") information, and *processes* refer to the physical events that "carry out" (or "perform" or "embody" or "instantiate") the operations. Thus, "information" and "operations" exist in the formal domain of *IP descriptions,* whereas "representations" and "processes" exist in the physical domain of objects and events in the world *when these are viewed as information processing.* Thus, we do not mean to imply that representations and processes are *merely* physical objects and events, but physical objects and events under an informational and operational description.

We have not yet said anything about what makes these systemic states count as representations that carry information about some other state of affairs. This is an important metatheoretical question within the IP framework, and some work has been done explicitly on it (e.g., Bobrow, 1975; Newell, 1980; Palmer, 1978; Rumelhart & Norman, 1984). The prevailing notions are that representations are defined by (1) being *used* as a surrogate for some referent world and (2) preserving the abstract informational structure of that referent world. These two aspects can be easily demonstrated in how a standard road map acts as a representation of the roads, towns, and spatial layout of the geographical region it depicts. To *use* the map as a surrogate of the region, one needs to establish a correspondence (or mapping) from geographical objects to map objects and geographical relations to map relations. In an actual road map, this correspondence is spelled out in the "key" and the various labels attached to map-objects. If a representation is to *work* as a surrogate, however, it also has to be reasonably accurate. This is where preserving informational structure comes in. Structure is preserved when the truth of statements about the referent world is preserved by the truth of the corresponding statements about its representation. For instance, true statements about the lengths of roads, directions of roads, distances between cities, and so forth correspond to true statements about the corresponding map entities: the lengths of lines, directions between lines, and distances between small circles.

Together, these two aspects of representation allow a model to be used as a surrogate of the world.

Unfortunately, space does not permit us to present even a small subset of the issues involved in deciding what sorts of internal representations people use in perceptual and cognitive processes. The reader is referred to Palmer's (1978) presentation for a more complete analysis of the nature of representation in IP theories and to Rumelhart and Norman's (1984) discussion for a survey of issues and specific assumptions that have been made in recent IP theories.

Flow Diagrams versus Programs as Psychological Theories.   We have proposed that IP theories are well-formed information flow diagrams plus mini-mapping theories of the operations within them. We now want to consider how this view of IP is related to the well-known claim that running computer simulation programs are IP theories of the mental processes that they simulate (e.g., Newell & Simon, 1963). Superficially, at least, they seem to be compatible, because they are both in the same line of theoretical analogy. Although they are definitely related, we see them as distinct claims, at least in the sense that IP theories are descriptions whereas running computer programs are events to be described.

According to the present view, a running simulation program is only an IP theory by virtue of the fact that it too can be described by a flow diagram plus mini-mapping theories of its components. If there were one unique flow diagram associated with each program, then there would be no difficulty in calling the program a psychological theory. However, any program can be described by (or is compatible with) many different flow diagrams at different levels of specificity. In fact, programs are often written by constructing a sequence of hierarchically embedded flow diagrams at more and more specific levels of detail (e.g., as shown in Fig. 3.1). Therefore, important problems arise in deciding *which* flow diagram corresponds to the theory allegedly embodied in the program.

The important theoretical issue for the simulation theorist concerns which flow diagrams he or she takes to be psychologically meaningful. For instance, there is a level of description (i.e., a flow diagram) that corresponds to the sequence of elementary logical operations the digital computer actually executes when it runs the simulation in "machine language." Almost nobody would take this level of description to be psychologically meaningful, and yet it is the most obvious level of flow diagram to identify with "the program." At a higher level, there is the flow diagram that reflects the statement-by-statement sequence of operations specific to the higher level programming language that the simulationist used: Lisp, Fortran, Pascal, APL, or whatever. It is very unlikely that even this level of description is psychologically meaningful, although it has been claimed that certain languages are much closer to the elementary IP operations of the mind than others (see Newell & Simon, 1963).

At some still higher level of description the operations represented by the flow diagram become plausible components of a psychologically reasonable IP theory of the mind. A simulationist might well want to claim, for example, that high-level flow diagram components like searching through a network structure from several nodes simultaneously (as in "spreading activation" theories) or matching one feature list against another for similarity *actually happen* in the mental process simulated by the program. Even in a high-level programming language, such components usually involve large chunks of "code" that include many ad hoc details, such as the programming tricks required to mimic parallel processes on serial machines. Clearly the latter are *not* part of the IP theory the simulationist had in mind, whereas the former, large-scale components of the higher level flow diagram *are* part of the theory. Thus, decisions about which components are psychologically real determine what level of description of the program constitutes the IP theory it embodies. Because there may be higher level flow diagrams that the theorist also wants to claim are psychologically meaningful, the theoretical interpretation of the program corresponds to drawing a line across the hierarchy of flow diagrams to separate those components that are psychologically meaningful ("above" the line) from those that are implementational details ("below" the line). The reason for wanting to keep the higher level flow diagrams as part of the psychological theory, of course, is that they may well be correct even though lower level ones are wrong.

This way of viewing simulation programs also makes clear one of their principle drawbacks as cognitive theories: The constraints of writing a complete, runable program require the theorist to specify much more than he or she actually needs to specify for the IP theory. This includes everything in the hierarchy of flow diagrams that exists "below the line." As anyone who has ever written a simulation program soon realizes, enormous amounts of time and energy must be expended in figuring out how to get the machine to do what is required, even though many of the details of how this gets done are not really part of the theory. The payoff for this additional work is the assurance that one's theory is actually capable of performing the task simulated and that one really has mini-mapping theories of each component operation in the flow diagram.

In summary, we are arguing that a simulation program *implies* an IP theory but is ambiguous about just what that theory is. Once the theorist has identified the level of flow diagram that separates meaningful theoretical statements from mere programming details, the theory attached to the simulation becomes clear. We view this analysis as a clarification of the program-as-theory idea rather than as a contradiction. We agree wholeheartedly with much of the spirit and the motivation behind the program-as-theory movement, such as specifying vague verbal theories more precisely and allowing their adequacy to be tested rigorously (Newell & Simon, 1963, 1972). Our objection is merely that simulation theorists should be more careful than they often have been in specifying the relation between their program as it runs on a computer from their psychological theory of the mental processes it simulates.

RELATIONS TO OTHER VIEWS OF COGNITION

We stated at the outset that one of our primary goals in trying to specify IP theory was to clarify its relation to other views of cognition. Having now stated explicitly at least some of what we believe are the principal assumptions underlying IP theory, we are in a position to contrast it with some other noteworthy approaches to cognitive theory in the history of psychology: cognitivism, behaviorism, and ecologism. We then turn our attention to some more contemporary views of cognition that are closely related to IP: computationalism (or "weak AI"), functionalism, and Turing-machine functionalism (or "strong AI"). Our initial intuition that IP is different from and weaker than these other contemporary views turns out to be correct when the underlying issues are examined carefully. IP is not so weak as to be meaningless or unfalsifiable, but it does make fewer substantive claims about the nature of human mentality than these related proposals.

Cognitivism

It is important to be clear at the outset that IP psychology, as described here, is *not* the same as "cognitivism," but a specific brand of it. As the term is used in psychology, *cognitivism* refers to a very broad theoretical position in which it is assumed that behavior can only be properly understood by postulating internal "cognitive" (or "mentalistic") states such as percepts, attitudes, beliefs, goals, memories, images, plans, and the like. This explicitly cognitivist stance was formulated vigorously by Tolman (1932) in response to the explicitly anticognitive viewpoint expressed in Watsonian behaviorism (Watson, 1913, 1925). Prior to this time, psychological theory was certainly "cognitive" in the sense we have defined, but it was only implicitly so. It took the challenge of the behaviorist alternative to bring the cognitivist viewpoint into focus.

Information processing is certainly an explicitly cognitivist approach in that its theories are based on such hypothetical internal states. However, IP goes well beyond simple cognitivism in making further assumptions about the specific *form* that such theories should take. It is these further assumptions—described here in terms of informational description, recursive decomposition, flow continuity, flow dynamics, and physical embodiment—that distinguish IP theories from other cognitive theories. Indeed, there are many cognitivists who simply do not ascribe to one or more of these assumptions, preferring to work within a looser (or at least different) set of theoretical constraints that are nevertheless quite "cognitive." Historically prominent examples include Freud, Piaget, Vygotski, Wertheimer, Kohler, Koffka, Bartlett, and, of course, Tolman. Thus, IP is correctly viewed as a proper subset of cognitivism: All IP psychologists are cognitivists, but not all cognitivists are IP psychologists.

Behaviorism

The relation between IP and behaviorism is far more complex, because (1) there are several different brands of behaviorism that need to be distinguished and (2) each brand includes somewhat different proposals with which IP is in agreement on some and opposed on others. Perhaps because IP arose historically as a reaction *against* behaviorism, there is a tendency to see them as diametrically opposed. As is often the case, however, the new approach has much more in common with the one it supplants than is initially acknowledged. This is clearly true of the relation between IP and behaviorism.

As initially proposed by Watson (1913, 1925), the behaviorist approach broke with the then-traditional introspective approach by identifying publicly observable behavior as the central concern of psychology rather than private mental experiences. This general proposal contains at least two quite different aspects that need to be distinguished, however: *methodological behaviorism* and *theoretical behaviorism*. The methodological proposal is that because subjective experiences are not scientifically observable, behavior is the proper object of study in psychology as an objective natural science. With this IP practitioners invariably agree, at least in the sense that the data on which theoretical issues in IP are decided are objective measures of overt behavior.

There is a more controversial extension of methodological behaviorism: namely, that because conscious experience is inherently unscientific, consciousness should play no role whatsoever in scientific psychology. On these grounds, radical behaviorists avoided all questions about "purely mental events" such as imagery and thought. Practitioners of the IP approach have rejected this extreme position in a number of different ways. First, many IP psychologists use personal introspection as a source of ideas and hypotheses about cognitive events. Of course, these must then be subjected to more rigorous evaluation by measuring observable behavior in others to be scientifically respectable, but this is a standard procedure for much IP work in cognitive psychology. Second, the behaviors that IP psychologists measure are often overt reports of subjective experiences, such as ratings of perceptual or conceptual similarity (e.g., Shepard & Chipman, 1970) or verbal "thinking aloud" protocols while solving a complex problem (e.g., Newell & Simon, 1972). Thus, subjective experiences are considered important enough to warrant explanation, but only insofar as they can be made public by behavioral criteria. Third, IP psychologists are decidedly more interested in and optimistic about the scientific study of "purely mental events" such as imagery, thought, and consciousness.

Far from banishing them as inherently unscientific, most IP psychologists have come to view them as valid and important topics that will yield to appropriate scientific methods. During the past decade or two, IP psychologists have made a great deal of progress on the topics of imagery (e.g., Kosslyn, 1980; Shepard & Cooper, 1982) and thought processes (e.g., Newell & Simon, 1972). This has been accomplished within the framework of methodological behaviorism by using objective measures such as reaction times and protocol analysis to anchor these "mental events" in observable behavior. There has lately been a resurgence of interest in consciousness itself, focusing on issues like why some things are conscious whereas others are not (Mandler, 1975; Shallice, 1972, 1978), whether a stimulus can affect IP events without itself becoming conscious (Dixon, 1971; Marcel, 1983a, b), and what sort of IP architecture is needed to account for consciousness (Johnson–Laird, 1983). Still, these projects are deemed sensible only to the extent that they can be grounded in objective behavioral measures, thus conforming in the end to the central tenet of methodological behaviorism.

Theoretical behaviorism concerns the nature of explanation in scientific psychology. "Radical behaviorism" is a theoretical view in which all accounts of behavior are couched in strictly "external" terms of environmental histories (cf. Riley, Brown, & Yoerg, this volume). Internal "mentalistic" constructs that could not be directly observed in behavior were rejected out of hand as improper theoretical objects. It is to this part of radical behaviorism that IP is fundamentally opposed. Indeed, it is this proposal that is rejected by all cognitivists, not just IP psychologists. Within the IP approach the behaviorist rejection of unobservable internal events is specifically opposed to the decomposition assumption, because this is the mechanism by which hypothetical "internal events" are generated in IP theories. (We shortly consider this issue of "unobservables" in more detail.) These theoretical strictures of behaviorism were too extreme to go unchallenged for long, even among otherwise devout behaviorists, and eventually they led to revisionist movements such as "neobehaviorism" and Tolman's "purposive behaviorism."

The neobehaviorist movement was initiated by Hull's (1952) introduction of "mediating" stimuli and responses within the organism (e.g., S–r–s–R) that were taken to be "internal surrogates" of observable S–R connections. Here we see a line of reasoning—strikingly similar to IP's decomposition assumption—in which the "primitives" were taken to be minimal associations between stimuli and responses, both external and internal. For this reason, neobehaviorism is an important theoretical precursor to IP. It has even been shown that such mediated S–R theories are formally equivalent to a particular class of finite automata (Suppes, 1969). There are important *pragmatic* differences between mediated S–R theories and IP theories, however, because the computer analogy brought with it a vast repertoire of concepts from computer science that could be used to specify the nature of the hypothesized internal events. These IP constructs—

including information structures such as lists, arrays, matrices, and so forth, plus operations such as encoding, storing, retrieving, transforming, comparing, deciding, branching, looping, and the like—are richer and more powerful tools for theorizing about mental events than were the neobehaviorists' simple associations among "covert stimuli" and "covert responses." Still, neobehaviorism accomplished the important step of lifting radical behaviorism's absolute ban on theories that appealed to internal processes in explaining behavior.

Tolman's (1932) "purposive" behaviorism went a step further in allowing openly "cognitive" constructs back into the theoretical arena. He argued convincingly for the importance of goals, hypotheses, plans, cognitive maps, and the like in understanding the behavior of rats as well as man. As we noted previously, Tolman's theoretical views are actually "cognitivist" rather than "behaviorist," although he remained a firm believer in the methodological tenets of behaviorism. We do not discuss the relation between Tolman and IP further here because an excellent discussion of this topic is presented elsewhere in this volume (Riley, Brown, & Yoerg).

The Role of Unobservables.   We have claimed that the primary difference between the IP and radical behaviorist approaches to theories of mind is the former's willingness—even eagerness—to postulate internal mental structures in accounting for observable behavior versus the latter's unwillingness to do so. If the IP approach is preferable to this radical form of behaviorism, the use of unobservable constructs in psychological theory must be justified. We do so by appealing to the well-documented use of unobservable entities in other sciences and by examining a few successful cases within psychology itself.

There is a long and important history to the use of unobservables in the natural sciences, and it includes some of the most profound discoveries of the last several centuries. Examples abound of scientists proposing initially unobservable constructs on the basis of purely "behavioral" research and later having their theories confirmed by more "direct" observation. Biologists such as Mendel proposed the existence of genes that carry hereditary traits on the basis of measured regularities in the characteristics of offspring, and this happened long before DNA was actually observed within cell nuclei. Physicists like Rutherford deduced the internal structure of atoms from measuring the scatter that resulted when they were bombarded by X-rays, again, many years before the existence of these subatomic particles was confirmed more directly. There have also been many important cases in which unobservables were postulated without any presupposition of direct observation, e.g., Newton's hypothesis of gravitational attraction and Darwin's concept of natural selection. More recently physicists have suggested that gravity may, in fact, be carried by an elementary particle, but this conjecture antedated considerably their success as "unobservable" constructs in physics. No one has yet supposed that the process of natural selection will itself turn out to be a directly observable "thing."

From such examples we can discern at least two important factors in the success of unobservables in scientific theories. The first is *adequate description:* The construct must provide a succinct and parsimonious account of results known at the time the theory is proposed. The second is *successful prediction:* They must figure centrally in generating novel hypotheses about the existence of new phenomena in substantially different circumstances, and these predictions must subsequently be confirmed. We submit that unobservable constructs of the sort found in IP theories are at least potentially adequate on both counts.

The criterion of adequate description is, of course, the reason for postulating unobservable constructs in the first place: It "makes sense" of some set of data or relates several different sets of data in ways not previously considered. The rationale for this justification of unobservables in psychological theory was developed quite nicely by neobehaviorists in defending the use of internal variables like hunger and thirst in their theories (cf. Tolman, 1932) and there is no need to restate their arguments here. As we said earlier, the move away from the stricture against unobservables was actually started by the neobehaviorists and merely continued and expanded by IP psychologists. There is certainly no problem in principle with IP constructs providing adequate descriptions of well-documented phenomena, and there are several noteworthy successes, such as the two-stage theory of color vision (cf. De Valois & De Valois, 1975) and the spatial frequency theory of spatial vision (cf. De Valois & De Valois, 1980).[9] Neither of these has achieved the status of, say, subatomic particles or gravity in physics, but each has provided a substantial framework for describing a large number of experimental results in its domain.

Successful prediction is the true hallmark of success for any scientific theory. It was repeated successful predictions that really convinced biologists of the existence of genes and physicists of the reality of subatomic particles. Repeated confirmation of a theory's predictions leads eventually to such a dense cluster of results around it that the theory displaces specific results in textbooks. There are at least a few good examples in psychology. For instance, color vision is usually presented in texts on perception almost exclusively by the theory with just a few examples of experimental procedures to give a feeling for the research. The same is generally true of the duplex theory of pitch perception. The situation is quite different in more complex cognitive domains, such as semantic memory and language understanding: Each of several competing theories is presented along with a few results that seem to support it, and it is the results, not the theory, that

---

[9]We are considering that psychophysical theories generally fall within the IP framework. Although much of this work predated the IP movement in cognitive psychology, our position is justified on the grounds that most psychophysically derived theories conform to all five assumptions aforementioned and to the whole spirit of the IP enterprise. Indeed, it was this kind of connection between IP and sensory processes that Lindsay and Norman (1972) developed so skillfully in their seminal textbook, *Human information processing*.

are emphasized as characterizing the domain in question. Such theories are "brittle" in the sense that they break down (or simply do not apply) when seemingly minor changes in procedure are introduced, and they often fail to make successful new predictions or succeed only under certain unusual conditions. There is no reason to suppose, however, that robust IP theories cannot someday be achieved in these areas as they have been in sensory domains; the problems are just a great deal more numerous and complex.

There is a third possible criterion of success that applies to at least some unobservable constructs proposed in science: *potential observability*. A construct is potentially observable if it is, in principle, capable of being measured directly, even if the means for doing so are not yet at hand. Not all unobservable constructs have this status, of course, as exemplified by gravity and natural selection. In psychology, a distinction has been made between "intervening variables," which do not imply potential observability, and "hypothetical constructs," which do (MacCorquodale & Meehl, 1948). Proposed IP components are clearly meant to be stronger than intervening variables, which merely redescribe empirical relations succinctly in somewhat different form. Because intervening variables are not meant to have any reality "inside the black box" (i.e., they claim only to specify *what* the mapping is, not *how* it is accomplished), they only play a role within the IP approach as part of mapping theories. IP theories, however, *do* make substantive claims about what goes on inside the head, so the internal operations they propose must be some species of hypothetical construct. This does not mean, however, that all such internal operations imply the existence of specific, isolable, and identifiable neurological mechanisms that embody them.

We believe that IP operations are potentially observable in the brain in just the same sense that programs are potentially observable in Turing machines. If the program is "hardwired" into the machine, it is *physically observable* in the wiring of its circuits. If it is implemented on a general-purpose machine, it is *functionally observable* in the behavior of the machine, but not physically observable in the sense of dedicated hardware components. In the latter case, the hardware constitutes the *architecture* on which the programs run, but this architecture only weakly constrains the programs that can run on it. In the case of the brain, peripheral operations seem to take place on "dedicated hardware" where there is some distinctly physical reality to its functional components. More central "cognitive" operations may well take place on a more general-purpose architecture. Most IP theorists who try to account for complex cognitive events find it hard to imagine that the brain has enough distinct neural circuits for all the necessary mental processes to be realized in dedicated hardware.

In summary, there is no good reason to avoid unobservable constructs in psychological theory and several good reasons to use them as needed. The natural sciences provide ample precedent for this, and psychology itself includes some successful examples. The kinds of unobservable constructs that appear in IP theories are, in principle, capable of both adequate description and successful prediction. Some may even be potentially observable in the "hardware" of the brain, although this is not a necessary claim.

Ecologism

Ecological psychology has been proposed, at least in part, as an alternative to IP psychology (e.g., Gibson, 1979; Shaw & Bransford, 1977). It is not easy to summarize the ecological approach, partly because it is not yet well defined, and partly because ecological psychologists themselves capture their approach partly in terms of negating the IP approach as they see it. Here we briefly discuss the ecological approach and examine its relation to the foregoing view of IP.

Generally speaking, ecological psychologists reject the computer program metaphor and the appeal to representations and processes as explanatory concepts in theorizing about perception and cognition. Rather, they view the organism from an evolutionary perspective—i.e., as a system whose primary purpose is self-survival and adaptation—and organisms in their environments as mutually constraining systems.

Ecological psychology is primarily derived from J. J. Gibson's approach to perception (1950, 1966, 1979). Gibson viewed perception as a biologically adaptive activity and emphasized the dynamic interaction between organisms and their environments. The centrality of the role that the environment plays in Gibson's view of perception was aptly and succinctly captured by Mace (1977): "Ask not what's inside your head but what your head's inside of."

Gibson asserted that there is information in complex patterns of stimulation available to the organism, corresponding to the important distal objects and events in its environment. This significant information is to be found in "higher order" variables that remain invariant over the visual transformations taking place as the organism actively explores the world around it. In his theory of "ecological optics" Gibson tried to identify and specify these invariants. According to his theory the active perceptual system "picks up" this information without the involvement of logical processes using specific knowledge about the world. This approach led him to the notion of "direct" perception.

One way to understand the idea of direct perception is in the historical context within which it was initially proposed. Gibson believed that perception was direct in the sense that, contrary to the Helmholtzian notion of "unconscious inference," it does not involve *epistemic* mediation. As we understand it, this argument does not necessarily deny that representations and processes play a role in perception, but only that it does not make use of *explicit* forms of knowledge and *logical* inference processes of the sort associated with thought, memory, and problem solving.[10] We do not see this view of direct perception as incompatible with the basic tenets of IP. As evidence for this, it is entirely possible to construct a "data driven" IP theory of perception that does not rely on explicitly represented "facts" or logical "deductions": Marr's (1982) theory is one prominent example, at least up to the point at which patterns are identified as instances of known types. Such IP theories can easily be seen as consistent with this weak interpretation of direct perception.

There is, however, a stronger interpretation of direct perception that seems to strike at the heart of the IP approach by rejecting the decomposition assumption. The goal of ecological optics is to specify the mapping from proximal stimuli to perceptual responses, and its contention is that this can be done by correlating physical invariants in the dynamic optic array with perceptual responses. Thus Gibson's theory is not concerned with the *mechanisms* that enable an organism to do this, except that the perceptual system detects the invariants by some sort of physiological "resonation" (Gibson, 1966). It is in this sense—namely, the lack of interest in specifying the nature of internal mechanisms—that Gibson rejects, if not the decomposition assumption itself, certainly the motivation behind it. Ullman (1980) presents an extended critical analysis of this view, and the interested reader is referred to his paper and the many commentaries that follow it for more information.

From the IP point of view, Gibson's theory is an important attempt to formulate a mapping theory of perception, because he was occupied almost entirely with *what* the mapping is to the exclusion of *how* it might be achieved. Thus, although his theory is *incomplete* from an IP standpoint, it is entirely compatible with the IP framework, because an ecological mapping theory of perception is the logical starting point for an IP theory of perception (see Marr, 1982). From Gibson's point of view, however, IP theories of perception are not compatible with his ideas, because he believed that psychological theories of internal mechanisms were irrelevant to understanding perception. Recent followers of Gibson's ecological approach claim that Gibson did recognize that information pickup involves processes, but from his brief allusions to resonating, optimizing, and

---

[10]We refer here to "explicit" knowledge and "logical" inference to distinguish the classical position of "unconscious inference" from some modern theories that seem to make use of knowledge and inference of a very different sort. One interesting example is Marr and Poggio's (1976) model for computing global stereopsis: The excitatory and inhibitory connections among the binocular processing units actually embody knowledge of the world (that the visual world is generally continuous in depth, at least over local regions) and of light (that because most surfaces are opaque, each point on an image generally comes from just one depth plane). Even so, this model does not seem to be in the spirit of Helmholtzian "unconscious inference," but more like a sort of "resonance" process of which Gibson might have approved. The difference between classical "unconscious inference" and this type of computational theory seems to be that the knowledge in the former case is explicit, whereas in the latter case it is implicit, and that the rules of inference in the former case conform to the standard logical conception, whereas in the latter case they do not.

the like, they infer that these processes have to be different from those suggested by a general-purpose device such as the modern digital computer (Carello, Turvey, Kugler, & Shaw, 1982). This assertion may constitute an argument against the computer program metaphor, but not necessarily against the IP approach as presented here.

It should be clear at this point that we do not see ecological psychology as incompatible with the basic tenets of IP. Why then, do ecological psychologist so often present their view as a reaction against IP? The answer to this question requires differentiating between theoretical principles of IP on the one hand and common practice of IP psychologists on the other. As noted previously there are not many mapping theories in psychology, and most current IP models focus almost exclusively on the internal structure (representations and processes) proposed to accomplish the mapping without any attempt to specify the ecological constraints that support the mapping in the first place. There have been some recent attempts among IP theorists to remedy this situation (e.g., Bregman, 1981; Marr, 1982; Shepard, 1981), but it is generally a criticism well taken. In summary, there is a clear difference in emphasis between the ecological and IP approaches as typically practiced, even though they are not theoretically as conflicting as they are often assumed to be.

Computationalism

As we have seen from the foregoing discussion of cognitivism, behaviorism, and ecologism, the most controversial assumption of the IP approach is that mental events are decomposable. For this reason, it would certainly be reassuring if somehow one could *prove* that this were true. As it turns out, a closely related problem has been studied by mathematical logicians in the "theory of computability" (see Johnson–Laird, 1983, for a psychologically motivated introduction). From this work by Church, Turing, and others, we know at least something about certain *conditions* under which an operation is decomposable. It turns out that *if* the mental mapping is an example of what is called a "computable function," then it can indeed be decomposed into a set of primitive functions that are combined according to well-specified rules, just as would be required for the decomposition assumption to be unequivocally true.

Probably the best known definition of a computable function is due to Turing (1936): A function is computable if it is the input–output mapping of a machine (now called a "Turing machine") that reads binary symbols from and writes binary symbols to an indefinitely long tape. The sequence of logical steps by which such a function is computed in such a machine is called an algorithm, and there are many different algorithms that can result in the same computable function. Indeed, it turns out that there are many different sets of "primitive functions" and rules for combining them that are, in principle, capable of generating the set of all computable functions: Turing machines, recursive functions, lambda calculus (Church), Post canonical systems, Markov processes, and others (cf. Newell, 1980). So if the mental mapping is actually computable, then the job of IP psychology amounts to discovering what the mind's primitive IP functions are and how they are composed into the larger, more complex algorithms of the human mind (see previous section on "The Role of Primitives"). Mental architecture is probably quite different from that of standard universal Turing machines (or modern digital computers), and a psychologically more plausible formulation has been described by Newell (1980).

We can now say that the decomposition assumption would be true if the mental mapping is a computable function. But is it? There are many functions that are not, so perhaps it is one of these. Unfortunately, no way is currently known to determine this analytically because there is no well-defined method for determining whether an arbitrary function is computable or not. The only alternative is to try to show that it *is* by finding an algorithm that "simulates" the mind. The goal is to program a computer so that it passes Turing's test: to behave so much like a person that experts cannot distinguish its behavior from that of a real person (Turing, 1950). Because such a program would, by definition, be a well-defined composition of primitive IP operations, its existence would prove by demonstration that mental decomposition is possible. Because an infinite number of other algorithms will produce the same computable function, there would still be the problem of finding the *right* decomposition, but at least we would know that such a decomposition exists. Psychologists would presumably play a central role in determining which of several alternative decompositions is correct.

This line of reasoning suggests an approach to cognitive theory that we call "computationalism" (or "simulationism"). Its proponents assume that the mental mapping is indeed a computable function, at least as a working hypothesis, and proceed to try to attain the goal presumed possible. Their method is to write computer programs (which are, by definition, computable) that try to simulate human behavior. Searle (1980) has called this sort of approach "weak AI": The programmer views the modern computer as an important tool for discovering things about the nature of mentality but does not assume that the programmed machine actually *has* mental states. Later we contrast this view with "strong AI" in which the computer is presumed actually to *have* the mental states that it simulates.

The primary difference between computationalism and IP concerns the logical relation between the assumptions of computability and decomposability. As we have said, computability implies decomposability, but does decomposability imply computability? It turns out that it does not, because the mental mapping, as a whole, may not be computable, yet it still may be possible to decompose it meaningfully into an IP theory. Perhaps the easiest way to see this is to suppose that there is one small part that is not computable, and that this part can be isolated in its own "black box" as an uncomputable primitive within the system. Then it is clear that the system could be decomposed in this way, even though its overall input–output mapping would not be computable. Indeed, there might be many such uncomputable components in the mind, but their existence does not necessarily preclude successful decomposition.

It is not obvious what this sort of analysis would be like, but Dreyfus (1979) and Searle (1983) have recently offered arguments suggesting that something like this might be true. They allow that some of human knowledge and mental operations may indeed be analyzable into component pieces—what Searle calls "the Network"—and this part may well be compatible with computationalism. However, they also argue that there will necessarily be some residue of complex yet fundamental skills, presuppositions, and stances toward the physical world— what they call "the Background"—that will defy all attempts at computational analysis. In truth, their reasons for claiming this are not entirely clear and have not yet had much impact on the beliefs of most computationalists. However, the critical point for the present discussion is that even if Dreyfus and Searle did turn out to be right and computationalism wrong, mental decomposition would still be a potentially valid assumption for cognitive psychology and IP a potentially useful approach to solving at least some of its problems. Its usefulness would depend on how much decomposition were possible before the intractible "Background" were reached, and how much would have been learned about the nature of mind as a result.

The possibility of decomposition without strict computability clarifies the relation between IP and weak AI (computationalism). Classical computationalists start with certain precisely stated primitive functions and show how to *compose* them into more complex functions. The resulting complex function is necessarily computable by definition. IP psychologists start with a complex function, which may or may not be computable, and proceed by trying to *decompose* it into flow diagrams. The components of these flow diagrams may or may not be themselves computable. Thus, computability is a *sufficient* condition for decomposition, but not a *necessary* one. Weak AI therefore places stronger constraints on a theory of mind than does IP. By the same token, of course, weak AI is less likely than IP to be correct.

We see, then, that IP psychologists are not necessarily committed to believing that the mind will ultimately be simulable on an appropriately programmed digital computer, because, strictly speaking, IP does not imply computability. This conclusion is consistent with the fact that serious doubts exist among a substantial subset of IP psychologists that mental events will ever be fully simulated on the sort of digital computers that are currently available. Perhaps someday different machines will be developed that will change such opinions, but they may also change the very definition of computability.

Functionalism

Functionalism was proposed by philosophers as a possible solution to the mind/body (or mind/brain) problem (e.g., Fodor, 1965; Putnam, 1960).[11] It assumes that the necessary and sufficient conditions for mentality are to be found in the functional organization of the brain rather than in its particular physical embodiment. This implies that any device that has the same functional organization as the human brain literally *has* mental states in exactly the same sense that people do. This includes all aspects of mentality, including intentionality, consciousness, and internal experiences.

The initial intuitive basis for this claim comes, once again, from the computer analogy. There is an important sense in which the same program (software) can be run on many different digital computers (hardware). The analogous implication for the mind/body problem is that the same "mind" might potentially be instantiated on a wide variety of physically different devices. The essence of functionalism, then, is that systemic organization defines the necessary and sufficient conditions for having mental states, and brains are merely the one material form in which this particular organization has been realized so far. Nothing in principle prevents other sorts of objects from having the same mental states people do, provided that they have the right sort of organization.

It is certainly true that many IP psychologists seem to reject the *spirit* of functionalism by taking certain aspects of neurology very seriously in their theorizing. For instance, several psychological IP theories have been proposed that rest importantly on neurological or quasineurological constructs such as excitation and inhibition (e.g., Hinton & Anderson, 1981; Posner, 1978), aftereffects due to priming (e.g., Posner, 1978), and even hemispheric specialization (e.g., Friedman & Polson, 1981). On closer examination, however, these proposals do not really conflict logically with functionalism. If true, they would only imply that brain properties like activation, inhibition, aftereffects, and so forth play some functional role in the nature of mind, and that for another physical object to have the same mental states it would presumably need to have the same functional properties. These might easily be realized in nonbiological objects such as a computer. Thus, even if such theories were correct in detail, they would not strictly imply that it is the *physical* properties of the central nervous system that are responsible for their role in mental events. However, these examples do demonstrate rather convincingly that many IP psychologists do not really "buy the functionalist line" that the hardware of the brain is uninformative about the nature of mind.

---

[11] The modern philosophical doctrine called *functionalism* should not be confused with the older psychological school also known as *functionalism*, which is associated with the work of James, Hall, Cattell, Dewey, Woodworth, and others. There is little, if any, connection between them.

A stronger argument against the claim that IP is equivalent to functionalism can be made on strictly logical grounds. It turns out that IP is weaker than functionalism, and the principle reason is that because IP theories are descriptions, they require only that some, not necessarily all, aspects of what makes an event "mental" can be captured by the flow diagrams. There may be certain aspects that are not captured, and these may be considered necessary conditions for something literally *having* mental states as opposed to merely *simulating* them. The most obvious candidate for such a mental aspect is consciousness: Qualitatively different phenomenal experiences might be necessary for something literally to *have* mental states, and yet IP theories might not be able to capture this aspect of mentality. One could be an IP theorist and a true dualist at the same time, for instance. Such a person would believe that, whereas IP flow diagrams specify the functional organization of the brain, internal experiences are required for it literally to have a mind, and these are quite independent of the specified functional organization. It is also possible, of course, that IP theories *will* be able to characterize consciousness in terms of flow diagrams, at least those aspects of it that are scientifically approachable, and several IP psychologists have proposed such theories (see Johnson–Laird, 1983; Marcel, 1983b; Shallice, 1978).

The important point in understanding the relation of IP to functionalism is that the validity of the IP approach does not stand or fall in terms of whether it captures *all* aspects of mental events, whereas functionalism does. Naturally, IP psychologists hope that IP theories will turn out to account for everything, but not many would feel that it had failed if it turned out to leave some mysteries unsolved. In this case, the "correct" flow diagram theory of the mind would turn out to be merely a *necessary,* but not *sufficient,* condition for having the sort of mental states that people do. It would be devastating to a functionalist, however, if it turned out this way. For example, Searle (1983, Epilogue) has argued against functionalism by suggesting that consciousness is inherent to specific biological processes occurring in brains, but this is not necessarily an argument against the IP approach as described earlier. In defense of functionalism, however, it should be noted that there is presently no scientific evidence in support of Searle's materialist, biological view, only his own intuitions. Consciousness may well turn out to be a problem whose solution will be found entirely within the realm of functional organization.

Turing-Machine Functionalism (or "Strong AI"). If a properly programmed computer has the same functional organization (i.e., implements the same algorithm) as the human mind, then it follows from functionalism that the machine would literally have a mind in exactly the same sense that people do. Indeed, this would be true of any machine implementing the same algorithm, including one made of electronic, mechanical, optical elements, or whatever.

This conjunction of computationalism and functionalism is usually called "Turing-machine functionalism" (e.g., Block, 1978; Block & Fodor, 1980; Fodor, 1980) and sometimes "strong AI" (Searle, 1980). Note that it would not be sufficient for the computer merely to duplicate the input–output mapping function of the human mind because many different algorithms (and, therefore, different functional organizations) can produce the same mapping.[12] Functionalism proposes that it is the *functional organization* that must be the same, and this is a much stronger constraint than just that the *mapping* be the same. For example, if one proposed an IP theory of consciousness that required that two processes run in parallel, a strictly serial computer that merely *simulated* parallelism by switching back and forth between them would not have the organization specified by the theory, even though it would exactly mimic its input–output function. Therefore, it need not be itself conscious but might well only mimic consciousness. It isn't just *what* gets done that matters, it's *how* it gets done. In any case, it should be clear that IP as characterized here is not equivalent to Turing-machine functionalism, because it does not strictly imply either computationalism or functionalism, much less their conjunction.

At this point we can summarize the foregoing discussion by putting it all into a single framework involving just two issues and the positions taken on them by each approach. The first issue concerns the *analyzability* of mental processes into functional components. The strong position is that mental processes are computable (computationalism and Turing-machine functionalism), and the weak position is that they are merely decomposable (functionalism and IP). Radical behaviorism and Gibsonian ecologism take the more pessimistic position that the question of analyzability itself is entirely misguided.

The second issue concerns the *logical implications* of functional organization for the nature of the human mind. The strong position here is that the functional organization is both necessary and sufficient for having mental states (functionalism and Turing-machine functionalism) and the weak position that it is merely necessary (computationalism and IP). Again, it is possible to hold the more pessimistic position that functional organization is logically unrelated to issues concerning the human mind (radical behaviorism and ecologism). Thus, the four meaningful conjunctions of the two positions on these two issues define the four principle modern views shown in Table 3.1. Of these, Turing-machine functionalism is the strongest and IP the weakest. Note that, by the same token, IP is the most general view and is compatible with all three of the other approaches.

---

[12]I thank Phil Johnson–Laird for pointing out this crucial distinction to me. The example that follows came from him.

TABLE 3.1
Logical Implications

		Necessary & Sufficient	Necessary	(Irrelevant)
	Computable	Turing-Machine Functionalism	Computationalism	-
ANALYZABILITY	Decomposable	Functionalism	Information Processing	-
	(Irrelevant)	-	-	Behaviorism & Ecologism

Summary and Conclusion

We have presented a metatheoretical view of the IP approach to cognition in terms of five central assumptions that underlie it. The first two assumptions—informational description and recursive decomposition—are the most critical. The third and fourth assumptions—flow continuity and flow dynamics—further specify the nature of the decomposition assumption, and the final assumption—physical embodiment—further specifies the informational description assumption. Together these five assumptions form the basis for constructing IP theories of mental processes in terms of information flow diagrams that represent the component operations and the temporal relations among them. Unless the operations of the flow diagram are taken to be primitives, the IP theory should also include a mapping theory of each operation.

We then contrasted this view of IP to other prominent approaches to cognitive theory: behaviorism, ecologism, computationalism (weak AI) functionalism, and Turing-machine functionalism (strong AI). Many of the differences among these views can be captured, at least schematically, by their stands on two fundamental issues: the extent to which mental processes are *analyzable* into functional components and the *logical* implications of this analysis in accounting for the nature of mental states. According to this analysis, IP is weaker than (but compatible with) computationalism, functionalism, and Turing-machine functionalism.

We believe that IP is currently the most viable theoretical approach to cognition, but this is obviously just our own opinion. We offer the foregoing analysis and discussion in the hope that it gives a clearer conception of the IP approach than has previously been available. Even if IP turns out to be fatally flawed in one or more ways, being clear about the underlying issues can only help in the ultimate goal of understanding cognition.

ACKNOWLEDGMENTS

We are grateful to the many people who read and criticized earlier drafts of this chapter: Phil Johnson–Laird, Tony Marcel, Saul Sternberg, and Richard Young plus the editors of this volume, Terry Knapp and Lynn Robertson. The initial draft was written while Steve

Palmer was visiting the MRC Applied Psychology Unit in Cambridge, England, and he wishes to thank Alan Baddeley for the opportunity to work there and Phil Johnson–Laird for the many hours of discussion that helped shape some of the ideas contained in this chapter. Preparation of the chapter was facilitated by a grant from the Alfred P. Sloan Foundation to the University of California, Berkeley, and by Grant BNS-8319630 from the National Science Foundation to the first author.

REFERENCES

Anderson, J. R. (1976). *Language, memory, and thought*. Hillsdale, NJ: Lawrence Erlbaum Associates.

Anderson, J. R. (1983). *The architecture of cognition*. Cambridge, MA: Harvard University Press.

Atkinson, R. C., & Shiffrin, R. M. (1968). Human memory: A proposed system and its control processes. In K. W. Spence & J. T. Spence (Eds.), *The psychology of learning and motivation: Advances in research and theory* (Vol 2). New York: Academic Press.

Baddeley, A. D. (1976). *The psychology of memory*. New York: Basic Books.

Block, N. (1978). Troubles with functionalism. In C. W. Savage (Ed.), *Perception and cognition: Issues in the foundations of psychology*. (Minnesota studies in the philosophy of science, Vol. 9.) Minneapolis: University of Minnesota Press. Reprinted in N. Block (Ed.), *Readings in philosophy of psychology* (Vol. 1). Cambridge, MA: Harvard University Press, 1980.

Block, N., & Fodor, J. A. (1980). What psychological states are not. In N. Block (Ed.), *Readings in philosophy of psychology* (Vol. 1). Cambridge, MA: Harvard University Press.

Bobrow, D. G. (1975). Dimensions of representation. In D. G. Bobrow & A. Collins (Eds.), *Representation and understanding: Studies of cognitive science* (pp. 1–34). New York: Academic Press.

Bregman, A. S. (1981). Asking the "what for" question in auditory perception. In M. Kubovy & J. R. Pomerantz (Eds.), *Perceptual organization*. Hillsdale, NJ: Lawrence Erlbaum Associates.

Carrelo, C., Turvey, M. T., Kugler, B. T., & Shaw, R. (1982). Inadequacies of the computer metaphor. In M. S. Gazzaniga (Ed.), *Handbook of cognitive neuroscience*. New York: Plenum.

Chomsky, N. (1965). *Aspects of the theory of syntax*. Cambridge, MA: MIT Press.

Craik, K. (1943). *The nature of explanation*. Cambridge, England: Cambridge University Press.

Dennett, D. C. (1978). *Brainstorms*. Cambridge, MA: MIT Press/Bradford Books.

De Valois, R. L., & De Valois, K. K. (1975). Neural coding of color. In E. C. Carterette & M. P. Friedman (Eds.), *Handbook of perception* (Vol. V): *Seeing* (pp. 117–166). New York: Academic Press.

De Valois, R. L., & De Valois, K. K. (1980). Spatial vision. *Annual Review of Psychology, 31*, 309–341.

Dixon, N. F. (1971). *Subliminal perception: The nature of a controversy*. London: McGraw–Hill.

Dretske, F. I. (1979). *Knowledge and the flow of information*. Cambridge, MA: MIT Press/Bradford Books.

Dreyfus, H. L. (1979). *What computers can't do*. New York: Harper Colophon Books.

Edwards, W. (1965). Optimal strategies for seeking information: Models for statistics, choice RT, and human information processing. *Journal of Mathematical Psychology, 2*, 312–329.

Edwards, W. (1968). Conservatism in human information processing. In B. Kleinmuntz (Ed.), *Formal representation of human judgment*. New York: Wiley.

Feldman, J. A. (1981). A connectionist model of visual memory. In G. E. Hinton & J. A. Anderson (Eds.), *Parallel models of human associative memory* (pp. 49–81). Hillsdale, NJ: Lawrence Erlbaum Associates.

Fitts, P. M., & Posner, M. I. (1967). *Human performance*. Belmont, CA: Brooks Cole.

Fodor, J. A. (1965). Explanation in psychology. In M. Black (Ed.), *Philosophy in America*. London: Routledge & Kagan Paul.

Fodor, J. A. (1968). *Psychological explanation*. New York: Random House.

Fodor, J. A. (1980). Methodological solipsism considered as a research strategy in cognitive psychology. *The Behavioral and Brain Sciences, 3,* 63–109.

Freud, S. (1933). *New introductory lectures on psychoanalysis* (A. Strachey, Trans.). New York: Norton, 1965.

Friedman, A., & Polson, M. C. (1981). The hemispheres as independent resource systems: Limited capacity processing and cerebral specialization. *Journal of Experimental Psychology: Human Perception and Performance, 7,* 1031–1058.

Garner, W. R. (1962). *Uncertainty and structure as psychological concepts*. New York: Wiley.

Gibson, J. J. (1950). *Perception of the visual world*. Boston: Houghton–Mifflin.

Gibson, J. J. (1966). *The senses considered as perceptual systems*. Boston: Houghton-Mifflin.

Gibson, J. J. (1979). *The ecological approach to visual perception*. Boston: Houghton-Mifflin.

Gibson, J. J., Olum, P., & Rosenblatt, F. (1955). Parallax and perspective during aircraft landing. *American Journal of Psychology, 68,* 372–385.

Hebb, D. 0. (1949). *The organization of behavior*. New York: Wiley.

Heidegger, M. (1962). *Being and time*. New York: Harper & Row.

Henle, M. (1978). Foreward to R. Revlin & R. E. Mayer (Eds.), *Human reasoning*. Washington, DC: Winston.

Hinton, G. E. (1981). Implementing semantic networks in parallel hardware. In G. E. Hinton & J. A. Anderson (Eds.), *Parallel models of associative memory* (pp. 161–187). Hillsdale, NJ: Lawrence Erlbaum Associates.

Hinton, G. E., & Anderson, J. A. (Eds.). (1981). *Parallel models of associative memory*. Hillsdale, NJ: Lawrence Erlbaum Associates.

Horn, B. K. P. (1975). Obtaining shape from shading information. In P. H. Winston (Ed.), *The psychology of computer vision*. New York: McGraw–Hill.

Horn, B. K. P. (1977). Understanding image intensities. *Artificial Intelligence, 8,* 201–231.

Hubel, D. H., & Wiesel, T. N. (1968). Receptive fields and functional architecture of monkey striate cortex. *Journal of Physiology, 195,* 215–243.

Hull, C. L. (1952). *A behavior system: An introduction to behavior theory concerning the individual organism*. New Haven: Yale University Press.

Inhelder, B., & Piaget, J. (1958). *The growth of logical thinking from childhood to adolescence*. London: Routledge & Kagan Paul.

Johnson–Laird, P. N. (1983). *Mental models*. Cambridge, England: Cambridge University Press.

Just, M. A., & Carpenter, P. A. (Eds.). (1977). *Cognitive processes in comprehension*. Hillsdale, NJ: Lawrence Erlbaum Associates.

Kahneman, D., & Tversky, A. (1973). On the psychology of prediction. *Psychological Review, 80,* 237–251.

Kosslyn, S. M. (1980). *Image and mind*. Cambridge, MA: Harvard University Press.

Lachman R., Lachman, J. L., & Butterfield, E. C. (1979). *Cognitive psychology and information processing*. Hillsdale, NJ: Lawrence Erlbaum Associates.

Leeuwenberg, E. L. J. (1971). A perceptual coding language for visual and auditory patterns. *American Journal of Psychology, 84,* 307–349.

Leeuwenberg, E. L. J. (1978). Quantification of certain visual pattern properties: Salience, transparency, and similarity. In E. L. J. Leeuwenberg & H. F. J. M. Buffart (Eds.), *Formal theories of visual perception*. New York: Wiley.

Lindsay, P. H., & Norman, D. A. (1972). *Human information processing: An introduction to psychology*, (1st ed.). New York: Academic Press.

Longuet–Higgins, H. C., & Prazdny, K. (1980). The interpretation of a moving retinal image. *Proceedings of the Royal Society of London, A, 254,* 557–599.

MacCorquodale, K., & Meehl, P. E. (1948). On a distinction between hypothetical constructs and intervening variables. *Psychological Review, 55,* 95–107.

Mace, W. M. (1977). James J. Gibson's strategy for perceiving: Ask not what's inside your head, but what your head's inside of. In R. Shaw & J. Bransford (Eds.), *Perceiving, acting, and knowing.* Hillsdale, NJ: Lawrence Erlbaum Associates.

Mandler, G. (1975). *Mind and emotion.* New York: Wiley.

Marcel, A. J. (1983a). Conscious and unconscious perception: Experiments on visual masking and word recognition. *Cognitive Psychology, 15,* 197–237.

Marcel, A. J. (1983b). Conscious and unconscious perception: An approach to the relation between phenomenal experience and perceptual processes. *Cognitive Psychology, 15,* 238–300.

Marr, D. (1982). *Vision.* San Francisco: Freeman.

Marr, D., & Poggio, T. (1976). Cooperative computation of stereo disparity, *Science, 194,* 283–287.

Marr, D., & Poggio, T. (1979). A computational theory of human stereo vision. *Proceeding of the Royal Society of London, B, 204,* 301–328.

McClelland, J. L. (1979). On the time relations of mental processes: An examination of systems of processes in cascade. *Psychological Review, 86,* 287–330.

McClelland, J. L., & Rumelhart, D. E. (1981). An interactive activation model of context effects in letter perception. Part 1: An account of basic findings. *Psychological Review, 88,* 375–407.

Merleau-Ponty, M. (1962). *Phenomenology of perception.* English translation. London: Routledge & Kagan Paul.

Meyer, D. E., Yantis, S., Osman, A., & Smith, J. E. K. (1984). Discrete versus continuous models of response preparation: A reaction time analysis. In S. Kornblum & J. Requin (Eds.), *Preparatory states and processes* (pp. 69–94). Hillsdale, NJ: Lawrence Erlbaum Associates.

Miller, J. (1982). Discrete versus continuous stage models of human information processing: In search of partial output. *Journal of Experimental Psychology: Human Perception and Performance, 8,* 273–296.

Newell, A. (1980). Physical symbol systems. *Cognitive Science, 4,* 135–183.

Newell, A., & Simon, H. (1963). Computers in psychology. In R. D. Luce, R. R. Bush, & E. Galanter (Eds.), *Handbook of mathematical psychology* (Vol. 1, pp. 361–428). New York: Wiley.

Newell, A., & Simon, H. (1972). *Human problem solving.* Englewood Cliffs, NJ: Prentice–Hall.

Newell, A., & Simon, H. (1976). Computer science as empirical inquiry: Symbols and search. *Communications of the ACM, 19,* 113–126.

Norman, D. A., & Bobrow, D. (1975). On data-limited and resource-limited processes. *Cognitive Psychology, 7,* 44–64.

Palmer, S. E. (1978). Fundamental aspects of cognitive representation. In E. Rosch & B. Lloyd (Eds.), *Cognition and categorization.* Hillsdale: NJ: Lawrence Erlbaum Associates.

Palmer, S. E. (1983). The psychology of perceptual organization: A transformational approach. In J. Beck, B. Hope, & A. Rosenfeld (Eds.), *Human and machine vision.* New York: Academic Press.

Palmer, S. E., & Bucher, N. (1981). Configural effects in the perceived pointing of ambiguous triangles. *Journal of Experimental Psychology: Human Perception and Performance, 7,* 88–114.

Piaget, J. (1950). *The psychology of intelligence* (M. Piercy & D. E. Berlyne, Trans.). London: Routledge & Kegan Paul.

Posner, M. I. (1978). *Chronometric explorations of mind.* Hillsdale, NJ: Lawrence Erlbaum Associates.

Putnam, H. (1960). Minds and machines. In S. Hook (Ed.), *Dimensions of mind.* New York: New York University Press.

Putnam, H. (1975). The nature of mental states. In H. Putnam (Ed.), *Mind, language and reality: Philosophical papers.* Cambridge, England: Cambridge University Press. Reprinted in N. Block

(Ed.), *Readings in philosophy of psychology* (Vol. 1). Cambridge, MA: Harvard University Press, 1980.

Rumelhart, D. E., & McClelland, J. L. (1982). An interactive activation model of context effects in letter perception (Part 2): The contextual enhancement effect and some tests and extensions of the model. *Psychological Review, 89,* 60–94.

Rumelhart, D. E., & Norman, D. A. (1984). Representation in memory. In R. C. Atkinson, R. J. Herrnstein, G. Lindzey, & R. D. Luce (Eds.), *Handbook of experimental psychology.* New York: Wiley.

Searle, J. R. (1980). Minds, brains, and programs. *The Behavioral and Brain Sciences, 3,* 417–457.

Searle, J. R. (1983). *Intentionality.* Cambridge, England: Cambridge University Press.

Shallice, T. (1972). Dual functions of consciousness. *Psychological Review, 79,* 383–393.

Shallice, T. (1978). The dominant action system: An information-processing approach to consciousness. In K. S. Pope & J. L. Singer (Eds.), *The stream of consciousness: Scientific investigations into the flow of human experience.* New York: Plenum.

Shannon, C. E. (1948). A mathematical theory of communication. *Bell System Technical Journal, 27,* 379–423, 623–656.

Shaw, R., & Bransford, J. D. (1977). *Perceiving, acting, and knowing: Toward an ecological psychology.* Hillsdale, NJ: Lawrence Erlbaum Associates.

Shepard, R. N. (1981). Psychophysical complementarity. In M. Kubovy & J. R. Pomerantz (Eds.), *Perceptual organization.* Hillsdale, NJ: Lawrence Erlbaum Associates.

Shepard, R. N., & Chipman, S. (1970). Second-order isomorphism of internal representations: Shapes of states. *Cognitive Psychology, 1,* 1–17.

Shepard, R. N., & Cooper, L. A. (1982). *Mental images and their transformations.* Cambridge, MA: MIT Press/Bradford Books.

Skinner, B. F. (1953). *Science and human behavior.* New York: Macmillan.

Sternberg, S. (1966). High-speed scanning in human memory. *Science, 153,* 652–654.

Sternberg, S. (1969a). The discovery of processing stages: Extension of Donders' method. In W. G. Koster (Ed.), *Attention and performance II.* Amsterdam: North Holland. (*Acta Psychologica, 30,* 276–315.)

Sternberg, S. (1969b). Memory-scanning: Mental processes revealed by reaction time experiments. *American Scientist, 57,* 421–457.

Suppes, P. (1969). A stimulus–response theory of finite automata. *Journal of Mathematical Psychology, 6,* 327–355.

Tolman, E. C. (1932). *Purposive behavior in animals and men.* New York: Appleton–Century–Crofts.

Townsend, J. T. (1971). A note on the identifiability of parallel and serial processes. *Perception and Psychophysics, 10,* 161–163.

Townsend, J. T. (1972). Some results on the identifiability of parallel and serial processes. *British Journal of Mathematical and Statistical Psychology, 25,* 168–199.

Townsend, J. T., & Ashby, F. G. (1983). Stochastic modelling of elementary psychological processes. Cambridge, England: Cambridge University Press.

Turing, A. M. (1936). On computable numbers, with an application to the Entscheidungsproblem. *Proceedings of the London Mathematical Society, Series 2, 42,* 230–265.

Turing, A. M. (1950). Computing machinery and intelligence. *Mind, 59,* 433–460.

Turvey, M. T. (1977). Contrasting orientations to the theory of visual information processing. *Psychological Review, 84,* 67–88.

Ullman, S. (1979). *The interpretation of visual motion.* Cambridge, MA: MIT Press.

Ullman, S. (1980). Against direct perception. *The Behavioral and Brain Sciences, 3,* 373–415.

Watson, J. B. (1913). Psychology as the behaviorist views it. *Psychological Review, 20,* 158–177.

Watson, J. B. (1925). *Behaviorism.* New York: Norton.

4 Why I Am Not A Cognitive Psychologist[1]

B. F. Skinner
Harvard University

The variables of which human behavior is a function lie in the environment. We distinguish between (1) the selective action of that environment during the evolution of the species, (2) its effect in shaping and maintaining the repertoire of behavior which converts each member of the species into a person, and (3) its role as the occasion upon which behavior occurs. Cognitive psychologists study these relations between organism and environment, but they seldom deal with them directly. Instead they invent internal surrogates which become the subject matter of their science.

Take, for example, the so-called process of association. In Pavlov's experiment a hungry dog hears a bell and is then fed. If this happens many times, the dog begins to salivate when it hears the bell. The standard mentalistic explanation is that the dog "associates" the bell with the food. But it was Pavlov who associated them! "Associate" means to join or unite. The dog merely begins to salivate upon hearing the bell. We have no evidence that it does so because of an internal surrogate of the contingencies.

In the "association of ideas" the ideas are internal replicas of stimuli to which I shall return. If we have eaten lemons, we may taste lemon upon seeing a lemon or see a lemon upon tasting lemon juice, but we do not do this because *we* associate the flavor with the appearance. They are associated in the lemon. "Word associations" are at least correctly named. If we say "home" when someone says "house," it is not because we associate the two words but because they are associated in daily English usage. Cognitive association is an invention. Even if it were real, it would go no further toward an explanation than the external contingencies upon which it is modelled.

---

[1]Reprinted with permission of *Behaviorism* and the author.

Another example is abstraction. Consider a simple experiment. A hungry pigeon can peck any one of a number of panels bearing the names of colors—"white," "red," "blue," and so on, and the pecks are reinforced with small amounts of food. Any one of a number of objects—blocks, books, flowers, toy animals, and so on—can be seen in an adjacent space. The following contingencies are then arranged: whenever the object is white, no matter what its shape or size, pecking only the panel marked "white" is reinforced; whenever the object is red, pecking only the panel marked "red" is reinforced; and so on. Under these conditions the pigeon eventually pecks the panel marked "white" when the object is white, the panel marked "red" when the object is red, and so on. Children are taught to name colors with similar contingencies, and we all possess comparable repertoires sustained by the reinforcing practices of our verbal environments.

But what is said to be going on in the mind? Karl Popper (1957) has put a classical issue this way: "We can say either that (1) the universal term "white" is a label attached to a set of things, or that (2) we collect the set because they share an intrinsic property of "whiteness." Popper says the distinction is important; natural scientists may take the first position but social scientists must take the second. Must we say, then, that the pigeon is either attaching a universal term to a set of things or collecting a set of things because they share an intrinsic property? Clearly, it is the *experimenter* not the pigeon who "attaches" the white key to the white objects displayed and who collects the set of objects on which a single reinforcing event is made contingent. Should we not simply attribute the behavior to the experimental contingencies? And if so, why not for children or ourselves? Behavior comes under the control of stimuli under certain contingencies of reinforcement. Special contingencies maintained by verbal communities produce "abstractions." We do attach physical labels to physical things and we collect physical objects according to labels properties, but comparable cognitive processes are inventions, which even if real, would be no closer to an explanation than the external contingencies.

Another cognitive account of the same data would assert that a person, if not a pigeon, forms an abstract *idea* or develops a *concept* of color. The development of concepts is an especially popular cognitive field. (The horticultural metaphor minimizes contributions from the environment. We may hasten the growth of the mind but we are no more responsible for its final character than farmers for the character of the fruits and vegetables they so carefully nourish.) Color vision is part of the genetic endowment of most people, and it develops or grows in a physiological sense, possibly to some extent after birth. Nevertheless, most stimuli acquire control because of their place in contingencies of reinforcement. As the contingencies become more complex, they shape and maintain more complex behavior. It is the environment that develops, not a mental or cognitive possession.

A passage from a recent discussion of the development of sexual identity in a child might be translated as follows: "The child forms a concept based upon what it has observed and been told of what it means to be a boy or girl." (A child's behavior is affected by what it has observed and been told about being a boy or girl.) "This concept is oversimplified, exaggerated, and stereotyped." (The contingencies affecting the behavior are simplified and exaggerated and involve stereotyped behavior on the part of parents and others.) "As the child develops cognitively, its concepts, and consequently its activities, become more sophisticated and realistic." (As the child grows older, the contingencies become more subtle and more closely related to the actual sex of the child.) Children do not go around forming concepts of their sexual identity and "consequently" behaving in special ways; they slowly change their behavior as people change the ways in which they treat them because of their sex. Behavior changes because the contingencies change, not because a mental entity called a concept develops.

Many mentalistic or cognitive terms refer not only to contingencies but to the behavior they generate. Terms like "mind," "will," and "thought" are often simply synonyms of "behavior." An historian writes: "what may be called a stagnation of thought prevailed, as though the mind, exhausted after building up the spiritual fabric of the Middle Ages, had sunk into inertia." Exhaustion is a plausible metaphor when a quiet period follows an active one, but it was behavior that became stagnant and inert, presumably because the contingencies changed. Certain social conditions ("the spiritual fabric of the Middle Ages") made people active. A second set of conditions, possibly produced by the very behavior generated by the first, made them much less so. To understand what actually happened, we should have to discover why the contingencies changed, not why thought became stagnant or inert.

Behavior is internalized as mental life when it is too slight to be observed by others—when, as we say, it is covert. A writer has pointed out that "the conductor of an orchestra maintains a certain even beat according to an internal rhythm, and he can divide that beat in half again and again with an accuracy rivaling any mechanical instrument." But is there an *internal* rhythm? Beating time is behavior. Parts of the body often serve as pendulums useful in determining speed, as when the amateur musician beats time with a foot or the rock player with the whole body, but other well-timed behavior must be learned. The conductor beats time steadily because he has learned to do so under rather exacting contingencies of reinforcement. The behavior may be reduced in scale until it is no longer visible to others. It is still sensed by the conductor, but it is a sense of behavior not of time. The history of "man's development of a sense of time" over the centuries is not a matter of cognitive growth but of the invention of clocks, calendars, and ways of keeping records—in other words, of an environment that "keeps time."

When an historian reports that in a given period "a wealthy, brilliant, and traditional governing class lost its will," he is reporting simply that it stopped acting like a wealthy, brilliant, and traditional governing class. Deeper changes are suggested by the term "will" but they are not identified. They could not have been changes in particular people, since the period lasted more than one lifetime. What changed were presumably the conditions affecting the behavior of members of the class. Perhaps they lost their money; perhaps competing classes became more powerful.

Feelings, or the bodily conditions we feel, are commonly taken as the causes of behavior. We go for a walk "because we feel like going." It is surprising how often the futility of such an explanation is recognized. A distinguished biologist, C. H. Waddington (1974), reviewing a book by Tinbergen, writes as follows:

> It is not clear how far he (Tinbergen) would go along with the argument of one of the most perceptive critical discussions of ethology by Suzanne Langer, who argues that each step in a complex structure of behavior is controlled, not by a hierarchical set of neural centers, but by the immediate feelings of the animal. The animal, she claims, does the next thing in the sequence, not to bring about a useful goal, or even as a move toward an enjoyable consummation, but because it actually feels like doing it at the moment.

Evidently Waddington himself goes along part way with this "perceptive view."

But suppose Langer is right. Suppose animals simply do what they feel like doing? What is the next step in explaining their behavior? Clearly, a science of animal behavior must be replaced or supplemented by a science of animal feelings. It would be as extensive as the science of behavior because there would presumably be a feeling for each act. But feelings are harder to identify and describe than the behavior attributed to them, and we should have abandoned an objective subject matter in favor of one of dubious status, accessible only through necessarily defective channels of introspection. The contingencies would be the same. The feelings and the behavior would have the same causes.

A British statesman recently asserted that the key to crime in the streets was "frustration." Young people mug and rob because they feel frustrated. But why do they feel frustrated? One reason may be that many of them are unemployed, either because they do not have the education needed to get jobs or because jobs are not available. To solve the problem of street crime, therefore, we must change the schools and the economy. But what role is played in all this by frustration? Is it the case that when one cannot get a job one feels frustrated and that when one feels frustrated one mugs and robs, or is it simply the case that when one cannot earn money, one is more likely to steal it—and possibly to experience a bodily condition called frustration?

Since many of the events which must be taken into account in explaining behavior are associated with bodily states that can be felt, what is felt may serve as a clue to the contingencies. But the feelings are not the contingencies and cannot replace them as causes.

By its very nature operant behavior encourages the invention of mental or cognitive processes said to initiate action. In a reflex, conditioned or unconditioned, there is conspicuous prior cause. Something triggers the response. But behavior that has been positively reinforced occurs upon occasions which, though predisposing, are never compelling. The behavior seems to start up suddenly, without advance notice, as if spontaneously generated. Hence the invention of such cognitive entities as intention, purpose, or will. The same issues were debated with respect to the theory of evolution and for the same reason: selection is a special causal mode not easily observed. Because controlling circumstances which lie in an organism's history of reinforcement are obscure, the mental surrogate gets its chance. Under positive reinforcement we do, as we say, what we are free to do; hence the notion of free will as an initiating condition. (I think it was Jonathan Edwards who said that we believe in free will because we know about our behavior but not about its causes.)

When we do not know why people do one thing rather than another, we say that they "choose" or "make decisions." Choosing originally meant examining, scrutinizing, or testing. Etymologically, deciding means cutting off other possibilities, moving in a direction from which there is no return. Choosing and deciding are thus conspicuous forms of behavior, but cognitive psychologists have nevertheless invented internal surrogates. Anatole Rapaport (1973) puts it this way: "A subject in a psychological experiment is offered a choice among alternatives and selects one alternative over others." When this happens, he says, "common sense suggests that he is guided by a preference." Common sense does indeed suggest it, and so do cognitive psychologists, but where and what is a preference? Is it anything more than a tendency to do one thing rather than another? When we cannot tell whence the wind cometh and wither it goeth, we say that it "bloweth where it listeth," and common sense, if not cognitive psychology, thus credits it with a preference. (List, by the way, is an example of a term with a physical referent used to refer to a mental process. It means, of course, to lean—as in the list of a ship. And since things usually fall in the direction in which they are leaning, we say that people lean toward a candidate in an election as a rough way of predicting how they will vote. The same metaphor is found in "inclination"; we are "inclined" to vote for X. But it does not follow that we have internal leanings and inclinations which affect our behavior.)

"Intention" is a rather similar term which once meant stretching. The cognitive version is a critical issue in current linguistics. Must the intention of the speaker be taken into account? In an operant analysis verbal behavior is determined by the consequences which follow in a given verbal environment, and consequences are what cognitive psychologists are really talking about when they speak of intentions. All operant behavior "stretches forward" a future even though the only consequences responsible for its strength have already occurred.

I go to a drinking fountain "with the intention of getting a drink of water" in the sense that I go because in the past I have got a drink when I have done so. (I may go for the first time, following directions, but that is not an exception; it is an example of rule-governed behavior, of which more later.)

So much for the cognitive internalization of contingencies of reinforcement and the invention of cognitive causes of behavior. Far more damaging to an effective analysis is the internalization of the environment. The Greeks invented the mind to explain how the real world could be known. For them, to know meant to be acquainted with, to be intimate with. The term cognition itself is related to coitus, as in the Biblical sense in which a man is said to know a woman. Having no adequate physics of light and sound nor any chemistry of taste and odor, the Greeks could not understand how a world outside the body, possibly some distance away, could be known. There must be internal copies. Hence cognitive surrogates of the real world.

The distinction between reality and conscious experience has been made so often that it now seems self-evident. Fred Attneave (1974) has recently written that "the statement that the world as we know it is a representation is, I think, a truism—there is really no way in which it can be wrong." But there are at least two ways, depending upon the meaning. If the statement means that we can know only representations of the outside world, it is a "truism" only if we are not our bodies but inhabitants located somewhere inside. Our bodies are in contact with the *real* world and can respond to it directly, but if we are tucked away up in the head, we must be content with representations.

Another possible meaning is that knowing is the very process of constructing mental copies of real things, but if that is the case how do we know the copies? Do we make copies of *them*? And is that regress infinite?

Some cognitive psychologists recognize that knowing is action but try to make the point by appealing to another mental surrogate. Knowledge is said to be "a system of propositions." According to one writer, "when we use the word 'see' we refer to a bridge between a pattern of sensory stimulation and knowledge which is propositional." But "propositional" is simply a laundered version of "behavioral," and the "bridge" is between stimuli and behavior and was built when the stimuli were part of the contingencies.

Representational theories of knowledge are modeled on practical behavior. We do make copies of things. We construct representational works of art, because looking at them is reinforced in much the same way as looking at what they represent. We make maps, because our behavior in following them is reinforced when we arrive at our destination in the mapped territory. But are there internal surrogates? When we daydream, do we first construct copies of reinforcing episodes which we then watch, or do we simply see things once again? And when we learn to get about in a given territory, do we construct cognitive maps which we then follow or do we follow the territory? If we follow a cognitive map, must we learn to do so, and will that require a map of the map? There is no evidence of the mental construction of images to be looked at or maps to be followed. The body responds to the world, at the point of contact; making copies would be a waste of time.

Knowledge is a key term in cognitive theory, and it covers a good deal of ground. It is often contrasted with perception. We are said to be able to *see* that there are three dots on a card but only to *know* that there are thirteen after counting them, even though counting is a form of behavior. After noting that one spiral can be seen to be continuous but that another can be discovered to be so only by tracing, Bela Julesz (1975) has said that "any visual task that cannot be performed spontaneously, without effort or deliberation, can be regarded as a cognitive task rather than as a perceptual one," though all the steps in that example are also clearly behavioral.

"Knowing how to do something" is an internal surrogate of behavior in its relation to contingencies. A child learns to ride a bicycle and is then said to possess knowledge of how to ride. The child's behavior has been changed by the contingencies of reinforcement maintained by bicycles; the child has not taken possession of the contingencies.

To speak of knowing *about* things is also to construct an internal surrogate of contingencies. We watch a football game and are then said to possess knowledge of what happened. We read a book and are said to know what it is about. The game and the book are somehow "represented" in our minds: we are "in possession of certain facts." But the evidence is simply that we can describe what happened at the game and report what the book was about. Our behavior has been changed, but there is no evidence that we have acquired knowledge. To be "in possession of the facts" is not to contain the facts within ourselves but to have been affected by them.

Possession of knowledge implies storage, a field in which cognitive psychologists have constructed a great many mental surrogates of behavior. The organism is said to take in and store the environment, possibly in some processed form. Let us suppose that a young girl saw a picture yesterday and when asked to describe it today, does so. What has happened? A traditional answer would run something like this: when she saw the picture yesterday the girl formed a copy in her mind (which, in fact, was really all she saw). She encoded it in a suitable form and stored it in her memory, where it remained until today. When asked to describe the picture today, she searched her memory, retrieved the encoded copy, and converted it into something like the original picture, which she then looked at and described. The account is modelled on the physical storage of memoranda. We make copies and other records, and respond to them. But do we do anything of the sort in our minds?

If anything is "stored," it is behavior. We speak of the "acquisition" of behavior, but in what form is it possessed? Where is behavior when an organism is not behaving? Where at the present moment, and in what form, is the behavior I exhibit when I am listening to music, eating my dinner, talking with a friend, taking an early morning walk, or scratching an itch? A cognitive psychologist has said that verbal behavior is stored as "lexical memories." Verbal behavior often leaves public records which can be stored in files and libraries, and the metaphor of the storage is therefore particularly plausible. But is the expression any more helpful than saying that my behavior in eating my dinner is stored as prandial memories, or scratching an itch as a prurient memory? The observed facts are simple enough: I have acquired a repertoire of behavior, parts of which I display upon appropriate occasions. The metaphor of storage and retrieval goes well beyond those facts.

The computer, together with information theory as designed to deal with physical systems, has made the metaphor of input-storage-retrieval-output fashionable. The struggle to make machines that think like people has had the effect of supporting theories in which people think like machines. Mind has recently been defined as "the system of organizations and structures ascribed to an individual that processess inputs . . . and provides output to the various subsystems and the world." But organizations and structures of what? (The metaphor gains power from the way in which it disposes of troublesome problems. By speaking of input one can forget all the travail of sensory-psychology and physiology; by speaking of output one can forget all the problems of reporting and analyzing action; and by speaking of the storage and retrieval of information one can avoid all the difficult problems of how organisms are indeed changed by contact with their environments and how those changes survive.)

Sensory data are often said to be stored as images, much like the images said to represent the real world. Once inside, they are moved about for cognitive purposes. There is a familiar experiment on color generalization in which a pigeon pecks at a disk of, say, green light, the behavior being reinforced on a variable interval schedule. When a stable rate of responding develops, no further reinforcements are given, and the color of the disk is changed. The pigeon responds to another color at a rate which depends upon how much it differs from the original; rather similar colors evoke fairly high rates, very different colors low rates. A cognitive psychologist might explain the matter in this way: The pigeon takes in a new color (as "input"), retrieves the original color from memory, where it has been stored in some processed form, puts the two colored images side by side so that they may be easily compared, and after evaluating the difference, responds at the appropriate rate. But what advantage is gained by moving from a pigeon that responds to different colors on a disk to an inner pigeon that responds to colored images in its mind? The simple fact is that because of a known history of reinforcement, different colors control different rates.

The cognitive metaphor is based upon behavior in the real world. We store samples of material and retrieve and compare them with other samples. We compare them in the literal sense of putting them side by side to make differences more obvious. And we respond to different things in different ways. But that is all. The whole field of the processing of information can be reformulated as changes in the control exerted by stimuli.

The storage of factual knowledge raises another problem. When I learn, say, to take apart the rings of a puzzle, it seems unlikely that I store my knowledge of how to do so as a copy of the puzzle or of the contingencies the puzzle maintains for those trying to solve it. Instead cognitive theory holds that I store a rule. Rules are widely used as mental surrogates of behavior, in part because they can be memorized and hence "possessed," but there is an important difference between rules and the contingencies they describe. Rules can be internalized in the sense that we can say them to ourselves, but in doing so we do not internalize the contingencies.

I may learn to solve the puzzle in either of two ways. I may move the rings about until I hit upon a response that separates them. The behavior will be strengthened, and if I do the same thing a number of times, I will eventually be able to take the rings apart quickly. My behavior has been shaped and maintained by its effects on the rings. I may, on the other hand, simply follow printed directions supplied with the puzzle. The directions describe behavior that separates the rings, and if I have already learned to follow directions, I can avoid the possibly long process of having my behavior shaped by the contingencies.

Directions are rules. Like advice, warnings, maxims, proverbs, and governmental and scientific laws, they are extremely important parts of a culture, enabling people to profit from the experience of others. Those who have acquired behavior through exposure to contingencies describe the contingencies, and others then circumvent exposure by behaving in the ways described. But cognitive psychologists contend that something of the same sort happens internally when people learn directly from the contingencies. They are said to discover rules which they themselves then follow. But rules are not *in* the contingencies, nor must they be "known" by those who acquire behavior under exposure to them. (We are lucky that this could be so, since rules are verbal products which arose very late in the evolution of the species.)

The distinction between rules and contingencies is currently important in the field of verbal behavior. Children learn to speak through contact with verbal communities, possibly without instruction. Some verbal responses are effective and others not, and over a period of time more and more effective behavior is shaped and maintained. The contingencies having this effect can be analyzed. A verbal *response* "means" something in the sense that the speaker is under the control of particular circumstances; a verbal *stimulus* "means" something in the sense that the listener responds to it in particular ways. The verbal community maintains contingencies of such a nature that responses made upon particular occasions serve as useful stimuli to listeners who then behave appropriately to the occasions.

More complex relations among the behaviors of speaker and listener fall within the fields of syntax and grammar. Until the time of the Greeks, no one seems to have known that there were rules of grammar, although people spoke grammatically in the sense that they behaved effectively under the contingencies maintained by verbal communities, as children today learn to talk without being given rules to follow. But cognitive psychologists insist that speakers and listeners must discover rules for themselves. One authority, indeed, has defined speaking as "engaging in a rule-governed form of intentional behavior." But there is no evidence that rules play any part in the behavior of the ordinary speaker. By using a dictionary and a grammar we may compose acceptable sentences in a language we do not otherwise speak, and we may occasionally consult a dictionary or a grammar in speaking our own language, but even so we seldom speak by applying rules. We speak because our behavior is shaped and maintained by the practices of a verbal community.

Having moved the environment inside the head in the form of conscious experience and behavior in the form of intention, will, and choice, and having stored the effects of contingencies of reinforcement as knowledge and rules, cognitive psychologists put them all together to compose an internal simulacrum of the organism, a kind of Dopplegänger, not unlike the classical homunculus, whose behavior is the subject of what Piaget and others have called "subjective behaviorism." The mental apparatus studied by cognitive psychology is simply a rather crude version of contingencies of reinforcement and their effects.

Every so-called cognitive process has a physical model. We *associate* things by putting them together. We *store* memoranda and retrieve them for later use. We *compare* things by putting them side by side to emphasize differences. We *discriminate* things one from another by separating them and treating them in different ways. We *identify* objects by isolating them from confusing surroundings. We *abstract* sets of items from complex arrays. We describe contingencies of reinforcement in *rules*. These are the actions of real persons. It is only in the fanciful world of an inner person that they become mental processes.

The very speed with which cognitive processes are invented to explain behavior should arouse our suspicions. Molière made a joke of a medical example more than three hundred years ago: "I am asked by the learned doctors for the cause and reason why opium puts one to sleep, to which I reply that there is in it a soporific virtue the nature of which is to lull the senses." Molière's candidate could have cited evidence from introspection, invoking a collateral effect of the drug, by saying: "To which I reply that opium makes one feel sleepy." But the soporific virtue itself is a sheer invention, and it is not without current parallels.

A conference was recently held in Europe on the subject of scientific creativity. A report published in *Science* (Maugh, 1974) begins by pointing out that more than ninety percent of scientific innovation has been accomplished by fewer than ten percent of all scientists. The next sentence might be paraphrased in this way: "I am asked by the learned doctors for the cause and reason why this should be so, to which I reply that it is because only a few scientists possess creativity." Similarly, "I am asked by the learned doctors for the cause and reason why children learn to talk with great speed, to which I reply that it is because they possess linguistic competence." Molière's audiences laughed.

Cognitive psychologists have two answers to the charge that the mental apparatus is a metaphor or construct. One is that cognitive processes are known through introspection. Do not all thinking persons know that they think? And if behaviorists say they do not, are they not either confessing a low order of mentality or acting in bad faith for the sake of their position? No one doubts that behavior involves internal processes; the question is how well they can be known through introspection. As I have argued elsewhere, self-knowledge, consciousness, or awareness became possible only when the species acquired verbal behavior, and that was very late in its history. The only nervous systems then available had evolved for other purposes and did not make contact with the more important physiological activities. Those who see themselves thinking see little more than their perceptual and motor behavior, overt and covert. They could be said to observe the results of "cognitive processes" but not the processes themselves—a "stream of consciousness" but not what causes the streaming, the "image of a lemon" but not the act of associating appearance with flavor, their use of an abstract term but not the process of abstraction, a name recalled but not its retrieval from memory, and so on. We do not, through introspection, observe the physiological processes through which behavior is shaped and maintained by contingencies of reinforcement.

But physiologists observe them and cognitive psychologists point to resemblances which suggest that they and the physiologists are talking about the same things. The very fact that cognitive processes are going on inside the organism suggests that the cognitive account is closer to physiology than the contingencies of reinforcement studied by those who analyze behavior. But if cognitive processes are simply modelled upon the environmental contingencies, the fact that they are assigned to space inside the skin does not bring them closer to a physiological account. On the contrary, the fascination with an imagined inner life has led to a neglect of the observed facts. The cognitive constructs give physiologists a misleading account of what they will find inside.

In summary, then, I am not a cognitive psychologist for several reasons. I see no evidence of an inner world of mental life relative either to an analysis of behavior as a function of environmental forces or to the physiology of the nervous system. The respective sciences of behavior and physiology will move forward most rapidly if their domains are correctly defined and analyzed.

I am equally concerned with practical consequences. The appeal to cognitive states and processes is a diversion which could well be responsible for much of our failure to solve our problems. We need to change our behavior and we can do so only by changing our physical and social environments. We choose the wrong path at the very start when we suppose that our goal is to change the "minds and hearts of men and women" rather than the world in which they live.

REFERENCES

Attneave, F. (1974). How do you know? *American Psychologist, 29,* 493–499.

Julesz, B. (1975, April). Experiments in the visual perception of texture. *Scientific American,* pp. 34–43.

Maugh, T. H. II. (1974). Creativity: Can it be dissected? Can it be taught? *Science, 184,* 1273.

Popper, K. R. (1957). *Poverty of historicism.* London: Routledge and Kegan Paul.

Rapaport, A. (1973). *Experimental games and their uses in Psychology.* Morristown, NJ: Silver Burdett Company, General Learning Press.

Waddington, C. H. (1974, February 3). How to succeed in nature without really trying. *New York Times Book Review,* pp. 2–3.

5 Bringing Cognition and Creativity into the Behavioral Laboratory

Robert Epstein
University of Massachusetts at Amherst
and
Cambridge Center for Behavioral Studies

Four categories of complex behavior have traditionally given praxists[1] trouble and, not surprisingly, have stimulated theories about cognition and creativity.

Novel Behavior. The most perplexing has been novel behavior. Humans and other organisms do things they have never done before and, occasionally, things no member of their species has ever done before. The mystery of novelty underlies most theories of creativity and has spurred such concepts as "generativity" in language production (Chomsky, 1965) and "productivity" in problem solving (Wertheimer, 1945).

Delays. Second, behavior often appears to be under the control of events that occurred in the remote past. Köhler (1925) notes a case in which some food was buried outside a chimpanzee's cage in full view of the chimpanzee. When the animal was released the next morning, it immediately unearthed the food. Few people would be content to speak of action at a distance in this situation, in part because we know that intervening events can change the outcome. Clearly, environmental events change organisms, and the changes often manifest themselves in subsequent behavior, even after long intervals of time have elapsed. We know very little about what those changes are. Meanwhile, control of behavior by temporally remote stimuli spurs theories of "memory."

---

[1]*Praxics*—a blend of "physics" and "praxis," the Greek for " behavior "—is a term I and others now use for the study of behavior. *Behaviorism,* properly speaking, is the name of a school of philosophy. For a fuller discussion of this terminology, see Epstein (1984d).

Covert Activity.   Third, thoughts, feelings, and so on are accessible only to oneself, and as long as that remains the case, speculative theories about their nature and significance will flourish.

Complex, Distinctively Human Behavior.   And finally, complex human behavior, such as language, or the behavior attributed to a self-concept, is often difficult to account for. When an environmental or biological account of distinctively human behavior is not apparent, people often appeal to a construct. Only humans sing "The Star Spangled Banner," but because one is taught in a conspicuous way to do so as a child, we don't bother with a construct. In contrast, many would insist that Francis Scott Key's composition, which is not easily traceable to either biological or environmental factors, was a product of creativity and various cognitive processes.

Creativity

Creativity is a natural category and, as such, is probably not worth trying to define (Epstein, 1980).[2] It is, moreover, a particularly elusive one. It is a judgment pronounced by a community on behavior or a product of behavior, and like all such judgments (for example, of "morality" or "beauty"), it differs from one community to the next and changes from time to time. A cubist painting would not have been judged creative in 15th-century Europe; it would have been burned. Western music critics wouldn't presume to be able to judge the creativeness of a traditional Japanese composition without special training in the criteria the Japanese use to make such a judgment.

The judgment also depends on who did what first. If Einstein had emerged from the patent office only to find that others had already proposed the theory of relativity, Wertheimer (1945) would not have bothered to determine what was so productive about his thought processes. Deviance alone is not sufficient for the judgment of creativity; it must be deviance that is valuable to other people.

The elusive judgment, furthermore, once made, can be retracted. A current popular song was no doubt judged a creation of the composer until he lost a plagiarism suit. The scientific works of a young academician were no doubt judged creative before it was discovered that he had stolen some of them from fellow scientists. Computer-generated poetry is never judged to be creative once its origins are revealed. The more we know about the sources of behavior, the less inclined we are to speak of creativity, or, to paraphrase Samuel Butler, creativity is only a word for man's ignorance of the gods.

Such a concept does not seem suitable for the laboratory. What is worth studying, however, is novelty. Novel behavior has to occur before a community

---

[2]Catania (1979) justifiably makes the same point about the word "learning."

can select some of it and call it "creative." Why it selects some and rejects others is no mystery; novelty itself is the mystery.

Sources of Novelty

At least four sources of novelty are readily accessible to laboratory study. Two—imitation and instructions—are social phenomena that involve conspicuous controlling stimuli; the others—variation and the spontaneous interconnection of repertoires—are individual phenomena that seem to be responsible for novelty's air of mystery. A discussion of these phenomena must be preceded by at least a few words about a rather troublesome problem: How do we *measure* novelty?

Measurement.   If we look only at behavior, our determination will be constrained by our level of observation. If we look at behavior too closely, we will judge all behavior to be novel, for we never do exactly the same thing twice. A rat sometimes presses the lever with one paw and sometimes with the other, and presses constantly vary in force and duration. We often seem to be repeating something we have done before, but that is only because we are so insensitive to detail (Epstein, 1982a). The same word, spoken twice, leaves easily distinguishable records on a spectrogram. Even an identical repetition could still be judged novel, because it is both unique in time and the product of a changed organism; as William James (1890) noted, we don't call two ticks of a clock the "same" tick.

On the other hand, if we overlook too much detail or summarize over too long a period of time, we will judge very little behavior to be novel. We would take no notice, for example, when Mozart sat down to write a symphony if he had already written one before. This is the problem addressed by Skinner in his "Generic Nature" paper in 1935, but his solution, unfortunately, is not applicable here, for we are not interested in a recurring unit of behavior but simply in one special instance.

Topography, in general, might mislead us, no matter what our level of analysis. A painter's hand may have moved (more or less) in every possible way it could have moved before she began work on the canvass before her. What will make this work unique is a new sequence of strokes. Perhaps, in our determination of novelty, our focus should be on new combinations of old behaviors.

Still other complications present themselves when we look exclusively at behavior: Is smoother or more forceful motor performance "novel"? How should we treat apparently "random" changes in behavior? One alternative is to look at the product of behavior, which is what researchers have tended to do (e.g., Goetz & Baer, 1973). We can in so doing establish fairly objective criteria for novelty suited to our domain of interest. We can look for uncommon words in a composition, for example, or block structures greater than a certain height, or new color combinations in a drawing. Though response product is a convenient measure, objective measures of behavior itself will be helpful in cases in which the relevant behavior is observable and in which observations are made at an appropriate level (e.g., Maltzman, 1960; Schwartz, 1980).

Imitation.   One important source of novelty is a social process—imitation. If you can do something you have never done before just because you see someone else doing it, you are capable of infinitely more behavior than you would be otherwise. Most of the novel behavior a child exhibits is imitated: blowing on hot food, playing "patty cake," turning door knobs, and so on. And as any linguist will attest, in the early years most words are acquired through imitation. Imitation can be either innate or learned; it can be specific to certain behaviors or generalizable to many; and it can occur either soon after a model has behaved or after a substantial delay.

Both innate and learned imitation have been studied as part of the Columban Simulation Project (Baxley, 1982; Epstein, 1981, 1984a).[3] Experiments on learned imitation revealed that pigeons imitate each other to some extent even without training (Epstein, 1984b).[4] Several experiments have been conducted in which a naive pigeon on one side of a clear partition watches a pigeon on the other side peck a ping pong ball, pull a rope, or peck a key for food reinforcement. Given access to similar operanda, the naive pigeon will imitate the leader at a low rate day after day without any reinforcement. Moreover, it will subsequently continue to peck or pull for several sessions without a leader present.

Instructional Control.   A second source of novelty in human behavior, also a social process, is instructions. The first time we drive a car or play the piano or bake a cake, we are usually following instructions. We could simulate the effect of instructions in producing new behavior by bringing several different responses under the control of different discriminative stimuli and then presenting the stimuli in new orders or by bringing the force of a response under the control of the size of some stimulus and then making the stimulus smaller or larger than it

---

[3]The rationale for using pigeons in such experiments is given at length elsewhere (Epstein, 1984a). Carefully constructed simulations of complex human behavior with nonhuman subjects can provide "plausibility proofs" of the role that certain environmental histories play in the emergence of the behavior. In some cases more definitive research cannot be conducted, usually for ethical reasons. The plausibility of such simulations rests on five factors: the topography of the behavior, the function of the behavior, the structure of the organism, the generality of the behavioral processes invoked, and evidence that humans have had the relevant histories. Not all the studies referred to in the present chapter meet these criteria. For a fuller discussion of these and related issues, see Epstein (1984a). The rationale is briefly stated in Epstein (1981).

[4]There is a previous report of spontaneous imitation in pigeons (Zentall & Hogan, 1976). In that report, however, the observing animals were technically not "naive," because they had been hopper trained, and the observed effect was small. There are perhaps hundreds of other investigations of both innate and learned imitation in both animals and humans (e.g., see Flanders, 1968; Miller & Dollard, 1941; Porter, 1910; Thorpe, 1963).

ever was before (cf. Catania, 1980). Human language will be considerably more powerful in this capacity than anything we can simulate with pigeons.

Variation.   A third and in many respects the most fundamental source of novelty is variation, nature's own source of novelty, both at the ontogenic and phylogenic levels. We speak of classes of responses, just as taxonomists speak of classes of organisms, because—although it is true that the same response never occurs twice—related responses covary. Like Darwin, we depend on variation to account for novelty, at least in some instances, and again, like Darwin, we know nothing about the underlying mechanism. We also depend on variation to produce novel behavior: We are able to "shape" behavior only because there is always a distribution of responses from which to make a selection. As long as the response we reinforce is not near the mode of the distribution, a new distribution will appear from which we can make another selection. By continuing to strengthen infrequent responses, we can eventually produce behavior that has never occurred before, as when we gradually increase the force requirement for a lever press in a classroom demonstration until a rat presses with a force equal to its own weight. Relatively little research has been done on variation per se; it is simply a fact about behavior which we make use of daily but which is otherwise quite mysterious.

Interconnection.   A fourth source of novelty is a phenomenon we might call "the spontaneous interconnection of repertoires" (cf. Hull, 1935). Separate repertoires of behavior can come together in new situations to produce blends, new sequences of behavior, or—by bringing an organism into contact with new contingencies—behaviors that have new functions. This is in many respects the most dramatic and mysterious source of novelty and is probably responsible for much of the behavior people call creative in science and the arts, as well as certain productive aspects of language (Place, 1981).

Several popular and highly speculative theories of creativity describe a similar process: Writer Arthur Koestler (1964), for example, attributed creativity to something he calls "bisociation," which is "any mental occurrence simultaneously associated with two habitually incompatible contexts." Rothenberg (1971), a psychiatrist, said that creativity is based on what he calls "Janusian thinking" (from Janus, the god with two faces), which is the ability "to conceive and utilize two or more opposite or contradictory ideas, concepts, or images simultaneously." Norman Maier (1929), a Gestalt psychologist, defined "reasoning," which was to him a creative process, as "the combination of isolated experiences." The mathematician Poincaré (1946) spoke of the collision of ideas, rising into consciousness "in crowds" "until pairs interlocked" in accounting for some of his achievements.

The combinatorial process just described is less speculative than the latter four, but if it works in covert behavior the way it works in overt behavior, it may be just the process about which Koestler and others were speaking. The spontaneous interconnection of repertoires is actually surprisingly accessible to laboratory study. It has occurred in a number of the Columban simulations. One was called "The Spontaneous Use of Memoranda" (Epstein & Skinner, 1981), which was a follow-up of the symbolic communication demonstration we did with Jack and Jill (Epstein, Lanza, & Skinner, 1980). After we established the original exchange, we changed the positions of the birds until each had acquired both the "speaker" and "listener" repertoires. Among other things, each subject had now learned to pair colors (red, green, and yellow) with letters (R, G, and Y) and letters with colors. When the partition that had separated Jack and Jill was removed and one bird was given access to both response panels at once, a new sequence emerged without our intervention: Those parts of the speaker and listener repertoires which were successful in this new situation became interconnected to form a new chain. A bird would peck a color hidden behind a curtain, peck (and thus illuminate) the corresponding black-on-white letter, cross to the other side of the chamber, *look back* at the illuminated letter, and, finally, peck the corresponding color key.

The repertoires that had been established prior to the test not only provided the makings of the new sequence, they also brought the pigeon into contact with new contingencies, according to which a peck at a letter key now served a new function—that of mediating the delay between a peck at the hidden color and a peck at a corresponding color on the other panel. Without providing any additional training, we conducted a series of tests over a 5-month period which indicated that these pecks were indeed functioning as memoranda. When the task was made easier, for example, the pigeons stopped pecking the letter keys; when the task was made more difficult, they began pecking them appropriately once more. When Jack was distracted by a loud noise before a peck at a color key, he would start and then *look back* at the illuminated letter key before pecking the corresponding color key.

An even more striking example of the spontaneous interconnection of repertoires occurred in our experiment on "insight" (Epstein, 1981; Epstein, Kirshnit, Lanza, & Rubin, 1984). A pigeon was trained both to push a box toward a target and to climb into a stationary box and peck a small toy banana. When the banana was placed out of reach and the box placed elsewhere on the floor of the chamber—a situation very much like the one with which Köhler (1925) confronted his chimpanzees—the two repertoires occurred one after the other, and hence the pigeon "solved the problem." We have conducted this experiment now many times and have varied the training histories to determine the contributions of a number of different experiences. For example, if brute force attempts to get at the banana by flying and jumping are extinguished before the test, the solution may occur rather quickly (in about a minute, for several birds). If such behavior is not extinguished, the pigeon will first attempt to reach the banana by brute force, as did Köhler's chimpanzees.

On the basis of various controls we have completed so far, we can give a tentative, moment-to-moment account of a successful performance. The test situation is a new one for the bird, so at first there may be very little behavior and then what appears to be competition between the climbing and pushing repertoires (stimuli are present which control both repertoires).[5] The bird manages to look "puzzled": It looks back and forth from banana to box, stretches toward the banana, motions toward the box, and so on. At some point the bird starts to push the box. If it had been previously trained to push the box toward a small green spot at the base of the chamber—one training scenario—it very clearly starts to push the box *toward* the banana. This, it now appears, is a matter of generalization, though not based on physical similarity but rather on the fact that behavior with respect to both the green spot and the banana had been reinforced. A bird trained to push the box toward the green spot but not to peck the banana or climb on the box did not push the box toward the banana when the banana was placed out of reach in the chamber.[6]

Once the bird has pushed the box in the neighborhood of the banana, it has arranged for itself a new stimulus—box under banana—which is the occasion upon which the second repertoire, climbing onto the box and pecking the banana, had been reinforced. We call this process "automatic chaining," because the bird has automatically arranged the discriminative stimulus for the second link of a two-component chain.

Reinforcement.   I have mentioned four sources of novelty but have managed to omit reinforcement. Psychologists have been using reinforcement to promote novelty for decades (e.g., Goetz & Baer, 1973; Maltzman, 1960); isn't it a source of novelty? Reinforcement, I submit, is probably not a source of novelty per se but rather: (1) It may stimulate activity and in so doing increase the amount

---

[5]Multiple repertoires can be made available in several ways. The first, which seems to apply in the version of the box-and-banana experiment just described, is multiple controlling stimuli: Compound, ambiguous, and novel stimuli should increase the likelihood of all the behaviors controlled by their constituents. There is some evidence that this is an orderly, quantifiable process (Cumming & Eckerman, 1965; Migler, 1964). A second phenomenon is the resurgence of previously reinforced behavior during extinction (Epstein, 1983, 1985a; Epstein & Medalie, 1983; cf. Epstein & Skinner, 1980; Hull, 1934; Leitenberg, Rawson, & Bath, 1970; Maltzman, 1955; Staddon & Simmelhag, 1971). Resurgence during extinction may be one of the most important determinants of behavior that is often mistakenly labeled—even by me—"spontaneous" (e.g., Epstein & Medalie, 1983; Epstein & Skinner, 1981).

[6]I have tested this interpretation by repeating the test with two other birds who have had such training and then testing them again after they have been trained to peck the banana. The pigeons pushed more directly toward the banana in the second test. Similarly, a child who has spotted a cookie jar on a table and then retrieved it by pushing a chair toward the table and climbing on the chair will more likely do so the next day to retrieve a toy car than to retrieve a roll of toilet paper, though the latter more closely resembles the cookie jar. Such behavior suggests a process akin to what some describe as "functional" categorization (e.g., Bruner, Goodnow, & Austin, 1956).

of variation we see in behavior. But almost any stimulus will do that; it needn't be a reinforcer. (2) By strengthening one response over another from the distribution of available responses, it can produce a new distribution in which, because behavior varies, new behavior occurs. Variation is the actual source of novelty in this case (cf. Fenner, 1980; Staddon & Simmelhag, 1971). (3) It can serve to establish a discrimination between what is new and not new. Given reinforcement, for example, for building novel block structures, a child would come to preserve structures that he (or she) hasn't seen before and destroy or alter structures like those he had already built. Similarly, if income and recognition are contingent on originality, an artist might push aside or alter a design that resembles that of another artist or another of his or her own works. Schwartz's (1980) finding that pigeons cannot learn to emit novel sequences of pecks indicates only that he could not establish the discrimination between old and new sequences, not that pigeons are incapable of significant novel behavior (cf. Pryor, Haag, & O'Reilly, 1969).

"Promoting Creativity."   Arieti (1976), Guilford (1950), Koestler (1964), Maltzman (1960), Osborn (1953), Skinner (1970, 1981), Torrance (1962, 1963), and many others have offered techniques for "promoting creativity." Many techniques, such as brainstorming, free association, spending time alone, daydreaming, "free thinking," and inactivity, provide circumstances under which behavior is free to vary or old behaviors are likely to come together in new ways.

Measures of Mind

In their influential text on theories of learning, Bower and Hilgard (1981) ask, "Do behaviorists confuse the subject matter of [psychology—which is to say, cognition] with the evidence available for drawing inferences about this subject matter?" (p. 211). A sentence or two earlier they query, "Is physics the science of physical things or the science of meter readings?" The rhetoric is misleading.

Let us assume that physics is indeed the science of physical things.[7] Praxics would seem to have a lot in common with it, for analysts of behavior use meters (videotape recorders, computers, cumulative recorders, event recorders, and so on) to measure physical things—events in behavior and the environment.

Hilgard and Bower overlook the fact that physicists use measuring devices, not to make inferences about physical things, but to measure them. The things

---

[7]Some physicists would debate the matter. According to Wheeler (1981), for example, quantum mechanics has taught us that "No elementary phenomenon is a phenomenon until it is a registered (observed) phenomenon"; that is, "until is has been brought to a close by an irreversible act of amplification" (pp. 24–25). Different registering devices, furthermore, provide different answers to the same question. According to this view, physics might be construed to be the science of meter readings.

they measure presumably exist. Praxists do the same. It is the cognitivists who are doing something unique—that is, using measuring devices to measure events in behavior and the environment, and then using the obtained measurements to speculate about a domain that can never be directly measured and whose very existence is uncertain.

("Cognition," after all, is just a nine-letter substitute for a four-letter word. What they're really interested in is Mind.)

Reaction Time.   The problem of measurement is not a trivial one for cognitivists, for there must always be some doubt about whether their measurements are making contact with the mental phenomenon in which they are interested. The problem is exemplified in the use of reaction time to make inferences about mental processes.

Oswald Külpe, a student of Wundt's, struck a near-fatal blow against the use of reaction time in his *Outline of Psychology* in 1893. Donder's subtraction procedure, he argued, is valid only if complicated tasks, such as discrimination or choice, preserve the simpler components of which the complicated task is supposedly composed. There is no way to know a priori that this is the case, because direct measurement of the processes is impossible. As Woodworth (1936) later put it, "Since we cannot break up the reaction time into successive acts and obtain the time of each act, of what use is the reaction time?" (p. 309). Külpe and contemporaries were also disturbed by contradictory and unreliable results. With the emergence of functional and behavioristic psychologies in the first two decades of this century, the use of reaction time as a means of inference about cognition lost its popularity.

With the rise of cognitive psychology in the 1950s and 1960s, however, reaction time has come into use again and in fact may now be psychology's most popular measure of behavior. But the old problems have not gone away. Because the object of study can never be measured directly, the same data are always subject to more than one interpretation. Consider the debate that has been raging since the 1950s about whether perception works by template matching (Selfridge & Neisser, 1960; Uhr, 1963) or feature detection (Selfridge, 1959), or the recent debate about whether the facts from which mental imagery is inferred require functional mental images (Kosslyn & Pomerantz, 1977) or a set of propositions (Pylyshyn, 1973), or the controversy over whether retrieval from short-term memory is a serial or a parallel process (Corcoran, 1971; Donahoe & Wessells, 1980; Sternberg, 1969, 1975). Data cannot resolve such debates because components of the various models (rehearsal buffers, storage bins, executive processors, tree structures, and so on) are not constrained by direct observations (of neural structures, for example), and hence, as Anderson (1978) has noted, the models can almost always be modified to take descrepant data into account.

Kosslyn and other "cognitive scientists" are not, for all the trappings, studying cognition; they are studying the effects of extremely complex histories, stimulus materials, and instructions on reaction times and other measures of behavior—and then showing how information-processing systems might behave in such ways. This enterprise can shed light on people only if people are information processors, a debatable assertion (Epstein, 1981, 1982b, 1984a).

Skinner and I conducted a modest program of research with a pigeon using reaction time. We first arranged contingencies to produce good waiting behavior and fast key pecks. An auditory ready signal of varying length preceded the onset of a keylight. If a peck occurred within a certain period of time, a feeder operated. The requirement was changed until we reached what appeared to be an asymptotically fast reaction, which was in the range of human simple reaction time (about 200 msec). We then added a discrimination: A peck produced food if the key became transilluminated with green and had no consequence if it became transilluminated with white. With the discrimination well established, the average reaction time to green increased over the simple reaction time. According to Donder's method, the difference in the two times should give us the time for "pure discrimination."

Using similar procedures with humans, Hick (1952) estimated this time to be about 110 msec, and Hyman (1953) found a difference of about 100 msec. The average difference for our pigeon was about the same—120 msec. This tells us that similar requirements produce similar changes in reaction time for humans and at least one pigeon. We add nothing to this fact by claiming that we have measured the time of "pure discrimination" in the pigeon. No doubt there are other correspondences between changes in reaction times in humans and pigeons (cf. Blough, 1977; Hollard & Delius, 1982). But why this is so—or not so—is a matter for the physiologist. Models of the mind can neither account for nor in any way shed light on such a coincidence.

Self-Concept

The concept of a self-concept exemplifies the dilemma of cognitive psychology and has provided an opportunity for demonstrating some advantages of a behavioral approach.[8] The behavior from which it is inferred fits into the fourth category of troublesome phenomena I outlined earlier: It is complex, distinctively human, and not easily traceable to environmental or biological factors. Like language, the behavior that comes under the rubric of "self" is acquired haphazardly over a period of years; in many cases the controlling stimuli are not observable by others.

Like "creativity," "self-concept" is a natural category and hence difficult to define. A wide variety of behavior is said to provide evidence for its existence: body-directed behavior in front of a mirror, pointing to one's picture, gazing at

---

[8]A more detailed analysis of this topic is given by Epstein and Koerner (in press) and Epstein (1985b).

one's picture longer than at another person's picture (for young children, anyway—perhaps, under some circumstances, adults would do the opposite), imitating a videotape of oneself more than a videotape of someone else, and so on. At least these are the measures used by psychologists who study the self-concept (e.g., Amsterdam, 1972; Gallup, 1970; Lewis & Brooks–Gunn, 1979). The verbal behavior said to show "self-knowledge"—describing one's thoughts, feelings, aches and pains, actions, and so on—would also seem to contribute to various notions of "self"; Skinner (e.g., 1945, 1957, 1963, 1974) has offered an account of verbal behavior of this type.

"Self-concept" is one of many psychological terms that are often reified. It is said not only to exist but to grow, in embryonic fashion (Lewis & Brooks–Gunn, 1979). It is, furthermore, mistakenly used to explain behavior that, at best, it only characterizes. Gallup (1979), for example, attributes a lack of behavior said to show self-awareness to a lack of "a sense of identity" and "a sufficiently well-integrated self-concept." That kind of explanation is no explanation at all. Because we can never test for the existence of self-concept independently of the existence of the behaviors said to show it, we can never test the explanation. And no explanation is given for why the self-concept itself may be lacking.

Such a concept obscures the search for more concrete determinants of the behavior. Because it functions grammatically as an explanation, no further explanation is sought. Yet more concrete explanations are usually available.

The rubric of self also mistakenly implies that all the various "self" behaviors have the *same* cause or causes—in the worst case, the cause is said to be the self itself. But, parsimony notwithstanding, it is absurd to think that mirror-directed behavior has the same determinants as an answer to the question "Where does it hurt?" and that a child comes to respond to photographs of its face differently than to photographs of other faces for still the same reasons. Each of the various behaviors said to show the existence of a self-concept demands its own investigation and analysis. A child has many thousands of learning experiences during its first few years of life, and physical maturation has profound effects. A child not only rapidly acquires a wide variety of self-controlled behaviors but many other complex behaviors, as well—verbal and other social behaviors, complex motor skills, and so on. That many "self" behaviors seem to be acquired more or less in unison (Kagan, 1981) is not surprising—after all, *many other* complex behaviors are also acquired during the same period. The first few years of life are a period of rapid acquisition; covariance is—indeed, it *must be*—the rule.

And what of parsimony? A different set of determinants for each of a dozen different "self" behaviors is hardly appealing. The parsimonious solution may prove to lie with a general set of principles of behavior change—one set of functions describing such phenomena as reinforcement, extinction, resurgence, automatic chaining, maturational factors, and so on—that cut across many different "self" behaviors, and, of course, many other behaviors, as well (cf.

Epstein, 1984c, 1985a). When a child selects its photograph from among a group of photographs, its behavior has the same functional characteristics as the behavior of a pigeon in a "delayed matching-to-sample" task. Similar principles might adequately describe both performances, and, in fact, it would be difficult at this point to rule out the possibility that similar neurophysiological processes underlie each performance. Automatic chaining must operate across many species and across many behaviors, verbal and nonverbal, self and nonself: An organism's own behavior changes its environment in such a way that the probability of subsequent behavior is changed. A student draws an arc on a geometry exam and, in so doing, creates new intersections where the point of the compass can rest. A pigeon pushes a box for the first time toward a suspended banana and, in so doing, sets up box-under-banana, the stimulus in whose presence climbing and pecking the banana had been reinforced in the past; the pigeon stops pushing, climbs, and pecks (see Epstein et al., 1984).

These matters aside, the behaviors that come under the rubric of "self" do seem to have one functional characteristic in common: They all seem to be controlled either by one's own body or by one's own behavior. I use "controlled" here in a technical sense: One's behavior or body is the setting for the "self" behavior; it is the stimulus to which one responds. One responds to one's mirror image—a reflection of one's body—in a special way. One answers the question "Where does it hurt?" by pointing to a location on one's body and the question "How do you feel?" by describing a state of one's body. One answers the question "What did you do last night?" by describing one's behavior.

So "self" behaviors are indeed self behaviors in some sense—they are "self"-controlled. But that does not justify the reification of the "self-concept"; nor does it tell us where these behaviors come from.

Mirrors.   When first confronted with a mirror, virtually all birds and mammals, including both human children and adults, react either with indifference or as if they are seeing another organism of their species (Dixon, 1957; Gallup, 1968, 1970; Lewis & Brooks–Gunn, 1979; von Senden, 1960; Wolff, 1943). A variety of fish, birds, and mammals engage in social or aggressive displays or attack their mirror images (Boutan, 1913; Gallup, 1968; Köhler, 1925, Lissman, 1932; Lopez, 1979; Ritter & Benson, 1934, Tinbergen, 1951). Unlike other animals, humans and chimpanzees, after sufficient exposure to a mirror, come to react to their mirror images as images of their own bodies (Gallup, 1979; Lewis & Brooks–Gunn, 1979), though there is at least one contradictory report with chimpanzees (Russell, 1978). This phenomenon—often labeled "self-recognition"—has been studied for at least a century (consider Darwin, 1877).

The modern literature on the topic begins with a paper by Dixon (1957). Human children, according to Dixon, are said to progress through four stages of behavior with respect to their mirror images. In the first few months of life, there is little reaction. Soon the child begins to react to the image as if it were another child, by smiling, playing, touching, vocalizing, and so on. The third stage is one of "testing" or "discovery," characterized by "repetitive activity while observing the mirror image intently, e.g., alternately observing a hand or foot and its mirror image, opening and closing the mouth with deliberation or rising up and down slowly while keeping [the] eyes fixed on the mirror image" (p. 253). Finally, when the child is between 18 and 24 months old, it begins to react to the image as a reflection of its own body.

In the late 1960s Amsterdam (1968, 1972) devised an objective test to determine whether a child had reached the final stage. A mother would smear some rouge on her child's nose and then encourage the child to look at a mirror. If the child touched its nose, it was said to be able to recognize itself. By age 2, most children would do this. Using a mirror to locate a mark on one's body that one cannot see directly is now said to be "the most compelling example of self-directed behavior" (Lewis & Brooks–Gunn, 1979, p. 212).

Gallup (1970) showed that the same effect could be obtained with chimpanzees. Four chimpanzees were exposed to a large mirror for a total of 80 hours over a 10-day period. Social behavior was observed to decline over this period and self-directed behavior (such as grooming) to increase. Then the animals were anesthetized and a red dye painted over an eyebrow bridge and on the top half of an ear. When the animals recovered, they were observed for 30 minutes in the absence of a mirror and for 30 minutes in the presence of a mirror. There were substantially more movements judged to be "mark-directed" in the presence of the mirror (virtually none without the mirror, and an average of 6 per animal with the mirror). Similar tests Gallup arranged with nonhuman primates other than chimpanzees produced negative results. Because he attributed the behavior to a self-concept, he concluded that only man and the great apes (chimpanzees, at least) have this cognitive capacity.

"Self-awareness" in the Pigeon.   Epstein, Lanza, and Skinner (1981) provided an alternative account of mark-directed behavior in the mirror test by showing that, after some rather simple training over a period of less than 15 hours, a pigeon, too, could use a mirror to locate a spot on its body which it could not see directly. We first trained the pigeon to peck at blue stick-on dots placed on different parts of its body. Then we added a mirror to the pigeon's chamber and reinforced pecks at blue dots placed on the walls and floor. Finally, we briefly flashed blue dots on the walls or floor when the pigeon could see them only in the mirror. It received food if it turned and pecked the position where a blue dot had been flashed. We then conducted the following test: A blue stick-on dot was placed on the pigeon's breast and a bib placed around its neck in such a way that it prevented the bird from seeing the dot. The pigeon was observed first for 3 minutes in the absence of a mirror and then for 3 minutes in the presence of a mirror. Three subjects were tested. Independent observers scored video tapes for "dot-directed" responses. None were observed when the mirror was absent,

and an average of 10 per bird were observed when it was present—greater than 10 times the rate of mark-directed responses that Gallup (1970) observed (Epstein, in 1985b).

One might conclude from this experiment either that (1) pigeons have a self-concept (few psychologists are likely to go to that extreme), (2) the mirror test is a bad test of self-concept (many will put their money here), or (3) as has already been asserted on other grounds, the self-concept is simply a superfluous scientific category.

These issues aside, we may also have in hand an account of the emergence of such behavior in chimpanzees and children (cf. Epstein, 1981, 1984a), for there is ample evidence that both chimpanzees and children who pass the mirror test have already acquired both of the repertories we established in our pigeons: They presumably have touched themselves many times in the places they must touch during the test, and they have had ample opportunities to come under the control of the contingencies of reinforcement which govern mirror use.

Contingencies.   Normally, moving toward an object brings it closer and ultimately produces contact with it; one must move in a special way—which most of us never learn perfectly—to produce contact with an object whose reflection we see in a mirror. A mirror thus provides a new set of relationships between one's movements and their consequences—a new set of "contingencies."

These contingencies are rather weak, which is to say that under most circumstances: (1) the reinforcement they provide comes with less effort and more immediately if one simply faces an object directly, and (2) there is no penalty for *not* coming under their control. One would expect, therefore, that only special circumstances would bring an organism's behavior under their control and that the more sensitive the organism's behavior is to its consequences, the more readily the control will be established.

A pigeon, needless to say, would not normally come under the control of these contingencies. We had to supplement them. Attending to an object in the mirror and then finding it in real space not only produced the natural consequence—contact with the object—it also produced food, a powerful, effective reinforcer for a hungry pigeon. The food only supplemented the natural contingency; it did not obliterate or override it. The pigeon's behavior had to be under the control of the correspondence between mirrored and real space in order for food to be delivered.

"Discovery."   The period of "testing" or "discovery" that Dixon (1957) described is undoubtedly the period during which a child's behavior comes under the control of the contingencies of reinforcement which govern mirror use. The child slowly learns the correspondence between the locations of parts of its body (and, presumably, of other objects) in real and mirrored space. Unlike the

pigeon, the child needs no trainer, but this means only that a child's behavior is so sensitive to its consequences that even occasional exposure to weak contingencies is sufficient for control to be established. Because the contingencies are weak, however, and because the exposure is occasional, it often takes months for control to be established. Presumably, given systematic training, a child or monkey could learn the task even faster than our pigeons.

The same two repertoires probably account for a pigeon's, a chimpanzee's, and a person's success in the mirror test—and hence for some of the behavior often explained by the mythical ''self-concept.'' The only impressive thing about chimpanzees and children is that they can acquire the second repertoire—albeit quite slowly—without explicit training. This is a matter of sensitivity to contingencies. *That* is how man and the great apes differ from other organisms, which should surprise no one.

Conclusions

Praxists have never really met the cognitivists' challenge because in restricting our research to simple behaviors and simple stimuli, we have ignored most of the complex phenomena that they investigate daily. Cognitivists and developmentalists have not found useful answers because they have not asked the right questions. There is little value in trying to determine what a mental structure looks like or how it grows. We achieve a more effective understanding by discovering how the behavior of an organism, both inside and out, is determined by environmental histories and genetic endowments, and ultimately, how changes in behavior are mediated by the body. A model of problem solving is no substitute for a determination of how genes and the environment produce effective behavior. A specification of deep structure or rules of transformation can't tell us where these things come from or how to put them into someone when they seem to be lacking. Attributing insightful behavior to insight is uninformative. Attributing behavior said to show self-awareness to a self-concept tells us nothing.

The time has come for praxists to answer the challenge by bringing complex behavior into the laboratory—in a sense, by giving the freely moving organism a little more freedom to move.

ACKNOWLEDGMENTS

This chapter is based on an invited address given at the 7th annual meeting of the Association for Behavior Analysis, Milwaukee, May, 1981. It was included as a chapter in a doctoral dissertation presented to Harvard University. The research and preparation of the manuscript was supported in part by National Science Foundation grant BNS-8007342 to Harvard, by National Institutes of Health grant MH32628 to the Foundation for Research on the Nervous System, and by a Sigma Xi Grant-in-Aid of Research. I am grateful to Murray Sidman and B. F. Skinner for comments and to Pierre Mayer for help in the reaction-time experiment. Requests for reprints should be sent to the author at the Cambridge Center for Behavioral Studies, 11 Ware Street, Cambridge, MA 02138.

REFERENCES

Amsterdam, B. K. (1968). *Mirror behavior in children under two years of age.* Unpublished doctoral dissertation, University of North Carolina, Chapel Hill.

Amsterdam, B. K. (1972). Mirror self-image reaction before age two. *Developmental Psychobiology, 5,* 297–305.

Anderson, J. R. (1978). Arguments concerning representations for mental imagery. *Psychological Review, 85,* 249–277.

Arieti, S. (1976). *Creativity: The magic synthesis.* New York: Basic Books.

Baxley, N. (Producer). (1982). *Cognition, creativity, and behavior: The Columban simulations.* Champaign, IL: Research Press.

Blough, D. (1977). Visual search in the pigeon: Hunt and peck method. *Science, 196,* 1013–1014.

Boutan, I. (1913). Le pseudo-language. Observations effectuées sur un anthropoide: Le gibbon (*Hylobates leucogenys Ogilby*). *Actes de la Societé linneenne de Bordeaux, 67,* 5–80.

Bower, G. H., & Hilgard, E. R. (1981). *Theories of learning* (5th ed.). Englewood Cliffs, NJ: Prentice-Hall.

Bruner, J. S., Goodnow, J. J., & Austin, G. A. (1956). *A study of thinking.* New York: Wiley.

Catania, A. C. (1979). *Learning.* Englewood Cliffs, NJ: Prentice-Hall.

Catania, A. C. (1980). Autoclitic processes and the structure of behavior. *Behaviorism, 8,* 175–186.

Chomsky, N. (1965). *Aspects of the theory of syntax.* Cambridge, MA: M.I.T. Press.

Corcoran, D. W. J. (1971). *Pattern recognition.* Baltimore: Penguin Books.

Cumming, W. W., & Eckerman, D. A. (1965). Stimulus control of a differentiated operant. *Psychonomic Science, 3,* 313–314.

Darwin, C. (1877). A biographical sketch of an infant. *Mind, 2,* 285–294.

Dixon, J. C. (1957). Development of self-recognition. *Journal of Genetic Psychology, 91,* 251–256.

Donahoe, J. W., & Wessells, M. G. (1980). *Learning, language, and memory.* New York: Harper & Row.

Epstein, R. (1980). Defining creativity. *The Behavior Analyst, 3*(2), 65.

Epstein, R. (1981). On pigeons and people: A preliminary look at the Columban Simulation Project. *The Behavior Analyst, 4*(1), 43–55.

Epstein, R. (1982a). A note on the mythological character of categorization research in psychology. *The Journal of Mind and Behavior, 3,* 161–169.

Epstein, R. (1982b). Representation: A concept that fills no gaps. *The Behavioral and Brain Sciences, 5,* 377–378.

Epstein, R. (1983). Resurgence of previously reinforced behavior during extinction. *Behaviour Analysis Letters, 3,* 391–397.

Epstein, R. (1984a). Simulation research in the analysis of behavior. *Behaviorism, 12,* 41–59.

Epstein, R. (1984b). Spontaneous and deferred imitation in the pigeon. *Behavioural Processes, 9,* 347–354.

Epstein, R. (1984c). The principle of parsimony and some applications in psychology. *The Journal of Mind and Behavior, 5,* 119–130.

Epstein, R. (1984d). The case for praxics. *The Behavior Analyst, 7,* 101–119.

Epstein, R. (1985a). Extinction-induced resurgence: Preliminary investigations and possible applications. *Psychological Record, 35,* 143–153.

Epstein, R. (1985b). On the Columban simulations: A reply to Gallup. *Contemporary Psychology, 30,* 410–418.

Epstein, R., Kirshnit, C., Lanza, R. P., & Rubin, L. (1984). "Insight" in the pigeon: Antecedents and determinants of an intelligent performance. *Nature, 308,* 61–62.

Epstein, R., & Koerner, J. (in press). The self-concept and other daemons. In J. Suls & A. Greenwald (Eds.), *Psychological perspectives on the self* (Vol. 3). Hillsdale, NJ: Lawrence Erlbaum Associates.

Epstein, R., Lanza, R. P., & Skinner, B. F. (1980). Symbolic communication between two pigeons *(Columba livia domestica). Science, 207,* 543–545.

Epstein, R., Lanza, R. P., & Skinner, B. F. (1981). "Self-awareness" in the pigeon. *Science, 212,* 695–696.

Epstein, R., & Medalie, S. (1983). The spontaneous use of a tool by a pigeon. *Behaviour Analysis Letters, 3,* 341–347.

Epstein, R., & Skinner, B. F. (1980). Resurgence of responding after the cessation of response-independent reinforcement. *Proceedings of the National Academy of Sciences USA, 77,* 6251–6253.

Epstein, R., & Skinner, B. F. (1981). The spontaneous use of memoranda by pigeons. *Behavior Analysis Letters, 1,* 241–246.

Fenner, D. (1980). The role of contingencies and "principles of behavioral variation" in pigeons' pecking. *Journal of the Experimental Analysis of Behavior, 34,* 1–12.

Flanders, J. P. (1968). A review of research on imitative behavior. *Psychological Bulletin, 69,* 316–337.

Gallup, G. G., Jr. (1968). Mirror-image stimulation. *Psychological Bulletin, 70,* 782–793.

Gallup, G. G., Jr. (1970). Chimpanzees: Self-recognition. *Science, 167,* 86–87.

Gallup, G. G., Jr. (1979). Self-awareness in primates. *American Scientist, 67,* 417–421.

Goetz, E. M., & Baer, D. M. (1973). Social control of form diversity and the emergence of new forms in children's blockbuilding. *Journal of Applied Behavior Analysis, 6,* 209–217.

Guilford, J. P. (1950). Creativity. *American Psychologist, 5,* 444–454.

Hick, W. E. (1952). On the rate of gain of information. *Quarterly Journal of Experimental Psychology, 4,* 11–26.

Hollard, V. D., & Delius, J. D. (1982). Rotational invariance in visual pattern recognition by pigeons and humans. *Science, 218,* 804–806.

Hull, C. L. (1934). The rat's speed-of-locomotion gradient in the approach to food. *The Journal of Comparative Psychology, 17,* 393–422.

Hull, C. L. (1935). The mechanism of the assembly of behavior segments in novel combinations suitable for problem solution. *The Psychological Review, 42,* 219–245.

Hyman, R. (1953). Stimulus information as a determinant of reaction time. *Journal of Experimental Psychology, 45,* 188–196.

James, W. (1890). *Principles of psychology.* New York: Henry Holt.

Kagan, J. (1981). *The second year: The emergence of self-awareness.* Cambridge, MA: Harvard Univeristy Press.

Koestler, A. (1964). *The act of creation.* New York: Macmillan.

Köhler, W. (1925). *The mentality of apes.* London: Routledge & Kegan Paul.

Kosslyn, S., & Pomerantz, J. (1977). Imagery, propositions, and the form of internal representations. *Cognitive Psychology, 9,* 52–76.

Külpe, O. (1895). *Outlines of psychology.* New York: Macmillan. (originally published in German in 1893.)

Leitenberg, H., Rawson, R. A., & Bath, K. (1970). Reinforcement of competing behavior during extinction. *Science, 169,* 301–303.

Lewis, M., & Brooks–Gunn, J. (1979). *Social cognition and the acquisition of self.* New York: Plenum.

Lissman, H. W. (1932). Die Umwelt des Kampffisches (*Betta splendens* Regan). *Zeitschrift für Vergleichende Physiologie, 18,* 62–111.

Lopez, F. (1979). Ausencia de autorreconocimiento en lobos (*Canis lupus signatua*) con exposcion en espejo. *Informes del Departamento de Psicologia General* (Universidad Complutense de Madrid), 2(3), 3–14.

Maier, N. R. F. (1929). Reasoning in white rats. *Comparative Psychology Monographs, 6,* 1–93.

Maltzman, I. (1955). Thinking: From a behavioristic point of view. *Psychological Review, 62,* 275–286.

Maltzman, I. (1960). On the training of originality. *Psychological Review, 67,* 229–242.

Migler, B. (1964). Effects of averaging data during stimulus generalization. *Journal of the Experimental Analysis of Behavior, 7,* 303–307.

Miller, N. E., & Dollard, J. (1941). *Social learning and imitation.* New Haven: Yale University Press.

Osborn, A. F. (1953). *Applied imagination.* New York: Scribner's.

Place, U. T. (1981). Skinner's *Verbal Behavior* II—What is wrong with it? *Behaviorism, 9,* 131–152.

Poincaré, H. (1946). Mathematical creation. In *The foundations of science.* Lancaster: Science Press.

Porter, J. P. (1910). Intelligence and imitation in birds: A criterion of imitation. *The American Journal of Psychology, 11,* 1–71.

Pryor, K. W., Haag, R., & O'Reilly, J. (1969). The creative porpoise: Training for novel behavior. *Journal of the Experimental Analysis of Behavior, 12,* 653–661.

Pylyshyn, Z. (1973). What the mind's eye tells the mind's brain: A critique of mental imagery. *Psychological Bulletin, 80,* 1–24.

Ritter, W. E., & Benson, S. B. (1934). "Is the poor bird demented?" Another case of "shadow boxing." *Auk, 51,* 169–179.

Rothenberg, A. (1971). The process of Janusian thinking in creativity. *Archives of General Psychiatry, 24,* 195–205.

Russell, I. S. (1978). *Medical Research Council Unit on Neural Mechanisms of Behavior: Progress report, 1975–1978.* Unpublished document, University of London.

Schwartz, B. (1980). Development of complex, stereotyped behavior in pigeons. *Journal of the Experimental Analysis of Behavior, 33,* 153–166.

Selfridge, O. G. (1959). Pandemonium: A paradigm for learning. In *The mechanisation of the thought processes.* London: H. M. Stationery office.

Selfridge, O. G., & Neisser, U. (1960, August). Pattern recognition by machine. *Scientific American, 203,* 60–68.

Skinner, B. F. (1935). The generic nature of the concepts of stimulus and response. *Journal of General Psychology, 12,* 40–65.

Skinner, B. F. (1945). The operational analysis of psychological terms. *Psychological Review, 52,* 270–277, 291–294.

Skinner, B. F. (1957). *Verbal behavior.* New York: Appleton–Century–Crofts.

Skinner, B. F. (1963). Behaviorism at fifty. *Science,140,* 951–958.

Skinner, B. F. (1970). Creating the creative artist. In A. J. Toynbee and others, *On the future of art* (pp. 61–75). New York: Viking Press.

Skinner, B. F. (1974). *About behaviorism.* New York: Knopf.

Skinner, B. F. (1981). How to discover what you have to say—a talk to students. *The Behavior Analyst, 4*(1), 1–7.

Staddon, J. E. R., & Simmelhag, V. L. (1971). The "superstition" experiment: A reexamination of its implications for the principles of adaptive behavior. *Psychological Review, 78,* 3–43.

Sternberg, S. (1969). The discovery of processing stages: Extensions of Donder's method. *Acta Psychologica, 30,* 276–315.

Sternberg, S. (1975). Memory scanning: New findings and current controversies. *Quarterly Journal of Experimental Psychology, 27,* 1–32.

Thorpe, W. H. (1963). *Learning and instinct in animals.* Cambridge, MA: Harvard University Press.

Tinbergen, N. (1951). *The study of instinct.* London: Oxford University Press.

Torrance, E. P. (1962). *Guiding creative talent.* Englewood Cliffs, NJ: Prentice–Hall.

Torrance, E. P. (1963). *Education and the creative potential.* Minneapolis: University of Minnesota Press.

Uhr, L. (1963). "Pattern recognition" computers as models for form perception. *Psychological Bulletin, 60,* 40–73.

von Senden, M. (1960). *Space and sight: The perception of space and shape in the congenitally blind before and after operation.* Glencoe, IL: Free Press.

Wertheimer, M. (1945). *Productive thinking.* New York: Harper.

Wheeler, J. A. (1981). Delayed-choice experiments and the Bohr-Einstein dialog. In *The American Philosophical Society and the Royal Society: Papers read at a meeting June 5, 1980* (pp. 9–40). Philadelphia: American Philosophical Society.

Wolff, W. (1943). *The expression of personality.* New York: Harper.

Woodworth, R. S. (1936). *Experimental psychology.* New York: Holt, Rinehart.

Zentall, T. R., & Hogan, D. E. (1976). Imitation and social facilitation in the pigeon. *Animal Learning and Behavior, 4,* 427–430.

6 Understanding Animal Cognition

Donald A. Riley
Michael F. Brown
Sonja I. Yoerg
University of California, Berkeley

Not many years ago, both the study of animal learning and of the reality and nature of cognitive processes in animals were at the center of psychology. Learning theorists held that principles of learning were sufficiently general that an understanding of the choice behavior of rats, pigeons, and monkeys in mazes and lever boxes would provide keys to the understanding of mental life and behavior in general including, of course, that of humans. The pervasiveness of this belief is too widely known to require documentation beyond noting the titles of the works by the dominant theorists of the time, such as Hull's *Principles of Behavior* (1943), Tolman's *Purposive Behavior in Animals and Man* (1932), and Skinner's *Behavior of Organisms* (1938).

Sometime between 1955 and 1965 a revolution occurred in experimental psychology. Suddenly, the number of papers on human cognition increased dramatically and, although the number of papers in animal learning did not decrease, the central impact of this research on the field as a whole rapidly declined. This change reflected, in part, a decline of faith in the assumption that the nature of the human mind could be revealed by the study of rats' behavior in mazes.

Since the late 1970s, however, a part of the field of animal learning has developed into the study of cognition in animals and has undergone a renaissance. Roitblat, Bever, and Terrace (1984), in the preface to a collection of works in this area, date the beginning of this development as 1976, the year that a conference was held on cognitive processes in animals (Hulse, Fowler, & Honig, 1978). In this chapter, we comment on three issues associated with this renaissance, all of which are concerned with the justification of research on cognition in animals. First, we describe the history of ideas about cognition in animals and explore the relationship between historical and modern theories.

Secondly, we address modern radical behaviorism and its criticism of the cognitive approach. The radical behaviorists have offered a sustained critique of cognitive psychology from within the field of animal learning. Its major thesis, clearly aimed at human as well as animal cognitive psychology, is that explanations of behavior that posit internal (nonphysiological) mechanisms are pseudoexplanations that rely on fictions. True explanations of behavior, they argue, must be historical in nature. We describe the radical behaviorists' objections and question them on a number of grounds, using examples of data and issues from the literature on animal cognition.

Finally, we examine the question of why the study of animal cognition and the comparison of cognitive processes in a variety of species is important. The earlier view that understanding general behavior (i.e., the behavior of animals in simple, arbitrary tasks) is the most direct route to an understanding of the human mind has clearly been rejected by most cognitive psychologists. In place of this notion, we describe several important reasons for the study of cognition in animals.

A SHORT HISTORY OF COGNITIVE THEORY IN ANIMAL PSYCHOLOGY

The first modern psychologist who attempted to address issues of cognition by way of the experimental study of behavior appears to have been Edward Tolman (1932). Whereas it is true that earlier investigators such as Thorndike (1911) and Morgan (1894) addressed issues related to animal cognition, it was not until Tolman and his rejection of Watsonian behaviorism that an individual appeared who was at the same time self-consciously behavioristic and avowedly cognitive. Tolman's psychology, both in its early forms (e.g., 1925, 1932) and in later forms (e.g., 1938), was an attempt to explain the achievements of animals with psychological concepts. This effort was reflected both in Tolman's descriptions of behavior as "molar," "purposive," and "cognitive," as well as in his proposed explanations of behavior, that is, in the characterization of the hypothetical intervening events as including knowledge about such things as what leads to what. In the following section we briefly describe the principle features of Tolman's purposive behaviorism and then characterize the changes that we believe have occurred in the development of contemporary animal psychology.

There are three important features of Tolman's psychology that should be made explicit. All three were characteristic of his concerns, and at least two were central to the resistance that Tolman's brand of purposive behaviorism generated in his theoretical appointments. Consideration of these features will help in understanding the relation between early and modern cognitive psychology.

First, in his rejection of Watsonian behaviorism, Tolman argued on epistemological grounds that cognition is a property of behavior. In contrast to Watson's preoccupation with the conditioned reflex, Tolman focused on behavior that (1) is goal directed, (2) requires that the animal engage in a pattern of interaction with objects in getting to such goals, and (3) reveals a tendency for the animal to discover and prefer easy solutions over hard ones. These three criteria, he said, identified the properties of molar as opposed to molecular behavior. His (Tolman, 1932) argument was that behavior that has these characteristics directly reveals purpose and cognition: "These purposes and cognitions are of its [behavior's] immediate descriptive warp and woof" (p. 10). Tolman's insistence that purpose and cognition were descriptive attributes of molar behavior as well as inferred causal mechanisms was less apparent in his later writing but his preoccupation with the kind of behavior he was describing was not (cf. Smith, 1982). Throughout his career, Tolman was concerned with the animal's molar achievements rather than its molecular movements, and he was the first psychologist to make this distinction of theoretical significance.

In their own way, his major contemporaries, Hull and Skinner, adopted the idea of molar behavior as the unit of behavior to be studied. Hull did so explicitly (e.g., Hull, 1930). Skinner (1935) did so by including as operants behaviors such as lever pressing that were lawfully related to reinforcement schedules. Such operants, like molar behaviors, are achievements rather than movements. For example, they are whatever behaviors depress the lever in an operant chamber. In this sense, Skinner agreed with Tolman, for whom the behavior of interest was getting to the goal rather than the muscle movements involved in doing so.

Second, Tolman's cognitive psychology was characterized by explanatory notions that had a strong mentalistic cast. Even in 1932, Tolman's explanatory concepts were descriptions of knowledge that the animal had about the world. Tolman's animals had certain properties that explained their behavior, such as knowledge of what leads to what or, as he called such intervening events, sign–gestalt expectations, means–end readinesses, and cognitive maps (1932, 1948). All such metaphors indicated that problem solution involves a change in animal's knowledge about the relations between environmental events.

This type of explanatory notion is one of the key differences between Tolman's psychology and those of other learning theorists. Hull's notions of what is learned were explicitly mechanistic and consisted of internal surrogates of stimulus–response connections. For Hull, the animal's apparent knowledge as reflected in its molar behavior resulted from concatenations of implicit responses made to implicit stimuli (e.g., 1930). For Tolman, on the other hand, the apparent knowledge in the animal's behavior reflected an underlying awareness of external contingencies.

This issue of what is learned (i.e., the content of learning) is still an important one. For example, Dickinson (1980), in his book on animal learning, discusses the nature of associations formed during classical conditioning. Does the animal learn facts ("declarative representations") or does it acquire response tendencies ("procedural representations")? Dickinson concludes that what is learned can be either declarative or procedural, depending on the conditions of learning.

The third aspect of Tolman's cognitive psychology lay in the source of his ideas. Tolman's use of cognitive processes as explanatory concepts stemmed at least in part from his own phenomenology. His affinity for Gestalt psychology also reflected this same bias. Tolman argued that we, as humans, seem to know what leads to what and seem to have cognitive maps of our environment that allow us to function in space. Because animals like rats are also spatial navigators, it is not unreasonable to suspect that they have similar cognitive devices. As Tolman (1938) said in a famous passage: "I, in my future work intend to go ahead imagining how, *if I were a rat,* I would behave" (p. 24). Certainly part of the resistance to Tolman's ideas was related to this reliance on phenomenology and the mentalistic explanations that were derived from it. Conversely, the attraction of Hullian psychology, apart from its apparent simplicity, was in its appeal to principles of conditioning as a source of ideas, that is to experimentally generated and observable facts. It should be emphasized that in neither case did the proponents regard the source of ideas as critical to the test of the theory, but certainly in the war of ideas the source of the weapons is important.

Whereas the Tolman and Hull camps were debating the issues of the learned product and of the necessary and sufficient conditions for learning, Skinner's radical behaviorism denied the need for theories (e.g., 1950). The denial took at least two forms: (1) a lack of concern for the identification of the mechanism of reinforcement and (2) a denial of the importance or perhaps the reality of the psychological processes intervening between the environment and behavior. Like Hull and Tolman, Skinner's radical behaviorism sought to explain molar behavior. It differs in its assertion that a theory of what is learned is both premature and misleading. The radical behaviorist insists that the explanation of behavior lies in the description of the past environmental events that have caused it; an insistence that leads to a preoccupation with response reinforcement history. In addition, modern radical behaviorists argue that because the cognitive enterprise focuses investigation on events intervening between stimuli and responses, it leads to a neglect of the true causes of behavior, thereby wasting valuable time and resources (Skinner, 1977). We explore these issues in some depth after we have considered the changes that have occurred between the cognitive psychology of Tolman's time and the study of animal cognition today.

In describing Tolman's position, we have emphasized three features: the type of behavior he chose to investigate, the nature of the intervening events that he hypothesized as explanations of the behavior, and the reliance on phenomenology as a source of ideas. This account ignores an issue that was of great concern to Tolman and his contemporaries, namely the role of reinforcement in learning. The lack of resolution of this problem may have contributed to the decline in the influence of animal learning on the field of psychology. However, a discussion of this issue would divert us from the main concerns of this chapter.

Modern cognitive psychology, as it has developed since 1950, has been stimulated in part by information theory and the rise of the modern computer (Miller, Galanter, & Pribram, 1960; Neisser, 1967) and by modern psycholinguistics (e.g., Chomsky, 1956). The cognitive revolution occurred when it was realized that there existed a mechanistic alternative to the reflex machines that S–R psychologists had been describing since the 1920s. The computer, with its multiple information storage and processing systems, set the stage for the view that processes much more complex than those previously posited (e.g., Hull's S–r–s–R) could be instantiated in an undeniably real entity. In this sense modern cognitive psychology differs importantly from Tolman's cognitive psychology with its use of phenomenology as a source of ideas.

There is, however, an additional difference between modern and Tolmanian cognitive psychology. As we indicated, Tolman was interested in describing the properties of behavior observed as animals solved complex spatial problems. He proposed cognitive processes because he felt that they best explained the problem-solving behavior of his subjects. But it was the behavior itself, and its explanation, that was central to his interests and those of his contemporaries. Much of modern cognitive psychology, in contrast, seems to have much less interest in behavior as such and in the explanation of behavior than it has in the understanding of internal processes for their own sake (cf. Bolles, 1983). Certainly most modern cognitive psychologists have little or no interest in molar behavior per se. Part of Tolman's attraction to molar behavior was because it seemed so difficult either to describe it or explain it by recourse to reflexes, an explanation he rejected. Modern cognitive psychologists, however, have long since rejected reflexology as a candidate for explaining cognitive processes. Consequently, they do not have a preoccupation with the molar/molecular distinction. Instead, there has been a tendency to use simple behaviors as indices of more complex internal processes. Thus, the behaviors that are measured are chosen to be as simple as possible, so that inferences about internal processes may be rigorously made. Among the favorite tools of the modern cognitive psychologist are signal detection and speeded reaction tasks. The simplicity of the behaviors produced in these tasks makes them most likely to permit rigorous inferences about the internal mechanisms controlling behavior.

The rise of the computer as a metaphor has provided a rich source of ideas for how cognitive systems might operate. If such ideas are compatible with phenomenology, so much the better. But, as before, the evaluation of an idea or theory is independent of its source and depends on its relation to the experimental facts of behavior. In this sense, modern cognitive psychologists, just as earlier ones, are *methodological* behaviorists; that is, they use behavior because they must do so in testing hypotheses. Modern cognitive psychology differs from its

Tolmanian predecessor both in the source of ideas and in its lack of concern for molar behavior. It is similar in its assumption that what the organism knows about the world (as inferred from experiments) determines behavior. It is also similar in its conviction that the study of such internal processes is interesting and fruitful.

As we indicated in the opening paragraphs, there has been since the mid 1970s a revival of interest in animal cognition. In part, this revival is directly attributable to the development of modern human cognitive psychology. Certainly much of the animal work has been influenced by work on human cognition, just the opposite direction of influence that predominated during the heyday of learning theories. The obvious question that arises from this reversal is what the role of animal research on learning and cognitive processes should be today. This is an issue that we return to in the last portion of the chapter. But certainly the question of animal mind is one that has fascinated people at least since Aristotle. If we now have adequate behavioral methods for investigating the human mind, then they should also be adequate for investigating the animal mind. Certainly, this has been part of the stimulus for much of the recent animal research.

MODERN RADICAL BEHAVIORISM AND ITS CRITIQUE OF COGNITIVE PSYCHOLOGY

A fundamental tenet of modern radical behaviorism is that all explanations of behavior are descriptions of environmental histories (cf. Blackman, 1983; Branch, 1982; Skinner, 1981; Staddon, 1973): a position that disallows the explanatory concepts used by both Tolman and modern cognitive psychology. The rejection of such hypothetical constructs is based on two epistemological views. The first of these says that cognitive processes have no basis in reality and, therefore, are not a proper subject of scientific investigation. Skinner (1977) believes that the cognitive processes assumed to intervene between controlling environmental events and behavior are "inventions." For him they are simply models of the external contingencies of reinforcement that in fact cause behavior. The contingencies have real existence in the sense that they are observable and so are the causal variables around which psychology should proceed. The cognitive processes, on the other hand, have no real existence, and therefore no causal efficacy. As such, a science of them is impossible.

A second criticism of cognitive psychology is a pragmatic one. One might argue that even if not real in any strict sense, cognitive models provide an efficient way of summarizing data and describing behavior under different conditions and therefore serve to facilitate further research. Skinner's (1977) objection to this view is that cognitive science is "a diversion which could well be responsible for much of our failure to solve our problems" (p. 10). Thus,

Skinner believes that the study of cognition will have a detrimental effect on the progress of behavioral science because it causes researchers to ask the wrong questions.

A closely related position of radical behaviorism has to do with the proper methodology of psychology. Cognitive psychologists rely heavily on the hypothetico-deductive method in which various hypothesized processes are evaluated in terms of their ability to predict behavior. Radical behaviorists object to the hypothesis formation stage of this research methodology. Skinner (1969) acknowledges the value of this general method for many fields of science but claims that this value depends on the fact that in these fields (e.g., astronomy, atomic physics) workers "cannot manipulate variables or observe effects as [they] should like to" (p. ix). He claims, however, that "behavior is one of those subject matters which do not call for hypothetico-deductive methods. Both behavior itself and most of the variables of which it is a function are usually conspicuous" (p. ix, exceptions to this rule are stated to involve only technical problems, e.g., the measurement of very small responses). Because the subject matter of psychology (behavior) is conspicuous, the argument goes, we as psychologists should use the allegedly more powerful Baconian method of induction.

Other positions are often attributed to radical behaviorism. In the field of animal learning, it is clear that conditioning occurs at different rates for different stimulus/reinforcer pairs (e.g., Garcia & Koelling, 1966). This has been argued to pose a problem for radical behaviorism because of its alleged assumption of equipotentiality of reinforcers (cf. Seligman, 1970). Herrnstein (1977) has argued convincingly, however, that whereas many radical behaviorists tacitly assume (or assumed) equipotentiality it is not a necessary part of their program. He points out that Skinner advocated the use of arbitrary responses in order to avoid the intrusion of such species-specific characteristics into investigations of more general phenomena.

Partly in response to the existence of such species differences in conditioning, Staddon and Simmelhag (1971; Staddon, 1973) have advanced a formulation of the behaviorist position that retains the fundamental characteristic of historical explanation but can deal with differences in performance under what seem at first to be identical environmental contingencies. Under this formulation, differences that the cognitive psychologist would attribute to differences in the internal state of the organism are instead attributed exclusively to aspects of the environment in the more remote past. These causes might be found in the contingencies operating during early development or in the contingencies operating through natural selection on the gene pool of the species in question. Such a view allows for species differences and nonplastic behavior, while retaining the radical behaviorist insistence on historical explanations and the inductive method. More importantly for the present discussion, this view results in a greatly expanded domain in which the radical behaviorist methodology should be applied. Presumably, before resorting to cognitive theories, one must be sure that there are no potential explanations of a behavior in the evolutionary history of the species in question. This view, however, would seem to stifle research on behavior that is caused by forces in the remote past. One certainly cannot manipulate such variables in the way that variables can be manipulated in operant experiments (except perhaps in species with very short life-spans such as *Drosophila*). It seems to us that a much better use of evolutionary considerations is to use them in generating hypotheses about the internal processes that proximately control behavior. We discuss this approach in the final section of this chapter.

A SAMPLE OF ISSUES IN ANIMAL COGNITION

Most cognitive theories are descriptions of processes that mediate the temporal "gap" between stimuli and responses. As such, these theories do not have as their main goal the prediction and control of behavior that modern radical behaviorists see as the goal of psychology. Rather, their goal is to understand, at the conceptual level, the structures and processes that produce the observed behavior. The only method the cognitive theorist has of testing hypotheses about the nature of these intervening events is testing the behavioral predictions of her/his theories. Therefore, the radical behaviorist notion that cognitive theories do not make behavioral predictions seems, on the face of it, to be quite false.

The radical behaviorist argument is more complex than this, however. The claim is that these predictions could be made just as well given knowledge of the antecedent conditions to which subjects had been exposed in the relevant experiments (and perhaps over the course of their lives and the evolutionary history of their species). The cognitive theories that experiments purport to test, on the other hand, are unnecessary for predicting the behavior, and there is no way to justify attributing the processes that the theory describes to the nervous system of the subject. As Epstein (1982) states: "[Many cognitive theorists use] behavioral data to construct models of information-processing systems that might generate similar data. [They do not tell] us what's inside, but rather how a computer might simulate behavior" (p. 377). Is such a criticism justified? The answer depends on the extent to which theories (1) make testable predictions about behavior in new situations that cannot be derived from knowledge of the environmental history of the subject, (2) lead to informative experiments and valuable knowledge that the radical behaviorist approach would not have, and (3) help guide research at other levels of inquiry, i.e., lead to new behavioral phenomena or do in fact help tell us "what's inside" at the neurophysiological level. In the following we describe several areas of investigation from the animal literature that seem to meet these criteria.

One issue that has become prominent in the animal cognition literature has to do with the nature of the "memory code" that mediates the delay in conditional discriminations between the conditional cue and the discriminative response. Imagine an animal that is trained to respond to stimulus X following the presentation of stimulus A and to stimulus Y following B. The events that mediate the delay could, for example, be distinctive behaviors associated with each conditional cue. The animal could lift its right leg following A and its left leg following B, for example, and the stimulus (X or Y) responded to subsequently could be cued by the leg currently lifted rather than by the nature of the conditional cue per se. Alternatively, the animal could store information about the nature of the previously seen conditional cue and use this information to determine its response ("retrospective coding"). Recently, the possibility that animals store information about the anticipated test stimuli (X or Y) rather than about the preceding conditional cues ("prospective coding") has been discussed (e.g., Honig & Wasserman, 1981; Roitblat, 1980). Evidence for all three types of coding processes has accumulated and current research focuses on understanding the conditions that produce different types of codes (cf. Honig & Thompson, 1982; Riley, Cook, & Lamb, 1981).

In an effort to experimentally discriminate between the use of retrospective and prospective memory codes, Roitblat (1980) used a three-alternative symbolic matching-to-sample task. Pigeons were required to peck one of three line orientations (or colors, depending on the subject) following presentation of one of three colors (or line orientations for the subjects presented with colors as samples). Two of the colors used were similar to each other whereas one was dissimilar to the others. Each of the samples was paired with one of the test stimuli and signalled that a peck to that stimulus would result in food. The pairings were such that the similar sample stimuli were paired with test stimuli that were dissimilar to each other, and the two dissimilar sample stimuli were paired with the test stimuli that were similar to each other. Roitblat varied the retention interval between the sample presentation and the test and found that the increase in errors that occurred as a result of increased retention interval was produced because birds increasingly pecked the test stimulus that was similar to the correct test stimulus rather than because they increasingly pecked the test stimulus associated with the sample that was more similar to the correct sample. Roitblat inferred from these data that the subjects must be retaining information that was isomorphic to the test rather than to the sample.

Recently, Cook, Brown, and Riley (in press) have obtained data that they used to infer that rats use both retrospective and prospective memory codes in the same task, the radial arm maze. In this maze, rats obtain small amounts of food from the ends of each of a number of arms (in this case, 12) that radiate out from a central platform. Rats have previously been found to learn quickly to visit each arm, seldom returning to a previously visited arm (e.g., Olton & Samuelson, 1976). A number of experiments have eliminated the possibility that smell, response biases, and a number of other nonmemorial processes are responsible for this ability (see Olton, 1978 for a review). Cook, Brown, and Riley interpolated 15-minute delays at various points in the choice sequence (after either the 2nd, 4th, 6th, 8th, or 10th choice) and measured the effect that these retention intervals had on the rats' ability to avoid arms chosen prior to the delay after being returned to the maze. They assumed that the retention of a greater amount of information leads to loss of more information. Given this assumption, a theory that states that rats remember the previously visited arms would predict that the delay will have the greatest effect when interpolated late in the choice sequence, when most of the arms have been visited and are being remembered. The prospective hypothesis, on the other hand, predicts a greater effect when most arms are yet to be visited (early in the choice sequence) and the subject is retaining a list of many to-be-visited arms. The results show that the delay has the greatest disruptive effect on accuracy when it occurs in the middle of the choice sequence (i.e., after the 6th choice). The delay has very little effect when it occurs either early (after the 2nd choice) or late (after the 10th choice). This suggests that rats remember retrospectively early in the choice sequence, but prospectively after the 6th choice. Thus, rats can use either type of memory and we have speculated that cognitive efficiency seems to determine which type of code is used at the time of the test, i.e., that the shortest list is used.

In both of these examples, a theory of the type of information that is retained during a stimulus-to-response interval makes predictions about the behavior of animals that can be tested and potentially disconfirmed. But do these examples meet the aforementioned criteria? The behavior that needs to be explained in the case of Roitblat's data is that as the time between sample stimulus offset and test stimulus presentation increases, errors increasingly come to be attributable to test stimulus similarity rather than sample stimulus similarity. In the case of the data from the radial maze, rats' performance is disrupted more by a delay occurring in the middle of the choice sequence than by a delay either early or late in the sequence. In his critique of Roitblat's (1982) discussion of the memory code question, Branch (1982) states that he has "yet to be convinced that postulating an internal structure on the basis of observed behavior, and then referring to that structure as a cause of the behavior, really adds a great deal to our ability to predict and control behavior" (p. 372). It appears to us, however, that an understanding of memory codes can add to our ability to predict behavior.

The theories supported by these experiments can be used to make predictions about behavior in situations other than the experimental conditions used to test the hypotheses. This ability to make subsequent predictions is at the heart of the hypothetico-deductive method. Knowledge of cognitive processes allows behavioral output to be predicted in novel situations that are not predictable from knowledge of historical antecedents.

For example, the cognitive processes implied by Cook, Brown, and Riley's data include the ability of the rats to translate information about previous events into knowledge about future actions. This allows us to predict, for example, that a rat in a 17-arm maze would be disrupted by a delay no more than a rat in a 12-arm maze if the delay occurred early or late in the choice sequence. If the delay occurred following either the second or fifteenth choice, for example, two locations would have to be remembered in the same way that two locations would be remembered following either the second or tenth choice in a 12-arm maze. If the delay occurred in the middle of the choice sequence (after the eighth choice when eight previous choices and nine future choices exist), however, a delay should have a greater effect in the 17-arm maze than in the smaller maze. Furthermore, in order to use a prospective "list" of the locations that remain to be visited on a given trial, the rat must be familiar with all the locations that exist in the maze. This implies that the pattern of results found by Cook, Brown, and Riley would not be obtained if rats were tested when they had only a limited amount of training in the maze or when they were transferred to a situation that forced them to use novel cues.

Roitblat's hypothesis that prospective codes are used under his experimental conditions allows confusion errors to be predicted with a completely different stimulus set than the one he happened to use. One can also use knowledge of memory-coding processes in matching-to-sample to predict the performance of subjects in transfer experiments, in which they are exposed to a new set of samples. If retrospective coding is used, then birds trained to peck red following a red sample and blue following a blue sample may be able to match a novel color immediately, because what is in memory is a representation of the stimulus that was previously seen. If prospective coding is used, however, transfer of performance to novel stimulus sets would not be possible, because prospective coding depends on exposure to the sample/test pairings that produce reinforcement (cf. Riley et al., 1981). Thus, to the extent that prospective coding is used, transfer should not be found. Knowledge of the principles that determine whether information is coded retrospectively or prospectively will allow even more specific predictions about performance in a wide variety of tasks.

These predictions are of the type that is normally used by cognitive psychologists in hypothesis testing. Some theories turn out to be false, meaning that they predict behavior incorrectly, as determined by behavioral tests of those predictions. This, in turn, leads to revision or rejection of those theories. For example, recent evidence of transfer of matching-to-sample performance to novel sample sets questions the generality of prospective coding in this paradigm (cf. Riley et al., 1981; also Lombardi, Fachinelli, & Delius, 1984; Wilkie, 1983). Transfer seems to occur only under limited conditions, however, and this, among other things, has led to hypotheses about the conditions that determine which type of memory code is used (Honig & Thompson, 1982; Riley et al., 1981). Perhaps even more important than the theory's correctness or incorrectness is its heuristic value. Interest in cognitive mechanisms stimulates research aimed at elucidating the nature of such mechanisms, just as interest in reinforcement histories stimulates research aimed at elucidating such histories.

Could a historical account of symbolic matching-to-sample behavior or performance in the radial maze do as well as a cognitive account in predicting behavior in variants of the basic procedures that led to the findings just outlined?

What would purely historical accounts of these data be like? What would be the determinants of behavior to which the radical behaviorists would appeal? None seem to be available in the contingencies of reinforcement. It may be possible to appeal to the developmental or evolutionary history of the individual or species involved, as has become common in many modern radical behaviorist treatments (Skinner, 1981; Staddon, 1973). As we argue later, this appeal to remote history in understanding behavior and its determinants is a valuable approach. However, it is addressed mainly at the question of ultimate causation and leaves open the question of the immediate determinants of behavior.

Although it is clear that much can be learned about the causes of behavior by looking at the evolutionary, developmental, and experimental history of the subject, the cognitive level of explanation is a way of summarizing the functional organization and structure of the nervous system (cf. Hebb, 1949). From the work on memory coding, it is clear that whatever the details of neurophysiology and neuroanatomy are they must include systems that store information in two different forms, namely in the form of recently encountered stimuli and in the form of anticipated stimuli. This knowledge of cognitive processes, however silent concerning the precise neurological processes involved, can allow us to better predict behavior in situations where historical accounts have much more difficulty.

The preceding example of memory coding was chosen largely because of our familiarity with it. Many other areas of research on animal cognition could also be used to make the same argument. Many of them are directly related to questions asked in the human literature. For example, Sands and Wright (1980, 1982) have studied the performance of a rhesus monkey in a serial probe recognition task of the type used extensively by Sternberg (e.g., 1969) and others. The familiar bowed serial position curve relating serial position of the probe items and accuracy was obtained for both monkeys and humans (Sands & Wright, 1980). Under conditions that resulted in few errors, reaction times increased with the number of items in the to-be-remembered list (Sands & Wright, 1982). This result is taken as evidence that the memory-scanning process hypothesized by Sternberg (1969) exists in monkeys. It seems to us that these effects are not amenable to historical analysis and we know of no attempt to explain them in such terms. What they do provide is a valuable clue about the general organization of the nervous system. No matter what the details of the underlying processes turn out to be, they must include a process that generates better retention of the first few items (primacy effect) and last few items (recency effect) than of the items in the middle of the list. Some attributes of the system also exist that result in a relation between the number of relevant stimuli presented and reaction time. Whereas the physiological processes that are involved in this phenomenon will, we hope, be determined in the future, it is of great value for cognitive psychologists to determine the basic properties and structure of the mechanism responsible. Given that the nervous system includes such a mechanism, an understanding of its properties will allow a variety of behavioral predictions that were not available before.

Another example of a cognitive process that has received recent attention involves the sensitivity of animals to temporal durations. Church, Roberts, and their colleagues (e.g., Church, 1978; Roberts, 1981, 1983; Roberts & Church, 1978) have labeled this process an "internal clock" and have used a variety of experimental procedures to isolate it from other cognitive processes and to determine its properties. For example, Roberts (1981) used a procedure he calls the "peak procedure." It is a modified discrete-trials, fixed-interval procedure in which rats usually receive food following a signal of a fixed duration. On less frequent probe trials, the signal is presented for a duration that is substantially longer than during the training trials. This procedure produces a function that relates response rate to the time that has elapsed since the onset of the signal. The "reading" of the clock is inferred from the point during probe trials at which response rate is highest. Under normal conditions, this point (known as "peak time") matches the point at which food is presented during training trials. Roberts (1981) showed that manipulations that typically affect performance in learning tasks have no effect on peak time. For example, if one signal predicts food on 80% of the training trials and a second signal predicts food on only 20% of the training trials, peak time during either signal is the same. However, the maximum response rate (which occurs at the peak time) is lower during the signal with a lower rate of reinforcement. Thus, the process that determines peak time is distinct from some of the other processes involved in performance. Roberts and others have shown that this process has many properties that are similar to those of a stopwatch (see Roberts, 1983 for a review). For example, there is a linear relation between signal duration and the time the animal seems to expect food. The internal clock can also be stopped and then either restarted or reset. The clock also appears to "time up" rather than "time down" (as a kitchen timer does). If a rat is trained to press one lever following a short signal and a second lever following a long duration, it will press the first lever on a probe trial in which no signal is presented. Thus, it treats zero seconds as "short" rather than as "long," indicating that the clock is "set" to zero prior to stimulus onset.

It is of interest to note that one behaviorist account of this phenomenon (Blackman, 1983) claims that "rather than reflecting the operation of a clock, the rat's behavior would now be said to have the properties of a clock in certain environmental conditions" (p. 46). The similarity between this distinction and the distinction drawn earlier between Tolman's early views of cognition as descriptive and his later view of cognitive processes as causal is striking. Certainly one can say that the rat's behavior has the properties of a clock, thereby avoiding the implication of causality. But clocks themselves have different properties that correspond to the structural organization of the clock: such as timing "up" or "down" and storing information or discarding it. These properties of clocks can both cause specific behavioral outcomes and can be inferred from behavioral experiments with the clock. Clearly then, one can infer causal mechanisms in the form of components of the clock from experimental data. Whether or not such mechanisms are to be regarded as "real" depends, in part, on how well the theory predicts data and in part on one's views concerning the validity of the hypothetico-deductive method.

This research on the internal clock used by rats has recently led to a series of experiments designed to determine the physiological substrates that underlie various cognitive processes. Meck (1983) used a number of pharmacological agents with known effects to show that behavioral changes attributed to (1) the speed of the internal clock and (2) the *memory* of the durations timed by the clock could be independently produced. These processes had been proposed as distinct in cognitive models based on behavioral data (Gibbon & Church, 1984). Meck argued that distinct physiological processes correspond to the proposed distinct cognitive processes. Meck, Church, and Olton (1984) showed that lesions of the hippocampus disrupt the ability of rats to perform in the radial maze as well as the effects of previously experienced durations on their subsequent behavior but do not disrupt their sensitivity to ongoing stimulus durations. Again, these various abilities correspond to cognitive processes that had been hypothesized as distinct based on behavioral data. Meck et al. proposed that the lesions they performed disrupted temporal and spatial working memory, but not the sensitivity of the internal clock. These comparisons and manipulations would not have been performed without the benefit of theories that distinguish among cognitive processes such as internal clocks, spatial memory, temporal memory, reference memory, and working memory. Thus, cognitive theories have led directly to experiments at the physiological level of analysis that a radical behaviorist program would not have inspired. Although we hasten to point out that particular cognitive theories can stand or fall without the benefit of physiology, this kind of interaction between the two levels of analysis supports the value of the study of cognition in general.

We have illustrated several examples of cognitive processes in animals that can be inferred from behavioral experiments and that can be used in predicting behavior and understanding its determinants. Many more are described in several recent collections (Hulse et al., 1978; Roitblat et al., 1984; Spear & Miller, 1981).

AN ANALYSIS OF THE RADICAL BEHAVIORIST/COGNITIVIST CONFLICT BY EXAMPLE: "SELF-AWARENESS" IN ANIMALS

One of few direct interactions between a cognitive theorist and modern radical behaviorists is the interchange between Gallup (1970, 1977, 1982, 1983) and Epstein and his colleagues (Epstein, this volume; Epstein, Lanza, & Skinner,

1981). Gallup (1969) introduced a procedure that he used to operationally define the notion of "self-awareness." Chimpanzees were first given simple exposure to mirrors. After varying amounts of exposure, a mark was placed on their body (e.g., above the eyebrow) that they could not perceive except by using the mirror. Gallup and others found that chimpanzees and orangutans exhibit mark-directed behavior under such conditions (i.e., they use the mirror in attempts to investigate the mark and/or to remove it from their body). Previous exposure to mirrors is necessary for such behavior. Despite numerous attempts with a great variety of species, no other nonhuman primates have shown this effect (cf. Gallup, 1983). Gallup has argued that the ability to use mirrors in guiding self-directed behavior implies that the subject possesses a "self-concept" or "self-awareness." By this he (Gallup, 1983) means a "cognitive category for processing mirrored information about [itself]" (p. 483). Thus, the "self" is argued to be a particular type of category that is apparently accessible to only a limited number of primates.

The necessity of invoking this cognitive process of self-awareness to explain mirror-guided, self-directed behavior was challenged by Epstein, Lanza, and Skinner (1981). They used a series of operant shaping procedures to train pigeons to peck dots on their own body that could only be seen by using a mirror. Epstein et al. first trained the birds to peck dots that they placed on parts of the pigeon's body that it could easily see. Later, the pigeons were placed in a mirrored chamber. Dots were flashed on the walls and ceiling in such a way that the bird could see them only in the mirror and it was reinforced for pecking the location on the walls or ceiling where the dot had appeared. Thus, it came to use the mirror to determine the location of dots. In the test, a dot was placed on the bird's body where it could see the dot only by using the mirror. Under these conditions, pigeons pecked the dot on their bodies in the presence of the mirror but not when the mirror was unavailable. Epstein et al. argue that these data indicate that the notion of a "self-concept" is not necessary to explain the self-directed behavior of Gallup's chimpanzees. Rather, the fact that similar behavior can be produced in pigeons shows that a historical account, in terms of the contingencies of reinforcement that existed in the chimpanzees environment, is possible. Consequently, cognitive interpretations are redundant.

Gallup (1982) has argued that "reinforcement works, but in and of itself this has no bearing on self-awareness or any other cognitive phenomenon" (p. 241). There is no doubt that some combination of complex historical events is necessary to produce the self-directed behavior of Gallup's chimpanzees. But, there is likewise no doubt that some set of processes in the nervous system serve as the proximate cause of the behavior. Hypotheses, in the form of cognitive models, are testable descriptions of the features of those processes and may lead to further knowledge of the behavior labeled "self-recognition" and its neural correlates in the same manner as have ideas about memory coding and internal clocks. Gallup's experimental data, like that of cognitive psychology in general, provides knowledge of the *functional organization* of the processes that produce behavior.

Such knowledge is of value whether or not it corresponds to or guides knowledge of the *structural organization* of those processes.

A problem with Epstein's demonstration is that it does not permit a comparison of the processes in the ape and the pigeon that are involved in self-directed behavior. Epstein indicates that a demonstration that the behavior can be produced in pigeons by providing the proper contingencies of reinforcement shows that there is no need to look beyond contingencies of reinforcement for an explanation of the apes' behavior. Whereas it is almost certain that there are such contingencies involved in producing the behavior in apes (and in humans), they tell us nothing about the internal processes that intervene. Whether the processes that are responsible for the behavior of Epstein et al.'s and Gallup's subjects are the same or different is an empirical question for which there is presently no evidence.

For example, it is doubtful that the relevant reinforcement histories in the two cases were similar. Gallup (1982) argues that the reinforcement histories were drastically different. The pigeons had been reinforced for pecking dots regardless of where they were. The chimpanzees, on the other hand, had not and were only interested in marks that appeared on their own bodies. Thus, whereas it is true that the reinforcement histories of the subjects may have been critical in both cases, it seems that those histories were quite different for pigeons and apes. Behaviorists have been critical of cognitive psychology because, they argue, its explanatory concepts do not facilitate further research on important issues. Salzinger (1973), for example, has argued that cognitive theories have a deleterious effect because they supply "answers by naming problems rather than by investigating them" (p. 376). It is true that Gallup has given a name to the proposed determinant of mark-directed behavior in his subjects. However, it is the radical behaviorist argument that only a simple case of reinforcement history is involved that may stifle research in this case.

If the behavior of Gallup's subjects were all that was of interest, then Epstein's experiment would indicate equivalence between pigeon and ape. But it is not only the behavior that interests Gallup. In addition, it is the internal processes that produce the behavior. This difference in the interests of radical behaviorists and those studying animals from a more cognitive perspective has become pronounced since the adoption of the information-processing approach. As we have argued, early theorists, such as Tolman, adopted cognitive theories because they seemed necessary in explaining the behavior of their subjects. It was the behavior that was of primary interest; intervening cognitive processes were merely one of several ways of explaining that behavior. The focus of much current research is an understanding of internal mechanisms *for their own sake* as well as their ability to explain behavior. Thus, the radical behaviorists' objections often fall on deaf ears not only because of disagreements about the most efficient or proper manner of explaining behavior, but also because cognitive psychology is oriented toward both explaining behavior and understanding the inferred mental events that cause behavior.

Although Epstein would prefer to wait for a physiological description of these internal events, the cognitive approach is to determine as many details of their functioning as possible by exploring their behavioral output. This is in essence what Gallup has attempted to do in hypothesizing that some process in the nervous system of humans and two species of apes can discriminate the "self" from the nonself. This hypothesis makes a number of predictions about the behavior of those animals who possess it and Gallup has tried to test these predictions (Gallup, 1982). Whether or not one believes that Gallup has indeed isolated a cognitive process that can reasonably be called self-awareness is not the issue here. What is critical is that Gallup wants to understand the processes that cause a particular behavior. That certain environmental histories are necessary for this behavior and that animals that presumably do not possess the hypothesized cognitive apparatus can be given a reinforcement history that produces the same behavior does not necessarily speak to the nature of the processes that produce it in the chimpanzee.

COMPARATIVE ANIMAL COGNITION

Thus far we have argued that the study of cognitive processes in animals is critical for a complete understanding of behavior. We have also maintained that it is necessary and profitable to use behavioral data to examine the general principles that underlie cognitive function. In the following section, we discuss the importance of species differences and ecology to the study of cognitive processes.

But before we launch our discussion of comparative cognition, we briefly address the question of why we should study nonhuman animals at all. The first reason is a practical one. For ethical and methodological reasons, certain types of experiments are impossible or impractical to conduct with human subjects. Nonhuman animals can, in this context, serve as model systems for questions of human cognition. Whereas the validity of such models has frequently been contested on logical and theoretical grounds, the approach has had a significant impact on the human literature.

The second reason for studying nonhuman animals is that they are, in varying degrees, phylogenetically related to humans, and understanding humans is one of the primary goals of cognitive psychology. Although there is no doubt that the human species is unique in certain ways, it is also true that it shares many characteristics with other species. This argument is one of evolutionary continuity and is as old as psychology itself (Darwin, 1872; Morgan, 1894; Romanes, 1884; Thorndike, 1911). The notion of continuity suggests that the study of other primates may be most informative, but we also share behavioral and cognitive abilities with other, more distantly related species to the extent that they have been exposed to similar selective pressures in the evolutionary past.

A final reason for the study of nonhuman cognition is that it is an exciting, diverse, and informative area of study independent of what it tells us about humans. Much can be learned about the nature of cognition through the study of the cognitive processes of divergent species that could never be learned by studying humans, and we have reviewed a subset of that literature previously. How interspecies comparisons and a consideration of ecology can contribute to the study of cognition is the subject of the present section.

Our interest in pursuing this issue reflects our belief that the study of animal behavior and the associated cognitive processes benefits from a consideration of their adaptive function. This approach should not be viewed as merely an adjunct to the more traditional approach described previously. Rather, viewing cognition as one product of evolutionary processes is vital to the development of a meaningful set of principles that account for the interrelations among animal, behavior, environment, and mental processes.

Many animals share common problems (e.g., where to find food, how to find a mate) and one evolutionary principle, i.e., *convergence*, states that common problems may produce common solutions, whether they be morphological, behavioral, or cognitive. The complementary principle is that of *divergence*. Animals that share a common ancestry but exhibit differences in morphology, behavior, or cognitive structure can be said to have diverged on those traits. Divergence is the result of differences in selective pressures between species, favoring the expression of certain traits in some species and not others. Similarities and differences among species on morphological, behavioral, and cognitive dimensions can be understood by considering phylogenetic relationships and the action of convergent and divergent evolution.

The use of the principle of convergence to compare behavior across species is a relatively recent development in psychology, though it has long been used in ethology. Ethologists such as Lorenz (1950) and Tinbergen (1951) adopted this approach from students of comparative morphology, arguing, as just stated, that behavior is subject to the same types of selective pressures as morphology. For example, it has been demonstrated that honey bees exhibit many of the same phenomena of classical conditioning characteristic of vertebrates (Bitterman, Menzel, Fietz, & Schafer, 1983). If the common ancestor of vertebrates and invertebrates did not have a nervous system capable of producing conditioning, then the similarity between these remote species must reflect the action of convergent evolution. Recently, several authors (Domjan & Galef, 1983; Johnston, 1981; Kamil & Yoerg, 1982; Shettleworth, 1983) have discussed the importance of the use of ecological and evolutionary principles in the study of learning and other classes of behavior traditionally within the realm of psychology that have, for the most part, been studied in ecologically arbitrary contexts. The arguments presented by these theorists, emphasizing the crucial role that ecology and evolution have in the determination of behavior and the principles that govern it, also apply to cognition, as we argue later.

Given adequate knowledge of the specific problems of survival a species encounters, it may then be possible to make predictions about its cognitive organization. For example, nectar-feeding animals all share the problem of deciding when to return to a nectar source that they have depleted in the past. If the solution to this problem has resulted in a particular cognitive organization in one species, do other nectar-feeding animals share this organization (how general is the cognitive phenomenon across species)? If so, do these animals exhibit this same cognitive organization in other similar problems (how general is the phenomenon within species)? If there are differences in the cognitive organization of species sharing common problems, can we explain those differences by appealing to phylogenetic relationships?

The interaction between a comparative/ecological analysis and animal cognition may take two forms that relate the traditional psychological emphasis on mechanism to the ethological emphasis on function. First, if the mechanism underlying a behavior is known, we may then inquire about the function of that behavior. Second, if the function of a behavior is known, we may then search for the mechanism governing it.

Understanding Function After Mechanism is Known.   Although data obtained in the laboratory with a limited set of species may reveal how certain cognitive processes are structured, a different approach is demanded to understand how such processes help the animal solve the problems of survival. Whereas this is not the primary goal of cognitive psychology, functional considerations can play an important role in furthering our understanding of basic cognitive processes. Students of evolution have long held that both structure and behavior, which depends on structure, are subject to the forces of natural selection. Because cognitive processes help to determine and are expressed in the organization of behavior, it is logical that such processes have also been selected over evolutionary time to accrue a relative survival advantage to the animals that possess them. Consequently, functional attributes of cognition are central to the more general questions about animal cognition, and our methods of addressing those questions should reflect this proposition.

As described in a previous section, Cook, Brown, and Riley (in press) found that rats on the radial arm maze use either prospective or retrospective coding depending on the point of interpolation of a delay. This analysis of the type of coding used provides information regarding the mechanism that produces accurate performance on the maze. This analysis also suggests testable implications about the possible function of this mechanism, that is, to reduce memory load. Thus, one finding that would be consistent with the reduction in memory load interpretation would be that the rat, after switching to prospective memory, would have a way of discarding the retrospective information. Cook et al. (in press) have provided data that support this conjecture.

Although the data may shed light on this aspect of the problem, they do not contribute to an understanding of why such a mechanism would have evolved. What advantage do rats that can code both retrospectively and prospectively have over other animals that cannot? How are these codes used by the animal to solve the problems of survival?

The answers to these questions is not known, but it may be instructive to consider how the answers might be sought. In order to code prospectively, an animal must be familar with the task, i.e., it must know that arms exist that it has not visited and have some way of representing the locations of those arms in some type of permanent memory system. In the natural world, only animals that are very familiar with their foraging area would be expected to have this type of reference memory and consequently would at least have the opportunity to code information about spatial locations prospectively. Species that would be expected to be able to code prospectively would likely be site tenacious and territorial. We would still expect these species to code retrospectively when that type of coding results in a shorter list of items to be remembered. In order to code retrospectively, the animal must only have the capacity to remember where it has already been.

From knowledge of foraging ecology, it should be possible to choose species that would be expected to be able to code both retrospectively and prospectively, and other species that would be able to only code retrospectively. These two sets of species could then be tested on the radial maze to see whether the differences in foraging ecology correlate with differences in coding mechanisms. If so, then one possible function of multiple memory coding will have been elucidated. Norway rats would be poor subjects for this experiment, even though the phenomenon was discovered in this species, because so little is known about their foraging ecology. The analysis of function will generally require psychologists to increase the diversity of the type of animals they study and will certainly require them to select species more carefully (cf. Kamil, 1984).

Understanding Mechanism After Function is Known.   Several researchers have argued that the study of animal behavior should start from a consideration of the behavior animals actually exhibit in attempting to solve the problems of survival (Johnston, 1981; Kamil & Yoerg, 1982; Rozin & Kalat, 1971). The argument is that the principles of behavior derived from the study of animals in ecologically and functionally arbitrary contexts may not reflect the relation between animal and environment that helped to determine the behavior and the principles that govern it. Consequently, research strategies that ignore these ecological principles will not reveal the most important learning processes or will do so only accidentally. Again, these arguments logically also apply to cognition.

A complete discussion of this argument is beyond the scope of this chapter, but the message to cognitive psychologists is clear. Consideration of the adaptive function of behavior can provide a meaningful, nonarbitrary framework in which to study cognition. Also, the diversity of animal life can provide the cognitive psychologist with a wide range of problems for study, allowing him/her to assess the generality of principles derived from the study of a limited set of species, and to discover new phenomena that support or result in the revision of existing principles.

An example of this is the current research on cache recovery in birds. Numerous bird species cache seeds in the ground or in trees that they later retrieve during periods of food shortage. Field studies of Clark's nutcrackers (Corvidae; *Nucifraga columbiana*) (Mattes, 1978; Swanberg, 1951; Tomback, 1980) and of marsh tits (Paridae; *Parus palustris*) (Cowie, Krebs, and Sherry, 1981) have yielded estimates of the accuracy of recovery of stored seeds (the proportion of probes resulting in the retrieval of a seed), which are impressive (e.g., 72% for nutcrackers; Tomback, 1980) and which suggest the use of spatial memory. By spatial memory we mean the ability of an animal to locate objects in space using the relative positions of other objects (e.g., halfway between the rock and the tree), as opposed to using objects as direct cues (e.g., under that rock, no matter where it is relative to other objects in space). But because testing hypotheses about the nature of the cognitive mechanisms (e.g., is the animal really using complex spatial relations as cues?) is very difficult in natural settings, laboratory studies of the role of spatial memory in the recovery of cached seeds have been conducted (Balda, 1980; Kamil & Balda, 1985; Sherry, 1982; Shettleworth & Krebs, 1982). The questions asked by these studies have a clear functional context, because the importance of seed recovery in nature has been demonstrated (Vanderwall & Balda, 1981). Having shown that birds will cache and recover seeds in the laboratory, researchers have begun to ask mechanistic questions about how accurate recovery is achieved and what characteristics of the underlying cognitive structures contribute to this behavior.

From a comparative perspective, two types of questions may be asked. First, how do the characteristics of this spatial memory compare to the characteristics of spatial memory elucidated by studies of other species with other experimental paradigms, such as rat memory in the radial arm maze, or the ability of chimpanzees to recover pieces of food hidden by an experimenter while they watched (Menzel, 1973)? In all these cases, the memory system exhibits a large capacity and can span relatively long delays (Shettleworth & Krebs, 1982). Such comparisons might lead to the conclusion that spatial memory is essentially similar in all species that exhibit it; that is, the comparison implies that certain principles of spatial memory structure are universal. This universality could reflect common evolutionary heritage or unavoidable constraints on the evolution of spatial memory structure. In either case, if these principles are indeed universal, our understanding of this aspect of cognition has been enhanced by comparative analysis.

More interesting, perhaps, is the second type of comparative question. How do these memory systems differ, and what is the explanatory basis for those differences? During recovery, marsh tits avoid revisits to sites already emptied of food (Shettleworth & Krebs, 1982; Sherry, 1982), a result that is consistent with considerations of foraging efficiency. Nutcrackers, however, often revisit emptied caches in the laboratory (Kamil & Balda, 1985). One possible explanation for these results is that the memory of which caches have already been visited is poorer for nutcrackers than for tits. As pointed out by Kamil and Balda (1985), however, nutcrackers in nature typically bury several seeds in each cache site, whereas tits store one seed per hole. Therefore, in nature, the payoff for revisiting sites may be higher for nutcrackers than for parids. This suggests the possibility that nutcrackers do remember previously visited sites but have a natural tendency to revisit them. The implications of these hypotheses could be evaluated in the laboratory using the radial arm maze or similar procedures. Given that the spatial memory of these birds is intimately connected with their ecology, an attempt can be made to relate behavioral and cognitive differences to disparate selective pressures arising from dissimilar ecologies.

The difference between tits and nutcrackers in frequency of revisits suggests another theoretical issue. Had the researchers decided to use a more traditional procedure (e.g., the radial arm maze) to explore the characteristics of spatial memory in caching birds, instead of initially testing them in a more ecologically relevant task, potentially important differences may not have been revealed or may have been uninterpretable, because the differences may relate to the ecological variables that would have been ignored. This underscores the importance of recognizing the function of cognitive systems, even if the stated goal is to discover how these systems are organized and what behavior they control.

Even if more traditional tasks do reveal interspecific differences, our ability to interpret them is limited unless we understand to which adaptive functions those differences relate. For instance, many corvids store food, but morphological and ecological data on the nutcracker indicate that it is the most specialized caching corvid (Vanderwall & Balda, 1981). If the selective pressures that have affected caching specialization have had isomorphic effects on spatial memory, then orderly species differences in reliance on cached food should be accompanied by orderly species differences in characteristics of spatial memory (Kamil & Balda, 1985; Shettleworth & Krebs, 1982). Such an analysis may provide information as to which characteristics of spatial memory are unique specializations and which are more general characteristics that may be expected to appear in any spatial memory system.

Finally, only a comparative analysis will inform us of the evolutionary history of cognitive processes. Although this is not now a central issue in cognition, it is clear that knowledge of which types of processes are primitive, which are recent developments, and which are unique specializations will make our understanding of animal cognition more complete. Gathering such knowledge is a complex task, but methods have been developed to discover the evolutionary history of certain behaviors (e.g., Greene, 1978). Similar methodology could conceivably be applied to the study of the evolution of cognitive processes. An example of this general approach is the study of animal communication to better understand the evolution of human language (cf. Parker & Gibson, 1979). In attempting to analyze the similarities and differences between nonhuman and human communication systems, the definition and necessary attributes of language have become more precise. Eventually, this analysis may reveal which attributes of human language are relatively primitive (i.e., are shared with the common ancestor of humans and whichever species also exhibit this attribute) and which attributes are unique specializations of our species.

SUMMARY

We have examined the history of ideas about animal cognition, illustrated their current state, and suggested some potential roles that the field might have in the future of psychology. We have also addressed the criticisms that have been made of the cognitive enterprise. The modern study of animal cognition has shifted from an interest in the explanation of molar behavior that characterized it earlier in this century to the use of behavioral tests to evaluate hypotheses about the nature of internal processes. In this respect, the modern enterprise is borrowing methods and concepts from the field of human information processing (cf. Blackman, 1983; Riley & Leith, 1976). It is clear that the cognitive processes that have been inferred are meant as descriptions of causal factors that are properties of the functional organization of the nervous system. These hypothesized mechanisms have predictive power in situations where historical analyses have difficulty predicting behavior. Finally, we have described how the study of cognitive processes is enriched by consideration of their function and argued for a more ecological approach to the study of cognition.

ACKNOWLEDGMENTS

Thanks are due to Robert Cook, Elenice Ferrari, Stephen Glickman, Mark Holder, Marvin Lamb, Seth Roberts, Lynn Robertson, and John Watson for helpful suggestions and comments on this manuscript and/or lively discussions of the ideas contained therein. Preparation of this chapter was supported by National Science Foundation Grant BNS-8317577 to D. A. Riley.

REFERENCES

Balda, R. P. (1980). Recovery of cached seeds by a captive *Nucifraga caryocatactes*. *Zeitshrift fur Tierpsychologie, 52*, 331–346.
Bitterman, M. E., Menzel, R., Fietz, A., & Schafer, S. (1983). Classical conditioning of proboscis extension in honeybees (*Apis mellifera*). *Journal of Comparative Psychology, 97*, 107–119.

Blackman, D. E. (1983). On cognitive theories of animal learning: Extrapolation from humans to animals? In G. C. L. Davey (Ed.), Animal models of human behavior. New York: Wiley.

Bolles, R. C. (1983). The explanation of behavior. The Psychological Record, 33, 31–48.

Branch, M. N. (1982). Misrepresenting behaviorism. The Behavioral and Brain Sciences, 5, 372–373.

Chomsky, N. (1956). Three models for the description of languages. IRE Transactions on Information Theory, 2, 113–124.

Church, R. M. (1978). The internal clock. In S. H. Hulse, H. Fowler, & W. K. Honig (Eds.), Cognitive processes in animal behavior. Hillsdale, NJ: Lawrence Erlbaum Associates.

Cook, R. G., Brown, M. F., & Riley, D. A. (in press). Flexible memory processing by rats: Use of retrospective and prospective information in the radial arm maze. Journal of Experimental Psychology: Animal Behavior Processes.

Cowie, R. J., Krebs, J. R., & Sherry, D. F. (1981). Food storing by marsh tits. Animal Behavior, 29, 1252–1259.

Darwin, C. R. (1872). The expression of emotion in man and animals. London: John Murray.

Dickinson, A. (1980). Contemporary animal learning theory, Cambridge: Cambridge University Press.

Domjan, M., & Galef, B. G. Jr. (1983). Biological constraints on instrumental and classical conditioning: Retrospect and prospect. Animal Learning and Behavior, 11, 151–161.

Epstein, R. (1982). Representation: A concept that fills no gaps. The Behavioral and Brain Sciences, 5, 377–378.

Epstein, R., Lanza, R. P., & Skinner, B. F. (1981). Self-awareness in the pigeon. Science, 212, 695–696.

Gallup, G. G., Jr. (1969). Mirror-image stimulation. Psychological Bulletin, 70, 782–793.

Gallup, G. G., Jr. (1970). Chimpanzees: Self-recognition. Science, 167, 86–87.

Gallup, G. G., Jr. (1977). Self-recognition in primates: A comparative approach to the bidirectional properties of consciousness. American Psychologist, 32, 329–338.

Gallup, G. G., Jr. (1982). Self-awareness and the emergence of mind in primates. American Journal of Primatology, 2, 237–248.

Gallup, G. G., Jr. (1983). Toward a comparative psychology of mind. In R. L. Mellgren (Ed.), Animal cognition and behavior. New York: North–Holland.

Garcia, J., & Koelling, R. A. (1966). Relation of cue to consequence in avoidance learning. Psychonomic Science, 4, 123–124.

Gibbon, J., & Church, R. M. (1984). Sources of variance in information processing models of timing. In H. L. Roitblat, T. G. Bever, & H. S. Terrace (Eds.), Animal cognition. Hillsdale, NJ: Lawrence Erlbaum Associates.

Greene, H. W. (1978). Behavior and phylogeny: Constriction in ancient and modern snakes. Science, 200, 74–77.

Hebb, D. 0. (1949). The organization of behavior: A neuropsychological theory. New York: Wiley.

Herrnstein, R. J. (1977). The evolution of behaviorism. American Psychologist, 32, 593–603.

Honig, W. K., & Thompson, R. K. R. (1982). Retrospective and prospective processing in animal working memory. Psychology of Learning and Motivation, 16, 239–283.

Honig, W. K., & Wasserman, E. A. (1981). Performance of pigeons on delayed simple and conditional discriminations under equivalent training procedures. Learning and Motivation, 12, 149–170.

Hull, C. L. (1930). Knowledge and purpose as habit mechanisms. Psychological Review, 37, 511–525.

Hull (1943). Principles of behavior. New York: Appleton–Century.

Hulse, S. H., Fowler, H., & Honig, W. K. (1978). Cognitive processes in animal behavior. Hillsdale, NJ: Lawrence Erlbaum Associates.

Johnston, T. D. (1981). Contrasting approaches to a theory of learning. *Behavioral and Brain Sciences, 4,* 125–173. (with commentaries and author's response)

Kamil, A. C. (1984). Adaptation and cognition: Knowing what comes naturally. In H. L. Roitblat, T. G. Bever, & H. S. Terrace (Eds.), *Animal cognition.* Hillsdale, NJ: Lawrence Erlbaum Associates.

Kamil, A. C., & Balda, R. C. (1985). Cache recovery and spatial memory in Clark's nutcracker (*Nucifraga columbiana*). *Journal of Experimental Psychology: Animal Behavior Processes, 11,* 95–111.

Kamil, A. C., & Yoerg, S. I. (1982). Learning and foraging behavior. In P. P. G. Bateson & P. H. Klopfer (Eds.), *Perspectives in ethology* (Vol. 5). New York: Plenum Press.

Lombardi, C. M., Fachinelli, C. C. & Delius, J. D. (1984). Oddity of visual patterns and conceptualized by pigeons. *Animal Learning & Behavior, 12,* 2–6.

Lorenz, K. (1950). The comparative method in studying innate behavior patterns. *Symp. Soc. Exp. Biol., 4,* 221–228.

Mattes, H. (1978). Der Tannenhaber im Engadin. *Munstersche Geographische Arbeiten, 3,* 87.

Meck, W. H. (1983). Selective adjustment of the speed of internal clock and memory processes. *Journal of Experimental Psychology: Animal Behavior Processes, 9,* 171–201.

Meck, W. H., Church, R. M., & Olton, D. S. (1984). Hippocampus, time and memory. *Behavioral Neuroscience, 98,* 3–22.

Menzel, E. W. (1973). Chimpanzee spatial memory organization. *Science, 182,* 943.

Miller, G. A., Galanter, E., & Pribram, K. H. (1960). *Plans and the structure of behavior.* New York: Holt, Rinehart, & Winston.

Morgan, C. L. (1894). *An introduction to comparative psychology.* London: Scott.

Neisser, U. (1967). *Cognitive psychology.* New York: Appleton–Century–Crofts.

Olton, D. S. (1978). Characteristics of spatial memory. In S. H. Hulse, H. Fowler, & W. K. Honig (Eds.), *Cognitive processes in animal behavior.* Hillsdale, NJ: Lawrence Erlbaum Associates.

Olton, D. S., & Samuelson, R. J. (1976). Remembrance of places past: Spatial memory in rats. *Journal of Experimental Psychology: Animal Behavior Processes, 2,* 97–116.

Parker, S. T., & Gibson, K. R. (1979). A developmental model for the evolution of language and intelligence in early hominids. *The Behavioral and Brain Sciences, 2,* 367–408. (includes commentaries and authors' response)

Riley, D. A., Cook, R. G., & Lamb, M. R. (1981). A classification and analysis of short-term retention codes in pigeons. *Psychology of Learning and Motivation, 15,* 51–79.

Riley, D. A., & Leith, C. R. (1976). Multidimensional psychophysics and selective attention in animals. *Psychological Bulletin, 83,* 138–160.

Roberts, S. (1981). Isolation of an internal clock. *Journal of Experimentl Psychology: Animal Behavior Processes, 7,* 242–268.

Roberts, S. (1983). Properties and function of an internal clock. In R. L. Mellgren (Ed.), *Animal cognition and behavior.* New York: North–Holland.

Roberts, S., & Church, R. M. (1978). Control of an internal clock. *Journal of Experimental Psychology: Animal Behavior Processes, 4,* 318–337.

Roitblat, H. L. (1980). Codes and coding processes in pigeon short-term memory. *Animal Learning and Behavior, 8,* 341–351.

Roitblat, H. L. (1982). The meaning of representation in animal memory. *The Behavioral and Brain Sciences, 5,* 353–406. (includes commentaries and author's response)

Roitblat, H. L., Bever, T. G., & Terrace, H. S. (1984). *Animal cognition,* Hillsdale, NJ: Lawrence Erlbaum Associates.

Romanes, G. J. (1884). *Mental evolution in animals.* New York: Appleton.

Rozin, P., & Kalat, J. W. (1971). Specific hungers and poison avoidance as adaptive specializations of learning. *Psychological Review, 78,* 459–486.

Salzinger, K. (1973). Inside the black box, with apologies to Pandora. A review of Ulric Neisser's *Cognitive Psychology*. *Journal of the Experimental Analysis of Behavior, 19*, 369–378.

Sands, S. F., & Wright, A. A. (1980). Serial probe recognition performance by a rhesus monkey and a human with 10- and 20-item lists. *Journal of Experimental Psychology: Animal Behavior Processes, 6*, 386–396.

Sands, S. F., & Wright, A. A. (1982). Monkey and human pictorial memory scanning. *Science, 216*, 1333–1334.

Seligman, M. E. P. (1970). On the generality of laws of learning. *Psychological Review, 77*, 406–418.

Sherry, D. F. (1982). Food storage, memory, and marsh tits. *Animal Behaviour, 30*, 631–633.

Shettleworth, S. J. (1983). Function and mechanism in learning. In M. Zeiler & P. Harzem (Eds.), *Advances in the analysis of behavior* (Vol. 3). New York: Wiley.

Shettleworth, S., & Krebs, J. R. (1982). How marsh tits find their hoards: The roles of site preference and spatial memory. *Journal of Experimental Psychology: Animal Behavior Processes, 8*, 354–375.

Skinner, B. F. (1935). The generic nature of the concepts of stimulus and response. *Journal of General Psychology, 12*, 40–65.

Skinner, B. F. (1938). *The behavior of organisms*. New York: Appleton–Century–Crofts.

Skinner, B. F. (1950). Are theories of learning necessary? *Psychological Review, 57*, 193–216.

Skinner, B. F. (1969). *Contingencies of reinforcement*. New York: Appleton–Century–Crofts.

Skinner, B. F. (1977). Why I am not a cognitive psychologist. *Behaviorism, 5*, 1–10.

Skinner, B. F. (1981). Selection by consequences. *Science, 213*, 501–504.

Smith, L. D. (1982). Purpose and cognition: The limits of Neorealist influence on Tolman's psychology. *Behaviorism, 2*, 151–163.

Spear, N. E., & Miller, R. R. (1981). *Information processing in animals: Memory mechanisms*. Hillsdale, NJ: Lawrence Erlbaum Associates.

Staddon, J. E. R. (1973). On the notion of cause, with applications to behaviorism. *Behaviorism, 1*, 25–63.

Staddon, J. E. R., & Simmelhag, V. (1971). The "superstition" experiment: A re-examination of its implications for the principles of adaptive behavior. *Psychological Review, 78*, 3–43.

Sternberg, S. (1969). Memory-scanning: Mental processes revealed by reaction-time experiments. *American Scientist, 57*, 421–457.

Swanberg, P. O. (1951). Food storage, territory, and song in the thick-billed nutcracker. In S. Horstadius (Ed.), *Proceedings of the 8th Ornithological Conference*, 545–554.

Thorndike, E. L. (1911). *Animal intelligence*. New York: Macmillan.

Tinbergen, N. (1951). *The study of instinct*. London: Oxford University Press.

Tolman, E. C. (1925). Purpose and cognition: The determiners of animal learning. *Psychological Review, 32*, 285–297.

Tolman, E. C. (1932). *Purposive behavior in animals and men*, New York: Appleton-Century-Crofts.

Tolman, E. C. (1938). The determiners of behavior at a choice point. *Psychological Review, 45*, 1–41.

Tolman, E. C. (1948). Cognitive maps in rats and men. *Psychological Review, 55*, 189–208.

Tomback, D. F. (1980). How nutcrackers find their seed stores. *Condor, 82*, 10–19.

Vander Wall, S. B., & Balda, R. P. (1981). Ecology and evolution of food-storage behavior in conifer-seed-caching corvids. *Zeitshrift fur Tierpsychologie, 56*, 217–242.

Wilkie, D. M. (1983). Pigeons' spatial memory: II. Acquisition of delayed matching of key location and transfer to new locations. *Journal of the Experimental Analysis of Behavior, 39*, 69–76.

7

J. J. Gibson's Ecological Theory of Information Pickup: Cognition from the Ground Up

William M. Mace
Trinity College

INTRODUCTION

The ecological approach presented in this chapter is that developed by James Gibson. It is not the only ecological approach to issues in psychology. Of the other ecological psychologists, Barker (1965) is best known *as* an ecological psychologist. Brunswik (1943, 1956) and Lewin (1943) used the term in commenting on one another as early as 1941. Brunswik (1943) gave Lewin credit for suggesting that he use the term *ecology* when discussing "the statistics of organism and environment" (p. 267).[1] Because Barker worked closely with Lewin, and Gibson took Lewin quite seriously (Gibson & Crooks, 1938/1982), Lewin, as well as Brunswik, undoubtedly deserves a good share of the credit for ecological concerns in psychology. Urie Bronfenbrenner (1979), a long-time colleague of Gibson's at Cornell, is yet another prominent psychologist who calls his work ecological psychology. There are undoubtedly similarities among all the psychologies that have been called ecological. Obviously, they all deem animal and human environments important for psychologists to study. However, the differences in the core problems they treat and their theoretical elaborations are large enough that they are best regarded as distinct.

There are a number of other articles that discuss the relevance of Gibson's work for cognition. Runeson and Bingham (1983), Turvey and Carello (1981), and Turvey, Shaw, Reed, and Mace (1981) dwell heavily on metatheoretical and philosophical aspects of Gibson's work as they relate it to cognition. Neisser

---

[1] I thank Professor Kenneth Hammond for pointing out the early Brunswik/Lewin references.

(1976, 1984) and Shepard (1984) show how Gibson's work can influence research on cognitive topics such as imagery and memory. The purpose of this chapter that distinguishes it from those papers is to review the immediate, straightforward extensions into cognitive areas that Gibson himself suggested.

The major claims of Gibson's ecological approach to perception are now well known (Fodor & Pylyshyn, 1981; Ullman, 1980): that perception of the environment is direct and unmediated by images or representations; that no form of memory, schemata, or other cognitive structure contributes to perception; that information is "in the world"; that perception is a matter of extracting invariants from the optic array; that perceiving is more like resonance than it is like "processing"; that the properties of the environment directly perceived include meaningful properties reflecting an animal's interests and utilities; that computation is not involved in perceiving; and that hidden as well as unhidden surfaces can be visually perceived.

What seems to be much less well known are the meaning of these claims and the foundations on which they rest. This chapter reviews the major components of the ecological approach with special attention to three somewhat neglected supporting concepts: within ecological optics, the concept of the ambient optic array and the lessons of the occluding edge; then, overarching Gibson's theorizing, the definition of perception.

Gibson's approach has two types of implications for cognition. First it elaborates perception itself in a way that does not require cognitive processes to be brought into perception to explain perception. Most theorists (e.g., Fodor & Pylyshyn, 1981; Hochberg, 1982; Rock, 1983) take it for granted that cognition is necessary to explain perception. Second, the ecological theory of perception, more precisely the theory of information pickup, not only does not utilize cognition to explain perception but extends perception to displace some apparently clear cases of cognition. Finally, there are suggestions of how Gibson's approach can form the foundation for an extended theory of "cognition" with a completely different scheme for classifying "processes."

Gibson's book (1966) on the mechanisms of perception devotes space to every perceptual "modality." His ideas are framed generally enough to apply to every "modality." The novelties proper to his perceptual theory apply to hearing, touching, smelling, tasting, and orienting as well as to vision. However, the bulk of his work was on visual perception, and most of the detailed theory is visual. Hence I describe the ecological approach to visual perception at great length. The implications for cognition that I present most easily follow from the visual theory.

THE THEORY OF INFORMATION PICKUP

Gibson called the theory of perception that developed within the ecological approach the theory of information pickup. If all the interlocking components of the theory have been fashioned to fit properly, then perception can be said to be a matter of an animal's picking up or detecting information. The words *picking up, detecting,* and others (such as *extracting*) used by Gibson imply prior existence of the information *as* informative structure. Obviously, to understand what Gibson meant by information pickup, then, one must carefully study what he meant by *information* and what he meant by *pickup.*

Information

Information refers to structure carried in media by light, mechanical energy, or chemical energy. The structure must be intrinsically *informative* about the sources of its structure by virtue of being lawfully specific to those sources of structure. The relevant contrast here is to concepts that would have stimulation be intrinsically informative of nothing more than its own existence. As stimulation, light rays, for example, are not informative about their sources. One cannot know from the light ray itself if its source is near or distant, a reflecting surface or a radiant surface. Receptors in an eye stimulated by a ray of light can at best be informed of the presence of the ray of light—and that, of course, is a vast oversimplification. Indeed given the complexity of nervous systems and the presence of spontaneous activity in them, theorists in the Johannes Müller tradition of specific nerve energies would say that one can be informed only of the activity of the nervous system itself. For perceivers to be informed about the sources of stimulation in such cases, they must make a large contribution by having a store of alternatives that are selected among according to those stimulating conditions.

In this view, in accord with classical information theory, the function of stimulation is to select among a "known" set of alternatives. It has no power of its own. A single lamp in the Old North Church belfry could mean "by land" to Paul Revere, "by day" to Gerald Ford according to one story, or any number of other things depending on the set of prearranged options. With no such prearranged options it is just a light high above the ground.

Most theorists of visual perception do not trace the uninformative nature of light back to individual light rays but to the ambiguities inherent in a single view. Even a *distribution* of intensities may arise from an indefinite number of environmental sources, hence such a distribution is also intrinsically uninformative. For a distribution of intensities to act informatively, a perceiver must have some means of *interpreting* or decoding the distribution according to a restricted set of possibilities.

One can frame the issue this way: Is seeing a light in a tower window high above the ground to be understood in the same way that Paul Revere learned of the British route or in some other way? Without denying the existence and utility of "Paul Revere" information, Gibson argued that there was a very different sense of information to be developed and that this was the more appropriate sense for understanding perception. In his sense of information the structure of light could be intrinsically informative. His theory implies that sensitivity to structure must exist in a perceiver but that there does not have to be an added interpretation process based on some prearranged code.

Development of the Ecological Concept of Information

Gibson's concept of information resulted from what began as a search for "higher order" variables of stimulation that would correspond to perceived properties of the world. His program of perceptual psychophysics was based on the hypothesis that what perceivers perceived was a function of stimulus patterning and that the relevant stimulus pattern was a function of the environment. According to Gibson (1960, 1982b), "If experience is specific to excitation, and excitation to stimulation, and stimulation to the external environment, then experience will be specific to the environment, within the limits of this chain of specificities" (p. 346). It was possible, he thought, that the presumed lack of correspondence between the environment and stimulation, and stimulation and perceptual experience, reflected a failure to discover the proper variables, not a failure of the correspondence.

The best known result of this program was Gibson's hypothesis that gradients of texture could act as unitary stimuli yielding perception of the slant of rigid surfaces relative to the line of sight (Gibson, 1947/1982a, 1950). If a gradient could be defined over an arbitrary number of different surface textures and yield the same perceived slant, it seemed justifiable to call the gradient a "stimulus" for slant perception. Because gradients are defined over textures and textures are already patterns, gradients are patterns of patterns. That is what Gibson meant by "higher order." With the key insight of "higher order" variables, it seemed that diligence and some cleverness would be sufficient to discover the true correspondences between stimuli and perception of the environment.

By the mid 1950s, however, Gibson began to reject the major assumptions of the psychophysical program (Gibson, 1982e). This must seem odd to many readers because the theory of information pickup does not, on the face of it, seem very different from "perception as a function of stimulation." Both say that optical patterning (for the case of vision) is the basis of perceiving the environment. So why the new terms? Why did Gibson regard the theory of information pickup as a radical new theory and the 1950 vintage ideas like texture gradients as merely "bright ideas" (Gibson, 1982e, p. 95)?

Ecological Information

So far we have said that Gibson regarded information as structure specific to its sources. To say more about information it would be helpful to turn again to light and vision and the new discipline Gibson called Ecological Optics. Ecological Optics is the theory of the lawful structuring of light by its sources at a level appropriate for perception. Hence it is where the theory of optical information is developed. Parallel disciplines studying the structuring of mechanical (for acoustics and haptics) and chemical (for taste and smell) energy could also be developed.

Gibson wanted to understand perception of the environment. From the foundations of physical, geometric, or physiological optics, to fully understand perception of the environment seems hopelessly complex. Any scientific discipline must work with simplified, idealized concepts in order to reason clearly and precisely. Gibson cut the Gordian knot tying perceptual theory to traditional branches of optics and formed concepts that abstracted directly over the animal and environment system, rather than waiting for elaborations of concepts from the other areas to build up to broad characterizations of environments. Instead of working with primitives such as points, lines, planes, and projections, he began with the ambient optic array.

The Ambient Optic Array

The ambient optic array is structured light *surrounding* a point of observation. It consists of multiple reflected light filling a medium. This means that there must be sources of light, reflecting surfaces, and a medium. With enough light bouncing from surface to surface, the medium becomes filled with light. The same set of reflecting surfaces that make the light-filled medium possible at all also accounts for differences of intensity in different directions from any point of observation. These differences exist by virtue of differences in arrangement (layout) relative to one another and to the illumination, differences in texture, and differences in pigment structure. Note that because this structure is a structure of differences it is invariant under changes of intensity of illumination.

The components of the array are a nested series of units with the earth–sky contrast being the first subdivision; that is, a terrestrial optic array is relatively light and untextured in the sky and darker and much more richly textured on the ground. The contrasting hemispheres corresponding to the sky and earth is a structure that is invariant under changes of illumination from day to night, and under changes in point of observation.

A number of conclusions can be drawn already. First, consider a homogeneous surround of light. It is ambient and it can cause receptors to fire, but there is *nothing* to see. There is nowhere to direct one's gaze and not even accommodation is possible. Gibson stressed that such light is *unfocusable*. To him this helped distinguish between a stimulus and stimulus information (or just information); that is, light can get to an eye and fire receptors but give rise to no perception. Gibson's interpretation of the Ganzfeld experiments attempting to show people homogeneous light was that visual perception literally fails under such conditions. It cannot work if there are no contrasts. It is a case of stimulation without information. In darkness, Gibson (1979) noted that visual perception fails for lack of stimulation *and* information. In homogeneous light, it fails for lack of information.

The language of stimuli implies something coming *from* the environment *to* an observer. In vision it implies light traveling from a source to an eye. The optic array (information), however, just exists. At the level of earth–sky, once one is born, one never goes outside of it (except for astronauts). One may obscure the sky or the earth by going into enclosures, but the sky and earth are always there as the outer limit on the array. At the level of places on the earth, eyes come to them, explore them, and leave for other places, perhaps to return, perhaps not. The motions of photons through the medium are assumed as a physical cause of illumination, but ecological optics begins after that with the assumption of an illuminated medium.

Because an optic array does not travel to observers but just exists, one can study the optical transitions from one region to another, and, for superordinate regions, transitions *within* them. The very stable features of an array, caused by very stable large-scale relations among surfaces, can support evolution. Gibson (1979) used the fact that animals with compound eyes, as well as animals with chambered eyes, show visually guided behavior (such as avoidance in the presence of an expanding shadow specifying a looming object; cf. Schiff, 1965) as evidence that they are designed to take advantage of information in the array even though they have no retinal images. Thus retinal images are not necessary for vision, but information is. Information, discussed this way, as something prior to animals phylogenetically, ontogenetically, and episodically, is real. It is not created by them or for them (except in senses described later in the discussion of affordances).

The stability and ubiquity of the sky–earth contrast makes it an effective absolute visual frame of reference for ecological optics. The sky–earth framework does not move. All changes of position are ultimately defined with respect to it. The clearest perceptual information for great distances or wide open spaces is information for a stretch of ground from a point of observation to the horizon; that is, the closest thing to the literal experience of "space" is to experience an uncluttered terrain. To present one literally with space would be to present a Ganzfeld and that experience, if anything, is like the experience of a heavy fog. It is certainly not an experience of vast "space." Even in his psychophysical days Gibson (1950) argued for the ground as a better framework for perception than any concept of "space." Hence he called his theory a *ground* theory in contrast to most other theories that he called *air* theories because they studied the perception of isolated objects, as if one were looking at birds or airplanes directly against a backdrop of the sky.

Perception occurs for *embodied* observers. This guarantees that no animal can see all 360 degrees of the ambient optic array at once. The body parts that an animal sees hide parts of the array. Thus eye turning relative to the array—by moving head or feet—is necessary to scan the whole array at any one place. The body of an observer causes part of the structure of an array at any observed place. It is an invariant across changes of location in the environment. It is an optical specification of "here" with the horizon as maximal "there." Thinking still of an open, flat terrain, one can understand that for a given height of the point of observation, there is a "here–there" dimension of distance invariantly specified under locomotion.

The frame of reference role of the sky–earth container (the ultimate terrestrial exterior treated optically as an interior) can be seen in the case of head movements relative to the horizontal. The horizon *is* the horizontal. An optic array sample with the horizon in the middle means that the head is level. This is a case where a fact about the observer ("here") is given in a fact about the maximal "there" (horizon). It is one reason for being uncomfortable with the distinction between "proximal" and "distal." If all one sees is the ground, one is looking down. If all one sees is the sky, one is looking up. An orientation of the eyes on this dimension is always specified in the optic array. Gibson maintained that such optical changes and nonchanges are used by perceivers to control their movements relative to the environment. Airplane pilots lose their sense of the orientation relative to the ground when flying in the middle of clouds and can be very surprised at what they see when they emerge. Dolezal (1982) showed that wearing tubes on the eyes to obscure peripheral vision of the body and ground at the feet caused a loss of the keen sense of head orientation relative to the midline of the body (is it to the left, right, how far?).

We have now developed enough to illustrate better what Gibson meant by defining information as structure specific to its sources. Consider the ambient optic array of a person alone on the prairie in the daytime. The optical structure is a nested one beginning with sky above and earth below. As one walks some of the subordinate structure of the earth is clarified by coming closer to it. Some is obscured by the body as one passes. The body is always visible, from feet on the ground to nose and eye sockets. There is optic flow outward from the horizon from the point being approached. The sky and earth remain stable throughout the walk. They both stretch to the horizon in all directions all the time. How could one simulate the optical structure of this situation without structuring by just the components of this situation? Can one make something look like "the outdoors" under conditions of free exploration without its *being* the outdoors? Even high-budget movies, with money for the technology of illusion, are made "on location." To the untutored eye, one might make a scene in Texas look somewhat like one in Kansas, but one cannot make a city studio look like a 5-mile walk in Kansas. And I certainly cannot imagine how one would specify *me* taking a long walk outdoors on the prairie without my taking a long walk on the prairie. Cinerama films and Disneyland displays that create vivid impressions of environments reinforce the point. Even to make an interesting approximation to an illusion of locomoting outdoors requires surrounding an observer as much as possible. But these surrounds are limited and one can readily find the boundaries—something one cannot do for the prairie until arriving at the mountains, and even then the mountains are connected to the prairie and the sky is still the same sky. The idea I am trying to convey rather imprecisely is that optical structure is lawfully determined by the surface layout (including the surfaces of the perceiver's body). Where this is true the structure is specific to its source and detecting the structure *is* detecting the source in surface properties. One does not detect something meaningless first and then interpret it meaningfully. There is only one step. That is the one Gibson referred to as information pickup. This does *not* say that the supporting processes for the act of pickup are not complex. There are many degrees of freedom to be coordinated. The alternative hypothesis, that there are two acts, one the detection of something meaningless and the other of interpretation, is equally simple relative to the underlying complex of supporting processes.

If this concept of information specific to its sources holds true for *any* cases, then information pickup is possible in those cases and a subject matter has been carved out. One can continue, asking "what other cases qualify?"

Invariants and Variants

As a structure surrounding an animal, an optic array can be explored or observed in the active sense of the word. For Gibson *observation* and other words for perceiving all designated active exploration. When this occurs, the array changes in some ways, but not in all. One way that the array of an idealized frozen environment changes occurs when an observer moves. Everything in the array flows (as alluded to previously) and there are regular exchanges of array components that are revealed and concealed (discussed more later). But within the flow some relations of components to one another stay the same. These invariants specify stable features of the environment. The changes, or variants, specify movement of the observer relative to the stable environment. Specification means the same thing it did before: In an ambient optic array, there is no other way the pattern of variants and invariants could come about. This point is when discussing the contributions of the theory of the environment and the theory of perceiving to the theory of information. The emphasis here is on the fact that specificity in an optic array depends on distinguishing variants and invariants and that these are natural concepts for an optic array. Because invariants are defined only with respect to variants, it follows that change is *necessary* to reveal nonchange. It also follows that systematic movements of an observer can be specified only relative to invariant structure. One could not see oneself locomoting or turning one's head in a Ganzfeld or in an ambient chaos.

An early example of an invariant in an optic array can be found in Gibson's early analysis of the gradient structure of optic flow generated by locomotion (Gibson, 1950; Gibson, Olum, & Rosenblatt, 1955). Originally he thought of the gradients of texture as higher order variables in the retinal image, but he considered the ecological optics interpretation to be a great clarification (Gibson, 1982e). In ecological optics, the optic array with its earth–sky "envelope" is the relevant frame of reference, not the eye, as in the retinal gradients; and the concept of invariants relative to variants replaced "higher order" variable. Gibson admitted that he never could say clearly what "higher order" meant, whereas the pairing of variants and invariants put mutual boundaries on them. The problem of "how high is higher order, and how does one count?" does not arise. This is not to say that all specific invariants and variants are immediately manifest without laborious research, only that the concept of invariant is much better than the concept of "higher order."

Gibson postulated four kinds of invariants that underlie change in the optic array that he reviewed together in the second appendix of his 1979 book: "those that underlie change of *illumination,* those that underlie change of the *point of observation,* those that underlie *overlapping samples,* and those that underlie a *local disturbance of structure*" (p. 310). The third kind of change in the list refers to something like head turning, which changes the sample of the same array but does not transform the array as would happen in moving to a new point of observation. The fourth refers to events, changes in the environment not due to the other three factors. Many invariants remain to be discovered. The program is young, but the classification of variants helps to be clear about what is meant by an invariant. There are explicit terms for structure specific to the world and for structure specific to the observer, for changes and nonchanges in each.

Optical Transitions: Occluding Edges and the Perception of Persistence

The construct of the ambient optic array naturally induces the study of orderly transitions as a fundamental part of optics. As structure produced by what an observer is *inside* of, it leads one to seek out the order that belongs to exploring a stable interior such as a room, a forest clearing, or a prairie; the order in making transitions from one interior to another; and the order in going around detached and attached objects. With a prior concept of the systematicity that *exists* in each case, one can get an idea of what is *possible* to detect on the basis of optical structure. None of these three cases has received much attention, although the latter is beginning to (Koenderink, 1984; Shaw, McIntyre, & Mace, 1974).

The most significant transition studied in ecological optics, according to Gibson, is the one that specifies an occluding edge. Opaque surfaces are among the primitives of the world assumed by ecological optics. By reflection, they make possible the ambient optic array in the first place, but they also hide many surfaces at any particular point of observation.

The place where one surface hides its own backside or a background surface relative to a fixed point of observation is an occluding edge. George Kaplan (1969; Gibson, Kaplan, Reynolds, & Wheeler, 1969) showed that such an edge could be optically specified by the progressive disruption of optical texture (developing a precise formulation of the optics of occlusion is still in its early stages; it is an important continuing task of ecological optics—cf. Mace & Turvey, 1983). Kaplan filmed a white sheet of paper, randomly spotted by blobs of ink, frame by frame. Each new frame was created by cutting a thin column out of its predecessor, sliding one side over to close the gap, and adding new random texture in the area left by the displacement. The operation was repeated at the same place to the same extent for all frames of any particular sequence. No margin was visible in any single frame. However, when the film was shown, one surface was seen clearly to be passing behind another at the place where the texture was removed from the display. This effect is as vivid as anything else one might see in a filmed display.

The main point is that even though the texture ''belonging to'' the occluded surface was going out of sight, the surface was seen to persist. What was perceived was not ''disappearance of texture,'' but ''disappearance-from-this-point-of-view'' with continued projection to some other point of view. There is a critical distinction to be made between disappearance of a surface from the face of the earth and disappearance of a surface from the view of a face. If a surface exists, then it does project into the optic array from some point of view. If it does not exist, it projects to no point of view. Gibson et al. (1969) showed that specifically different optical transitions can be demonstrated. They showed that *disappearance* is a vague, imprecise term because a visible surface can go out of sight from a point of view in at least three ways: being covered, turning around itself, going into the distance. Two other ways to specify persistence despite ''disappearance'' that can be distinguished are turning off the lights in an enclosed place and closing one's eyes. A surface can go out of existence in more ways: evaporation and sublimation, fading and increasing transparency, and consumption by eating were demonstrated in their film. Melting, breaking, crumbling, and exploding are other possibilities. Each of these is a distinctively different optical transition. Thus if one can detect a transition as a unit, then these changes can, in principle, be distinguished on the basis of optical information.

If the occlusion transition is different from the others and is detected as such then persistence of the occluded surfaces is specified. This is not to say that the unseen can be seen. One cannot see the rude faces being made behind one's back. But such faces are not usually made to be persisting structure. They are changed when one turns around and are distinguished from, say, the back wall of the room that remains connected to the floor, the adjoining walls, and ceiling throughout repeated inspections. The ordering of views that are possible is determined by the persisting structure of the array created by the room, and detecting this persisting structure is to detect the arrangement of the surfaces of the room.

The persistence specified in occlusion makes it possible to perceive environmental surfaces as connected and as existing concurrently. Not only does the disappearance of a surface by occlusion specify its persistence, but a surface that comes into sight by ''disocclusion'' is seen to preexist; that is, seeing it revealed is not confused with seeing it come into existence. That which is viewed ''now-from-here'' can be perceived as connected with those surfaces that are not seen by virtue of occlusion.

As we have seen, the ecological optics analysis of the ambient optic array into variants and invariants allows the separation of that which belongs to the environment from that which belongs to the self. The point of view belongs to the self. As it changes, in Gibson's theory of information, one can perceive when it is the point of view changing and when it is the environment changing. When the point of view changes in a stable environment, the persistence of that environment is specified by invariants in two of the four classes listed earlier. A consequence of the optics of occlusion is that as one uncovers new surfaces by exploration, one is extending the amount of connected, concurrently existing surface that one has detected. This is very important when we get to Gibson's definition of perception.

Information—Recapitulation and Affordances

Information is structure lawfully structured by its sources. For vision it is optical structure. We have reviewed some of the concepts required to make this work, especially in the optic array. It is important to stress, even though it must be brief in this chapter, that as an ecological concept, *information* requires a theory of what there is to be perceived as well as the informative optical structure. "What there is," in turn, requires that a fair amount be included about the animal as well as the environment. What there is to be perceived (visually here) must be limited to properties that can be shown to structure light and to do so at a level accessible to animals. Gibson's theory of the ecological environment to be perceived divides it into substances, media, and the surfaces formed by their boundaries. Even these are ecological concepts, because what counts as substance or medium (water is the main ambiguous case) depends on the animal. As already indicated, surfaces are the primary object of perception for Gibson.

Gibson (1982d) listed these perceivable properties of surfaces: The property of being rigid, viscous, or fluid; the property of being radiant or reflecting; the property of high to low reflectance of the incident light; the property of having uniform or nonuniform reflectance; the property of being smooth or rough (and if rough, whether texture is coarse or fine and the form it takes); the property of being dull or shiny; the property of being opaque or transparent; the property of being at a higher or lower temperature than the skin. He added that surfaces are not discrete and denumerable like detached objects, that they do not have location but rather layout, that they do not have the physical sense of color, and that they do not have the geometrical sense of form. Gibson (1979) defined places, attached objects, detached objects, and their changes (events) and asserted that these too could be perceived.

Affordances are the last and most important item on the list of what can be perceived. Gibson coined the term affordance to designate the utilities of surface and medium properties and their combinations for animal activities. Besides Gibson (1979), discussions of affordances may be found in Gibson and Spelke (1983), Turvey et al. (1981), and Warren (1984). The activities of an animal in an environment imply the ability to perceive the opportunities to perform and to control those activities. To walk is to be able to distinguish surfaces and their arrangements that allow walking from those surface arrangements that do not. Affordances are objective properties of the ecosystem. Whether something can be walked on, grasped, or swung from is a fact that depends on the size and abilities of an animal and the material structure of the environmental features. Affordances are ecological properties inasmuch as they do depend jointly on the properties of animal and environment for their determination.

What is important to note is that there are some such features that are optically distinct. One can study, as Warren (1984) did for stair climbing, the extent to which useful properties are specifiable in optical structure. If so, then in principle the information could be detected and the property perceived. The material requirements for action put heavy constraints on what can be specified and hence could ever be said to be perceived. Contra Fodor & Pylyshyn (1981), properties like "grandmother" and "shoe" *as such* are not likely candidates for being specifiable and hence perceivable in the sense of information pickup. Properties that make some shoes useful for protecting feet presumably *are* specified, but this is not to say that shoes *qua* shoes are specified. If I am seeking foot protection, a shoe box may be more appropriate than my son's baby shoes.

What it Means to Perceive Reconceived

To keep the theory of information pickup coherent and plausible, great care must be taken to *define* what it is to perceive. Gibson's version is a surprising twist of the traditional Aristotelian version. It is an information-based criterion. Here is one of his later definitions (Gibson, 1979):

> To perceive is to be aware of the surfaces of the environment and of oneself in it. The interchange between hidden and unhidden surfaces is essential to this awareness. These are existing surfaces; they are specified at some points of obser-vation. Perceiving gets wider and finer and longer and richer and fuller as the observer explores the environment. The full awareness of surfaces includes their layout, their substances, their events and their affordances. Note how this defini-tion includes within perception a part of memory, expectation, knowledge, and meaning—some part but not all of those mental processes in each case. (p. 255)

Of most direct importance for discussing cognition is the role Gibson gave to existing surfaces. They get the role that the "present" played in classical theo-ries. Since at least Aristotle, perception has been distinguished from memory and expectation by having the responsibility for sensing the present, whereas memo-ry was defined as a faculty responsible for the past and expectation for the future.

Thus time as represented by the past–present–future sequence is the basis for classifying processes or faculties. By distinguishing between information for the changing point of view and for persisting surfaces, Gibson underscored the fact that the traditional demarcation of perception, memory, and expectation is defined relative to the observer. He proposed to have the delineation be tied to the persisting, presently existing surfaces instead! Thus, no matter how long it takes to reveal and build the awareness of a connected set of surfaces, up to a lifetime, that total awareness of the existing world is perception. A large connected surface such as the territory in the Louisiana Purchase would take a long time to explore. But for Gibson, the logic of it is of a piece with detecting persisting properties of the surfaces extending slightly to the left and right of one's current head position. As long as the information being detected belongs to concurrently persisting surfaces, the detection of their invariant properties constitutes perception.

Persisting surfaces in an environment can be explored reversibly. They can go out of sight (hearing, touch, etc.) from some point of view, but as long as they exist, information for them must continue to be available and the possibility of exploring them remains within the environment. One can, in principle "get there from here" because "there" is connected to "here." Some real pathway exists. When one explores back and forth on such a reversible pathway, persistent properties of surfaces can emerge.

The perceiving conceived by Gibson is an animal's achievement of controlled and controllable "contact" with the environment. It is an activity, an activity of the *whole body* acting on and in the environment to obtain information, the major point of Gibson's book on perceptual systems (1966). Thus Gibson talked of *obtaining* and *extracting* information. Obtaining and extracting in this sense requires coordinated movement. Walking closer to something one wishes to clarify perceptually is a functional part of whatever modality or modalities are guiding the investigatory act; that is, the legs function perceptually by bringing one in a perceptually controlled way to a place where nested adjustments of head turning, eye pointing, lens accommodation, hand positioning, finger movement, and so forth can perform their clarifying functions—all as a single coordinated act. In this case, leg movement (in the context of maintaining a perceptually controlled stable posture) controls perception by moving the appropriate sensitive surfaces to a desired place, and leg movement is controlled by perception by slowing down and halting when the desired place is reached (keep in mind that a myriad of detailed adjustments of the legs and body are also being perceptually guided).

Other properties of perceiving in Gibson's analysis of information are continuity and nested organization. Gibson used the image of animals being immersed in a sea of energy that contains information. This information can be analyzed in a nested way from global to local, with the most global being the contrast between ground and sky that, for vision, provides the ultimate information for orientation of the whole body. In a completely enclosed architectural space, floor, walls, and ceiling provide the local objects to be perceived for stable posture even though a full analysis returns to the earth–sky. A stable posture is a prerequisite for any other controlled activity and "means of support" is the "object" that must be perceived for this overall stability. On a good day (and night), a person or animal preserves a controlled posture relative to the earth the whole time. This means perceiving some global nonchange within which other changes occur, changes that themselves are nonchanges relative to subordinate changes. Changes involved in performing activities occur *within* the context of global orientation. I might say that I perceive the paper in front of me for some purpose, but a full inventory of what I am perceiving is hard to imagine. It would include my orientation to the room, the house, and the outdoor layout. It would include my orientation to my chair, my desk, and my pencil, and these would involve numerous fine-tuning adjustments that I am not focally aware of. I am aware of all these in the sense that I am controlling bodily adjustments for purposes of exploration and manipulation (which includes sitting still), but not in the sense that I can list them explicitly in words. Perceiving, thought of this way, cannot quit, not just because the life process goes on, but also because the earth–sky, and some more local properties for any particular animal, remain as persisting objects of perception for one's whole life. Neither perceiving nor all the objects of perceiving start and stop during one's lifetime.

A final example of a property of perceiving follows from Gibson's argument that information in the world is inexhaustible. Because information is inexhaustible, perceiving does not change its focus because a "correct" or "matching" percept was computed. Rather, perceiving is guided by the practical requirements of an animal's goals, achievements, and circumstances. An animal has to perceive enough of its environment to accomplish its goals, but that's all. There is no final right or wrong. Moreover, perceiving can get better. If there is always more structure that can be clarified with more exploration, then the possibility for more perceiving is always present.

The upshot of these remarks is to emphasize that the perceiving Gibson described does not come in percepts. It is nested from global to local, and a description of what is being perceived at any particular moment would have to acknowledge all levels.

What Perceiving Is Not.   Another way to try to clarify what perceiving is in the theory of information pickup is to say what it is not: (1) To perceive is not to have an experience. Dreams are nonperceptual experiences because they are not based on the active pickup of information in an ambient optic array. When one is sleeping in the ambient array, one is not exploring it. The surfaces in dreams are often not connected to one another and certainly not to persisting surfaces that can be visited, left, and revisited as specified in reversible occlusion. Most theorists agree that not all experiences are perception. Rock (1983) makes it very clear that perception is to be distinguished from other cognition by its connection to "stimuli"; (2) to perceive is not to experience something occasioned by a stimulus. Because of what I already know, I might see a spot on the horizon over a vast expanse of water and say, "Aha! Here comes the QE II with 749 passengers." However, so far as optical information goes, all I can detect at such a distance is that there is something out there on the water. Without a telescope I could not distinguish the QE II from an oil tanker. I could certainly not orient specifically to the layout of surfaces on the QE II. This is an important case because some theorists like Dretske (1981), who say a great deal that is agreeable to and helpful to an ecological perception theorist, would allow this as a case of detecting information if what one sees can select among alternatives a person knows; (3) the last case suggests the need to say clearly that to identify correctly based on perceiving is not perceiving; (4) to perceive is not to arrive at an explicit description in a system of representation as many workers in artificial intelligence define it (Marr, 1982). For Gibson, perceiving involves modulating the complex adjustments of the body performing goal directed activities in the environment. It is action theory, dual to perception theory, that gives perception its semantic closure (Pattee, 1982; Shaw & Turvey, 1981); (5) to perceive is not merely to experience structure as Gestalt psychology suggests. For Gibson it is to experience structure specific to oneself in a persisting layout of surfaces; (6) to perceive visually is not merely to experience light. Remember that in a Ganzfeld, Gibson argued that perceiving literally failed for want of proper "objects," that is, information.

PERCEPTION AND COGNITION

Gibson recognized a clear distinction between the achievements of perception (perceptual knowledge) and the achievements of thought (conceptual knowledge). He did not believe that one could wave one's hand and say that everything was one or the other—or even a mix in the senses found in cognitive approaches to perception. To clarify the distinction between the two kinds of knowledge he offered the following set of contrasts (Gibson, 1974): For perception, the environment consists of substances, medium, and surfaces, not tiny particles like atoms or large astronomical bodies. For perception, the earth is flat, not round. The earth does not move. It is an absolute frame of reference for motion. Gravity is perpendicular to the substratum (things fall *down*). The environment is always upright. Only changes within a moderate range of times are perceptible as such (Shaw, McIntire, & Mace, 1974; Shaw & Pittenger, 1978 have disagreed with Gibson on this point). Illumination reaches a steady state instantly, the speed of light being irrelevant for perception. Finally, perception of the self is always specified and therefore possible ecologically. Gibson argued that it was a mistake to use the conceptual entities and facts of abstract science (such as "space") as if they were possible objects of perception. It was certainly a mistake to use concepts and facts of abstract science as standards of "veridical" perception from which to judge error and illusion.

On the other hand Gibson did believe that the ecological approach offered a firm foundation for a general understanding of knowledge and he did not believe that there was a categorical boundary between perceptual and conceptual cases. Characteristically, he developed a classification scheme, based on the theory of information pickup, to show a *graded* series of cases linking perceptual and conceptual knowledge without blurring what he took to be natural distinctions.

Direct Perception and Cognition

The definition of perception quoted earlier is a definition of what he called *direct perception*. Direct perception means that observers perceive themselves in the environment, surrounded by it, and in relation to it. This is implied by the ambient array in that, to be ambient, the array must be around the observer and it must be occupied by an observer. Another way Gibson defined direct perception was to say that it was extracting information from the ambient array, where ambient has the implications just mentioned. Gibson's treatment of the perception of persistence and change, invariants and variants in the optic array, allowed him to distinguish the part that belongs to an observer and the act of observation from that which belongs to the environment. Both can be observed simultaneously. The concurrent registration of invariants and variants is necessary to make any of his other claims plausible.

Memory and Expectation.   Both change and nonchange must be registered over time. Does this mean that the theory of perception depends on memory to provide the link between past and present necessary to perceive change and persistence? If so, how does it work? What evidence and theory from research on memory would help us understand the apprehension of persistence and change? What is *meant* by memory? If all that is meant is that an animal and its abilities persist over time, then calling it memory adds no explanatory value. Such persistence is required to support the function of information pickup described, but that is necessary for any process to have continuity.

Consider the case of looking at a paper bag on the table in front of you— bearing in mind that in ecological terms it is not a paper bag but a connected set of detached surfaces, mostly surrounding air, and offering a myriad of affordances from carrying groceries to filling a sandbox (carefully) to covering one's face at Halloween. After first looking straight at the bag, you turn to the left so that the texture of the object disappears by occlusion. You can look back at it if you like, to scrutinize it more. Do you know that you can look back at it because you remember it and its location? If you do look back at it, bringing it progressively into view, how is retrieving the view in the structured optic array related to retrieving "a memory"? What if it disappeared by melting? Would you still look for it in the same way?

Gibson stressed the importance of recognizing the differences among types of transitions. If you can discover the difference between melting and going out of sight by occlusion, how do you do that? On Gibson's account, these cases differ in orderly ways. Orderly optical consequences of a change can constitute information—even if it occurs over time, even if it continues to occur for a very long time. The question then is whether or not the information can be detected. It would seem that either *everything* is memory here, or everything is perception and nothing is memory. Setting up this opposition, in light of Gibson's analysis, is pointless because it does not matter what words one uses to designate the process if one admits that information exists and is detected. That is why Gibson talked about information pickup. It is more precise. He did think information pickup was the best explanation of perception as he defined it, but the activity of extracting invariants and variants that specify persistence and change is the main point no matter what one calls it.

The same can be said for *expectation*. If one maintains that one turns in the right direction toward the bag to scrutinize it because one *expects* it to be at a particular place in the sequence of views, what is added? Why should one appeal to three separate processes to explain the apprehension of the layout of a persisting unified structure (the room, its furniture, the observer)? This would draw attention away from the fact that there are riches of orderliness in the changing and persisting optic array structure of a person exploring the room.

It is difficult to see how appeals to memory and expectation could ever work in the first place if the order did not exist. But if the order exists and that order *is* what is ultimately ascertained (by whatever process), then why not refer to the process in a unitary fashion by calling it perception or information pickup? This does not absolve science of the need to probe more into the details of the pickup process, but it is a very different guide to what one would look for.

Affordances.   The previous discussion on affordances should have made it clear that this is a way to bring meaning into the theory of information pickup without having to invest an animal with concepts to do so. The key is to make intrinsic scaling and grouping work in the theory. The argument is that a certain rough fit between an animal's actions and the perceptible environment is constrained by evolution in the first place. The variables must be nonspooky ones that have physical reality in order to have ecological reality. For instance, a ledge is a good height for sitting (for a person) if one can look down and see it about level with one's knees. One does not have to have a metric scale in the head. A ledge is too high to crawl up on easily for most people if its supporting level surface is at eye level or above (measured by whether or not one can see this surface).

The Case of Surfaces That No Longer Exist.   As one explores the ambient array in direct perception, the set of connected surfaces that one can put in order expands. As long as the surfaces persist, those that go out of sight can be brought back into sight and can, therefore, continue to be part of the process of extracting invariants from the ambient optic array. The more one does this, the more one can reveal about the environment—without limit. Exploration over time can reveal more about the large-scale structure of an environment (the Lewis and Clark expedition) or the fine structure (a connoisseur of fine paper). What if surfaces are explored and later destroyed when one is not looking? Then the optical occlusion is not reversible because the surfaces are not available to any point of observation. New surfaces can be discovered connected to the persisting surfaces. There is information for a change of layout.

In Gibson's proposed classification, the awareness of surfaces that did exist, but no longer exist, is a distinct case from the awareness of surfaces that continue to exist. He said that *that* could be thought of as a kind of memory (1979). The advantage of this method of classification is that it is information based. Information for surfaces in these phases of existence can be defined. The "past" and the "future" relative to the "present" have never been well defined and do not seem like proper foundations for a distinction as important as that of *perception, memory, and expectation.* To define perception as an apprehension of something in the present as distinct from memory as apprehension of that which has been perceived implies that one can tell when perceiving quits and memory begins. Gibson's suggestion avoids that problem. For him, perceiving *never* quits during a lifetime, but surfaces can cease to exist.

The Case of Surfaces That Come into Existence.   The case symmetric to the previous one is that of surfaces coming into existence. The optical transitions to transform existing materials and surfaces into new ones should also be orderly enough to discover. To be aware of such surfaces in relation to persisting ones and a point of observation would be a case of planning or expectation in this new proposal.

Impossible Surfaces.   Finally one could consider the case of being aware of surfaces that could not exist and perhaps even differentiate the ways that they could not exist. These would be surfaces that could not be connected to previously existing, presently existing, or future surfaces.

Indirect Perception

The previous cases can be thought of as extensions of direct perception in that they are defined relative to an observer at some place in the environment. These were extensions of direct perception because they were defined in terms of awareness of surfaces, with no mediators.

A second method of classifying types of cognition is on the dimension of direct to indirect. Indirect perception is direct perception of something that in turn contains information for other surface layouts and points of view. Gibson distinguished three broad classes—information mediated by instruments, information mediated by pictures, and information mediated by symbols (including words).

In each case, the possibilities for exploration are very different from those in the ambient array. A picture, for example, can yield, at best, something like the texture of a tree from a particular distance. Looking more carefully at the picture yields more detail about the paint and the canvas, not about the tree. Looking closely at something in the environment yields new nested structure (e.g., the texture of individual pieces of bark) and is one of Gibson's criteria for perceptually distinguishing real things from others, such as pictures. Instruments (telescopes, microscopes) yield information about the environment but in a way that is disconnected from the perception of self in the ambient array. Symbols, of course, raise the problems of codes and such. Apprehension based on symbols is the extreme case of indirect perceiving. It is quite remote from direct perception within Gibson's taxonomy.

To recapitulate, Gibson's theory of information pickup clearly groups problems together in new ways. It is much more important to think about what cases belong to common groupings (and why) than it is to name the groupings (cognition, perception, memory, etc.). By taking the apprehension of environmental surfaces as the fundamental problem, Gibson showed that traditional topics reappeared (or disappeared) in a new light. It is a rich framework for research—a beginning, not an ending.

These are considerations for how one might pursue cognition from an ecological grounding. They call for filling out and testing.

REFERENCES

Barker, R. G. (1965). Explorations in ecological psychology. *American Psychologist, 20,* 1–14.
Bronfenbrenner, U. (1979). *The ecology of human development: Experiments by nature and design.* Cambridge, MA: Harvard University Press.
Brunswik, E. (1943). Organismic achievement and environmental probability. *Psychological Review, 50,* 255–272.
Brunswik, E. (1956). *Perception and the representative design of psychological experiments* (2nd ed.). Berkeley: University of California Press.
Dolezal, H. (1982). *Living in a world transformed.* New York: Academic Press.
Dretske, F. I. (1981). *Knowledge and the flow of information.* Cambridge, MA: MIT Press/Bradford Books.
Fodor, J. A., & Pylyshyn, Z. W. (1981). How direct is visual perception?: Some reflections on Gibson's "Ecological Approach." *Cognition, 9,* 139–196.
Gibson, E. J., & Spelke, E. S. (1983). The development of perception. In P. Mussen (Ed.), *Handbook of child psychology: Vol. III Cognitive development.* In J. H. Flavell & E. M. Markman (Eds.), New York: Wiley.

Gibson, J. J. (1950). *The perception of the visual world.* Boston: Houghton–Mifflin.

Gibson, J. J. (1966). *The senses considered as perceptual systems.* Boston: Houghton–Mifflin.

Gibson, J. J. (October, 1974). *A note on the relation between perceptual and conceptual knowledge.* Unpublished manuscript, Cornell University.

Gibson, J. J. (1979). *The ecological approach to visual perception.* Boston: Houghton–Mifflin.

Gibson, J. J. (1982a). Perception and judgment of aerial space and distance as potential factors in pilot selection and training. In E. Reed & R. Jones (Eds.), *Reasons for realism. Selected essays of James J. Gibson.* Hillsdale NJ: Lawrence Erlbaum Associates. (Reprinted from J. J. Gibson. *Motion picture testing and research.* Aviation Psychology Research Reports, No. 7. Washington, DC: U.S. Government Printing Office, 1947.)

Gibson, J. J. (1982b). The concept of the stimulus in psychology. In E. Reed & R. Jones (Eds.), *Reasons for realism. Selected essays of James J. Gibson.* Hillsdale NJ: Lawrence Erlbaum Associates. (Reprinted from *American Psychologist,* 1960, *15,* 694–703.)

Gibson, J. J. (1982c). Ecological optics. In E. Reed & R. Jones (Eds.), *Reasons for realism. Selected essays of James J. Gibson.* Hillsdale NJ: Lawrence Erlbaum Associates. (Reprinted from *Vision Research,* 1961, *1,* 253–262.)

Gibson, J. J. (1982d). What is involved in surface perception? In J. Beck (Ed.), *Organization and representation in perception.* Hillsdale, NJ: Lawrence Erlbaum Associates.

Gibson, J. J. (1982e). A history of the ideas behind ecological optics: Introductory remarks at the workshop on ecological optics. In E. Reed & R. Jones (Eds.), *Reasons for realism. Selected essays of James J. Gibson.* Hillsdale NJ: Lawrence Erlbaum Associates.

Gibson, J. J., & Crooks, L. E. (1982). A theoretical field-analysis of automobile-driving. In E. Reed & R. Jones (Eds.), *Reasons for realism. Selected essays of James J. Gibson.* Hillsdale NJ: Lawrence Erlbaum Associates. (Reprinted from *American Journal of Psychology,* 1938, *51,* 453–471.)

Gibson, J. J., Kaplan, G., Reynolds, H., & Wheeler, K. (1969). The change from visible to invisible: A study of optical transitions. *Perception & Psychophysics, 5,* 113–116.

Gibson, J. J., Olum, P., & Rosenblatt, F. (1955). Parallax and perspective during aircraft landings. *American Journal of Psychology, 68,* 372–385.

Hochberg, J. (1982). How big is a stimulus? In J. Beck (Ed.), *Organization and representation in perception.* Hillsdale, NJ: Lawrence Erlbaum Associates.

Kaplan, G. (1969). Kinetic disruption of optical texture: The perception of depth at an edge. *Perception & Psychophysics, 6,* 193–198.

Koenderink, J. J. (1984). The internal representation of solid shape and visual exploration. In L. Spillman & B. R. Wooten (Eds.), *Sensory experience, adaptation, and perception.* Hillsdale, NJ: Lawrence Erlbaum Associates.

Lewin, K. (1943). Defining the 'field at a given time.' *Psychological Review, 50,* 292–309.

Mace, W. M., & Turvey, M. T. (1983). The implications of occlusion for perceiving persistence. *The Behavioral and Brain Sciences, 6,* 29–31.

Marr, D. (1982). *Vision.* San Francisco: W. H. Freeman.

Neisser, U. (1976). *Cognition and reality.* San Francisco: W. H. Freeman.

Neisser, U. (1984). *Toward an ecologically oriented cognitive science* (Emory Cognition Project (Report #1). Atlanta, Georgia: Emory University, Dept. of Psychology.

Pattee, H. H. (1982). Cell psychology. *Cognition and Brain Theory, 5,* 325–341.

Rock, I. (1983). *The logic of perception.* Cambridge, MA: MIT Press/Bradford Books.

Runeson, S., & Bingham, G. (1983). *Sight and insights: Contributions to the study of cognition from an ecological perspective on perception* (Uppsala Psychological Reports, No. 364). Uppsala, Sweden: University of Uppsala, Dept. of Psychology.

Schiff, W. (1965). Perception of impending collision. *Psychological monographs, 79,* No. 604.

Shaw, R. E., McIntyre, M., & Mace, W. M. (1974). The role of symmetry in event perception. In R. B. MacLeod & H. L. Pick, Jr. (Eds.), *Perception: Essays in honor of James J. Gibson.* Ithaca, NY: Cornell University Press.

Shaw, R. E., & Pittenger, J. B. (1978). Perceiving change. In H. L. Pick, Jr. & E. Saltzman (Eds.), *Modes of perceiving and processing information*. Hillsdale, NJ: Lawrence Erlbaum Associates.

Shaw, R. E., & Turvey, M. T. (1981). Coalitions as models of ecosystems. In M. Kubovy & J. Pomerantz (Eds.), *Perceptual organization*. Hillsdale, NJ: Lawrence Erlbaum Associates.

Shepard, R. (1984). Ecological constraints on internal representation: Resonant kinematics of perceiving, imagining, thinking, and dreaming. *Psychological Review, 91*, 1–47.

Turvey, M. T., & Carello, C. (1981). Cognition: The view from ecological realism. *Cognition, 10*, 313–321.

Turvey, M. T., Shaw, R. E., Reed, E. S., & Mace, W. M. (1981). Ecological laws of perceiving and acting: In reply to Fodor & Pylyshyn (1981). *Cognition, 9*, 237–304.

Ullman, S. (1980). Against direct perception. *The Behavioral and Brain Sciences, 3*, 373–415.

Warren, W. H., Jr. (1984). Perceiving affordances: Visual guidance of stair climbing. *Journal of Experimental Psychology: Human Perception and Performance, 10*, 683–703.

8

From Gestalt to Neo-Gestalt

Lynn C. Robertson
University of California, School of Medicine, Davis
and
Veterans Administration Medical Center, Martinez

The emergence of Gestalt psychology is richly documented (e.g., Boring, 1950; Henle, 1980; Hochberg, 1979; Wertheimer, 1974). Its refutations of atomism, associationism, and structuralism are well known, and its impact on psychology would be difficult to deny. Yet, Gestalt psychology never reached the pinnacle of popularity in America enjoyed by behaviorism, nor was it subsumed intact into modern cognitive psychology when the latter began to surface in the late 1950s. Wolfgang Köhler (1959), one of the founders of Gestalt psychology, felt rather strongly that Gestalt theory had been neglected—neither disproved nor transformed in any meaningful way. In direct contrast, Helson (1969) (a supporter of the Gestalt school) suggested that Gestalt psychology succeeded because it influenced the field of psychology more than any other theoretical outlook either prior to or contemporaneous with it. In 1964 Hilgard suggested that Gestalt psychology had been so thoroughly integrated into modern psychology that it was no longer recognizable as something that could be contrasted with other positions. Even prior to Köhler's proclaimed defeat, Boring (1950) felt that it had "died of its own success."

If Gestalt psychology was integrated into mainstream psychology by the 1960s, it is puzzling that we are now seeing references to "neo-Gestalt" or "Gestalt-like" or "Gestalt-oriented" approaches (e.g., Beck, 1982; Kahneman & Henik, 1981; Perkins, 1982; Restle, 1982). It appears that a contrast is again believed to exist—that there is indeed something special about Gestalt psychology that is not reflected in recent theories of cognition.

What is this "neo-Gestalt"? What sorts of contemporary research activities fit into this category? How do theories that arise from this activity compare with Gestalt psychology as it was originally proposed? In order to address these

159

issues, I outline the ideas of the Gestalt psychologists and then discuss the relationship of the Gestalt position to some contemporary theories and models of cognition.

I separately discuss some exemplary phenomena, the principles that Gestalt psychologists felt governed these phenomena, their theoretical notions of representation, and their endorsement of the phenomenological method as acceptable scientific practice. These categories (phenomena, principles, theory, and methodology) were interconnected in Gestalt psychology. They formed a unified whole that Gestalt psychologists directed at all psychological issues. However, in contrast to its own thesis, Gestalt psychology has been fractured and applied piecemeal in contemporary accounts. Certain categories have been well integrated into some theories, whereas other categories have had substantial influence on other theories, but little of Gestalt psychology survives as a package, at least in theories that currently dominate the field. Although there is a small but thriving group of Gestalt psychologists in Europe, I restrict my discussion of current theories to those that are prominent in mainstream cognitive psychology and are well represented in English and American journals. There is no attempt to be exhaustive. Rather, some specific examples are discussed as indicative of a modern "Gestalt-like" approach.

PHENOMENA

Gestalt psychology gave us literally hundreds of examples of perceptual phenomena. The original observations that motivated the movement actually came from a member of the Graz School in Vienna. Christian von Ehrenfels noted that a melody is recognized independent of the key in which it is played and suggested that there was a "form-quality" or "Gestalt" that was added to the elemental sensations.

Max Wertheimer was impressed with Ehrenfels demonstrations but did not believe that Gestalt was an extra element. Instead he argued that the "Gestalt" was the fundamental unit itself and pointed out that this notion went beyond the realms of psychology. In physics there were organized fields that produced whole units, and these could be found in the physiology of the brain and in conscious experience.

Wertheimer began his study of Gestalts by investigating apparent movement, which he termed the *phi* phenomenon (Wertheimer, 1912/1961). When two lights alternate in blinking on and off at a certain rate calculated as a function of the distance between the two lights, the perceiver does not see two lights blinking as would be expected by an account in terms of elemental sensations. Rather a single light appears to move from one position to the other. The perceptual system structures the whole event as something other than what is physically presented: The individual flashes of light are organized in a way that gives rise to perceived motion, a property not actually present in the display at all.

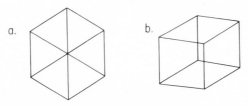

FIG. 8.1.   (a) appears 2-dimensional, whereas (b) appears 3-dimensional.

Gestalt structuring is not unique to events that happen over time. An align-ment of dots on a page is perceived as a line although no line actually exists. Perception "fills in" the empty spaces, as if the dots were connected. Perception can also add a dimension where none is present in the stimulus. Although we are likely to perceive a two-dimensional pattern when we look at Fig. 8.1a, the pattern in Fig. 8.1b appears three dimensional. Furthermore, the panel that defines the "front" of the cube of Fig. 8.1b can change as we stare at the pattern. This occurs despite the fact that the stimulus remains constant. Again, the perceptual system structures the stimulus as something other than what is physically given.

There are many such examples that cut across modalities and are relevant to other activities besides perception. The demonstrations are too numerous to list here, and I have given just a sample of the types of phenomena that support the Gestalt contention that perception was different from the simple summing of elemental sensations. The reader is referred to Koffka (1935) and Goldmeier (1982) for many other examples of perceptual and memory phenomena, to Duncker (1945), Wertheimer (1945/1982), and Köhler (1925) for examples in problem solving, and to Johannson (1950) for many more examples of perceived motion.

PRINCIPLES

Gestalt psychologists (like Köhler, 1969) emphasized perception because they felt it was the "most readily available subject matter" (p 33). Although they studied "higher order" cognition as well, they believed that the principles that applied to perception were the same principles that would apply to any other cognitive system; that is, representations of objects, events, or problems were organized such that they followed a certain set of rules. These rules, laws, or principles were thought to be relevant to everything from brains to social systems.

The principles of organization are often discussed as innate mechanisms of perception. This is due to the Gestalt psychologists' vigorous attacks on theories formulated by atomistic psychology in Germany and later by Behaviorists in the United States. Gestalt psychology was stamped as nativistic and continues to be so categorized by many secondary accounts (Boring, 1950; Gregory, 1970;

Hochberg, 1979). However, principles are neither learned nor genetically given. Rather, that which is given and that which is learned allow certain principles to become evident. As Köhler (1950/1961) explains: "It is . . . a mistake if all unlearned functions are attributed to achievements of evolution. For, quite apart from such achievements, unlearned functions are bound to exhibit certain characteristics which they share with actions in the inanimate world" (p 72). Because this is so often misconceived and Gestalt psychology is so often claimed to have held that all principles of perception were innate, a brief clarification is in order before discussing principles per se.

In the biological sciences, when one lists the principles that govern evolution, there is no confusion between these principles and the process of evolution itself. Principles of how evolution occurs are not passed via DNA from one member of a species to the next, nor do they develop as species develop. Rather, the way in which species arise and the way in which genes are passed follow certain principles. These principles hold whether we are speaking of earlier or later times in the course of evolution, and they apply whether earlier species are amoebas or seaweed. The principles of evolution tell us whether seaweed or amoebas are more likely to develop into bears or roses. By charting the course of this development, the laws become evident. Likewise, the laws of learning can tell us whether an organism is more likely to act in one way or another, and the laws of organization can tell us whether a group of sensations is more likely to be perceived as a unit or as separate parts. The principles are not innate, and they are not learned. According to Köhler (1969):

> If for one reason or another, the concentration of a certain chemical differs from one part of the tissue fluid to surrounding parts, diffusion will at once begin to equalize the concentration. This is dynamics; under comparable conditions the same process would occur everywhere in inanimate nature. What have the genes to do with this? And what inheritance? (p 88)

The argument has been made that it is not the principles per se but the mechanisms responsible for the discovery of the principles that are at issue. Gestalt psychologists felt it was the other way around—that the principles of dynamics were responsible for the way in which mechanisms could act. Köhler (1969) states:

> Obviously, such concepts as genes, inherited, and innate should never be mentioned when we refer to the basic, purely dynamic phase of processes in nervous systems. For, if we use these concepts . . . we implicitly violate the main premise of evolutionary theory, namely, that evolution, genes, inheritance, and so on never really change dynamics as such. By the mere juxtaposition of the terms "learned" and "inherited" as though the words indicated an "either-or" alternative, we commit the same mistake. (p 89)

The acts that the mechanisms performed were governed by forces that were neither learned nor innate.

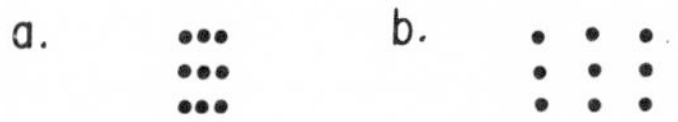

a.   •••   b.   • • •
          •••   • • •
          •••   • • •

FIG. 8.2. (a) is perceptually grouped as 3 horizontal lines, whereas (b) is grouped as 3 vertical lines due to the Factor of Proximity (adapted from Wertheimer, 1923/1938).

Laws of Organization

The original list of the laws of organization as they were presented by Wertheimer (1923/1938b) included the following "factors." By reviewing this list we can see the types of concerns that motivated the movement in the first place.

1. Factor of Proximity. The relative distance between objects will determine their grouping into subunits. For instance, the pattern in Fig. 8.2a is perceived as three horizontal lines, and the one in Fig. 8.2b is perceived as three vertical lines.

2. Factor of Similarity. Objects similar to one another tend to be grouped together. Similarity, in fact, could overrule the law of proximity. For instance, in Fig. 8.3a the natural grouping is by proximity, and we see groups of two dots *ab/cd/ef/gh*, whereas in Fig. 8.3b the law of similarity is a stronger organizing principle, and we see *a/bc/de/fg/h*.

3. Factor of Uniform Destiny or "Common Fate." Objects that covary in space over time will be grouped together. If *a, c,* and *e* of Fig. 8.4a were all shifted upward and then downward in certain time intervals, *ace* and *bdf* would exhibit uniform destiny by the covariation and due to the motion the organization of the field would become *ace/bdf,* again overruling the law of proximity.

4. Factor of Objective Set. Objects that are "a part in a sequence" will be grouped together. Fig. 8.4a looks like six dots equally spaced, but if preceded by Fig. 8.4b and then by Fig. 8.4c, it is more likely to appear as three groups of two dots.

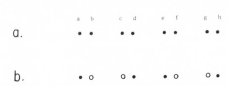

FIG. 8.3. (a) is grouped by proximity, whereas (b) is grouped by similarity due to the Factor of Similarity (adapted from Wertheimer, 1923/1938).

FIG. 8.4.   (a) is perceived as 6 equally spaced dots but as 3 sets of 2 dots when preceded in time by (b) and (c) due to the Factor of Objective Set (adapted from Wertheimer, 1923/1938).

5. Factor of Direction.   Parts that are "good continuations" of other parts will be grouped together. In Fig. 8.5, line segment *a, c* appears grouped, whereas *b* is a separate subunit despite the fact that *b* is closer to *c* than is *a*. This occurs because *a* to *c* has the same direction.

6. Factor of Closure.   Parts that enclose a region will tend to be grouped together. Figure 8.6a appears as a circle next to a diamond, rather than as one unit alone or as some differently parsed configuration such as shown in Fig. 8.6b.

7. Factor of "Good Curve."   The factor of closure may be overcome by good continuation of a curve. Despite the fact that *a, b,* and *c* in Fig. 8.7 are closed figures they are not seen as separate. Rather, the figure is seen as a smooth curve cutting through a square wave pattern.

8. Factor of Experience or Habit.   Parts that have become associated through drill or habit may become more distinct and less likely to be grouped according to the preceding principles. Unlike the other factors, Wertheimer did not italicize or capitalize this factor, perhaps to emphasize its subservient position in his list of organizing principles. He felt that this factor was only operative when organization was not due to any other factor.

To this list we can add the Law of Prägnanz and the Law of Configuration. The Law of Prägnanz was introduced as a guiding principle or heuristic. Simply stated (Koffka, 1935) it meant that "psychological organization will always be as 'good' as the prevailing conditions allow" (p. 110). The Law of Configura-

FIG. 8.5.   Despite the fact that *b* is closer to *c*, *a* and *c* are perceptually grouped together due to the Factor of Direction (adapted from Wertheimer, 1923/1938).

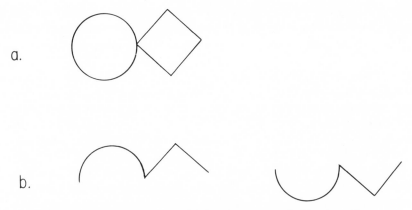

FIG. 8.6. The figure appears as a circle next to a square in (a) not as a figure parsed horizontally as in (b) (adapted from Wertheimer, 1923/1938).

tion was that the whole was *different* from the sum of its parts. Goodness and the Law of Prägnanz remained undefined but included properties such as regularity, simplicity, and symmetry. Koffka, and more recently Attneave (1982), likened this principle to the formation of a soap bubble. The forces both inside and outside the bubble will equalize the film of the soap to a form that will have maximum volume for the minimum surface. Its simplest form given the forces in empty space is a sphere. The bubble can be pushed and pulled by the introduction of a different force (e.g., wind or contact with an object), but the new form will still be in balance given the various forces operating upon it. The best form given the constraints will arise. The Law of Prägnanz is complementary to the Law of Configuration. A sphere, for instance, is not perceived as a set of local arcs but as a whole, symmetrical surface about an infinite number of axes that run through its center.

Current Theories and the Law of Prägnanz

Contemporary theories of perception have directed a great deal of attention to defining figural "goodness" (or "good Gestalt") and, although agreeing with Koffka that properties such as symmetry and regularity are inherent in a "good"

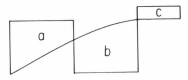

FIG. 8.7. Sections *a, b,* and *c* do not appear as individual units despite their closure due to the Factor of Good Curve (adapted from Wertheimer, 1923/1938).

form, have tried to go beyond Koffka in articulating precisely what defines it. One of the most influential theories of goodness has been proposed by Garner (1974). He analyzed pattern goodness from an information theoretic viewpoint by pointing out that the alternative forms that a pattern could be, but was not, were as important as what the pattern was. The set of alternatives was defined with respect to a set of specified transformations. The number of different patterns generated by applying a set of rotations and reflections (i.e., the degree to which this set of alternatives was redundant) defined a measure, called "rotation and reflection" (R & R) subset size, which was inversely related to how "good" a pattern was. If all the transformations of a pattern resulted in the same form, the resulting R & R subset size would be one, corresponding to a very "good" pattern. If all the transformed patterns were different, the resulting R & R subset size would be large, corresponding to poor patterns. In fact, figures with a small R & R subset size are judged as "better" and are more easily learned, recognized, recalled, sorted, and discriminated than figures with a large R & R subset size. Within this conceptualization, actual mental processes of rotations and reflections need not take place. Rather the transformations represent the number of possible forms in a set, which in turn defines goodness.

In a similar vein, but from a somewhat different perspective, Palmer has suggested that better forms are more symmetrical under a set of transformations (Palmer, 1982, 1983). Rather than emphasizing the number of different figures produced by rotations and reflections, Palmer focuses on the set of transformations over which the whole figure (or local parts of it) is "symmetrical" in the mathematical sense of being invariant (unchanged) after a transformation. Thus, the degree of both overall and subregional symmetry predicts the pattern's "goodness." In Palmer's approach symmetry is not restricted to the bilateral symmetry that Gestalt psychologists emphasized. Rather, it includes other types of symmetries by adopting the mathematical formulation of symmetry in terms of group theory (see Rosen, 1983; Weyl, 1952). In this context symmetry for a given figure includes any spatial transformation that maps the pattern onto itself, including rotations through an angle about a central point, reflections about an axis, translations through a directed distance, and dilations (expansions or contractions) about a point by a scalar. Within Palmer's model, then, goodness is defined by the subset of symmetries, both more global and more local, for a given figure relative to the set of all possible symmetries. A circle, for instance is a better figure than a square because a circle maps onto itself bilaterally about an infinite number of central axes. Another example is that a series of circles as in Fig. 8.8a is a better and more unified figure than the series in Fig. 8.8b because the translational symmetries are not as great. Figure 8.8c is not as good a figure as 8.8a or 8.8b., because the global and local symmetries in a and c are not aligned.

Other perceptual theories such as *coding theory*—later called *structural information theory* (Leeuwenberg, 1971, 1982a; Restle, 1979, 1982) do not rely as

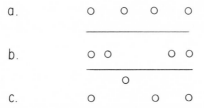

FIG. 8.8.   The patterns in (a), (b), and (c) are perceived differentially due to different symmetry relations between the elements and overall form.

heavily on such properties as symmetry but rather emphasize the role of redundancy (symmetry being a subset of redundancy). In this respect coding theory is like information theory, which had previously been used by Hochberg and Brooks (1960), Hochberg and McAlister (1953), and by Attneave (1954) to describe the conditions under which two-dimensional patterns would appear three dimensional. In coding theory the description (or code) assigned to a pattern by a perceiver will be in the simplest possible terms as determined by a set of rules for simplifying pattern descriptions. The code for a pattern is represented symbolically by a sequence of directional changes, and redundancies in such codes are removed by applying the rules to reduce the number of symbols in the code. The simpler the code in terms of the number of symbols it contains, the better the pattern will be. A square, for instance, is a better figure than a rectangle because it has fewer symbols in its reduced code. The primitive code for each is equal in number of symbols. For example, a rectangle could have a primitive code of s_v, a, s_h, a, s, a, s_h, a where s_v = vertical side, a = angle, and s_h = horizontal side, and a square could be coded s, a, s, a, s, a, s, a where s = side and a = angle. The code for rectangle can be reduced to two symbols $[s_v a]$ $[s_h a]$, whereas, the square can be reduced to one symbol $[sa]$. In any given figure there are multiple possible codes, but the one that has the fewest parameters will be the better description.

   Coding theory has been applied in various domains including brightness contrast (Leeuwenberg, 1982b), motion perception (Restle, 1979), figural completion of occluded forms (Buffart, Leeuwenberg, & Restle, 1981), gait perception (Cutting, 1981), and in somewhat altered form to pitch sequences (Deutsch & Feroe, 1981). In each of these studies subjects tended to perceive alternatives that could be most simply coded. Coding theory, then, has been quite successful at predicting the perceived organization of stimuli in a variety of domains. However, any coding theory (of which structural information theory is one) is critically dependent on the selection of primitives. For instance, if a square and a rectangle were each bisected horizontally and vertically and each of the resulting four regions were considered primitives, the reduced codes for the two figures would be equal. The goodness of squares and rectangles would be the same if one began with bisecting regions and different if one began with lines and angles.

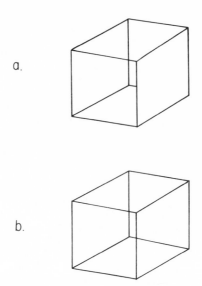

a.

b.

FIG. 8.9.   The pattern in (a) can reverse like the one in (b), although (b) is a "better" figure (adapted from Peterson & Hochberg, 1983).

As Cutting and Proffitt (1982) also point out, the selected coding scheme over all alternative coding schemes is of critical importance.

Garner's, Palmer's, and Leeuwenberg's models are examples of Gestalt-like approaches to pattern perception. The Law of Prägnanz is not accepted as it was originally proposed, yet the contemporary approaches are of the same general sort. They hold that a pattern will be perceived in its simplest form or the simplest code will be selected given the prevailing constraints, and they suggest a metric for defining simplicity. Garner has done this with reference to the rated goodness of a figure, and Palmer and Leeuwenberg have done so with respect to the manner in which a pattern will be perceived, either in terms of symmetries and orientation or in terms of form.

Lest it be thought that the only hurdle to a modern day Law of Prägnanz is determining the metric, I should mention that certain compelling perceptual findings are difficult to interpret within any model that suggests a system operating under a minimum principle. For instance, an altered Necker cube (see Fig. 8.9a) is seen to reverse in the same way as a regular Necker cube (see Fig. 8.9b) despite the fact that one interpretation of the altered cube of Fig. 8.9a is not nearly as "good" as the alternative (Peterson & Hochberg, 1983). The pattern in Fig. 8.9a should not be reversible, and yet it is. This effect is difficult to explain if the perceptual system seeks a minimum. A post hoc explanation offered by Pomerantz and Kubovy (1981) and by Goldmeier (personal communication) is that, when Fig. 8.9a is perceived as facing upward and toward the viewer, it is not an impossible figure at all but one of several possible views of a wire cube with one incomplete wire. Thus, the cube in 8.9a will more often or more easily be seen pointing downward and toward the viewer but will periodically change to point upward (which is what Peterson and Hochberg found), because that particular configuration, although not as "good" of a figure, is possible.

Current Theories and the Law of Configuration

That the whole is different from the sum of its parts is almost certainly the hallmark of Gestalt psychology. In fact, Hochberg (1981) claims that if the whole is not different than the sum of its parts, then there is no Gestalt psychology. This overstates the issue because Gestalt psychologists granted that there were conditions under which part information would be perceived piecemeal, but that many, if not most, "parts" would be perceived in the context of an overall pattern (Koffka, 1935). Wertheimer distinguished these two types of phenomena by using the terms aggregates and wholes (1922/1938a). Hochberg's statement, however, does demonstrate the extent to which this law represents the Gestalt position, and it is true that the emphasis on wholism (or holism) was historically a good way to refute atomistic theories prevailing in early decades of this century both here and in Germany. The law led to other developments such as field theory and the doctrine of isomorphism, and for this reason, I spend some time discussing it.

Under the influence of the information-processing approach to cognition, the Law of Configuration has been recast as the "whole is prior to" the parts (Neisser, 1967). Although the Gestalt psychologists did use such terms as *before* or *prior to,* this did not refer to serial processing of information at different stages. Rather, the experienced whole could transform a perceived part even if the part was processed first. The whole was "prior to" the part as it would finally be perceived. For instance, the perception of a note can be changed by the note (or notes) following it. This clearly does not mean that the second note must be heard before the first one. Rather, the second note changes the perceived *quality* of the first note.

However, even when "the whole is prior to the part" is interpreted in information-processing terms, there is some evidence supporting the claim. The strongest contemporary evidence in visual processing was presented by Navon (1977). He found that letters at a more "global" level of a hierarchically constructed pattern (Fig. 8.10) were responded to faster and detected earlier than letters at a more "local" level. (In Fig. 8.10 the large F constitutes the global level, whereas the small Rs constitute the local level). Furthermore, global information interfered with recognition of local letters, but local information did not affect recognition of global letters. Both Navon (1977) and Broadbent (1977) interpreted these findings as suggesting that preattentive processes operated first on the global form, and focal attention occurred thereafter. Although the stage in which global precedence occurs has been questioned (Miller, 1981; Robertson &

R   R   R   R

R

R   R   R

R

R

FIG. 8.10.   A hierarchically constructed figure with a global ("F") and local ("R"s) level (adapted from Robertson & Palmer, 1983).

Palmer, 1983), the finding that the global level is responded to sooner than the local level is highly replicable within given constraints and is difficult to explain within atomistic approaches.

Global precedence is not a matter of the absolute size of the letters at each level. Navon found that response times were equal when responding to single letters in isolation that were either the size of the local or the global form. There is something disturbing, however, about the idea that size does not matter. Surely, in a pattern modeled after Fig. 8.10, a global F subtending an area larger than the retina would not slow response times to a local R that was within retinal viewing. Such a large form would necessarily take several glances to recognize and should not, therefore, interfere with processing the local letter. In fact, when the visual angle of a pattern such as in Fig. 8.10 is varied in such a way that both levels are increased in size together, reaction time to the local level becomes faster than to the global level when the entire pattern subtends more than about seven degrees of visual angle (Kinchla & Wolfe, 1979).

Results such as these point to an inherent difficulty for Gestalt psychology and for Gestalt-like approaches. Parts and wholes are relative. Cognition does not operate at the most wholistic level every time a person must make a decision. The problem then is to define the highest or lowest level at which perception (or any other cognitive process) will operate in any given situation. At which level does the perceptual system begin to form units? Hochberg (1982) formulates this as the problem of grain and argues that if the grain or resolution of a percept cannot be identified a priori, then there is little recourse but to assume that perception proceeds from objectively definable smaller units to build larger units. It is unclear, however, how small these units should be. Is the smallest unit as large as a dot made by a pencil or as large as one made by a felt marker? Should the unit be a feature (Gibson, 1967; Treisman & Gelade, 1980)? Atomism appears to "solve" the problem of grain by arbitrarily defining grain as that which is phenomenally realized to be either something like the smallest point or the simplest feature. Thus, the phenomenally given grain (whether fine or coarse) is no more arbitrary than so-called more "objective" measures of grain.

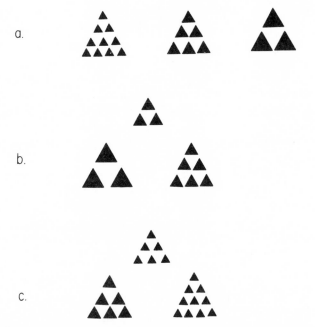

FIG. 8.11. Figures with many elements appear more texture like than figures with fewer elements (a). The proportional enlargement is judged more similar to the standard in (b), whereas the unproportional enlargement is judged more similar to the standard in (c) (adapted from Kimchi & Palmer, 1982).

Even if we could agree on a grain size to study perception, we could not confine it to an absolute quantity. There are certain stimulus sizes at which perception changes qualitatively, and these are defined relatively. In several elegant experiments using hierarchically constructed patterns (see Fig. 8.11), Goldmeier (1936/1972) and later Kimchi and Palmer (1982) found that as the size of elements increased and their number decreased (Fig. 8.11a), they appeared more and more form like, and as their size decreased and their number increased they appeared more and more texture like. Furthermore, the proportional enlargement of a pattern (Fig. 8.11b lower left pattern) was judged more like a standard (upper figure in Fig. 8.11b) even though the grain of the standard and the lower right pattern were objectively the same, whereas in Fig. 8.11c the proportional enlargement was rejected, and the lower right pattern was judged more like the standard. In Fig. 8.11b the elements were perceived as forms within the larger form, whereas in Fig. 8.11c they were perceived as texture.

These findings suggest that perceptual grain is a relative value that depends on many properties of the stimulus field. In a pattern with few, relatively large elements, structures at both global and local levels may be seen as forms, whereas in patterns with many, relatively small elements, structures at the local level will be perceived as texture, and those at the global level will be perceived as form. Perceptual grain can be empirically defined and can change with changes in the *relationship* between different levels of stimulus structure. The properties of the overall form can change the *quality* of the perceived elements.

In this section so far I have examined some contemporary attempts to articulate the Law of Prägnanz (or good form) and have discussed some evidence that bears on the Law of Configuration. The discussion is by no means exhaustive but does include some current accounts of perception that are indicative of a Gestalt-like approach to perceptual organization. These approaches are Gestalt like as they relate to phenomena and principles. They accept the phenomena as important clues about perceptual organization that warrant explanation and further investigation, and they go beyond Gestalt psychology in formulations of a Law of Prägnanz and a Law of Configuration. None of the models discussed in this section incorporate the more theoretical notions of Gestalt psychology such as field theory, and psychophysiological isomorphism, nor are they derived mainly from phenomenological methods (all of which are discussed in later sections). To this extent they are only partly Gestalt in nature.

Current Theories and Laws of Grouping

We should not leave this section on principles without examining the continued interest in phenomenal grouping and its relationship to cognitive functioning. Perhaps the best representative of a Gestalt-like approach to Gestalt phenomena may be found here. This area is best exemplified in the work of Pomerantz and colleagues (see Pomerantz, 1981, for a review) and by Banks and Prinzmetal (Banks, Larson, & Prinzmetal, 1979; Banks & Prinzmetal, 1976; Prinzmetal, 1981, Prinzmetal & Banks, 1977) in visual perception.

Banks and Prinzmetal supported the importance of Gestalt laws of grouping by showing that the addition of elements in a pattern could actually improve detection of a target. When subjects were told to detect a target such as "T" among a set of like structures, they were faster at responding that the target was present when it was in a group such as in Fig. 8.12a than in Fig. 8.12b. This occurred despite the fact that there were more "distractor" elements in 8.12a than in 8.12b. The distractor elements were evidently perceived as more strongly grouped in Fig. 8.12a than in Fig. 8.12b, and the target was phenomenally more isolated and easier to detect.

These findings are difficult to explain within feature detection models. Figure 8.12a clearly has more features, yet the target is detected more rapidly than in Fig. 8.12b where there are fewer features. Pomerantz (1981) cited this work—the findings of which are consistent with several of his own studies on unit formation—to support the notion that perception at a global level begins with analysis of "emergent features." Emergent features are features that do not exist in the individual parts and are only reflected in the wholes. For instance, a line or angle in Fig. 8.1a does not have closure, but the figure as a whole does. (For a

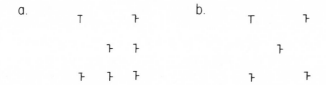

FIG. 8.12.   Responses to a target ("T") are faster in (a) than in (b) (adapted from Banks & Prinzmetal, 1976).

more thorough discussion, see Palmer, this volume). In Pomerantz's model emergent features are not something that result from local processes, although analyses at more local levels may in fact be happening. Rather they are the givens for a higher level of analysis occurring on the configuration as a whole. In this sense, Pomerantz captures the basic spirit of Gestalt psychology by examining the principles that govern grouping and suggesting that the global percept can be directly given without referencing piecemeal operations that still may be going on in parallel. Adding a part to a stimulus can produce a situation in which new processes are used, ones that are different from those that may be operating on the local elements.

THEORY

The overriding dictum of Gestalt psychology was that organization did not arise from the simple association of parts. Rather the parts were organized as a result of their functional role within a whole. The parts could be local elements or the *relationship* between local elements. Both elements and their relations were perceived as they functioned within the whole. This was made most clear by Wertheimer in a statement about the limitations of von Ehrenfel's notions. Recall that von Ehrenfel believed that the Gestalt was something in addition to the parts. A series of say six tones included the six tones plus a seventh element—the melody. Wertheimer (1925/1938c) remarked:

> But other explanations were also proposed. One maintained that in addition to the six tones there were intervals—relations—and that these were what remained constant. In other words, we are asked to assume not only elements but relations between elements as additional components of the total complex. But this view failed to account for the phenomenon because in some cases the relations *too* may be altered without destroying the original melody. (p 4)

The strength of the whole would change the perception of parts to differing degrees. Strong or "good" wholes affected the perceived parts more than weak wholes. This premise required more than a demonstration of phenomena and a list of principles. If Gestalt psychology was to be taken seriously, it needed a formulation of how units of analysis that contained parts could be organized without first analyzing those parts. Köhler borrowed liberally from field theory in physics in his proposal that the electrical potentials in the brain functioned to produce an electromagnetic field. The relative intensity of current in different areas of the field and the resistance of cortical tissue governed the degree to which sensations would be perceived as a unit or segregated into subunits. This neurological theory predicted certain functional relationships between different parts of the brain and also between sensory and cortical representations. The sensory mosaic was represented by projections to the cortex that resulted in an electrical field. The forces within this field were "functionally related to the stimulus as perceived." There was assumed to be an isomorphism between *experienced* perceptions and brain processes (Köhler, 1938/1966, 1940).

In Gestalt psychology the doctrine of isomorphism was developed in conjunction with the theory of brain fields. For Gestalt psychologists fields were the organizing structures at all levels of description. Experienced units were organized as they were because forces repelled certain regions and attracted other regions. The brain worked at both molar and molecular levels, but it was the molar level that was represented by the electrical brain fields. There was in Gestalt theory an isomorphism between patterns *as experienced* and their representation in "brain fields" that need not be isomorphic with the external environment. Units experienced as distinct would be relatively isolated at the physiological level, and units that were experienced as proximate would be proximate at the physiological level. As Köhler (1947) noted: "The principle of isomorphism demands that in a given case the organization of experience and the underlying physiological facts have the same structure" (p 301).

Köhler's premature jump to brain fields damaged the Gestalt movement severely. It was inconsistent with certain neurophysiological findings. Most significantly, Lashley, Chow, and Semmes (1951) found that insulating a part of the cortex, which would change the electrical field, did not radically alter perceptual organization in monkeys as Köhler's theory predicted it would. Although the theoretical notion of field theory to account for the perception of wholes disintegrated, this apparently occurred, at least in part, because Köhler applied field theory to the nervous system. If he had used field theory to model organization at a more abstract cognitive level, he might have been much more successful. What he essentially proposed was that organization could be spatially represented with regions of various densities of interaction and that "forces" could change the configuration of the representation. In fact, in the area of social psychology, Lewin (1951) adapted field theory to an abstract model of social interaction and, as a result, was much more successful. Lewin's formalized theory led directly to Heider's influential attribution and balance theories (Heider, 1958). The flavor of Lewin's theory is, in fact, similar to some contemporary spatial representation models. For this reason it is worth briefly working through some of his formulations.

Lewin (1936, 1951) suggested that the way to understand wholes, subwholes, and distinct wholes, whether in a physical, psychological, or social system, was by a spatial representation of regions with distance dynamically changing as a result of tensions or "forces." The forces changed the length of a "path" in topological space between two points. Distance was measured as the number of intervening regions between two regions, which is different from Euclidean geometry where distance is measured by some metric. However, as the number of regions increases in topological space, the distances between points begin to approximate Euclidean distances. Thus, a space with many regions will be similar in topological and Euclidean space in terms of the relative distance between points.

Briefly, Lewin assumed that any given region in psychological space contains a certain degree of dependence on and independence of any other given region. Dependence was defined as the degree to which one region must change to produce a change in the other, and independence was the inverse of dependence. "Simple dependence" was based on proximity; that is, any region (x) is more dependent on its neighboring region (n) than on a distant region (y). Simply stated, an area in psychological space is more affected by a change in a neighboring region than by a change in a distant region. For instance, given a series x, n, y, if n were to split into two regions, the distance between x and y would increase (the "path" between the two would become longer). If y were split into two regions the distance between x and n for all intents and purposes would remain the same, but the relationship between x and y would be weakened. Actually, the split of y would slightly strengthen the relationship between x and n because the relative dependence between x, n and x, y would change. We can restate this relationship by saying that as the *density* of a region that incorporates x, n, and y changes, the relative dependence between regions will change. This becomes important later when we examine theories of similarity space to account for judgments of similarity. For the moment, the important point concerning Lewin's theory is that he used the concepts of field theory in an abstract spatial model to represent relationships between regions of a psychological field.

Current Representational Theories and Fields

There are numerous instances in contemporary theories that rely on the notion that knowledge can be represented spatially (e.g., Shepard, Kilpatrik, & Cunningham, 1975) with processes producing changes in the "distance" between two points (Goldmeier, 1982; Krumhansl, 1978, 1983a,b). For instance, we can represent psychological distance in a metric space such that the distance between exemplars of the category "bird"—say robin and penguin—is greater than the distance between say robin and sparrow (Shepard, 1958). If subjects are asked how similar each is to the other, a configuration such as in Fig. 8.13a may result. The adequacy of this type of spatial representation has been questioned, because,

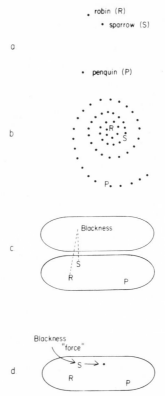

FIG. 8.13. Possible spatial representation of psychological distance between exemplars of the category "birds" (a) with density of points surrounding an exemplar represented in (b). The distance between exemplars may change with a qualification (blackness) in both a static (c) and dynamic (d) representation but in different ways.

for example, the similarity judgment of robin to penguin may be different from the judgment of penguin to robin, a finding that violates the symmetry axiom of geometrical distance metrics (Tversky, 1977). The spatial model, however, can survive this criticism if one considers other parameters. Krumhansl (1978) suggests that the density of points in an area may be one variable producing asymmetries. In categories, for instance, the number of birds similar to robins may be greater than those similar to penguins. The density of points in the region of "robin" would then be greater than those in the region of "penguin" as shown in Fig. 8.13b. If subjects calculated the sentence "a robin is similar to a penguin" (distance from robin to penguin) differently from "a penguin is similar to a robin" (distance from penguin to robin), they could do so by first referring to the source (the subject of the sentence) and then the destination (the object of the sentence). In each sentence the source and the destination would be in different density regions and could result in different similarity judgments. Just as in Lewin's theory the overall configuration of points can change the psychological distance between a source and its object as a function of the distribution of objects and the density of points (or regions).

Krumhansl has found that her model can account for similarity data quite well (Krumhansl, 1978, 1982). The difference between her model and a model based on field theory is that "density" in field theory is a dynamic property (changing with a force), whereas density in Krumhansl's model is a static parameter; that is, the points in Fig. 8.13b could move in Lewin's model, but in Krumhansl's model they would not.

More recently, Krumhansl (1983a) has developed a hierarchical system in which other parameters besides density and spatial distance may influence the "perceived" similarity between two points. For instance, if one were to qualify a bird by a color adjective and ask how similar a black sparrow is to a robin, one may find that black sparrows are less similar to robins than sparrows in general. How might one account for this finding? Either a point in the structure representing "black sparrow" must already exist, or blackness is an independent parameter that either moves the point "sparrow" a certain distance or creates a longer path in some other way. Krumhansl's more recent model suggests that a longer path is created by imposing a second spatial manifold that would, in the example, represent "blackness." The representation of birds in Fig. 8.13c is related to a representation of blackness via an effect of the "blackness space" that changes the path between two points in the "bird space." This "effect" could readily be called a *force*. It could either change the distance between two points in a uniform space as Lewin's model would suggest, or it could temporarily change the form of the space itself. In Krumhansl's model blackness is extrinsic to the static representation of birds. In Lewin's model blackness would exert a "force" on the underlying representation that would temporarily change the relationship between points (Fig. 8.13d).

Thus, the dependence of sparrow and robin could be represented in a dynamic system by the degree to which a change in one produces a change in the distance between the two. Although heterogeneous models such as recently proposed by Krumhansl (1983a) can maintain a static structure that changes judgments via the processes imposed upon the structure, there is no reason, in principle, why a more dynamic representation could not account for asymmetries in similarity judgments.

In fact, more recently, Goldmeier (1982)—Wertheimer's only living student—has suggested a dynamic system to account for changes in memory for visually presented forms. He demonstrated through a series of converging findings that forms that are "near-singular" (close to the prototype of a set, but not as "good" as the prototype) were more often confused with the prototype or what he calls "singular" forms than with an equally distant "nonsingular" form. Points are dynamic in a directionally systematic way if they are near a point that represents singularity. Points in regions more distant from singular representations remain unaffected by the singularity and simply fade nondirectionally with time.

Current Processing Theories and Fields

In a very different vein from representational models, there are some quite elegant information-processing models that are neurologically derived, at least in part, and suggest certain operations that appear similar to Köhler's brain field theory. Perhaps the best example is Marr and Poggio's (1976) first model of stereopsis in random dot stereograms. When dot stereograms are viewed binocularly, the laterally displaced dots in the two frames will, after some amount of viewing time, appear as in depth. Marr and Poggio have suggested that the visual system begins by comparing dots at each location from each eye and determining whether there is a match (dots at a given location in each stereogram or no dots at that location) or a mismatch (dot in one stereogram but not in the other). These are then represented by interconnecting nodes. The resulting matrix is weighted by positive and negative potentials along rows, columns, and diagonals. This configuration is the input for the first of a series of computations that essentially "relax" the system through reiterations into the "best" overall stereoscopic perception. The algorithm performs the computation at each stage guided by the strength of interaction between nodes that are weighted according to proximity. It then outputs a matrix that is again passed through the computation (see Marr, 1982, and Frisby, 1979, for a more complete description). At each pass the "field" is changed. The system is dynamic, and the end product is the result of a series of calculations based on the entire set of local interactions. The process is like field theory in the sense that a change in one region will affect every other region to varying degrees (that depend on how far away they are), and the overall pattern will settle into an equilibrium state. In Marr and Poggio's system and in other models similar to theirs (e.g., Rosenfeld, 1982), processing mechanisms are dynamic.

These models, however, begin with pieces (dots in the case of Marr & Poggio) and construct the experience of the whole from computations on these pieces. The result in the end is a new form that was not represented in the original input. What Marr and Poggio suggest (and they may very well be right) is that the system must "get beyond" a simple textured field and perform a point by point analysis in order to restructure the pattern as a whole.

The Gestaltists, however, did not consider experienced wholes as forms created from molecular operations on the parts. Gestalt psychologists were critical of the idea that atomistic processes at even sensory levels (in the Marr & Poggio case, quasisensory levels) somehow produced either a string of associated parts or a string of parts plus a whole. Marr and Poggio's theory is Gestalt like in the sense that it has certain similarities to field theory in its dynamically changing representation, but it violates an essential ingredient of the Gestalt school in the sense that it does not emphasize the role of wholes from the very beginning.

I grant that it would appear impossible to see stereopsis of random dot stereograms without some sort of point by point or region by region comparisons between input to the two eyes, and I am not trying to say that Gestalt psychologists denied local sensations. It was the nature of the field as a whole, however, that would govern the parts and their relations and, thus, govern the comparisons that would be made. For instance, surfaces with small and many points may be compared on a column by column basis, and surfaces with larger and few points may be compared on a point by point basis. The field as a whole will govern the process to solution,

Current Theories and Isomorphism

Just as field theory and psychophysiological isomorphism were interconnected in Gestalt psychology, Shepard's second-order isomorphism is interconnected with his model of internal representation (Shepard, 1975; Shepard & Chipman, 1970). Rather than suggesting that relations as perceived are isomorphic with physiological structures, he claims the isomorphism is between relations as perceived and the underlying *mental* representation. His studies of mental rotation (see Shepard & Cooper, 1982) led him to suggest further that the experienced similarity between the metric of the representation and the percept allowed for the experienced similarity between perception of an externally rotating object and an imagined rotating object. Whatever the states of the system while perceiving a transformation, they were similar to the states while imagining a transformation.

Shepard's theoretical view has been highly effective in generating data that support his contention of an internal metric space. (This concept should not be confused with the use of space to represent knowledge as discussed in a foregoing section. Rather I am talking here about the representation of space per se.) That transformations occur in some sort of ''mental space'' is no longer at issue, although the nature of the representation that is transformed continues to generate a great deal of debate (Hinton & Parsons, 1981; Koriat & Norman, 1983; Robertson & Palmer, 1983; Shepard & Cooper, 1982). Whatever the nature of the representation, it appears to traverse a path in internally structured space similar to one through which external objects are perceived to traverse in external space. The relationship between points in both perceived and imagined events appear, at least in part, to be isomorphic. Shepard, then, has retained from Gestalt psychology the notion of isomorphism between experience and an underlying representation, but he has abstracted the representation and avoided the difficulties of Köhler's doctrine of psychophysiological isomorphism that proposed that the structure of experience was isomorphic with the structure of brain fields.

METHODOLOGY

Gestalt psychologists were not phenomenologists in the strict philosophical sense. Husserl, who founded phenomenology, argued that consciousness was an entity apart. It was distinct and could not be compared to physical systems (see Merleau–Ponty, 1964). To Gestalt psychologists, however, conscious experience was not unique. The structure of experience was believed to be a result of the same principles that structured inanimate systems.

Gestalt psychology has been labeled phenomenological because of its methods more than for its philosophy. Köhler (1938/1966) distinguishes between method and philosophy as follows:

> 'Phenomenalism' . . . is . . . to be clearly distinguished from that of 'phenomenology.' Phenomenalism is a definite view of the universe—the monistic view that it consists exclusively of 'phenomena'—plus certain arguments by which this view is supported. Phenomenology, on the other hand, is a *method* which we may use whether or not we share the Phenomenalist's views. (p. 90)

Gestalt methods were quite simply to ask subjects to report experiences such as what they saw when viewing stimuli or what they were thinking while solving problems.

Because Gestalt psychology emphasized that experience was part of the universal order, experience itself was a bonafide unit of study, and the most direct way to access experience was by asking subjects to report it. Experience could change just as bodies or behavior could change, and its progression from one state to another could, therefore, be charted with reference to independent variables just like any other dependent variable.

"Phenomenological method" in this context is not referring to the more contemporary methods employed by Giorgi (1970) and his followers, examples of which can be found throughout the *Journal of Phenomenological Psychology*. Gestalt psychologists did not suggest that the subject should go "beyond ordinary experience," nor did they feel that a researcher must be *trained* to "suspend prior beliefs" or "be a certain kind of person" (Keen, 1975). In fact, they were quite adamant that experiential reports should be naive and untutored, in reaction against the trained introspectionism of Structuralist psychology. Gestalt psychologists would, however, agree with at least one of the tenets of present day phenomenological investigation—that it was the pattern of experience that was important.

It was on this issue of patterns of experience, in fact, that Gestalt psychology rejected classical Wundtian Introspectionism. Gestalt psychology wanted to examine ordinary experience and felt that special training of subjects to report "raw" sensations was neither necessary nor desirable. Cognitive structures or patterns of cognition would be uncovered through the careful study of experience.

By far the most prominent criticism of the methods used by Gestalt psychologists is that they were not objective. There were no right or wrong answers to which responses could be compared. Responses were not timed in order to examine what properties of a stimulus were processed in what stage of perception. Stimuli were not masked in order to stop information flow. Degraded stimuli of any kind were seldom used. To the Gestalt psychologists organization revealed itself in experience, and subjects could tell you what that experience was.

In contemporary approaches to cognition, subjective reports in the tradition of Gestalt psychology are becoming more respected even in the technologically oriented areas of information-processing psychology. Subjective ratings of perceived "goodness" are standard measures in the study of perceptual organization (Garner, 1974; Krumhansl, 1983b; Palmer, 1975). Ratings of subjective similarity form the basis of a great deal of work (e.g., Goldmeier, 1936/1972; Kimchi & Palmer, 1982; Krumhansl, 1978; Shepard & Chipman, 1970; Tversky, 1977). Subjective reports of perceived orientation or shape or size are often used to test various hypotheses about perception (Palmer, 1980; Rock, 1973; Rock, this volume) and are even collected from brain-damaged patients to test theories of altered perception (Robertson & Delis, 1985). Theories of categorical perception have been extended to tonics in musical sequences by using subjective reports (Krumhansl, 1983b), and Wertheimer's methods of studying the phi phenomenon have been employed by Shepard and Zare (1983) to examine the perceived path of motion between alternating lights when a barrier is placed between them.

These examples indicate the value many contemporary cognitive psychologists place on their subjects' experience and in this sense concur with the Gestalt appreciation for phenomena. It is clear, however, that using phenomenological methods does not make one a phenomenologist, nor does it make one a Gestalt psychologist.

CONCLUSION

Is there a neo-Gestalt movement? The answer, of course, depends on what would make a theory or model neo-Gestalt. The prefix "neo" does not mean it would be just like Gestalt psychology, but it should at least incorporate or emphasize the defining characteristics of Gestalt psychology. What are these characteristics? First, Gestaltists emphasized that organization was directly given in experience. It did not occur indirectly through a set of preconscious calculations in which parts were interrelated to build a whole. Second, there was a strong opposition to atomism at all levels of enquiry. Physiological atomism was attacked as strongly as Structuralism. Third, there was a heavy emphasis on configuration and goodness. The whole was in general different from the sum of its parts, and it was as good as the prevailing conditions would allow. Fourth, and perhaps more important than the other three, there was an emphasis on uniform principles of organization. The principles that applied to perceptual organization would not only apply to other cognitive functions such as memory and problem solving but also to social systems and to such diverse things as the relation of a person's ego to his or her culture. The search for organizing principles of perception was expected to pay off in all domains of psychology.

I begin by examining how the information-processing approach in general fits into this framework. This exercise should tell us whether references to "neo-Gestalt" are simply restating something that has been with us since the information-processing approach emerged, or whether information processing is something entirely different. Many articles during the development of cognitive psychology suggested a relationship between information processing and Gestalt psychology (e.g., Shepard, 1968; Wertheimer, 1974). If neo-Gestalt means keeping Gestalt terms but studying the stages of processing that result in Gestalt phenomena, then most of modern cognitive psychology could reasonably be called neo-Gestalt, but if it means keeping with the basic criteria as outlined previously, then information processing and Gestalt psychology are independent.

First, in information processing the phenomenally realized organization is the end product of a number of stages of decisions and transformations. The final organization that emerges in consciousness is typically represented in the large box marked "Output" at the end of a flow-chart-like structure. How this information gets from preconscious states to conscious states is not well specified. The assumption is that when an operation (or possibly a suboperation) is finished, it outputs the final organization, and it is the processing stages that occur before experience that explain the phenomenal organization. Where information-processing models end, however, is where Gestalt psychology began. The Gestaltists did not deny unconscious processing (see Kóffka, 1935). They just did not think that it was very important. If preconscious processing was the same as the experienced organization (e.g., if the whole was before the parts), then it added very little, and if it was different, then it was hard to see its relevance because the properties of the parts could be changed by the experienced whole. Second, information processing does not take a stand on atomism. Some models are atomistic. They suggest that pieces get glued together to form a unit. Other models are more "holistic." They emphasize properties such as symmetry or suggest that configurations of a represented set of points determine organization. Third, some information-processing approaches emphasize configuration and simplicity of form, and some do not. Fourth, the information-processing approach, although applied to areas outside cognitive psychology, does not necessarily have as its goal to define the organizing processes of areas beyond cognition.

It appears that information processing, in general, is not an extension of Gestalt psychology nor can it be labeled as neo-Gestalt. (Michael Wertheimer, 1983, has also recently come to a similar conclusion). This is not to say that information-processing approaches are misguided. I am simply pointing out that they cannot in themselves be considered Gestalt-like. Information processing is neutral to the concerns of Gestalt psychology.

Are certain realms of modern cognitive investigation captured in the term neo-Gestalt? Clearly, certain tenets of Gestalt psychology have been borrowed and utilized in theoretical issues surrounding cognitive functioning. The phenomena are more frequently discussed, the principles are becoming more clearly stated, studies of grouping continue to generate interest, and, although the theoretical notions of psychophysiological isomorphism have not survived, psychophysical isomorphism is a viable alternative. Some of the concepts underlying field theory have their modern-day analogue in spatial models of representation and to some degree to certain visual processing models, but field theory was not a necessary precursor to the development of such models. Although subjective report methods have enjoyed increased popularity, they are seldom tolerated as a sufficient experimental test and are typically followed by studies designed to collect more objective measures. In short, many of the cognitive theories discussed in this chapter deemphasize experience as a mode of study; they may oppose atomism and embrace notions of Prägnanz and configurationism, but with few exceptions they do so in a way that adds a whole at the end of a stage of processes rather than begins with wholes; some theorists may even imply that these principles should be a heuristic for all psychological investigation, but this is seldom stated explicitly. Modern theorists, then, generally do not emphasize the defining characteristics of Gestalt psychology as a unitary school of thought. There are, however, many modern theories that are consistent with some specific characteristics of the Gestalt school, and many of these have been discussed in the present work.

Is there a renewed interest in Gestalt psychology? The answer is an emphatic "yes." Contemporary cognitive theories that rely on the summing of parts are vigorously questioned. In present-day information-processing views of cognition, the parts at issue may not be elementary sensations but can rather be such things as features (Gibson, 1967; Treisman & Gelade, 1980). These approaches hold that the system works by concatenating the parts, whatever they may be. Computers work very well this way, but human perceptual systems often do not comply. For instance, integral dimensions are separated only with conscious effort (Garner, 1974), and symmetry (a wholistic attribute) is extremely influential in early perceptual processing (Corballis, 1976; Palmer, 1982; Rock, 1973). These observations are among the reasons that attempts to formalize configural processes are generating a great deal of interest. Configural notions have also been extended to the organization of categories. Categories can be represented very well by spatial models in which the degree of similarity between members of a category and the density of points around an exemplar can predict subjective judgments. Partly as a result of such endeavors, subjective reports are acquiring new dignity.

One could argue that it is futile or at least a waste of time to attempt to categorize theories into such things as Gestalt-like or neo-Gestalt. Yet there is a reason to classify research styles. Schools of inquiry have an internal dynamics. Gestalt psychology is unique because it had to grow up twice, first in Germany and then again in the United States. The second time it did not quite succeed as well as the first, but it was remarkable for its productivity. An analysis like the present one helps to capture the ingredient that made this school so innovative and led psychology from narrow psychophysics to the full richness of a cognitive science. In this sense, one can discover a neo-Gestalt movement, liberated from the confines of associationism and concerned with the value of our own experience of thought. Fundamentally, however, Gestalt psychology was and is a way of thinking, and that is the light in which it should be compared to other ideas.

ACKNOWLEDGMENTS

I wish to give special thanks to Erich Goldmeier, Carol Krumhansl, Stephen Palmer, and Irvin Rock for their painstaking reading of earlier drafts of this chapter. If I have failed to make my arguments clear, it is despite their efforts. In addition I wish to thank Rutie Kimchi and Terry Knapp for stimulating dialogue that helped to form my thinking. I also thank James Cutting and William Mace for directing me to many helpful resources.

REFERENCES

Attneave, F. (1954). Some informational aspects of visual perception. *Psychological Review, 61,* 182–193.

Attneave, F. (1982). Prägnanz and soap bubble systems: A theoretical exploration. In J. Beck (Ed.), *Organization and representation in perception.* Hillsdale, NJ: Lawrence Erlbaum Associates.

Banks, W., Larson, D., & Prinzmetal, W. (1979). Asymmetry of visual interference. *Perception and Psychophysics, 25,* 447–456.

Banks, W., & Prinzmetal, W. (1976). Configurational effects in visual information processing. *Perception and Psychophysics, 19,* 361–367.

Beck, J. (Ed.). (1982). *Organization and representation in perception.* Hillsdale, NJ: Lawrence Erlbaum Associates.

Boring, E. (1950). *A history of experimental psychology.* New York: Appleton–Century–Crofts.

Broadbent, D. E. (1977). The hidden preattentive processes. *American Psychologist, 32,* 109–118.

Buffart, H., Leeuwenberg, E., & Restle, F. (1981). Coding theory of visual pattern completion. *Journal of Experimental Psychology: Human Perception and Performance, 7,* 241–274.

Corballis, M. (1976). *The psychology of left and right.* Hillsdale, NJ: Lawrence Erlbaum Associates.

Cutting, J. (1981). Coding theory adapted to gait perception. *Journal of Experimental Psychology: Human Perception and Performance, 7,* 71–87.

Cutting, J., & Proffitt, D. (1982). The minimum principle and the perception of absolute, common and relative motion. *Cognitive Psychology, 14*, 211–246.

Deutsch, D., & Feroe, J. (1981). The internal representation of pitch sequences in tonal music. *Psychological Review, 88*, 503–522.

Duncker, K. (1945). On problem-solving (L. S. Lees, Trans.) *Psychological Monographs, 58* (Whole No. 270).

Frisby, J. (1979). *Seeing.* Oxford: Oxford University Press.

Garner, W. (1974). *The processing of information and structure.* Hillsdale, NJ: Lawrence Erlbaum Associates.

Gibson, E. (1967). *Principles of perceptual learning and development.* New York: Appleton–Century–Crofts.

Giorgi, A. (1970). Toward phenomenologically based research in psychology. *Journal of Phenomenological Psychology, 1*, 75–98.

Goldmeier, E. (1972). Similarity in visually perceived forms. *Psychological Monographs, 8* (Whole No. 29). (Originally published, 1936)

Goldmeier, E. (1982). *The memory trace: Its formulation and its fate.* Hillsdale, NJ: Lawrence Erlbaum Associates.

Gregory, R. (1970). *The intelligent eye.* New York: McGraw–Hill.

Heider, F. (1958). *The psychology of interpersonal relationships.* New York: Wiley.

Helson, H. (1969). Why did their precursors fail and the Gestalt psychologists succeed? *American Psychologist, 24*, 1006–1011.

Henle, M. (1980). The influence of Gestalt psychology in America. In R. W. Rieber & K. Salzinger (Eds.), *Psychology theoretical-historical perspectives.* New York: Academic Press.

Hilgard, E. (1964). The place of Gestalt psychology and field theories in contemporary learning theories. In E. R. Hilgard (Ed.), *Theories of learning and instruction.* Chicago: The National Society for the Study of Education.

Hinton, J., & Parsons, L. (1981). Frames of reference and mental imagery. In J. Long & A. D. Baddeley (Eds.), *Attention and performance* (Vol. 9). Hillsdale, NJ: Lawrence Erlbaum Associates.

Hochberg, J. (1979). Sensation and perception. In E. Hearst (Ed.), *The first century of experimental psychology.* Hillsdale, NJ: Lawrence Erlbaum Associates.

Hochberg, J. (1981). Levels of perceptual organization. In M. Kubovy & J. R. Pomerantz (Eds.), *Perceptual organization.* Hillsdale, NJ: Lawrence Erlbaum Associates.

Hochberg, J. (1982). How big is a stimulus? In J. Beck (Ed.), *Organization and representation in perception.* Hillsdale, NJ: Lawrence Erlbaum Associates.

Hochberg, J., & Brooks, V. (1960). The psychophysics of form: Reversible-perspective drawings of spatial objects. *American Journal of Psychology, 73*, 337–354.

Hochberg, J., & McAlister, E. (1953). A quantitative approach to figural "goodness." *Journal of Experimental Psychology, 46*, 361–364.

Johannson, G. (1950). *Configurations in event perception.* Stockholm: Almquist & Wiksell.

Kahneman, D., & Henik, A. (1981). Perceptual organization and attention. In M. Kubovy & J. R. Pomerantz (Eds.), *Perceptual organization.* Hillsdale, NJ: Lawrence Erlbaum Associates.

Keen, E. (1975). *A primer in phenomenological psychology.* New York: Holt, Rinehart, & Winston.

Kimchi, R., & Palmer, S. (1982). Form and texture in hierarchically constructed patterns. *Journal of Experimental Psychology: Human Perception and Performance, 8*, 521–535.

Kinchla, R., & Wolfe, J. (1979). The order of visual processing: "Top-down", "bottom-up" or "middle-out." *Perception and Psychophysics, 25*, 225–231.

Koffka, K. (1935). *Principles of Gestalt psychology.* New York: Harcourt, Brace, & World.

Köhler, W. (1925). *The mentality of apes.* New York: Harcourt Brace.

Köhler, W. (1940). *Dynamics in psychology.* New York: Live right.

186   ROBERTSON

Köhler, W. (1947). *Gestalt psychology*. New York: Liverright. (Originally published in 1929)
Köhler, W. (1959). Gestalt psychology today. *American Psychologist, 14*, 727–734.
Köhler, W. (1961). Psychology and evolution. In M. Henle (Ed.), *Documents of Gestalt psychology*. Berkeley: University of California Press. (Reprinted from *Acta Psychologica, 7*, 1950)
Köhler, W. (1966). *The place of value in a world of facts*. New York: Liver right. (Originally published, 1938)
Köhler, W. (1969). *The task of Gestalt psychology*. Princeton, NJ: Princeton University Press.
Koriat, A., & Norman, J. (1984). What is rotated in mental rotation? *Journal of Experimental Psychology: Learning, Memory and Cognition, 10*, 421–434.
Krumhansl, C. (1978). Concerning the applicability of geometric models to similarity data: The interrelationship between similarity and spatial density. *Psychological Review, 85*, 445–463.
Krumhansl, C. (1982). Density versus feature weights as predictors of visual identifications: Comment on Appleman and Mayzner. *Journal of Experimental Psychology: General, 111*, 101–108.
Krumhansl, C. (1983a). *Set-theoretic and spatial models of similarity: Some considerations in application*. Paper presented at the meeting of the Mathematical Psychology Society.
Krumhansl, C. (1983b). Perceptual structures for tonal music. *Music Perception, 1*, 28–62.
Lashley, K. S., Chow, K. L., & Semmes, J. (1951). An examination of the electrical field theory of cerebral integration. *Psychological Review, 58*, 123–136.
Leeuwenberg, E. (1971). A perceptual coding language for visual and auditory patterns. *American Journal of Psychology, 84*, 307–349.
Leeuwenberg, E. (1982a). Metrical aspects of patterns and structural information theory. In J. Beck (Ed.), *Organization and representation in perception*. Hillsdale, NJ: Lawrence Erlbaum Associates.
Leeuwenberg, E. (1982b). The perception of assimilation and brightness contrast as derived from code theory. *Perception and Psychophysics, 32*, 345–352.
Lewin, K. (1936). *Principles of topological psychology*. (F. Heider & G. Heider, Trans.). New York: McGraw-Hill.
Lewin, K. (1951). *Field theory in social science*. New York: Harper & Bros.
Marr, D. (1982). *Vision*. San Francisco: W. H. Freeman.
Marr, D., & Poggio, T. (1976). Cooperative computation of stereo disparity. *Science, 194*, 283–287.
Merleau–Ponty, M. (1964). *The primacy of perception*. (J. M. Edie, Trans.). IL: Northwestern University Press.
Miller, J. (1981). Global precedence in attention and decision. *Journal of Experimental Psychology: Human Perception and Performance, 7*, 1161–1174.
Navon, D. (1977). Forest before trees: The precedence of global features in visual perception. *Cognitive Psychology, 9*, 441–474.
Neisser, U. (1967). *Cognitive psychology*. New York: Appleton–Century–Crofts.
Palmer, S. (1975). The effects of contextual scenes on the identification of objects. *Memory and Cognition, 3*, 519–526.
Palmer, S. (1980). What makes triangles point: Local and global effects in configurations of ambiguous triangles. *Cognitive Psychology, 12*, 285–305.
Palmer, S. (1982). Symmetry, transformation, and the structure of perceptual systems. In J. Beck (Ed.), *Organization and representation in perception*. Hillsdale, NJ: Lawrence Erlbaum Associates.
Palmer, S. (1983). The psychology of perceptual organization: A transformational approach. In A. Rosenfeld & J. Beck (Eds.), *Human and machine vision*. New York: Academic Press.
Perkins, D. (1982). The perceiver as organizer and geometer. In J. Beck (Ed.), *Organization and representation in perception*. Hillsdale, NJ: Lawrence Erlbaum Associates.
Peterson, M., & Hochberg, J. (1983). Opposed-set measurement procedure: A quantitative analysis of the role of local cues and intention in form perception. *Journal of Experimental Psychology: Human Perception and Performance, 9*, 183–193.

Pomerantz, J. (1981). Perceptual organization in information processing. In M. Kubovy & J. R. Pomerantz (Eds.), *Perceptual organization*. Hillsdale, NJ: Lawrence Erlbaum Associates.

Pomerantz, J., & Kubovy, M. (1981). Perceptual organization: An overview. In M. Kubovy & J. R. Pomerantz (Eds.), *Perceptual organization*. Hillsdale, NJ: Lawrence Erlbaum Associates.

Prinzmetal, W. (1981). Principles of feature integration in visual perception. *Perception and Psychophysics, 30,* 330–340.

Prinzmetal, W., & Banks, W. (1977). Good continuation affects visual detection. *Perception and Psychophysics, 21,* 389–395.

Restle, F. (1979). Coding theory of the perception of motion configurations. *Psychological Review, 86,* 1–24.

Restle, F. (1982). Coding theory as an integration of Gestalt psychology and information processing. In J. Beck (Ed.), *Organization and representation in perception*. Hillsdale, NJ: Lawrence Erlbaum Associates.

Robertson, L. C., & Delis, D. C. (1985). "Part-whole" processing in unilateral brain damaged patients: Dysfunction of hierarchical organization. *Neuropsychologia,* in press.

Robertson, L., & Palmer, S. (1983). Holistic processes in the perception and transformation of disoriented figures. *Journal of Experimental Psychology: Human Perception and Performance, 9,* 203–214.

Rock, I. (1973). *Orientation and form*. New York: Academic Press.

Rosen, J. (1983). *A symmetry primer for scientists*. New York: Wiley.

Rosenfeld, A. (1982). Relaxation processes for perceptual disambiguation in computer vision. In J. Beck (Ed.), *Organization and representation in perception*. Hillsdale, NJ: Lawrence Erlbaum Associates.

Shepard, R. (1958). Stimulus and response generalization: Tests of a model relating generalization to distance in psychological space. *Journal of Experimental Psychology, 55,* 509–523.

Shepard, R. (1968). (Review of U. Neisser's *Cognitive Psychology*). *American Journal of Psychology, 88,* 285–289.

Shepard, R. (1975). Form, formation and transformation of internal representations. In R. Solso (Ed.), *Information processing and cognition: The Loyola symposium*. Hillsdale, NJ: Lawrence Erlbaum Associates.

Shepard, R., & Chipman, S. (1970). Second-order isomorphism of internal representations: Shapes of states. *Cognitive Psychology, 1,* 1–17.

Shepard, R., & Cooper, L. (1982). *Mental images and their transformations*. Cambridge, MA: MIT Press/Bradford Book.

Shepard, R., Kilpatrick, D., & Cunningham, J. (1975). The internal representation of numbers. *Cognitive Psychology, 7,* 82–138.

Shepard, R., & Zare, S. (1983). Path-guided apparent motion. *Science, 220,* 632–634.

Treisman, A., & Gelade, G. (1980). A feature-integration theory of attention. *Cognitive Psychology, 12,* 97–136.

Tversky, A. (1977). Features of similarity. *Psychological Review, 84,* 327–352.

Wertheimer, Max (1938a). The general theoretical situation. In W. D. Ellis (Ed.), *A source book of Gestalt psychology*. London: Kegan Paul, Trench, Trubner. (Originally published, 1922)

Wertheimer, Max (1938b). Laws of organization in perceptual forms. In W. D. Ellis (Ed.), *A source book of Gestalt psychology*. London: Kegan Paul, Trench, Trubner. (Originally published, 1923)

Wertheimer, Max (1938c). Gestalt theory. In W. E. Ellis (Ed.), *A source book of Gestalt psychology*. London: Kegan Paul, Trench, Trubner. (Originally published, 1925)

Wertheimer, Max (1961). Experimental studies in the seeing of motion. In T. Shipley (Ed.), *Classics in psychology*. New York: Philosophical Library. (Originally published, 1912)

Wertheimer, Max (1982). *Productive thinking*. Chicago: University of Chicago Press. (Originally published, 1945)

Wertheimer, Michael (1974). The problem of perceptual structures. In E. C. Carterette & M. P. Friedman, *Handbook of perception (Vol. I)*. New York: Academic Press.

Wertheimer, Michael (1983, August). *Max Wertheimer: Modern cognitive psychology and the Gestalt problem*. Paper presented at the meeting of the American Psychological Association, Anaheim, CA.

Weyl, H. (1952). *Symmetry*. Princeton, NJ: Princeton University Press.

9 Cognitive Intervention in Perceptual Processing

Irvin Rock
Rutgers University

Perception is a mode of cognition but it should be studied separately from other aspects of cognition. Perception is cognition because it concerns apprehension and the acquisition of knowledge or information. It should be studied separately, however, because it is based on the stimulation of sense organs and in that crucial respect is different from other modes of cognition.

If this were all there were to be said about the matter, a chapter on perception might be inappropriate for a book entitled *Approaches to Cognition*. But suppose perception were to be based upon thought-like operations? In that event (though the end product of its causal operations is phenomenologically distinct from other modes of cognition, concerning as it does the appearance of things and events) the operations themselves may well be the same or similar to those that underly the end products of thinking and problem solving. Thus we can learn about the operations of thinking by studying perception.[1] In this chapter I make this argument by comparing a sensory theory of a curious illusion with a problem-solving theory. Contrary to the nature of a purely sensory approach, the problem-solving approach implies an intervention in the lower level processing of sensory information by higher level cognitive activity.

THE ILLUSORY-CONTOUR PHENOMENON

In the illustration following, one spontaneously perceives a rectangular white figure on top of a set of black octagons and lines. There are several aspects of this experience that are not readily predictable on the basis of a perceptual theory that

---

[1]The Gestalt psychologists made this argument but the other way around, namely, that thinking was perception like rather than that perception was thought like.

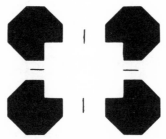

FIG. 9.1.   Illusory-contour figure perceived as a white rectangle covering four black octagons. From Kanizsa (1974). Reproduced by permission of the *Italian Journal of Psychology.*

emphasizes direct physiological processing of the proximal input. "Proximal input" refers to the stimulus impinging on the cells of the sense modality sensitive to a particular form of energy. In the case of vision, it refers to an image represented on the retina. This image only contains portions of black octagons plus a few line segments, and according to a sensory theory of perception that is what should be seen, and nothing more.

What is seen, however, is a rectangle that appears to have contours not only in the regions of the black fragments but between them as well. Such perceived contours are variously referred to as "subjective," "cognitive," or "illusory." I use the last of these terms, illusory, because it is theoretically neutral and descriptively correct. The perceived contours are illusory because there is no sharp discontinuity of luminance in the drawings such as ordinarily exists when we see contours. Needless to add, there are also no such discontinuities present in the retinal image of the drawing. A second illusory aspect of what is perceived in viewing the illustration is that the rectangle appears whiter than the white of the page surrounding it. A third illusion is that the black fragments tend to appear as complete black octagons.[2]

Of course, if it were the case that these illusory aspects were of the nature of *non*-sensory *interpretations* of the proximal stimulus, i.e., if we *perceived* only incomplete black fragments but interpreted them as representing octagons behind a rectangle, then we could conclude that *perception* qua sensory experience was indeed a direct reflection of the proximal input. Earlier theorists such as Titchener (1926) made precisely this argument, *sensation* being held to be in accord with the stimulus and *interpretation* to represent judgments about what the sensation represented in the world. Illusions were thought of as errors of judgment (Wundt, 1907).

---

[2]The same kind of illusory effects occur with a reversal of the lightness values shown in Fig. 9.1. In other words, in the negative of this display, the fragments and lines are all white and the background black. In that event one perceives a blacker than black figure with illusory contours, occluding white fragments. In the remainder of this chapter, however, only the version shown in the various illustrations is discussed.

Whereas it is admittedly difficult to resolve questions of this kind, a simple appeal to phenomenology, to how things look, argues strongly for the belief that the illusory contours and lightness of the rectangle in our illustration are indeed true direct perceptions. One *sees* the contours and the lighter or whiter color of the rectangle. The impression of completion of the black fragments is perhaps more debatable. One might reasonably argue on the basis of phenomenology that one *perceives* incomplete fragments but interprets them as complete. As I try to show on the basis of evidence, however, even in this case the argument is incorrect.

If, then, these are indeed perceptual effects, how can we explain them if there is no stimulus directly representing them on the retina? This is nothing less than the central problem of perception. How is it that we typically perceive the world the very way we do, as three dimensional, the objects of which maintain their size, shape, lightness, position, and orientation, despite variability and, therefore, despite the inadequacy of the proximal stimulus that represents such objects. Whether the perceptual outcome is veridical or illusory, the problem of explanation is the same, because it is often the case that a perceived property is not represented in the proximal input.

THE SENSORY THEORY: CONTRAST

A solution to the problem has been suggested. It is known that regions adjacent to those of high luminance, e.g., white ones, tend to appear darker than would otherwise be the case, and regions proximal to those of very low luminance, e.g., black ones, tend to appear lighter than would otherwise be the case. Thus a gray region surrounded by black appears to be lighter than an equally gray region surrounded by white. A mechanism to explain such contrast, as it has been called, has been invoked, namely, lateral inhibition. The more intense stimulation of the cells adjacent to those stimulated by the gray region is said to have the effect of diminishing the rate of discharge of the latter cells, as was demonstrated directly in the Horseshoe Crab, Limulus, (Ratliff, 1965). Assuming that rate of discharge is the neural correlate of perceived lightness, such an inhibitory effect should indeed alter the perceived lightness of the gray region, or at least of that part of it near enough to the white region to be so affected. No such inhibition would occur for gray regions adjacent to black ones, so that these cells would discharge more rapidly and thus give rise to the perception of a lighter color. One might refer to this as lightness enhancement based on the elimination of or release from inhibition.[3]

---

[3]Whereas contrast is a fact of perception, lateral inhibition may not be the mechanism responsible for it. Moreover, it is unlikely that rate of neural discharge is the neural correlate of perceived lightness (see Gilchrist, 1979). However, for purposes of the present discussion, I regard contrast as a sensory theory of the illusory-contour effect because it has always been held to be based on lower level or peripheral neural processing.

FIG. 9.2.   The Hermann grid. Dark illusory squares are perceived at the intersections of the white spaces, particularly those seen in peripheral vision. The effect is attributed to the greater inhibition occurring at these intersections based on the summation from white regions on all four sides.

From this analysis it follows that white regions adjacent to the black fragments in the illustration ought to appear to be whiter than white regions more remote for them. Each black fragment ought to appear surrounded by a halo of white that gradually declines in whiteness until it blends into the prevailing white color of the background as a whole. This is obviously not what is perceived. However it can be further argued that such contrast is below threshold unless there is a summation effect in a given region. This is precisely what is alleged to occur in the Hermann grid (Fig. 9.2), in which the white vertical and horizontal spaces between black squares only appear noticeably dark where they intersect each other. These intersections are surrounded on four sides by white, whereas the white regions elsewhere in the vertical or horizontal spaces are surrounded by white on only two sides. In Fig. 9.1, the white gap in the corner of each black fragment is surrounded by black on two sides and here is where the contrast effect should be strongest. Assuming that such an effect does occur, it remains to be explained why the *entire* inner rectangular region appears "extra white" when the contrast-enhancement effect from the black octagons would be expected to affect only the corner gap in each of them.

To deal with this problem another phenomenon has been invoked. It is now known that the important information about a region's lightness is given at its edges rather than by its luminance throughout. Without going into further detail, the evidence for this assertion derives from two opposite deductions that follow from this edge-information hypothesis. If an edge around a region is simulated by creating the necessary sharp gradient of luminance difference, then the entire region appears to have the uniform lightness predictable from that edge (and not the lightness predictable from the region's actual luminance). This is the so-called Craik–O'Brien illusion demonstrated by Cornsweet (Cornsweet, 1970; Craik, 1966; O'Brien, 1958). Conversely, if the edge surrounding a region of a given luminance is eliminated—as by a stabilized image—then the lightness of the region is governed not by its luminance but by the information provided by the next spatially surrounding edge that is present in the array (Krauskopf, 1963). This effect has been described as one of assimilation or spreading, and for convenience is referred to here as the "assimilation effect." The relevance of the assimilation effect for our illusory-contour example is fairly obvious. The contrast-generated extra whiteness in the gap between the black fragments presumably spreads throughout the inner rectangular white region.[4]

In short, the contrast theory seeks to explain the illusory-contour phenomenon in terms of the lightness effect. If a region appears to be different in lightness than its surroundings, then, ipso facto, it will have a perceptible boundary or outer contour. As we see later, it is possible to reverse this argument and maintain that it is the illusory contour that is fundamental and brings about the lightness effect.

The contrast theory has nothing to say about the completion effect, i.e., the experience of the black regions as complete octagons occluded by the white rectangular "figure." However, as noted earlier, it might be maintained that this effect is not genuinely perceptual and is simply an interpretation tacked on by the cognitive apparatus as a way of making "sense" of the presence of the white rectangle and the incompletion of the black octagons. Complete octagons or what perception represents in the scene are thus simply identified, categorized, judged, interpreted, or inferred.[5]

One can characterize this approach as proceeding in an ascending direction, beginning with the lowest levels of sensory processing and ending with a cognitive interpretation. In the jargon of contemporary information-processing psychology, the process would be described as "bottom up." At no point is it necessary to believe that processing is guided by or affected by stored knowledge, or expectations, mental set, internal hypotheses, or the like. It seems reasonable, to the writer at least, that if one can adequately explain a particular

---

[4]However, one wonders why no contrast effect can be discerned when only a single fragment with a gap is presented. The assimilation hypothesis is based on the presumption that what spreads is a differential contrast that begins at the fragments. It would, therefore, have to be further maintained that it is a below-threshold contrast effect at each fragment corner that spreads and rises above threshold in the central region via summation. Moreover, not all fragments used to create illusory-contour figures are of this kind, i.e., have gaps. In such cases, therefore, there is the problem of explaining why contrast would spread only toward the locus of the illusory figure.

[5]There are examples of illusory contour in which completion of visible fragments or stratification of the percept in three dimensions does not occur, and still other examples where a lightness (or brightness) effect does not occur. For example, see Ware (1981). However, in the best known and most frequently studied cases, these effects do occur. The theoretical analysis in this chapter is directed at such cases in an attempt to deal with all three aspects, the illusory contour, the illusory lightness, and the completion effect, but it does not follow that factors held to be crucial for these cases are necessary for all cases of illusory-contour perception.

perceptual phenomenon in this way it is to be preferred, for reasons of simplicity or parsimony if nothing else.

CRITIQUE OF THE SENSORY THEORY

The fact is, however, in the writer's opinion, that the case for the sensory, bottom-up approach to the illusory-contour phenomenon and to many other phenomena of perception is weak.[6] Of course one can always take refuge in the argument that we still know so little about the workings of the brain that we cannot yet explain many complex phenomena in terms of sensory mechanisms. But if the facts about a phenomenon such as illusory contour are such as to suggest logically the inadequacy of a bottom-up approach, that is another story. In what follows I try to indicate that this is indeed the case for the illusory-contour effect. I, therefore, use it as a detailed example to make a case for a cognitively based inference theory of perception.[7] I presume it will be clear from this example how one might deal with other facts of perception in terms of the same kind of theory. The theory is predicated on the assumption that perceptual processing proceeds in a bottom-up direction, but only to a point, after which top-down processing enters the picture. My argument is not simply that cognitive operations such as recognition enter at some point, because that is perfectly consistent with bottom-up processing, i.e., that the later stages of processing entail recognition and identification. Rather my argument is that cognitive factors affect perception itself, i.e., affect perceptual properties such as form, depth, and lightness.

There seems to be some confusion about the meaning of the terms *bottom-up* and *top-down*. They sometimes are used interchangeably with the terms *physiological* and *psychological*. In my opinion, not only is this kind of definition wrong philosophically, because *all* psychological events including the alleged cognitive events in question are based on physiological brain events, but it misses the important point about the bottom-up, top-down distinction. The essence of that distinction concerns the *direction* of the sequence of events that determines the outcome under study. When the determination is bottom-up, the sequence follows an orderly, logical progression in which one event would only

---

[6]Other sensory theories of illusory contour are possible such as one that is based on the activation of contour-detector neurons by the contours of the fragments that are present. Such activation then presumably spreads across the gaps between fragments. But apart from other difficulties with this kind of theory, it does not address the central fact of the lightness effect. It seems likely, therefore, that a viable sensory theory would have to be a contrast theory and that is why I selected it for analysis here.

[7]Many points I bring out are identical to or similar to those made by others, such as Kanizsa (1955, 1974), Gregory (1972), and Pritchard and Warm (1983) both with respect to limitations of a sensory or contrast theory and to features of a more cognitively based approach.

be expected to occur when a lower level one had preceded it. For example, sensory transduction *follows* energy input but *precedes* neural transmission to the brain; or recognition follows perception. The highest cognitive levels of processing can occur in a bottom-up sequence, but they occur only toward the end of that sequence. Thus, the outcome of one stage of processing is not affected by a higher stage.

When, however, the determination is top-down, the sequence departs from the orderly, logical progression. Higher level stages affect lower level stages. Here, for example, the processing of a part might, paradoxically enough, depend on the processing of the whole, or, strange as it may seem, the adequate perception of an object might depend on its recognition. As for the illusory-contour phenomenon, I argue that its perception, including the contour, figure-ground organization and lightness of the figure, depends on "hypotheses" that are triggered by certain lower level or earlier stages of perception.

The first point to make, one that seems to have been overlooked by most investigators (but see Kennedy, 1976), is that despite the presence of the appropriate stimulus figure the illusory percept need not occur at all. Naive observers not expecting such an effect may perceive a drawing such as that in Fig. 9.3 as four black forms, resembling photo mounts. With continued viewing their perception may or may not undergo a reversal in which a white diamond is seen in the central area. Accompanying this reversal are the features referred to earlier: The diamond is extra white, it has illusory contours, and it appears to partially occlude either four black rectangles or one black cross.

If the illusory figure is the result of bottom-up processing based on contrast, it ought to occur within a short period of time, milliseconds, and, apart from the latency question, it certainly ought to be an ineluctable outcome. Instead—and this is another point that has been overlooked—it appears to be the result of figure-ground reversal. At the outset, the central region is ground. Only the black fragments are figural and this is why they can be perceived and recognized as photo mounts. Their innermost contours are organized as belonging to *them* and

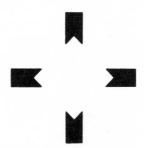

FIG. 9.3.   Figure perceived as four black photo mounts by naive observers or as a white diamond covering either four black rectangles or one black cross. After Kanizsa (1974). Reproduced by permission of the *Italian Journal of Psychology*.

FIG. 9.4.   Pattern that ought to give rise to an illusory-contour figure according to a contrast theory. After Kanizsa (1974). Reproduced by permission of the *Italian Journal of Psychology.*

thus give them shape. When the reversal occurs, those contours belong to and give shape to the white diamond, which becomes figure. The black fragments no longer look like irregular shapes but like the visible portions of rectangles or of a large cross. Thus we see that the illusory figure is perceived if and only if figure-ground reversal occurs. Such reversal, I argue, is not a bottom-up process. In our laboratory we have found that reversal often does *not* occur when subjects are uninformed that they are viewing figures that can be reversed, such as Rubin's well-known vase and faces figure or reversible perspective figures similar to the Necker cube (Girgus, Rock, & Egatz, 1977). Knowing about reversibility is a critical factor, which means that, to the extent that this is demonstrable, by definition, top-down processing occurs.

A further difficulty for a sensory theory is that illusory-figure percepts do not occur with some patterns at all even for informed subjects, although they ought to occur if contrast is the underlying cause. Figure 9.4 is an example. The reversal is unlikely to occur here because a white rectangular figure in the center would usurp the inner borders of the black crosses. These contours would then belong to the rectangle, and that means that the crosses would be occluded by the rectangle, would be ground with respect to the rectangle. They would, therefore, not be crosses at all. They would be incomplete figures, the shape of which could be the one shown in Fig. 9.5.

So we see that to achieve the illusory-contour figure in this example entails giving up the initial perception of four corner crosses. One might speculate that the perceptual system is loathe to surrender that percept because it is "good" in the Gestalt sense of the term, or alternately because it is familiar and already

FIG. 9.5.   How each corner fragment (or cross pattern) of Fig. 9.4 might appear if it is perceived as occluded by a central white rectangle.

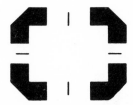

FIG. 9.6. Modification of Fig. 9.4 produced by truncating each cross. This pattern yields an illusory-contour percept. From Kanizsa (1974). Reproduced by permission of the *Italian Journal of Psychology*.

complete. A somewhat different argument is that it would be quite a coincidence if what the proximal stimulus produced by Fig. 9.4 represented is an inner rectangle partially covering four irregular objects such as shown in Fig. 9.5. The coincidence is that regular, symmetrical, familiar, and, therefore, complete proximal stimuli of crosses do not emanate from crosses in the scene at all. Rather they would emanate from four corner figures such as that shown in Fig. 9.5. In other words, although crosses are projected to the retina that is only a coincidence, because no crosses are present in the display. What is present are irregular shapes such as the one shown in Fig. 9.5 and a rectangle in front of them. By accident, or coincidence, these are so positioned that the unoccluded part of the irregular shape projects to the eye as a perfect cross. I return later to this notion of coincidence.

A final point about Fig. 9.4 is this. One might be inclined to dispute my assumption that the contrast theory ought to predict the illusory-contour effect here. Perhaps the stimulus is inadequate for some other reason. But Fig. 9.6 would seem to support my contention. For in this case one *does* perceive the illusory figure, and yet the corner fragments contain the same components of the crosses in the region most proximal to the critical inner corners. The fragments in Fig. 9.6 were devised by *cutting out* part of the crosses so as to make them potentially incomplete structures. Now they are very compatible with the "solution" of an inner white rectangle that partially occludes black corner objects that have the shape of hexagons.

The next fact to consider is that illusory-contour figures can be achieved from patterns that do not contain solidly colored fragments, which one would think are necessary to yield contrast. As can be seen in Fig. 9.7, patterns containing only

FIG. 9.7. Pattern consisting of lines rather than solid black fragments that nonetheless yields a vivid illusory-contour figure. From Kanizsa (1974).

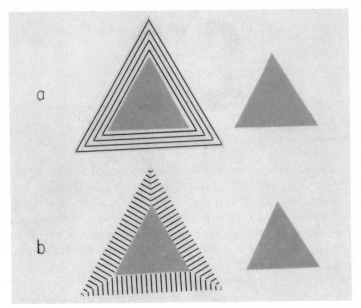

FIG. 9.8.   (a) The two inner gray triangles are equal in lightness and appear about equal despite the presence of black lines surrounding the triangle on the left; (b) the two inner gray triangles are equal in lightness, but the one on the left appears lighter than the one on the right, presumably because of end-of-line contrast. From Frisby & Clatworthy (1975).

lines give rise to some very striking illusory figures in which the extra whiteness seems, if anything, to be more compelling than in those patterns with solid black regions.[8] Although one might consider this fact alone—i.e., that the illusion occurs with such patterns—formidable evidence against the contrast theory, advocates of the theory have presented arguments and evidence that strong contrast effects occur at the ends of lines (Brigner & Gallagher, 1974; Day & Jory, 1978; Frisby & Clatworthy, 1975; Jory & Day, 1979; Kennedy, 1979). The presumption is that whereas a dark line, via contrast, enhances the lightness of regions on its sides, it does so all the more for regions at its ends. Why this should be so is not understood except for the speculation (based on physiological research on receptive fields of the retina of cats) that the presence of a line end on the retina in a certain location would maximally reduce the inhibition within a receptive field in that retinal region. For more details on this argument, see Frisby and Clatworthy (1975).

---

[8]Note that in such figures there is hardly any physical contour at all that can be incorporated into the outer boundary of the illusory-contour figure. Virtually the entire illusory contour must derive from internal processing that is not based on a physical contour.

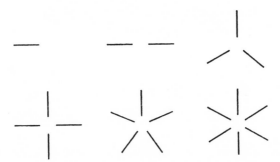

FIG. 9.9.   Patterns of the kind devised by Ehrenstein (1941) that yield an illusory white circle, presumably because of end-of-line contrast. From Frisby & Clatworthy (1975).

In support of this kind of theory are demonstrations such as those shown in Fig. 9.8. Patterns in which lines are *orthogonal* to a critical gray target figure (8*b*) create more of a lightness contrast effect than those in which the lines are parallel to the gray figure (8*a*). In the versions of the effect discovered by Ehrenstein (1941) shown in Fig. 9.9, the more line ends that converge at the center, the stronger is the lightness (extra-whiteness) effect. The trouble with these demonstrations, however, is that they can be explained in other ways. The superior contrast in Fig. 9.8b based on orthogonal surrounding lines can be understood as an example of the Benary effect (Benary, 1924). The gray triangle in *b* appears to be occluding a background of lines and, therefore, to be *on* those background lines, whereas the one in *a* may appear to be surrounded by a pattern of lines and, therefore, not necessarily *on* a background of lines. The belongingness of one region to another with which it contrasts in lightness is known to enhance contrast even when all else remains equal. See the further discussion following of the Benary effect.

As to the effects in Fig. 9.9, they would seem to be examples of the lightness effect associated with illusory-contour figures. Evidence for the end-of-line contrast hypothesis cannot simply be examples where illusory contours and the lightness effect occur when the fragments consist of lines, because that is the phenomenon the hypothesis is intended to explain. Lightness effects independent of illusory contour figures must be demonstrated. The extra whiteness in Fig. 9.9 only seems to occur for the patterns with at least three converging lines. Because such an illusory-figure percept becomes stronger with the addition of more lines, it is not surprising that the lightness effect does too. Note that the effect is accompanied by figure-ground reversal (the inner white region becomes a circular figure) and by an impression of some occlusion of the lines by that figure. In this connection, it is interesting to note that, unlike the other patterns, the three-line pattern is ambiguous: When the central region simply appears as background, no lightness effect occurs; when it is seen as figure, the lightness

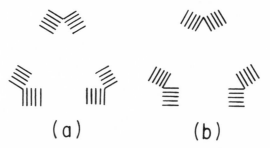

FIG. 9.10.   Whereas (a) yields an impression of a central white triangle, (b) does not. From Frisby & Clatworthy (1975).

effect does occur. This pattern then is useful in revealing that the lightness effect is linked to the achievement of an illusory occluding figure. Facts such as this question the sensory contrast theory.

End-of-line contrast enhancement has also been invoked to explain the superior lightness effects in Fig. 9.10a as compared to b. In a, ends of the lines of the corner fragments are orthogonal to the inner triangular region, whereas in b they are not. However, these differences can again be accounted for in terms of the achievement of illusory-contour figures in a but not b. Why this should be so is discussed later. Thus, it remains to be seen whether support will be forthcoming for an end-of-line contrast theory.[9] At the moment such a theory seems ad hoc; whereas from the standpoint of a problem-solving theory, the occurrence of illusory contour figures based on line patterns is as predictable and understandable as that based on solidly colored patterns.

AN OUTLINE OF A PROBLEM-SOLVING THEORY

In the foregoing critique of a bottom-up sensory theory, the argument in favor of a cognitive or top-down process in perceiving a figure with illusory contours has been implicit. What is the nature of such a process and how should we understand the sequence of events? My own view—which of course is not the only possible one of this kind—follows.

The Formation of the "Hypothesis."   For some finite period of time the pattern is perceived, literally, as several circumscribed figures (the fragments) on a homogeneous background. This occurs on the basis of known principles of

_____

[9]There are examples where an illusory contour or a diffuse illusory contour bounds a region undergoing an illusory lightness effect in the absence of any kind of completion or stratification effect (see Kennedy, 1976, 1978, 1979; Richardson, 1979). In these cases an entirely different mechanism may be at work than the one proposed here.

FIG. 9.11.   A pattern that typically does not *spontaneously* yield an illusory-contour effect when viewed by naive observers but yields a curved triangle percept when the illusory figure is achieved.

perceptual organization. (See the chapter by Robertson in this volume for a discussion of such principles.) Each fragment is a closed region surrounded on all sides by a uniform region of a differing luminance. Such surroundedness is a known principle of figure-ground organization. The processing will stop here if the pattern of lines and other fragments is not too "good" (the use of which term in this context I explain shortly), as in Fig. 9.11, and if no set or expectation is created to guide the system to try to perceive anything else, and certainly if attention is not drawn to the pattern as when it is embedded in a "noisy" context (See Fig. 9.12). Nothing else but these figural fragments will be perceived even with prolonged inspection. This much then might be the result of bottom-up processing.[10] I refer to it as the stage of the literal solution.

If, however, as is generally the case in the illusory-contour patterns, the fragments resemble familiar figures with a region missing, then it is plausible to suppose that a hypothesis will be generated that an object is occluding the missing region. If only one such fragment is given, such a hypothesis will die on the vine as it were. It receives no support. Familiarity is not the only possible basis of an impression of incompletion. An otherwise symmetrical object with a region missing that eliminates the symmetry might also trigger the hypothesis. Often familiarity and symmetry reinforce one another because the incomplete fragment is both familiar and potentially symmetrical (an incomplete circle, square, or the like).

Incompletion is not the only possible cue to the hypothesis of an occluding object. The alignment of the edges of the gap in the fragments *across* fragments can serve as a cue. In an experiment in our laboratory, we constructed fragments

---

[10]This assumes that perceptual organization, in this case figure–ground organization, is bottom-up rather than itself being a matter of problem solving. Such an assumption is debatable. Other questions also arise such as the nature of the process that yields specific shape and the role of attention. I argue elsewhere that the perception of shape is based on a process of propositional description and requires attention but for the sake of the discussion of illusory-contour perception these problems can be set aside (see Rock, 1983).

FIG. 9.12.   A pattern that typically does not yield an illusory-contour effect when viewed by naive observers. From Rock & Anson (1979).

that did not suggest incompletion of the fragments themselves (Rock & Anson, 1979). (See Fig. 9.13.) Nonetheless if certain edges were aligned, i.e., collinear, a figure with illusory contours was perceived in the central region. To be sure, each fragment then appeared as if a gap in one region was occluded by an opaque white figure, but that impression was part of the phenomenal *outcome*. The gap did not function as a *cue* in the sense of appearing as an incomplete part of the fragment prior to the emergence of the hypothesis. When the critical edges were arranged so as *not* to be aligned across fragments (as in Fig. 9.11), then very few subjects perceived an illusory figure. For in this case there is neither the cue of incompletion nor of alignment. In this experiment, needless to say, subjects were naive about the possibility of perceiving illusory figures. I hasten to add that the *reader*, who is not naive, will experience no great difficulty in achieving the illusory figure here. (It looks like a triangle whose sides are curved.) This suggests that still another cue to the hypothesis is set, expectation or knowledge. Once the hypothesis is cued (however, it may be cued) the issue then is: Can it be sustained?

The more contour alignment in the stimulus pattern, the more likely it is that it will be noticed and the sooner it will be noticed. That is why patterns such as

FIG. 9.13.   A pattern in which the corner fragments do not suggest incompletion nonetheless typically yields an impression of a central white triangle, presumably because of alignment of the edges of the corner gaps across fragments. From Rock & Anson (1979).

those in Fig. 9.7 will seem to lead immediately to the figure-ground reversal that brings about the illusory-contour percept. This is what I meant before by "good" illusory-contour patterns. Although the illusory-contour figure is experienced as immediate, I maintain that it is preceded, however fleetingly, by an earlier stage of processing, the literal perceptual solution.

Maintaining the Hypothesized "Solution."   The observer constructs the perceptual solution that has been cued, if and only if it has been cued, by incorporating the visible fragments into it in a fitting way. The solution must account for the proximal stimulus or rather for the components that are part of the literal solution. The constructed solution is that of a white object covering the black fragments (or line fragments). This entails figure-ground reversal. The central region is no longer ground.

The shape of the constructed figure must account for the orientation of the edges of the fragments. That is why its shape must be curvilinear as in Fig. 9.11 if its edges across the fragments are not aligned. Whereas in many cases one might say that the shape of the illusory figure is constrained by the orientation of the edges of the fragments, i.e., the direction of the illusory figure's edge is a continuation of the orientation of the physically given contour in the fragment, that is not necessarily the case. For instance, in Fig. 9.11 the edges of the triangular openings are in fact straight. The phenomenal shape of the illusory figure, however, is that of a curved triangle. From the standpoint of a problem-solving approach, if a figure is constructed to fit the requirements of an object occluding the three corner fragments, then in this instance its edges must be curvilinear. This is a good example of the principle that the solution must *conform* to the proximal stimulus.

Because the illusory figure is covering the fragments, *their* precise phenomenal shape depends on a number of factors. If the critical cue was that a fragment looked like an incomplete circle, then, of course, the fragment's shape in the perceptual solution would be that of a circle. But if the cue merely suggested covering of the fragment by a figure, then the precise completion would follow certain principles such as good continuation or parsimony.

Above all, if the solution is to be viable, there must be adequate *stimulus support* for it. What this means is simply this. Wherever the solution—considered as a description of a particular object or arrangement of objects—would entail the presence of a certain stimulus feature, then it must be present for that perceptual solution to survive. If not present, its absence must be accounted for. For example, if the solution is an outline figure, then a pattern with only *some* of the outline in it will not support that solution (Fig. 9.14a). But a pattern, in which the missing segments of outline are replaced by an occluding figure, *does* support that solution (Fig. 9.14b). If the solution is a solid, opaque object covering various fragments, then each corner or turning point in that object must be supported by a stimulus. The illustration in Fig. 9.15a is instructive in this

FIG. 9.14. (*a*) A pattern that does not "support" the perception of a triangle although it undoubtedly cues that perception. From Gregory (1972); (b) this pattern does support the perception of a triangle although it contains only the same same fragments of such a triangle as are present in *a*. Reproduced by permission from *Nature, 238*, pp. 51–52, © 1972 Macmillan Journals Limited.

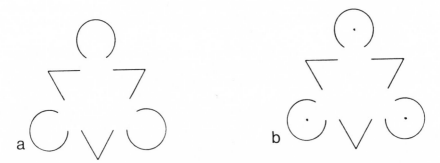

FIG. 9.15. (a) A pattern that may cue the presence of a central triangle but does not provide adequate support for such a percept; (b) with the addition of corner dots, a central white illusory triangle *is* perceived. After Kanizsa (1974).

FIG. 9.16. Despite the addition of extra lines along the perimeter of a central triangular region, no illusory white triangle is perceived. From Kanizsa (1974). Reproduced by permission of the *Italian Journal of Psychology*.

FIG. 9.17.   In comparison to Fig. 9.16, this figure yields a vivid impression of a central white figure although, except for the end points of lines, none of the contours of such a figure are physically present. From Kanizsa (1974). Reproduced by permission of the *Italian Journal of Psychology*.

regard. The incompletions and alignments are such as to strongly suggest an occluding figure. But if the corners of such a suggested figure solution are not represented by dots, as in Fig. 9.15b, the necessary support is missing. One can perceive parts of the figure, but it is vague and indeterminate in its corner regions without the presence of the dots. It is the necessity for stimulus support that distinguishes perception from other modes of cognition such as imagination or thought.

Internal consistency is critical. If the solution is that an opaque figure is present, of a lightness identical to that of the surrounding background, then its physical borders will only be visible where it happens to occlude a region (fragment) of a differing lightness. Most of the illustrations shown here are of this kind. It would be inconsistent then if certain other parts of the borders of the hypothesized figure were included in the stimulus pattern. Why are they visible and not the remainder of the figure? This analysis may explain why a pattern such as the one shown in Fig. 9.16 is not a good one for producing illusory-contour figures. It undoubtedly generates the hypothesis of an inner triangle. But it fails to support it because of the internal inconsistencies that arise. Figure 9.17 works quite well, but when some contours are added as in Fig. 9.16, the effect disappears. This occurs despite the fact that the added contours are along the locus of points that would constitute the illusory contour. Although the presence of these contours puts less of a burden on constructive processes, the illusion is not likely to occur.

The logic here is as follows: Given either solidly colored fragments or line fragments, the hypothesis is tenable that an opaque covering figure is present that is not visible for the most part because it has the same lightness as the overall background. However, it *is* visible, i.e., is revealed, where it covers another object such as the fragment. When the fragments consist of lines, as in Fig. 9.17, the lines are seen to terminate where they are occluded by the opaque object. The locus of points along the ends of the lines is perceived as the edge of the illusory figure and the lines of the fragment are seen as continuing under that edge, as part of complete shapes.

When however, the fragments are modified as is illustrated in Fig. 9.16, no consistent solution can be achieved. If the new lines here are to be perceived as visible regions of the border of the illusory figure, it is not evident why they are visible. If they are revealed because they are the outer contours of the illusory figure, there is an inconsistency with the fact that no such contour is visible *between* the fragments. If on the other hand, the new lines are organized as belonging to the fragments, as an inner border, then the observer continues to perceive them as he or she would before any hypothesis is entertained that the fragments are ground for an occluding figure. In this case no contradiction or inconsistency arises, but that organization does not allow for the emergence of an illusory-figure effect. In fact the presence of the new lines tends to "close" the fragments so that they appear to be complete figures. Thus the motive for constructive processes based on incompletion does not arise. It becomes very difficult to reverse figure and ground.

It seems clear then that from a problem-solving theoretical perspective, the pattern in Fig. 9.16 is not likely to generate an illusory figure. Whether a bottom-up theory such as is based on contrast can deal with this fact is not clear. The argument would have to be that the new, added lines serve to eliminate the end-of-line contrast effect.

A blatant contradiction is, of course, an internal inconsistency par excellence. It would be inconsistent if one were able to see through the central region hypothesized to be a solid *opaque* figure (unless conditions were such as to suggest and support a *transparency* solution). In our laboratory we investigated the effect of a striped pattern seen within the central region of an illusory-contour pattern (Rock & Anson, 1979). When depth cues such as retinal disparity or motion parallax led to an unequivocal impression that the stripes were behind the fragments, the observers were unable to perceive an illusory figure (See Fig. 9.18*b*). When, however, the stripes were seen as in front of the fragments, the illusory figure was perceived (Fig. 9.18*c*). Thus the detrimental effect of the stripes in *b* was not of some inhibitory kind based simply on the mere presence of such contours in the vicinity of the region expected to be seen as a figure with illusory contours.

A similar effect based on contradiction was demonstrated by Gregory and Harris (1974). They used a pattern like the one shown in Fig. 9.19 (but with only a single dot in each corner of the occluding triangle). By means of stereoscopic presentation the dots were made to appear behind or in front of the border-line triangle. When they appeared in front, the illusory-contour effect was enhanced, but when they appeared behind it was diminished or eliminated. Obviously the dots cannot represent the corners of an *occluding* triangle if they are *behind* the rest of the figure.

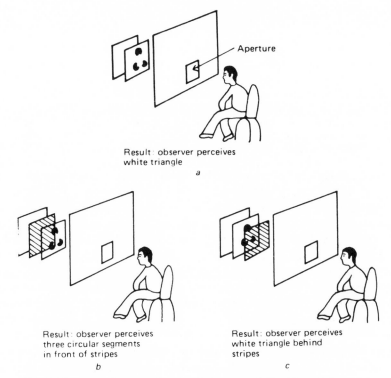

FIG. 9.18. (a) An illusory white triangle is seen occluding black circles at its corners; (b) the illusory triangle is not seen, presumably because it would be incompatible with depth information that the critical region is not opaque; (c) an illusory triangle is perceived despite the presence of stripes in the central region. However, here the stripes are seen as in front of the triangle. From Rock & Anson, (1979).

FIG. 9.19. A pattern in which an inverted white illusory triangle is not likely to be perceived unless one is alerted to it or looking for it, but which, once perceived, is as adequate as when it emerges spontaneously.

FIG. 9.20. Perceptual rationalization. Rather than preventing the illusory-contour perception, the oblique lines are perceived as parts of an elongated diamond that go above or below the illusory white rectangle. From Kanizsa (1974). Reproduced by permission of the *Italian Journal of Psychology.*

The Lightness Effect. How is the lightness effect to be explained? The absence of any support for the borders of the illusory figure ought to oppose the perception of such a figure. The hypothesis once entertained ought to be rejected. One possibility is that the perceptual system *invents* a lightness difference in order to *rationalize* the illusory-contour solution.[11] Such a process would have the effect of accounting for the perception of the contour on the basis of a lightness difference between the illusory figure and its background. An interesting fact supports this interpretation. If the illusory pattern of Fig. 9.21a is outlined as in Fig. 9.21b, the lightness effect is very much diminished (Coren & Theodor, 1975; Kennedy, 1979; Parks, 1979; Parks, Rock, & Anson, 1983). The contour eliminates the need for an invented lightness difference because its presence explains why the figure's borders are visible. Were the lightness effect the direct result of contrast, it is hard to see why it would be all but eliminated by the addition of the outline. In fact, one might reasonably expect that the presence of physical contours would facilitate a contrast effect. After all, the contour line itself should induce some contrast that ought to summate in the central region. Moreover, such contours would serve the purpose of indicating the boundaries of the region of the assimilation effect.

It is possible that the lightness effect *is* the result of contrast, but of a special kind. It is one that *depends on* the construction of the illusory contour figure, so it is a very different theory than one in which the illusory figure *results* from contrast, as discussed earlier. It has been known for over a half century that the effectiveness of contrast is very much a function of figure-ground organization (Benary, 1924). As is illustrated in Fig. 9.22, the two small gray triangles are equal in lightness. In both cases, the hypotenuse is adjacent to a white region and the legs to black regions. On the basis of a purely quantitative approach, the two

---

[11]There are many examples of rationalization in perception. The common denominator for its occurrence would seem to be the presence of an inconsistency. Rather than relinquish a particular solution that is favored, the perceptual system achieves an interpretation of the contradiction that is consistent with that solution. Another example of this in illusory-contour perception is shown in Fig. 9.20. Some of the lines if seen *behind* the central region would contradict the interpretation of that region as an opaque object. Hence they are perceived as weaving in and out, in front of that opaque object where necessary and behind it where necessary.

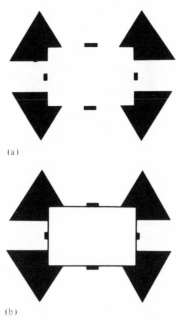

(a)

(b)

FIG. 9.21.   The typical extra-whiteness effect accompanies the perception of the illusory rectangle percept in (a), but such an effect is much weaker in (b) where the rectangle's contours are physically present. From Parks, Rock, & Anson (1983).

grays should undergo the same degree of contrast with their surroundings and appear equal in lightness. But, as the reader can see, the triangle that appears to be *on* the black cross, to belong to it, appears to be lighter than the one that appears to be *on* the white background. The effect is substantial, being almost as great as the magnitude of contrast that occurs in the better known lightness contrast effect discussed earlier (Gilchrist, 1985). Belongingness thus governs or influences contrast; the gray triangles interact more with the region to which they "belong" perceptually than they do with regions that are equally adjacent but to

FIG. 9.22.   The Benary effect. Although the two triangles are the same gray, the one on top that appears to be on the black cross is perceived as lighter than the one below. After Benary (1924).

FIG. 9.23. The white region that is perceived to be *on* or to belong to the background (the curved cross) appears whiter than the enclosed white region that does not (the square). After Kanizsa (1975).

which they do not "belong." This effect itself can be regarded as one that challenges a purely bottom-up account of contrast.

The Benary effect can be invoked to explain the lightness effect in illusory-contour figures but only after the appropriate figure–ground organization has occurred. If no such reorganization has occurred, one only perceives black figural fragments on a white ground. Whereas, if reorganization has occurred, then the illusory figure is perceived to lie *on* the black corner fragments. The illusory figure would then be expected to contrast more with the black fragments than would the white regions surrounding the fragments on all other sides. That a white region will appear to be whiter than it would otherwise appear to be as a result of just such a perceptual organization is clearly shown in Fig. 9.23. It is quite reasonable then to suppose that such an effect will occur when this organization happens with an illusory-contour display. But, to repeat, it can only be expected to occur after the illusory-figure percept is achieved.

At the moment then there are two possible explanations of the extra whiteness effect that are compatible with a problem-solving approach.[12] One is that it is of

---

[12]One might think that the perceived lightness of surfaces on the achromatic scale would be a perceptual property governed directly by sensory input such as luminance or by ratios of luminance or by sensory mechanisms such as lateral inhibition and thus have little to do with cognitive operations. If so, it follows that illusory effects such as the extra whiteness of illusory-contour figures discussed in this chapter would be explicable in terms of anomalies of sensory processing, such as contrast. But it has been known for years that perceptual factors including figure–ground organization and be-longingness affect lightness perception (Benary, 1924; Coren, 1969; Kanizsa, 1975; Wolff, 1935). Moreover, the recent work of Gilchrist (1977, 1979) has shown, among other things, that depth organization has a profound effect on lightness perception, and that the perceptual system discriminates between edges produced by reflectance differences from those produced by illumination differences. It is now possible to view lightness perception in terms of certain cognitive operations performed on input information relevant to luminance, the latter probably in the form of ratios of luminance at edges. (See Gilchrist, 1979 and Rock, 1983 for an elaboration of this way of thinking about lightness perception.) Thus the hypotheses put forward here about the extra whiteness in illusory-contour figures are in keeping with such an approach.

FIG. 9.24.   Little if any extra-whiteness effect occurs in *b* where the rectangle's contours are physically present in comparison to *a* where they are not. This suggests that the Benary contrast effect requires solid black regions and does not occur with contour lines. After Kanizsa (1974).

the nature of a cognitive invention. The other is that it results from that kind of contrast that depends on figure–ground perceptual organization, which in this case means perceptual reorganization. In both cases, the effect is secondary to the prior emergence of the illusory-contour organization rather than being the primary effect. There are two facts that favor the first explanation, namely: (1) Introducing actual contour lines where otherwise only illusory contours would be seen all but eliminates the whiteness effect. The Benary type of effect should certainly survive this change; (2) the lightness effect not only occurs but often is even more striking when line fragments replace solid black ones. It seems unlikely that the Benary type of effect would be very strong for line-figure patterns, and, indeed, very little if any extra whiteness effect occurs when actual contours are introduced instead of illusory contours in patterns where the fragments are line figures (see Fig. 9.24). Also only a slight contrast effect occurs when gray regions are embedded in a pattern of lines orthogonal to the edges of such regions (see Fig. 9.8).

There is, however, one remaining problem for the cognitive-invention theory. The illusory figure could just as well be lighter or darker than the surrounding region. Either direction of a lightness "invention" would solve the problem of rationalizing the perceptibility of the illusory figure borders. Why then is the choice one in which this figure appears *whiter* than the white background? Perhaps contrast only plays a role in resolving this ambiguity. It sets the direction or "sign" of the effect. With black fragments, solid or line, the perceptual system "decides" that the lightness of the illusory figure that differentiates it from the overall background is opposite in color to that of the covered fragments, namely white.

The Problem of Preference.   If a pattern can be perceived as an array of fragments, why is there a preference to perceive instead an illusory figure partially occluding the fragments? If, as I have suggested, hypotheses arise that something else is present or that there is some as yet unexplained relationship among the fragments, still one must ask why the perceptual system pursues these possibilities. Problem solving requires motivation.

The answer I suggest is that the literal solution is not satisfactory. Once the incompletion of the several fragments is detected, the perceptual system seeks an explanation. Once the alignment of the edges across fragments is detected, the system seeks an explanation of this as-yet unexplained coincidence. The illusory-figure solution elegantly accounts for the incompletion and/or the alignment.

The manifestation of a preference for one "solution" over another occurs often in perception. Moreover, once the preferred solution has been achieved, it is generally maintained and it is difficult to revert back to the nonpreferred, literal solution. Given the ambiguity of the proximal stimulus, some principle or principles must guide the system in the selection of a particular perceptual interpretation. The Gestaltists suggested that it is the simplest solution that is preferred (Koffka, 1935). In the case of illusory-contour patterns, whereas it is probably correct to say that *the fragments* become simple or more regular when the illusory occluding figure percept occurs, it is also the case that the solution of a figure partially occluding fragments is more complicated than the one in which only the fragments are seen for the following reason. Something must be *added* to what would otherwise be perceived, namely, the occluding figure. The empiricists would maintain that the selection is based on past experience. If that is translated to mean that the preference is for a recognizable, familiar figure, then it is worth noting that the fragments are often themselves familiar (e.g., circles with cutouts), whereas the illusory figure need not be.

Although simplicity and past experience may well play a role in the selection process,[13] I suggest another principle. The perceptual system seeks to account for regularity in the stimulus, both spatial and temporal, in such a way that it is explained as *caused* by the object or event giving rise to it rather than accepting it as mere coincidence. The reader is referred to a more complete discussion of this principle elsewhere (Rock, 1983). To make it clear here, I give an example concerning an entirely different phenomenon. The preferred perception of Fig. 9.25 is that of a transparent rectangle in front of a checkerboard type of background. It is possible to perceive this array differently, as a set of several regions of differing reflectances. That would be the literal solution, because it is perfectly correlated with the differing luminance values of the regions. But that solution leaves unexplained the fact that the four inner regions happen to compose a square and, more importantly, that the lightnesses of each of these regions change precisely along an edge aligned with the edge at which other regions change *their* lightnesses. All this is coincidence as far as the literal solution is

---

[13]Earlier (p.196, Fig. 9.4) we encountered an example where simplicity or past experience can be invoked to explain the *resistance* to the illusory-contour solution. A tendency to avoid coincidence would equally well explain this outcome.

FIG. 9.25.   A transparency pattern. After Metelli (1974).

concerned. But, in the transparency solution, it is explained: A tilted, partially transparent, square is in front of a checkerboard pattern. It is this rejection-of-coincidence principle I am invoking to explain the preference for the illusory-contour solution over the literal "fragment" solution in the examples under discussion. The incompletions and contour alignments are accounted for by the presence of the occluding figure.

The Completion Effect.   What can be said about the third feature of illusory-contour figures, the perceptual completion of the fragments? Because completion when achieved is essentially the same as with ordinary objects or drawings, where illusory contour does not enter in, e.g., Fig. 9.26, it is helpful to consider this more general case. Patterns of this kind have long been discussed under the heading of "interposition." They are regarded as a source of depth perception . . . indeed interposition is thought to be one of the major pictorial cues to the perception of depth. Proximal stimuli of this kind are generated very frequently in daily life, because they occur whenever one object occludes another. Although interest has been mainly in achieved depth, part of the phenomenal outcome is completion of the occluded object.

Various theories of the interposition effect have been offered, and there is some measure of agreement that factors of organization such as good continua-

FIG. 9.26.   A typical interposition pattern in which the preferred mode of perception is of one object occluding another (complete) object behind it rather than of two objects in the same plane joined together as in a mosaic.

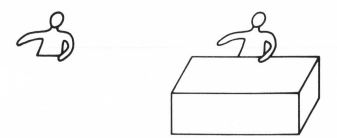

FIG. 9.27.   Although the same part of a person is represented in *a* and *b*, in *a* the person is seen as truncated, whereas in *b* the person is seen as amodally completed. From Kanizsa & Gerbino (1982).

tion play a role (Helmholtz, 1867; Ratoosh, 1949). This can account for the common contour belonging to the figure seen as in front. The common contour as shown in Fig. 9.26 is the contour between the two intersections of contours, the so-called T junctions. Although the pattern gives rise to the impression of one object in front of another, rather than to two objects in one plane fitting together as in a mosaic, and although the object seen as behind is perceived as a completed circle, it must be acknowledged that the occluded object does not appear precisely as it would were it entirely visible. The term *amodal completion* has been used to describe this experience.

Recent research supports the view that amodal completion is based on direct perceptual processing and is not merely a matter of interpretation (Kanizsa & Gerbino, 1982). What is implied here is illustrated in Fig. 9.27 in which the same visible portion of an object is shown with and without the presence of the occluding object. One can make the same *interpretation* of the incomplete object in both cases, but the fact is that in version *b* it *looks* like a complete object, whereas, in version *a* it looks like a truncated object. Indeed the ubiquity of interposition in the vision of animals and people in everyday life argues for the assumption that the completion of the occluded object is mediated by a perceptual rather than an interpretive process. Kanizsa and Gerbino (1982) have shown that the completion process has certain consequences or functional effects that would only be expected to occur if it were a perceptual process.

In an experiment performed by Gerbino and Salmaso (1985), subjects had to compare a double-figure pattern with a single, simultaneously present, figure and to press a key as soon as they recognized the single figure in the double figure. In Fig. 9.28, A is an example of a single figure used. The double figure did not always contain the single figure but, if it did, the figure was either entirely visible, C, partially occluded, B, or truncated, D. The time required to respond was about as brief for an occluded, amodally completed figure, B, as for an entire figure, C, whereas the time required to respond to a truncated version of the single figure, D, was significantly greater. In other words, the partially occluded figure contained in the comparison pattern looked about as much like

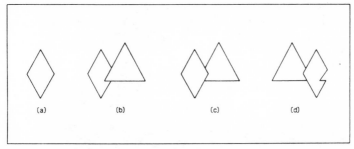

FIG. 9.28.   The reaction time to identify the presence of the target figure *a* in *b*, where it is only amodally represented, is almost as rapid as in *c* where it is entirely represented, whereas in *d*, the reaction time to identify the presence of a diamond is significantly increased although the truncated representation is physically and categorically identical to that in *b*. After Gerbino & Salmaso (1984).

the single figure as did a completed comparison figure . . . at least to the extent that a measure as sensitive as reaction time revealed little difference, whereas a truncated comparison figure (exactly the same as the directly visible parts of the occluded comparison figure) looked different from the single figure.

Therefore, as regards illusory-contour figures, it seems reasonable to say that the amodal completion of the fragments is as much a fact of perception as is the illusory contour and the extra whiteness of the illusory figure. On the face of it, there is nothing about the fragments in the illusory-contour pattern that ought to lead any bottom-up theory to predict their perceptual completion. Unlike the more typical interposition pattern, there is no central contour between two enclosed regions giving rise to a T junction at their intersections. One might, therefore, say that whereas the perception of partial occlusion of the fragments and of their completion is the phenomenal outcome it is not an outcome predictable on the basis of processes directly triggered by the stimulus.

However, it might be argued that once contrast occurs the newly emerging borders of the illusory figure transform the pattern in the vicinity of the fragments such that it now resembles an interposition pattern. Contrast alters the situation so that completion occurs as a second stage of processing for whatever reason it occurs in more typical interposition patterns. To my knowledge, no advocate of a contrast theory has proposed such an explanation or even addressed the problem of completion in illusory-contour figures. In any event, for a contrast or bottom-up theory, the completion effect is not central to the illusory-contour phenomenon and at most is epiphenomenal in this context. From a problem-solving point of view, however, the completion effect is a fundamental part of the "solution." It is top-down, a hypothesis imposed on the stimulus as it were, rather than a perception that would be expected to occur without such cognitive intervention. There is simply nothing about the stimulus per se that could be expected to lead to processing that would culminate in an interposition outcome.

FIG. 9.29. A fragmented representation of a man sitting on a bench. From Mooney & Ferguson (1951).

FINAL REMARKS

That a perception can occur either spontaneously or only after it has been suggested or otherwise facilitated is a fact that has generally been ignored by investigators. Although spontaneous perception may or may not indicate bottom-up processing, the other, facilitated, kind would surely seem to indicate top-down processing. The recognition of drawings such as the one in Fig. 9.29 is difficult and often requires prolonged inspection leading to the discovery of clues or requires being told what it represents. At that point more happens than just identification; the drawing looks different than it did before. In these cases it is hard to deny the claim that accessing relevant memories is affecting the final perception.

In this example, the stimulus is itself not adequate to lead to the final perception. Rather it leads first to some other perception, one that more literally corresponds to the stimulus input. There are various other examples of this kind, but
in these other examples it is at least debatable whether the cognitive contribution
to the outcome is based on accessing memories. Consider the phenomenon of
transparency in pictures (Fig. 9.25) discussed earlier. The transparency effect
does not always occur or does not occur right away. A hint is often necessary.
The dependency of the achievement of the effect on being informed of this option
does not necessarily mean that the memory of prior transparency perceptions is
the critical factor. The transparency solution may be available in one's repertoire
regardless of how it got there. But the important point is that in all such cases
where facilitation is required, one cannot understand the outcome without assuming that some form of cognitive representation is having an effect on the processing of sensory data.

These examples are instructive because they stop the action, as it were, in the
normal rapid processing that leads to the final, preferred, world-mode perception. They thus serve to bring out the two stages or phases of perceptual problem
solving. We see that some cue is needed to lead to the appropriate solution. In
these cases, that cue is either absent from the stimulus (or from the literal
solution to which it gives rise), not noticed, or the cue is camouflaged. It is,
therefore, worth emphasizing that despite this, the final percept, once it occurs,
can be perfectly adequate. To come back to the illusory-contour effect, a pattern
such as the one in Fig. 9.19 (and in other illustrations in this chapter) may not
spontaneously yield the effect until one is told where to look and what to look
for, but once this is known, the effect can be every bit as adequate as when the
effect spontaneously arises without a cue.[14]

If these various examples illustrate adequate perception despite poor cuing,
then there are also examples of the opposite, inadequate perception despite good
cuing. Figures 9.4, 9.14a, and 9.16 are examples of this kind. The key factor is
the quality of stimulus support. It must be adequate if the cued perception is to be
adequate. Needless to say, conditions can be such that neither the cue nor the
stimulus support is adequate, or they can be such that both are adequate. An
element in a pattern can have the dual role of serving as a cue (or as part of a cue)
and as stimulus support. The line segments between the corner fragments
orthogonal to the illusory contours in some figures in this chapter (Fig. 9.1, 9.6,
9.7, 9.15b, 9.17, 9.21a) serve in both of these capacities: Their inner ends are
aligned with the edges of the corner fragments, so that they are part of the

---

[14]Incidentally this figure was constructed to duplicate the features in a drawing previously used
by Gregory (1972) and interpreted by Frisby and Clatworthy (1975) in terms of end-of-line contrast.
My point in this regard is that the extra-whiteness effect only seems to occur *after* one realizes that
there are three points here that define a triangle occluding line segments. It is not merely a matter of
attention to the critical region. It is a matter of perceptual organization. Yet from the standpoint of a
contrast theory, the extra-whiteness effect should occur upon directing one's gaze to the appropriate
region.

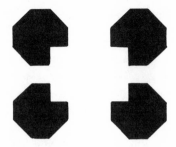

FIG. 9.30.   The illusory figure seen in Fig. 9.1 is poorer if the short line segments that provide additional stimulus support are removed.

alignment cue and thus improve it. But they also support the solution because of their location in the long stretch of space between fragments, appearing as longer lines, parts of which are occluded. Such *local* support is needed to yield the illusory contour *throughout* the empty space between corner fragments. Thus, Fig. 9.1 is improved by the presence of the line segments as can be seen by comparing it to Fig. 9.30 where they are eliminated. So we see that there is another meaning to "good patterns" other than the one concerning cuing discussed earlier.

Some further comment about the role of past experience in perceptual problem solving is warranted. The solving of a problem should not be identified with prior experience, as the Gestaltists were at pains to point out although such experience, if relevant, will often be utilized in the process (Duncker, 1945; Wertheimer, 1945). Understanding of the problem, reformulating the problem, searching for an appropriate object or method of solution are not processes that are reducible to past experience. In perception, in the case of the illusory-contour effect, we have seen that the cue of incompletion quite probably is generally based on experience, because it is through such experience that we know what configurations are incomplete departures from the norm. But the cue of alignment is not necessarily based on past experience. The hypothesis of the presence of an occluding opaque object need not necessarily derive from any experience with object occlusion in daily life. Phylogenetic "experience" is an alternative possibility. It is unlikely that the lightness effect, whether it be a cognitive intervention or a kind of contrast based on figure–ground organization, derives in any way from prior experience. Finally, the viability of a cued solution that depends on stimulus support and internal consistency and the preference for that solution over the initial, literal solution are characteristics of the perceptual process rather than contents in the mind that are acquired by previous perceptual experience.

In short "cognitive intervention" is not to be regarded as equivalent to "the effect of acquired knowledge" on perception. Moreover, where past experience does enter in, it should not be regarded as knowledge in the ordinary sense of the word. It is a central characteristic of perception that it is largely immune to any effect based on having information about what is or is not actually present in the environment. For example, illusions do not cease on learning that what is perceived is illusory. Perception is autonomous with respect to conscious thought and knowledge. Thus it is likely that when past experience does affect perception, it does so in the form of specific memories of prior perception or in the form of unconscious rules acquired in the past. However, this is a topic that cannot be pursued further here (see Rock, 1983 for a more thorough discussion).

Does the critique of the bottom-up, sensory approach and the advocacy of a top-down, cognitive theory imply rejection of brain explanations of perception? Not at all, at least not for this writer. It does imply rejection of most current attempts to derive perceptual phenomena from known sensory and neurophysiological mechanisms. It also implies rejection of the bottom-up model of brain explanation of many perceptual phenomena. But in the long run there is no reason why brain mechanisms will not be uncovered that underly psychological events such as "hypotheses" that will account for the application of such hypotheses to sensory data. Such ultimate discoveries will be all the more likely if scientists who study the brain are looking for mechanisms of this kind, because the findings of psychologists have shown that these more complex kinds of processes, rather than simpler sensory processes, are implicated.

REFERENCES

Benary, W. (1924). Beobachtung zu einem Experiment uber Helligkeitskontrat. *Psyhologisch Forschung, 5,* 131–142. (Reprinted in W. Ellis, *A source book of Gestalt Psychology,* Selection 8, The Humanities Press, 1950)

Brigner, W. L., & Gallagher, M. B. (1974). Subjective contour: apparent depth or simultaneous brightness contrast? *Perception and Motor Skills, 38,* 1047–1053.

Coren, S. (1969). Brightness contrast as a function of figure-ground relations. *Journal of Experimental Psychology, 80,* 517–524.

Coren, S., & Theodor, L. H. (1975). Subjective contour: The inadequacy of brightness contrast as an explanation. *Bulletin of the Psychonomic Society, 6,* 87–89.

Cornsweet, T. N. (1970). *Visual perception.* New York: Academic Press.

Craik, K. J. W. (1966). *The nature of psychology.* Cambridge, England: Cambridge University Press.

Day, R. H., & Jory, M. K. (1978). Subjective contours, visual acuity and line contrast. In J. C. Armington, J. E. Krauskopf, & B. Wooten (Eds.), *Visual psychophysics: Its physiological basis.* New York: Academic Press.

Duncker, K. (1945). On problem solving. *Psychological Monographs, 58,* 1–112.

Ehrenstein, W. (1941). Uber Abwandlungen der L Hermannschen Helligkeitserscheinung Zeitschrift fur Psychologie, *150,* 83–91.

Frisby, J. P., & Clatworthy, J. L. (1975). Illusory contours: Curious cases of simultaneous brightness contrast? *Perception, 4,* 349–357.

Gerbino, W., & Salmaso, D. (1985). Un analisi processuale del completamento amodale. *Giornale Italiano de Psicologia, XII,* 97–121.

Gilchrist, A. (1977). Perceived lightness depends on perceived spatial arrangement. *Science, 195,* 185–187.

Gilchrist, A. (1979). The perception of surface blacks and whites. *Scientific American, 240,* 112–126.

Gilchrist, A. (1985, in press). Lightness contrast and failure of constancy: A common explanation. *Perception and Psychophysics.*

Girgus, J., Rock, I., & Egatz, R. (1977). The effect of knowledge of reversibility on the reversibility of ambiguous figures. *Perception & Psychophysics, 22,* 550–556.

Gregory, R. L. (1972). Cognitive contours. *Nature, 238,* 51–52.

Gregory, R. L., & Harris, J. P. (1974). Illusory contours and stereo depth. *Perception & Psychophysics, 15,* 411–416.

Helmholtz, H. von. (1867). *Treatise on physiological optics* (Vol. III). (Trans. from 3rd German ed., edit by J. P. C. Southall). (Dover Publications, 1962. First publ. in the Handbuch der Physiologischen Optik, Voss)

Jory, M. K., & Day, R. H. (1979). The relationship between brightness contrast and illusory contours. *Perception, 8,* 3–9.

Kanizsa, G. (1955). Margini quasi-percettivi in campi con stimolazione omogenea. *Revista di Psicologia, 49,* 7–30.

Kanizsa, G. (1974). Contours without gradients or cognitive contours? *Italian Journal of Psychology, 1,* 93–113.

Kanizsa, G. (1975). Some new demonstrations of the role of structural factors in brightness contrast. In S. Ertel, L. Kemmler, M. Stadler (Eds.), *Gestaltheorie in der modernen psychologie.* Darmstadt: Steinkopff.

Kanizsa, G. (1976, April). Subjective contours. *Scientific American, 234,* 48–51.

Kanizsa, G., & Gerbino, W. (1982). Amodal completion: Seeing or thinking? In J. Beck (Ed.), *Organization and representation in perception.* Hillsdale, NJ: Lawrence Erlbaum Associates.

Kennedy, J. M. (1976). Attention, brightness, and the constructive eye. In M. Henle (Ed.), *Vision and artifact.* New York: Springer.

Kennedy, J. M. (1978). Illusory contours not due to completion. *Perception, 7,* 187–189.

Kennedy, J. M. (1979). Subjective contours, contrast, and assimilation. In C. F. Nodin & D. F. Fisher (Eds.), *Perception and pictorial representation.* New York: Praeger.

Koffka, K. (1935). *Principles of gestalt psychology.* New York: Harcourt Brace Jovanovich.

Krauskopf, J. (1963). Effect of retinal image stabilization on the appearance of heterochromatic targets. *Journal of the Optical Society of America, 53,* 741–744.

Metelli, F. (1974). The perception of transparency. *Scientific American, 230,* 90–98.

Mooney, C. M., & Ferguson, G. A. (1951). A new closure test. *Canadian Journal of Psychology, 5,* 129–133.

O'Brien, V. (1958). Contour perception, illusion and reality. *Journal of the Optical Society of America, 48,* 112–119.

Parks, T. (1979). Subjective figures: Does brightness enhancement depend upon subjective boundary definition? *Perception and Psychophysics, 26,* 418.

Parks, T. E., Rock, I., & Anson, R. (1983). Illusory contour lightness: A neglected possibility. *Perception, 12,* 43–47.

Pritchard, W. S., & Warm, J. S. (1983). Attentional processing and the subjective contour illusion. *Journal of Experimental Psychology: General, 112,* 145–175.

Ratliff, F. (1965). *The Mach bands: Quantitative studies on neural networks in the retina.* New York: Holden–Days.

Ratoosh, P. (1949). On interposition as a cue for the perception of distance. *Proceedings of the National Academy of Science, 35,* 257–259.

Richardson, B. L. (1979). The nonequivalance of abrupt and diffuse illusory contours. *Perception, 8,* 589–593.

Rock, I. (1983). *The logic of perception.* Cambridge: Bradford Books/The MIT Press.
Rock, I., & Anson, R. (1979). Illusory contours as the solution to a problem. *Perception, 8,* 665–681.
Titchener, E. B. (1926). *A textbook of psychology.* New York: Macmillan.
Ware, C. (1981). Subjective contours independent of subjective brightnesses. *Perception & Psychophysics, 29,* 500–504.
Wertheimer, M. (1945). *Productive thinking.* New York: Harper.
Wolff, W. (1935). Induzierte Helligkeitsveranderung. *Psychologische Forschung, 20,* 159–194.
Wundt, W. (1907). *Outlines of psychology* (4th German ed.) (C. H. Judd, Trans.), Stechert.

10 Toward a Computational Neuropsychology of High-Level Vision

Stephen Michael Kosslyn
Harvard University

Visual processes in humans have recently been studied from three distinct perspectives, with only the barest amount of cross fertilization among them. In this chapter we consider a way of melding the approaches of Artificial Intelligence (AI), Cognitive Psychology, and Neuropsychology, and explore the advantages of such a hybrid approach. Each of the individual approaches has its strengths and weaknesses, but these are different for each of them; by combining the three, we are in a position to take advantage of each one's strengths and may be able to circumvent each one's weaknesses. Although I believe that most of the observations offered in this chapter generalize to the study of all cognitive abilities, I restrict the examples to vision. Vision has been the subject of intense study in the three disciplines, and the evidence seems clear at least in this case that there is much to be gained by combining the approaches.

The focus in this chapter is on just those events that take place near the end of the visual-processing sequence that originates at the eyes. These events can be considered "mental" because they can be affected by one's knowledge and beliefs (whereas processes carried out by low-level systems, such as those localized at the retina, presumably are not affected by one's knowledge and beliefs). The study of high-level, "mental" events presents problems that are not as severe when one studies "low-level" processing, which is closely tied to properties of the stimuli. In low-level vision, an analysis of the geometry of surfaces and the optics of light places strong constraints on how information must be processed, as is discussed shortly. By the time we get to high-level processing, however, these properties of the stimuli have been transformed numerous times in numerous ways. How can we best go about trying to understand the last phases of the sequence of transformations? This task is a little like constructing a ship at sea, with each piece floating freely. Once we have nailed down a few of the pieces, the job will become easier; but how do we characterize the initial pieces? Let us briefly review the key features and limitations of the approaches currently taken in AI, Cognitive Psychology, and Neuropsychology.

THE COMPUTATIONAL APPROACH

One way of trying to understand the nature of vision is to consider what would be necessary to program a computer to see. In so doing, one is first led to ask about the purposes of vision and then is led to consider what problems must be solved in order for it to serve these ends. At the most general level of analysis, vision serves two general functions: First, it allows one to identify objects and events in the environment. Central to this capacity is the ability to compare representations of input to stored representations of previously seen objects. Second, it allows one to navigate around in the environment (without bumping into objects), and conversely, to avoid or intersect other objects that are moving. Central to this capacity is the ability to represent metric spatial relations and to update them efficiently as the organism or part of the environment moves. In addition, one can store visual input, which allows one to reason about objects and events in their absence (e.g., to consider whether one's hand could fit into a certain hole one remembers being of a specific size and shape). Central to this capacity is the ability to ''re-present'' objects and events to oneself in their immediate absence and to operate on these representations in a way that allow one to anticipate what would happen should the analogous actual operations be performed in the real world.

In trying to understand even one of these capacities, researchers very quickly discovered the usefulness of positing a modular design, with separate mechanisms being used to carry out distinct aspects of performance. Thus, researchers in AI developed theories of the *processing modules* used in vision. A processing module is a ''black box'' that carries out specific computation or computations. By ''computation'' I mean, roughly, a meaningful (i.e., informationally interpretable) transformation of an input. The theorist specifies the nature of the computations performed by various modules.

A *theory of a computation* specifies four things: the purpose of the computation, the information to be used in performing a computation, a description of what is being computed, and assumptions that must be met for the successful use of the computation (i.e., specification of its boundary conditions, see Marr, 1982). For example, consider a theory of a computation used in low-level vision to detect edges of objects. The information available is an intensity array, with intensity values specified for each point on the image. The computation posited by the theory discovers places where the intensity changes rapidly, which are assumed to correspond to edges of represented surfaces. What this computation does can be described as finding the zero-crossings in the second derivative of the function relating intensity and position. If light is arranged correctly, as in a movie, the system will be fooled—seeing edges where none exist. (The actual theory is more complicated, involving a convolution of the image with a function representing the output from the very early processors; however, this brief presentation is sufficient for present purposes. See Marr, 1982, Chapter 3.)

Researchers in AI do not stop with theories of processing modules and their constituent computations. Rather, in order actually to build a working program one must also formulate a theory of *how* a computation is actually accomplished on-line. Each "black box" can be opened up, so to speak, and its internal workings described. Indeed, a theory of processing modules (and their associated computations) is a way of organizing sets of representations and processing operations into coherent units; that is, a processing module is presumed to correspond to a mechanism that accomplishes the computations that constitute the module. The on-line operation of this mechanism can be described by a theory of the *algorithm* for a given task. The algorithm specifies step by step how a computation or set of computations is carried out.

To get a feel for the distinction between a computation and the algorithm that carries it out, think of the number of different ways one could perform a computation like multiplication; one could add one of the numbers to itself over and over, convert the numbers to logs and add the exponents, etc. The actual procedure follows an algorithm, and numerous different algorithms can be used to carry out the same computation.

In the course of developing theories of the algorithms used, a theory of the *functional architecture* is developed. (Newell & Simon, 1972, are primarily responsible for introducing the idea of a functional architecture to psychology.) A theory of the functional architecture specifies the kinds of representations (e.g., Roman numerals, numbers in log base 10, etc), buffers (places where representations can be stored), and processing operations (such as addition, matching, and substitution) that can be used in the algorithms that actually carry out the computations (see Kosslyn, 1984, for a more detailed discussion of the concept of a functional architecture). A given component of the functional architecture (e.g., a buffer) in principle might be used by different algorithms that carry out different computations (e.g., the same buffer can be used to store two numbers being added or multiplied); alternatively, it might be used only by one algorithm, which carries out only a single computation.

A "computational theory," then, is a theory that: (1) specifies the processing modules (and the constituent computations) used in performing a set of tasks; (2) specifies the representations, buffers, and processing operations used in carrying out the computations; and (3) specifies the precise sequence of steps used to perform a set of tasks. Incomplete computational theories are today the rule rather than the exception, but all computational theories are directed at eventually specifying these three aspects of information processing.

Limitations of the approach

On Marr's view, the core of a theory of how information is processed is the theory of the computation. The notion of a theory of the computation is relatively novel for cognitive psychology, and it is worth exploring the force of Marr's views. Marr (1982) argues that the information available and the purpose of a computation often virtually dictate what the computation must be. This sort of theory can sometimes be almost like a solution to a mathematics problem, arising through logical analysis of the nature of the problem to be solved and the input available to solve it. That is, if the task is very well defined and the input is highly restricted, a specific computation may seem almost logically necessary. Furthermore, Marr claims that once a computation is defined the task of characterizing the representations and processes used in carrying out an algorithm is now highly constrained: The representation of the input and the output must make explicit the information necessary for the computation to serve its purpose (e.g., picking out likely locations of edges), and the representations must be sensitive to the necessary distinctions, be stable over irrelevant distinctions, and have a number of other properties (see Marr, 1982, Chapter 5).

To return to the example of the computation for detecting edges that was discussed previously, note that once we have described the purpose and the input, we have almost defined what has to be computed. In addition, once the theory of the zero-crossings computation was formulated, the theory of the representation of the output of the computation was highly constrained: It needed to have primitives that were likely to correspond to physically-meaningful properties of the geometry of surfaces and had to make explicit places where zero crossings exist. Marr's "primal sketch" uses short line segments, bars, blobs, and the like to connect contiguous zero crossings, producing a representation with properties that are desirable as input to later computations that derive characteristics of surfaces and shape.

Marr's strong claims about the priority of the theory of the computation do seem appropriate for some of the problems of low-level vision, but only because there are such severe constraints on the input (posed by the nature of the world and the geometry of surfaces) and because the purpose of a computation is so well defined (e.g., to detect places where intensity changes rapidly, to derive depth from disparities in the images striking each eye, to recover structure from information about changes on a surfaces as an object moves). In cognition, the situation is somewhat different: First, the basic abilities in need of explanation— analogous to our ability to see edges or to see depth in vision—must be discovered. For example, with the advent of new methodologies, our picture of what can be accomplished in mental imagery has changed drastically (e.g., see Shepard & Cooper, 1982). Second, the input to a "mental" computation often is not obvious, not necessarily being constrained by some easily observed property of the stimulus. One must have a theory of what is represented before one can even begin to specify the input to the computations. Third, the optimal computation will depend in part on the kinds of processing operations that are available; presumably, over the course of evolution new computations developed in part by taking advantage of the available processing resources. Thus, developing a theory of the functional architecture—which specifies the types of structures and processing operations available—would seem to go hand in hand with developing a theory of a cognitive computation.

This conclusion is illustrated by problems with some of Marr's own work on "high level" vision. Marr posits that shapes must be stored using "object-centered" descriptions, as opposed to "viewer-centered" descriptions. In an object-centered description an object is described relative to itself, not from a particular point of view. Thus terms such as *dorsal* and *ventral* would be used in an object-centered description, as opposed to terms such as *top* and *bottom*, which would be used in a viewer-centered description. Marr argues that because objects are seen from so many different points of view, it would be difficult to recognize an object by matching viewer-centered descriptions of input to stored representations. However, this argument, based on a theory of the purpose of a computation, rests on implicit assumptions about the kinds of representations and processes available in the functional architecture. If there is an "orientation normalization" preprocessor, the argument is obviated: In this case, a viewer-centered description could be normalized (e.g., so the longest axis is always vertical) before matching to stored representations. And in fact, we do "mentally rotate" objects to a standard orientation when subtle judgments must be made (see Shepard & Cooper, 1982). Furthermore, the mere fact that we do seem to normalize the represented orientation, at least in some cases, casts doubt on the power or generality of object-centered representations (if object-centered descriptions are made, it simply is not clear why orientation normalization would be necessary). In fact, when the matter was put to empirical test, Jolicoeur and Kosslyn (1983) found that people can use both viewer-centered and object-centered coordinate systems in storing information and seem to encode a viewer-centered one even when they also encode an object-centered one, but not vice versa.

Similarly, one could easily take issue with Marr's assumption that the representations are genuine 3-dimensional representations, as opposed to "2½-D" representations, where one only stores the visible depth information (and not the occluded parts—as opposed to an actual 3-D representation, which stores all parts, as would occur in a stick figure or pattern of points in a 3-D array). Furthermore, one can even question whether shape representations used in recognition are distinct from those used in navigation and visual reasoning (as is involved in deciding whether a jar can fit on a particular space in the refrigerator). If not, then the input to the recognition computation is apt to be quite different from what was assumed by Marr.

The point is that a logical analysis of requirements on computations is not enough: At least for high-level abilities, the specifics of a computation will depend to some extent on what types of representations and processing operations are available in the functional architecture. One can only discover the actual state of affairs empirically, by actually studying the way the brain works.

Although the computational approach is not sufficient in and of itself to lead one to formulate a correct theory of information processing, it does have a lot to contribute to the enterprise: Thinking about how one could build a computer program to emulate a human ability is a very useful way of enumerating alternative processing modules, functional architectures, and algorithms. Not only does this approach raise alternatives that one may not have otherwise considered, but it eliminates others by forcing one to work them out concretely enough to reveal their flaws (the Guzman approach to vision is a good example; see Winston, 1975).

THE COGNITIVE PSYCHOLOGY APPROACH

The approach in cognitive psychology has been solidly empirical. Researchers have developed methodologies that make use of response times, error rates, and various judgments and have developed ways of using these methodologies to draw inferences about underlying mechanisms. Indeed, cognitive psychologists have developed methods for studying the separate components of information processing. These methodologies have become very sophisticated and powerful, allowing researchers to observe quite subtle regularities in processing. As we saw in the previous section, such data place strong constraints on theories of processing: because processing takes place in real time, there will always be measurable consequences of any given sequence of activity—and if the wrong pattern of responses occurs, a theory can be ruled out.

Although psychologists occasionally focus on the nature of an algorithm a subject is using (particularly if the subject is an expert at the activity, e.g., see Simon & Simon, 1978), they usually have been interested in studying specific components of the functional architecture (e.g., a short-term memory buffer; organization of a long-term memory network; types of production rules). Properties of components of the functional architecture are revealed when a person is engaged in a specific kind of information processing that presumably requires use of those components. However, it has proven difficult to draw firm conclusions about the underlying architecture or algorithms because of two general problems: structure/process tradeoffs and task-demand artifacts.

Structure/process tradeoffs

Anderson (1978) demonstrated that given any set of data, more than one theory can always be formulated to account for the data. His proof rests on the pervasive possibility of "structure/process tradeoffs." That is, what in one theory are properties of a given representation operated on by a specific process are in another theory properties of a different representation operated on by a different process (and this process compensates for the difference in representations, producing the same input/output characteristics when the representation is operated upon). The "analogue/propositional" imagery debate provides a good illustration of this point. For example, consider the results of experiments on "mental rotation" (see Shepard & Cooper, 1982, for a review), in which subjects require increasingly more time to compare two similar figures that are presented at increasingly disparate orientations. The "analogue theories" posit a representation that *depicts* the objects. In such a representation, (1) each part of the representation corresponds to part of a stimulus such that, (2) the distances among parts in the representation (where "distance" is defined functionally—as are distances among cells in an array in a computer) preserve the actual distances among the corresponding parts. These representations are like patterns of points in an array in a computer, and rotation is accomplished by shifting the points incrementally—with more shifts being required to effect a greater change in the represented orientation (see Kosslyn, 1980, 1981).

In contrast, "propositional theories" posit that objects are always represented in terms of descriptions. In this case, each part is described as being in a certain position relative to another part (e.g., attached to the left and oriented 45° up), and "rotation" consists of altering the relations incrementally (e.g., changing the number representing the angle from 45° to 90° in 15° steps). Thus, greater "rotations" require more time.

The two types of theories mimic each other, but in a rather uninteresting way: They are created ad hoc simply to account for the data. What is required are constraints on the theories, a source of motivation for selection of the specific representations and processes. Why should information be represented depictively or propositionally? Why is the transformation apparently done incrementally? Computational considerations are one possible source of constraint (e.g., a depictive representation makes explicit all metric spatial relationships among an object's parts, which is very useful for performing certain kinds of computations). However, we saw earlier that computational constraints in and of themselves are not sufficient—and in fact the observation of how the system functions (i.e., the dependence of response time on angle) put constraints on computational theories themselves.

Anderson (1978) drew some very pessimistic conclusions from the possibility of structure/process tradeoffs, but others such as Hayes–Roth (1979) and Pylyshyn (1979) were less gloomy. The upshot of the debate seems to be that it is possible to derive firm inferences about processing mechanisms from behavioral data, but it is very difficult to do so. One argument to be developed in this chapter is that neuropsychological data are powerful supplements to the usual behavioral data and greatly diminish the ease of using structure/process tradeoffs to concoct alternative theories.

Task demands

Another problem in interpreting behavioral data is the possibility of task demands, which is especially severe in studies of visual thinking. That is, subjects may respond (e.g., by taking longer to rotate an image of an object oriented at a greater angle) because they believe—perhaps unconsciously—that this is what the task requires them to do. Part and parcel of understanding the task may be to mimic the analogous real-world event (cf. Pylyshyn, 1981). If so, then data from many studies of mental imagery may say nothing about the nature of the underlying mechanisms but only reflect the subjects' understanding of tasks, knowledge of physics and perception, and ability to regulate their response times.

Although the problem of task demands has been brought to our attention primarily in the imagery literature (see Kosslyn, Pinker, Smith, & Shwartz, 1979, and commentators on that paper), it is applicable to many domains in cognitive psychology. There is no way to ensure that subjects are not unconsciously producing data in accordance with their "tacit knowledge" about perception and cognition and their understanding of what the task requires them to do. In contrast, neurological maladies not only produce behavioral deficits of various types, but sometimes the patients are not aware of the nature of these deficits (as is discussed later for "unilateral visual neglect"). Thus, these types of data might profitably supplement the usual cognitive data if for no reason other than to rule out task-demands accounts of data; some neurological patients cannot be responding to task demands because they are unaware of what they cannot do. And such data are useful for other purposes, as discussed in the following section.

In short, the strong suit of the cognitive psychologists is their sophisticated methodologies and the well-described phenomena discovered in the laboratory. However, although these phenomena can be used to rule out theories that posit specific structures operated on by specific processes, they are difficult to use to pin down the properties of the separate components of the functional architecture. As is discussed shortly, neuropsychological data help to put two important kinds of constraints on theories of how information is processed: constraints on the nature of the processing modules, and constraints on the representations and processing operations used in the modules. However, these data are most useful if construed within a theoretical framework—which can be provided using a computational approach—and if approached with sensitive methodologies—which have been developed in cognitive psychology.

NEUROPSYCHOLOGICAL APPROACHES

It is important to begin by distinguishing between two related, but distinct, neuropsychological projects: On the one hand, one can focus on the theory of functioning. In this case, one would use neuropsychological data (e.g., behavioral dysfunction following brain damage) to help formulate and evaluate a computational theory. On the other hand, one can focus on the brain per se. In this case, one would try to characterize different brain loci (e.g., cerebral hemispheres) or patterns of activation in terms of the computations they support. In this chapter the focus is on the theory of functioning, although in developing such a theory we may discover interesting facts about the role of specific brain structures. A good computational theory will provide a "road map" to guide investigations of the operation of the organ itself, and may even be a necessary prerequisite to understanding how the brain itself works.

The fact that cognition is something the brain does is so obvious it seems barely worth stating. But because of this fact, if a theory of cognitive processing is correct, then the various distinctions made in the theory must be respected by the brain. For example, if a theory claims that shape and color are extracted by separate mechanisms, then separate mechanisms must exist in the brain (which need not be localized in distinct regions, however). The nature of the brain introduces a number of constraints for theories of cognition: The theory should be able to explain why certain abilities are lost together whereas others can be lost separately. It should also be able to explain why patterns of brain activity are more or less similar for different sorts of tasks. Furthermore, theories must obey the broad constraints imposed by the nature of the mechanism itself; for example, if a theory posits that items are searched at a rate exceeding the firing time of neurons, the theory must be incorrect. Thus, it makes sense to look at data that bear on the functioning of brain mechanisms when formulating and testing theories of cognition.

Neuropsychological data are of two broad classes: First, and by far the most predominant, are data on behavioral dysfunction following brain damage. The damage can be endogenous (e.g., following a stroke or development of a tumor) or exogenous (e.g., following head injury or surgery, as in split-brain patients). Second, and of more recent vintage, are data on dynamic changes within an intact brain performing specific cognitive tasks. These data are obtained primarily by using EEG (electroencephalograph), ERP (event-related potentials), PET (positron emission tomography), Xenon-133 regional cerebral bloodflow, and NMR (nuclear magnetic resonance) techniques. Each technique has different advantages and drawbacks, and to a large extent they complement one another.

There is a rich literature on the neuropsychology of high-level vision, which can be of real value in constraining computational theories. John Hughlings Jackson is usually credited with making the first substantive observations on visual deficits following brain damage. In 1874 he described a way in which the cerebral hemispheres might be specialized, proposing that the posterior part of the right hemisphere is the "chief seat of the revival of images in the recognition of object, places, etc." (pg 101). This inference was based on the problems a patient with a lesion in this area had in knowing where she was. In 1876 Jackson described what is now known as "visual agnosia" (also called "mind-blindness''); this patient failed to recognize her nurses, got lost frequently when travelling familiar routes, and often did not know objects, persons, or places. This malady resulted from a lesion in the posterior right hemisphere. Patients suffering from visual agnosia are not blind: These patients can compare two shapes reliably when both are visible, but they cannot visually recognize what an object is (although many can recognize objects by touch). This sort of agnosia has been well documented in the literature (see Benton, 1982). By 1910 a number of visual/spatial deficits following brain damage had been identified, including difficulties in reading, locating objects in space, and ''neglect'' (ignoring) of objects that lie off to one side of the viewer. In addition, various theorists (e.g., Reichardt, 1918; Rieger, 1909—discussed in Benton, 1982) hypothesized that spatial/practical functions and verbal/conceptual functions are carried out by distinct mechanisms, which might be localized to the cerebral hemispheres (with verbal/conceptual on the left, spatial/practical on the right).

Recent reviews of the literature on visual deficits following brain damage (e.g., Benton, 1982; DeRenzi, 1982; Ratcliff, 1982) reveal that various clinical signs are fairly common following damage in particular regions of the brain (e.g., neglect of the left side often follows damage to the right parietal lobe), and that various deficits can be dissociated. For example, patients can have difficulty in copying objects (by drawing or constructing a model) but have no visual discrimination problems, or vice versa (Costa & Vaughan, 1962). In addition, considerable effort has been made in trying to identify various functions with one hemisphere or the other (see Springer & Deutsch, 1981).

Perhaps the most important conceptual development in the brain-damage literature is the formulation of the logic of the ''double dissociation.'' If some behavioral deficit reflects damage to a specific processing mechanism (e.g., for performing some sort of shape discrimination), and at least part of this mechanism is distinct from other processing mechanisms, then one should find cases where the ability is spared whereas other abilities are disrupted (e.g., perhaps discriminating orientation) and vice versa. (It is the ''vice versa'' that produces the ''double'' dissociation.) This sort of data provides very strong evidence for a particular set of processors in the system.

In addition to dissociations, one also finds associations. If a patient cannot perform task X, in many cases he or she also will be unable to perform task Y. This sort of result could indicate that the same aspect of the functional architecture is recruited in performing both tasks, and that component no longer functions effectively. However, one must be careful here: It could be that different functions happen to be carried out by the same (or nearby) neural tissue, and hence the association of deficits following brain damage in a given region says nothing about shared functions in different tasks. Thus, careful tests must be devised to ensure that processing is disrupted in the same way in different tasks in order to provide evidence that the tasks share a processing component (I discuss an example of this in the next section).

Limitations of the approach

There are two limitations evident in the neuropsychological literature that are of particular interest here: First, the theories have not been very sophisticated. For example, "localizing oneself in space" is usually considered a single ability in the neuropsychological literature, whereas a computationally oriented theorist would be inclined to decompose this ability into various encoding, representation and retrieval operations. Similarly, visual agnosia is described ("mind-blindness"), but the underlying causes of the deficit have not been explained; a computational approach would lead one to attempt to characterize the nature of the representations (or properties thereof) that may be lost or to characterize the nature of the failure of processes that encode perceptual information, match it to stored input, and/or make use of the stored information.

The computational approach has recently had an influence in neuropsychology and appears to be a promising avenue for future work. For example, Moscovitch (1979) distinguishes between low-level "stimulus features" (presumably processed by both hemispheres) and higher order processes (which may be localized in one cerebral hemisphere). This distinction helps to explain why hemispheric specialization only appears for some phenomena. A more detailed computational analysis might reveal that a given type of stimulus feature (e.g., places where intensity changes most rapidly) might rely on a computation that is localized in a given region, whereas others might rely on computations localized in other regions. Thus, guided by such notions a closer look might reveal subtleties that are not evident in the available data. An analogous case is our study of image generation, discussed in the following section, which illustrates how a computational analysis can illuminate neuropsychological phenomena.

The second limitation evident in many neuropsychological studies with humans is a lack of sophisticated methodologies. Much neuropsychological work centers on administering standardized tests to various patient populations and looking for differences in performance. These tests, however, do not necessarily tap distinct underlying processing mechanisms, and performance on them may be related in a complicated way to underlying deficits.

In short, neuropsychological data provide another source of constraint on theories of high-level visual processing. They have the potential of being especially useful in identifying processing modules, given the logic of "double dissociation." Let us now consider in more detail some of the potential benefits of combining the three approaches.

COMBINING THE APPROACHES

The logic of dissociations and associations in deficits is a very powerful way of developing and testing computational theories if it is yoked with the methodologies and analytic techniques developed by the cognitive psychologists. The methodologies developed by cognitive psychologists for the most part can be adapted for use in neuropsychological studies (much as many of them have been adapted to study cognitive processes in children; e.g., see Siegler, 1978). However, this has not been done by the few researchers who have used neuropsychological data to place constraints on explicit computational theories of high-level vision. For example, Marr (who was perhaps the best computational theorist, and thus worthy of such close examination) was very impressed by Warrington and Taylor's (1973) findings on the failure of patients with parietal-lobe damage to recognize misoriented objects (e.g., buckets viewed from the top). Marr concluded that this failure demonstrated that objects are stored as descriptions, and that such descriptions are formed by assigning a major axis to an object and then minor axes (of attached parts) off of it; when buckets were seen top down, one presumably had difficulty locating the major axis. However, from above, patients problems may have had nothing to do with axis assignment: perhaps they were unable to "mentally rotate" objects into a canonical orientation during the recognition process. This possibility is, of course, directly testable by applying the methodologies of contemporary cognitive psychology to brain-damaged populations.

To summarize, each of the three approaches discussed previously has something to offer, and each is complemented by the other two. The computational approach is especially useful for generating hypotheses about processing mechanisms: Thinking about the requirements of the task at hand and how one would need to program a computer to perform it is a good way of generating alternative theories. In addition, this approach provides a way of testing complex theories, by actually building a computer program that emulates cognitive processing (see Newell and Simon, 1972). Precise theories of on-line brain functioning may well be so complex that many of a theory's implications will be derived only by using simulation models.

Neuropsychological data offer constraints both on theories of processing modules and theories of the functional architecture. The finding of double dissociations allows one to argue that abilities involve at least some specialized processing modules. In addition, as is illustrated shortly, the finding of specific deficits that generalize across tasks of a given type can be used to implicate specific representations and buffers. However, neuropsychological data are open to multiple interpretations (just as are any other data) and must be approached analytically.

The methods of cognitive psychology can be profitably used analytically to investigate computational hypotheses about neuropsychological phenomena. These methods allow one to isolate the variables responsible for an effect, and often specific variables can be identified as reflecting the operation of distinct computations (e.g., using Sternberg's, 1966, additive factors methodology). In addition, once there are prior reasons for positing a specific modular composition of the system, the standard techniques of cognitive psychology become more powerful: Once a module is defined, the number of "degrees of freedom" is reduced for possible structure/process tradeoffs. That is, without modularity constraints, any part of the system can be invoked in combination with any other part to explain a specific result; but if a result can be shown to rest on the operation of a specific module—which is distinct from other modules—the explanation of the result becomes more constrained. Once well-specified classes of alternative theories are defined, cognitive psychologists are better able to specify which phenomena will distinguish among competing accounts (e.g., see the mental rotation case discussed previously as treated in Chapter 8 of Kosslyn, 1980).

Thus, the three approaches complement each other. The very rich neuropsychological phenomena place strong constraints on computational theories, especially when the tools of cognitive psychology are used to precisely characterize the phenomena. In addition, the computational approach provides useful guidelines about which phenomena are worth detailed scrutiny (as illustrated earlier in the discussion of Marr's use of Warrington and Taylor's findings). Furthermore, theory development will become much more challenging—and potentially rewarding—if we combine the requirements from all three disciplines: The theory must not only explain the neuropsychological phenomena and the data from normal subjects, but ultimately must be capable of guiding one to build a computer model that actually emulates the behavior of normal and brain-damaged subjects. Unlike the case in cognitive psychology, where it is easy to construct numerous alternative theories, we will be lucky to formulate even a single theory that meets these criteria.

SOME EXAMPLES OF A COMPUTATIONAL NEUROPSYCHOLOGY OF HIGH-LEVEL VISION

It is probably most useful to provide some concrete examples of how this combined "computational neuropsychological" approach can be used. Let us begin by very briefly considering the key aspects of the Kosslyn and Shwartz computational theory of visual mental imagery, and then consider some examples of (1) how available data in the neuropsychological literature bears on the theory; (2) how behavioral dysfunction following brain damage can be used to test and help develop the theory; and (3) how PET scanning studies can be used to test the theory.

The key claims of the Kosslyn and Shwartz theory can be divided into two classes, pertaining to representations and processes. With regard to representations, the theory claims that the experience of "having an image" reflects the existence of a depictive representation in a visual short-term memory buffer. Such a representation depicts in the same way that a pattern of points in an array in a computer can depict an object (see Kosslyn, 1983). This representation occurs in a buffer (which is a component of the functional architecture) that functions as an array, with patterns within it comprising the image itself. The image is a temporary representation, which is created on the basis of information stored in long-term memory. We claim that visual memories of objects are stored in long-term memory in terms of (1) perceptual memories, organized into "chunks" that correspond to parts of objects (e.g., a dog's body, legs, etc. might be stored in distinct units) and (2) descriptions, which indicate how the chunks are arranged.

With regard to the processing modules themselves, which make use of the representations, let us consider here only those used in generating an image (i.e., creating a short-term memory representation on the basis of information stored in long-term memory). Previous research has suggested that image generation is not a single computation. Rather, generation seems to involve a processing module that actually activates stored perceptual information (called PICTURE in our theory), another that "looks" for locations where other parts belong on partially completed images (called FIND in our theory), and yet a third (called PUT in our theory) that uses descriptions (e.g., "a cushion is flush on a chair's seat") to position additional parts onto an imaged object (see Kosslyn, 1981, for a brief overview). For example, in imaging a chair the PICTURE processing module would activate the main form of the chair (called a "skeletal image" in our theory), and in order to image the cushion on the seat the FIND processing module would locate the seat, and the PUT processing module would use the location information (plus its "understanding" of the meaning of the relation "flush on") to provide input to the PICTURE module so that the cushion would be imaged at the correct position relative to the seat. The PUT processing module is putatively responsible for looking up the description of the part and its relation, and uses this information to invoke the FIND and PICTURE modules appropriately.

This theory is based on computational and empirical arguments: On the computational side, the creative properties of image generation (e.g., as involved in creating a scene from previously isolated elements, such as Ronald Reagan shaking hands with George Washington)—which are useful in visual reasoning—demand some process that coordinates separately stored encodings. And if images can be formed at different sizes and locations, then new parts must be imaged relative to previously placed ones (not relative to some absolute coordinates), which requires "finding" the parts of previously imaged portions of an object before positioning new portions. On the empirical side, it has been found that the ease of forming an image depends in part on the "discriminability" of the location at which it is to be put on an imaged object. This result supports the idea that one inspects a partially completed image in the act of integrating in new parts (see Farah & Kosslyn, 1981; Kosslyn, Reiser, Farah, & Fliegel, 1983). In addition, findings that people can use descriptions to arrange items into an imaged scene forces one to posit some computation(s) that use descriptions to position segments of an image (see Kosslyn, 1980; Kosslyn et al., 1983).

It is possible, however, to argue that the data (which consist of reaction times collected from normal subjects) reflect task demands or the like. And one could argue on computational grounds that the PUT and PICTURE modules are not distinct, that activation of the stored information is simply one aspect of the PUT module's operation. Hence it is desirable to have stronger data supporting the proposed computational decomposition.

Data in the literature: an example

There is already information in the literature on brain damage that seems to have direct bearing on the nature of the representations and processes used in imagery. These data indicate that specific deficits are general across a class of tasks and seem to implicate problems in processing an array-like image of the sort posited by our theory. In particular, Bisiach and Luzzatti (1978) report that two patients with unilateral visual neglect (i.e., they ignored visual input on the left side) also showed corresponding neglect in their images of scenes encoded prior to the stroke. When asked to image a plazza from a particular point of view and describe what they "saw," they mentioned only objects that should have been to their right side; when then asked to image it from the opposite side, these patients reported "seeing" objects that now were on their right—which were the very ones ignored immediately before, when they were "viewing" from the opposite perspective! This phenomenon was also found when a patient imaged a familiar room from different perspectives. In later work, Bisiach, Luzzatti, and Perani (1979) used a more objective task and found the same results: These sorts of patients neglect half of their mental images. It is of especial interest that the patients lacked metaknowledge about their malady. They were unaware that they neglect the left side—which puts strain on an attempt to explain the data in terms of "task demands" based on "tacit knowledge" (as was discussed in the section on cognitive psychological approaches).

These data, then, are exactly what one would expect if our theory is correct, and images are array-like spatial representations with parts on the left side. Unfortunately, these patients also had slight "field cuts" on the left side. Thus, we cannot infer from these results whether the "mind's eye" (the tests used by the FIND processing module, in our theory) were selectively ignoring half of the representation, or whether half of the functional array in which images occur was disrupted. However, in principle the matter could be settled if patients could be located with neglect but no field cuts.

Evidence collected to test the theory: Brain damage

A recent review concluded that there is data suggesting that imagery is localized in the left, right, or both hemispheres; there was no unambiguous evidence for its localization in the right hemisphere, as is assumed in the common wisdom (see Erlichman & Barrett, 1983). And in fact, Farah (1984) reviewed the neuro-psychological literature and found evidence that different imagery abilities may be localized differently; in particular, she argued that image generation requires mechanisms that occur in the left hemisphere. But even here the story is not so clear-cut, with some results contradicting the generalization. However, unlike earlier theories of imagery, ours posits that the act of generating an image requires the operation of three processing modules working in concert. And it need not be the case that all computations involved in exercising a given ability are localized in the same place (or even nearby) in the brain. Our theory might, then, offer a way to sort out what now is a muddy picture in the neuro-psychological literature.

Kosslyn, Holtzman, Farah, and Gazzaniga (in press) have performed a large set of experiments designed to examine the claim that the module that coordi-nates multiple parts into a single image (the PUT processing module) is distinct from the PICTURE and FIND modules. We began by testing image generation of letters of the alphabet in the two isolated hemispheres of a split-brain patient. In our first series of experiments we asked the subject to make spatial judgments about letters of the alphabet, deciding from memory whether upper case letters were composed only of straight lines or included some curves. Robert Weber and his colleagues have demonstrated convincingly that normal subjects require im-agery in order to make these judgments from memory (see Kosslyn, 1980, for a review of this work). We reasoned that most adults have seen so many letters that if asked to image one, they do not image a specific letter they once saw (e.g., on page 43, line 5 of yesterday's *New York Times*). Rather, they use a stored description of the letter to generate a "prototypical example." For example, an upper case "a" might be stored as "two lines meeting at the top joined half way down by a horizontal line." The PUT processing module uses such a description to assemble an image (using stored images of lines), and hence the letter-classifi-cation task should be very difficult if the PUT module were not operating effectively.

To test this idea, we flashed a lower case letter into the left or right visual field, which presents the stimulus to the right or left hemisphere, respectively. Because our subject had his corpus callosum severed, the stimulus could be processed only by one hemisphere. We asked our subject to decide whether or not the upper case version had any curved lines (pressing one button if it did, another if it did not). He showed a huge left-hemisphere advantage. This was interesting in part because his left hemisphere showed superior ability at lan-guage and inference, both of which involve serial processing of symbols, and we posit that the PUT module performs serial symbol manipulation. Various control conditions were conducted to show that the right-hemisphere deficit was not due to its failing to understand the instructions, to know the association between upper and lower case letters, to retain an image, to inspect an image, to make the judgment, to generate a response, or to combine together separate stages of a task. The deficit seemed to be in generating the image from stored information.

In order to implicate a deficit in the operation of the PUT module per se, we needed to show a dissociation between this task and other imagery tasks that putatively do not require this module. Thus, in other experiments we used stimuli that presumably need not be imaged from a description of parts in order to perform the task. In one, names of animals were presented to one hemisphere or the other. If the named animal was larger than a goat, the subject was to press one button; if a goat was larger, he was to press the other button. Now both hemispheres performed essentially perfectly, and there was absolutely no difference in response times. This task has been shown to require imagery when the to-be-compared objects are close in size (e.g., goat vs. hog; see Chapter 9 of Kosslyn, 1980). In this case, however, only the global shapes (the ''skeletal images'') are necessary, not the parts. Similarly, the two hemispheres were equally good at evaluating whether an object is higher than it is wide—which also requires imagery, but does not require adding details to the imaged object. (This task was quite difficult, and neither hemisphere performed perfectly— eliminating the possibility of ceiling effects.)

One could argue that the right hemisphere simply has problems in generating images of letters because they are language-related materials. Thus, it is of interest that in another task the right hemisphere failed miserably when given the same names of animals used in the size-comparison task. Now, however, the question was, do the animal's ears protrude above the top of its skull? If so, the subject pressed one button; if not, he pressed another. In this task, an image of the ears must be correctly positioned relative to the head, and it is this positioning operation that apparently is difficult in the right hemisphere of this patient.

Taken together, the results served to implicate a distinct PUT processing module: Both hemispheres were comparable in their abilities to form and evaluate images of global shapes, which requires the PICTURE and FIND modules, but the right hemisphere showed a selective deficit in tasks that should require the PUT module to perform.

The point is, then, that we can directly test our computational theory by taking advantage of the idea that one or another computation may be localized in a cerebral hemisphere in this patient. We recently have been repeating the studies done with split-brain patients, now using normal subjects and looking for reaction-time differences. The preliminary results indicate small reaction-time differences in normal right-handed male subjects may mirror the dramatic effects we found with the split-brain subjects. However these effects are so small that they would not be noteworthy in the absence of the neuropsychological findings. Because the neuropsychological effects are almost qualitative, these sorts of results have the potential of supplying strong evidence for or against computational theories.

In addition, this sort of approach may well help untangle the convoluted story of how abilities are (or are not) localized in the brain. For example, we now need to administer image generation tasks that do or do not require integration of parts using descriptions, and discover whether patients having different sorts of lesions have selective difficulties with the different tasks.

Evidence from intact brains: PET scanning

Drawing inferences from research on brain-damaged patients is slightly suspect because mental functions in a damaged brain might have become organized in ways different from an intact one. Thus, it is useful to obtain convergent measures using an entirely different methodology. The Cornell Medical College and Harvard Psychology groups are just now planning PET scanning studies. The logic here is as follows: To the extent that tasks share similar processing, there should be similar patterns of activation in the brain. Further, if a theory claims that the same processing module is used in two tasks, then we may find (but not necessarily) that the same region or regions are activated in both cases. If we do not find this, we must discover how context shifts which parts of the brain are involved in which functions. The initial studies we are conducting are very simple: For example, we will ask subjects to listen to names of common objects, and to image the sound of the object (e.g., a train), its visual appearance, or both at the same time. If our theory is correct, parts of visual cortex—but not auditory cortex—should be activated when one forms a visual image but not an auditory one, and vice versa when one forms an auditory image. (After they finish imaging the words—and the PET scanning is over—we will test the subjects' recognition memory for sounds and pictures, expecting to find better memory for items imaged in the modality being tested; this will provide a check that subjects actually followed the instructions.) In addition, we hypothesize that the two systems will operate independently, even when one forms a multimodal image (which will cause activation of the regions activated when visual or auditory images were formed in isolation). In later experiments we plan to ask subjects to participate in various imagery tasks that putatively share greater or lesser numbers of processing modules, and will examine the similarity and overlap of activation during each task (for an example of how this logic can serve to illuminate the nature of individual differences, see Kosslyn, Brunn, Cave, & Wallach, 1984).

In this case, then, the theory serves to provide a framework for interpreting very complex neuropsychological data. In addition, the techniques of cognitive psychology allow us to design tasks to test the theory using these sorts of data. The three approaches, from AI, cognitive psychology, and neuropsychology, clearly complement each other.

CONCLUSIONS

In summary, the time seems ripe for a marriage of AI, cognitive psychology, and neuropsychology. Each field has built up a considerable dowry but has also revealed limitations. The marriage seems likely to be mutually beneficial. Whether a combined approach will indeed provide a major leap forward is, of course, something only time will tell. But it would not be surprising if the study of cognition were greatly enhanced by considering the brain. Cognition is, after all, something the brain does.

ACKNOWLEDGMENTS

Preparation of this report was supported by a grant from the Alfred P. Sloan Foundation, and the original research described herein was supported by NIMH grant MH 39478 and ONR contract N00014-82-C-0166. The author wishes to thank Martha Farah, Tommy Poggio, Lynn Robertson, and Eric Wanner for valuable comments on an earlier draft of this chapter.

REFERENCES

Anderson, J. R. (1978). Arguments concerning representations for mental imagery. *Psychological Review, 85,* 249–277.

Benton, A. (1982). Spatial thinking in neurological patients: Historical aspects. In M. Potegal (Ed.), *Spatial abilities: Developmental and physiological foundations.* New York: Academic Press.

Bisiach, E., & Luzzatti, C. (1978). Unilateral neglect of representational space. *Cortex, 14,* 129–133.

Bisiach, E., Luzzatti, C., & Perani, D. (1979). Unilateral neglect, representational schema and consciousness. *Brain, 102,* 609–618.

Costa, L. D., & Vaughan, H. G. (1962). Performances of patients with lateralized cerebral lesions: Verbal and perceptual tests. *Journal of Nervous and Mental Disease, 134,* 162–168.

DeRenzi, E. (1982). *Disorders of space exploration and cognition.* New York: Wiley.

Erlichman, H., & Barrett, J. (1983). Right hemispheric specialization for mental imagery: A review of the evidence. *Brain and Cognition, 2,* 55–76.

Farah, M. J. (1984). The neurological basis of mental imagery: A componential analysis. *Cognition, 18,* 245–272.

Farah, M. J., & Kosslyn, S. M. (1981). Strategy and structure in image generation. *Cognitive Science, 4,* 371–383.

Hayes–Roth, F. (1979). Distinguishing theories of representation: A critique of Anderson's "Arguments concerning mental imagery." *Psychological Review, 86,* 376–392.

Jackson, J. H. (1915). On the nature of the duality of the brain. *Brain, 38,* 30–103. (Originally published in 1874)

Jackson, J. H. (1876). Case of large cerebral tumor without optic neuritis and with left hemiplegia and imperception. *Royal London Opthalmological Hospital Reports, 8,* 434–444.

Jolicoeur, P., & Kosslyn, S. M. (1983). Coordinate systems of visual representations in memory. *Cognitive Psychology, 15,* 301–345.

Kosslyn, S. M. (1980). *Image and mind.* Cambridge, MA: Harvard University Press.

Kosslyn, S. M. (1981). The medium and the message in mental imagery. *Psychological Review, 88,* 46–66.

Kosslyn, S. M. (1983). *Ghosts in the mind's machine.* New York: Norton.

Kosslyn, S. M. (1984). Mental representation. In J. R. Anderson & S. M. Kosslyn (Eds.), *Tutorials in learning and memory: Essays in honor of G. H. Bower.* New York: W. H. Freeman.

Kosslyn, S. M., Brunn, J., Cave, K. R., & Wallach, R. W. (1984). Individual differences in mental imagery ability: A computational analysis. *Cognition, 18,* 195–243.

Kosslyn, S. M., Holtzman, J. D., Farah, M. J., & Gazzaniga, M. S. (in press). A computational analysis of mental image generation: Evidence from functional dissociations in split-brain patients. *Journal of Experimental Psychology: General.*

Kosslyn, S. M., Pinker, S., Smith, G. E., & Shwartz, S. P. (1979). On the demystification of mental imagery. *Behavioral and Brain Sciences, 2,* 535–581. (including "peer review" commentaries)

Kosslyn, S. M., Reiser, B. J., Farah, M. J., & Fliegel, S. L. (1983). Generating visual images: Units and relations. *Journal of Experimental Psychology: General, 112,* 278–303.

Marr, D. (1982). *Vision.* San Francisco: W. H. Freeman.

Moscovitch, M. (1979). Information processing and the cerebral hemispheres. In *Handbook of behavioral neurobiology* (Vol 2: Neuropsychology). New York: Plenum.

Newell, A., & Simon, H. A. (1972). *Human problem solving.* Englewood Cliffs, NJ: Prentice-Hall.

Pylyshyn, Z. W. (1979). Validating computational models: A critique of Anderson's indeterminacy of representation claim. *Psychological Review, 86,* 383–394.

Pylyshyn, Z. W. (1981). The imagery debate: Analogue media versus tacit knowledge. *Psychological Review, 88,* 16–45.

Ratcliff, G. (1982). Disturbances of spatial orientation associated with cerebral lesions. In M. Potegal (Ed.), *Spatial abilities: Developmental and physiological foundations.* New York: Academic Press.

Shepard, R. N., & Cooper, L. A. (1982). *Mental images and their transformations.* Cambridge, MA: MIT Press.

Siegler, R. S. (Ed.). (1978). *Children's thinking: What develops?.* Hillsdale, NJ: Lawrence Erlbaum Associates.

Simon, D. P., & Simon, H. A. (1978). Individual differences in solving physics problems. In R. S. Siegler (Ed.), *Children's thinking: What develops?* Hillsdale, NJ: Lawrence Erlbaum Associates.

Springer, S. P., & Deutsch, G. (1981). *Left brain, right brain.* San Francisco: W. H. Freeman.

Sternberg, S. (1966). High-speed scanning in human memory. *Science, 153,* 652–654.

Warrington, E. K., & Taylor, A. M. (1973). The contribution of the right parietal lobe to object recognition. *Cortex, 9,* 152–164.

Winston, P. H. (1975). *The psychology of computer vision.* New York: McGraw-Hill.

11 Cognitive Neuropsychology

Dean C. Delis
Veterans Administration Medical Center, Martinez, California
University of California, Davis

Beth A. Ober
Veterans Administration Medical Center, Martinez, California

In this chapter, we provide an introduction to neuropsychological investigations of cognitive processes. Because there have already been several excellent reviews on the interplay between cognitive psychology and neuropsychological studies with normal subjects (i.e., laterality experiments, cf. Hardyck, 1983; Moscovitch, 1979), we focus on neuropsychological investigations of brain-damaged patients. Following a brief history of the development of cognitive neuropsychology, this chapter examines how an integration of the findings from both normal functioning subjects and brain-injured patients enhances our understanding of cognitive processes and, where applicable, their relationship to brain structures. Selective examples of this integrative approach are given in the areas of visuospatial processing, memory, and language. The chapter concludes with a discussion of the caveats in generalizing from brain-damaged to normal cognition as well as the benefits that could be derived from a greater interchange between cognitive psychologists and neuropsychologists.

HISTORICAL PERSPECTIVE

The history of neuropsychology has paralleled the history of psychology in general. In the late 1800s, a time when Wundt, Titchener, and James conducted pioneering investigations on the structure of mental events, several European neurologists documented the decline of mental activities following focal lesions in the brain (Boring, 1950). Broca and Wernicke launched the field of neuropsychology with discoveries of two qualitatively different types of aphasia arising from discrete lesions in frontal and temporal regions of the left hemisphere.

243

Korsakoff documented a selective disturbance in memory for recent events that Gudden associated with mammillary body lesions in chronic alcoholics. Déjerine reported a relationship between arrested reading skills and left occipital–parietal lesions. Leipman described syndromes of apraxia (disorders of skilled movements) that were associated with either left-hemisphere or corpus-collosum damage. (See Hécaen and Albert, 1978 and Luria, 1976 for discussion of these historical antecedents.)

Despite the early enthusiasm generated by these investigations, and their acknowledged import for philosophical issues such as the mind–body problem (Schaff, 1973), the study of the relationship between mental activities and brain structures (i.e., mind–brain relationships) fell into relative quiescence from the 1920s through the 1950s. Contributing to this decline was the growing popularity of behaviorism. Neuropsychological investigators began focusing more on CNS correlates to behaviors such as eating, sleeping, sex, fight, and flight in non-human animals than on the seemingly nebulous constructs of mental abilities in humans. In addition, the equipotential notions of antilocalizationists such as Head (1920) and Lashley (1937) discouraged further elaboration on the discoveries of the 19th-century neurologists.

A renewed interest in the investigation of mental dysfunction in the brain-damaged patient occurred with the advent of cognitive psychology in the 1960s. The emphasis in cognitive psychology at that time was on the development of information-processing models, which attempt to characterize mental activity in terms of levels or stages of cognitive processing. More recently, these stage models have evolved into more complex models, with specific component processes posited within each stage (Kosslyn, this volume; Shallice, 1981). Not only have these approaches fostered a steady burgeoning of research on normal cognition, but they have also proven to be powerful methods for characterizing the mental architecture of the brain.

In the early 1960s, several independent neuropsychological laboratories began to investigate specific cognitive processes in brain-injured patients. The ''Boston Group'' (Geschwind & Kaplan, 1962; Goodglass, 1968; Goodglass & Kaplan, 1972) revived the early theories of Broca, Wernicke, Déjerine, and Leipmann on the aphasias and apraxias and more accurately characterized the spared and impaired processes of these syndromes. Hécaen in France (Hécaen, 1962; Hécaen & Albert, 1978) and Luria in the Soviet Union (Luria, 1966, 1973) similarly elaborated on the cognitive processes that underlie the aphasias, apraxias, agnosias, and acalculias. Milner (1966), in her famous case study of H.M., provided strong evidence of a neuropsychological reality for the distinction first advanced by James (1890) between short- and long-term memory. Sperry and Gazzaniga (Gazzaniga, 1970; Sperry, 1964) made the startling discovery that cognitive processes in one hemisphere could be disconnected and isolated from the cognitive processes in the other hemisphere following commissurotomy (e.g., successful naming occurred when stimuli were selectively presented to the left hemisphere but not to the right hemisphere of split-brain patients).

In the last decade, the continued development of sophisticated theories of normal cognitive processes has assisted neuropsychologists in more precisely mapping the organization of cognitive processes in the brain. At the same time, findings in neuropsychology have provided concurrent support for theories of normal cognition (e.g., Cermak & Butters, 1972), have assisted in determining the independence of component processes by their "separability" in the brain (e.g., Delis, Robertson, & Efron, in press), and have called attention to distinctions between cognitive processes previously unacknowledged in the study of normal functioning individuals (e.g., Cohen & Squire, 1980).

VISUOSPATIAL PROCESSING

In neuropsychology, visuospatial processing refers to a number of abilities, including visual attention, visual perception, constructional skills (e.g., drawing, block construction), memory for visual stimuli, and imagery. Compared to the large number of studies on aphasia and amnesia, there were relatively few investigations conducted during the 1960s and 1970s that attempted to utilize constructs developed in cognitive psychology to characterize visuospatial dysfunction following brain damage. Within the past few years, however, an increasing number of researchers have begun to investigate whether focal brain lesions disrupt specific processes of visuospatial functioning.

Visual Attention

Among a growing number of cognitive psychologists who have developed and empirically tested theories of normal cognition and then investigated the merits of the resulting theories in brain-damaged cognition is Michael Posner. In visual detection experiments with normal subjects, Posner and his colleagues have shown that attention can be dissociated from eye movements (Posner, 1980). They have also provided evidence for different operations underlying attention. For example, detection of a target stimulus in the periphery is facilitated if the target is preceded by a peripheral cue; however, if no target occurs in the periphery following the peripheral cue and the subject must then detect a target at the original fixation point, an inhibition of detection occurs (Posner & Cohen, 1984). Because different aspects of attention can be facilitated or inhibited, Posner and Cohen have posited specific elementary operations in normal attention such as moving towards a target and disengaging from a target in order to move towards a new target.

Utilizing this model, Posner, Walker, Friedrich, and Rafal (1984) investigated the attentional capacities of those brain-damaged patients who have been most frequently reported to show attentional deficits—patients with unilateral parietal-lobe lesions. In earlier neuropsychological investigations, attention was regarded as a unitary function that was either spared or impaired. Posner et al. found evidence, however, suggesting that attention is disrupted following parietal-lobe insults in a highly selective manner. The locus of the parietal-lobe patients' difficulty in detecting targets was not in moving towards initial target sites, but in disengaging from one site in order to detect another target. If it had been found in this study that all the proposed elementary operations of visual attention were equally impaired following parietal lesions, then the data would have indicated that attention is disrupted in a unitary manner, a result that would have been of little theoretical import for cognitive psychologists. However, the findings in the Posner et al. study give a neuropsychological reality to the notion of separate operations in normal visual attention. In addition, these findings enhance our understanding of the neuroanatomical correlates of attentional processes by more precisely describing the role of the parietal lobe in the operations of visual attention.

Processing of Parts and Wholes

A distinction between processing of parts and wholes has been intrinsic to many theories of normal perception (see Robertson, this volume). The possibility that the brain has evolved to favor processing of "parts and details" versus "wholes and configurations" in different cerebral regions was first suggested by neuropsychologists in the 1940s (Patterson & Zangwill, 1944). Subsequent research with commissurotomized patients, unilateral brain-damage patients, and neurologically intact subjects in laterality experiments has produced a large body of evidence indicating that the two cerebral hemispheres represent a division of labor in processing parts and wholes (Levy–Agristi & Sperry, 1968; Sergent & Bindra, 1981; Warrington, James, & Kinsbourne, 1966). For example, Kaplan has reported that the drawings of left-hemisphere-damage (LHD) patients often lack internal details, whereas the drawings of right-hemisphere-damaged (RHD) patients frequently have omitted or distorted outer configurations (Kaplan, 1983). These studies have concluded that the left hemisphere is superior for detailed, analytic processing, whereas the right hemisphere is superior for configural, holistic processing (see Bradshaw & Nettleton, 1981, for a review).

Despite the heuristic appeal of the analytic/holistic theory, this distinction has been criticized extensively (cf. Moscovitch, 1979). The commonest criticism is that the concepts "detailed or analytic" versus "configural or holistic" are vaguely and inconsistently defined across investigations. Researchers tend to infer (often in a posthoc manner) that a particular task involves more detail-analytic or configural-holistic processing without explicitly operationalizing these constructs. Another criticism is that neuropsychological investigations claiming support for the analytic/holistic theory often do not control for differential linguistic processing. As Moscovitch (1979) noted, internal details of a stimulus are often more easily verbalized than configural features, possibly predisposing them to greater left-hemisphere processing. We see, therefore, that these past investigations with brain-injured patients have not provided cognitive psychologists with a definitive neuropsychological reality to the notion of differential processing of parts and wholes.

In our laboratory, Lynn Robertson, Robert Efron, and the first author have been investigating the merits of the detail/configural dichotomy while attempting to overcome the methodological problems of past neuropsychological studies that have claimed support for this distinction. To accomplish this, we have utilized hierarchically constructed visual stimuli that consist of two levels of structure: A global (larger) form constructed from the repetition of smaller (local) forms (see Fig. 11.1). These stimuli are methodologically superior to stimuli traditionally used in part–whole or detail-configuration experiments (e.g., faces, incomplete figures) because (1) the two levels of structure are explicitly demarcated, and (2) the same type of form can exist at the global and local levels, enabling a highly controlled test of response differences at these two levels of structure while maintaining similar stimulus parameters. Investigations by cognitive psychologists in which hierarchical stimuli made of letters were presented centrally to normal subjects have found evidence for levels of perceptual processing that correspond to the global and local levels of structure (Kinchla & Wolfe, 1979; Navon, 1977; Robertson & Palmer, 1983). Sergent (1982) presented hierarchical letter stimuli to the visual half-fields of normal subjects and found a left visual-field advantage (putatively a right-hemisphere superiority) for identification of the global letter and a right visual-field advantage (putatively a left-hemisphere superiority) for identification of the local level.

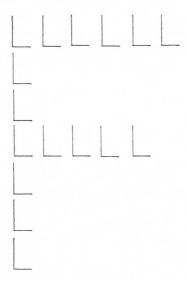

FIG. 11.1.   Example of a hierarchically constructed stimulus consisting of a global level (i.e., "F") and a local level (i.e., "L's").

In one study, Delis, Robertson, and Efron (in press) asked normal and unilateral brain-damaged subjects to study hierarchically constructed stimuli and then tested their memory for these stimuli in a forced-choice recognition experiment. Two categories of stimuli were used: linguistic symbols (letters created from letters) and nonlinguistic symbols (forms created from forms). As would be predicted from Sergent's (1982) results, the RHD patients recognized significantly more local forms relative to global forms, whereas the LHD patients recognized significantly more global forms than local forms. These findings occurred for both the linguistic and nonlinguistic symbols. Thus, the side of the cerebral lesion differentially affected processing at the global and local levels.

In a second experiment, Robertson and Delis (1984) employed a more perceptual task to evaluate the notion that more global and more local levels of a stimulus are processed differentially in the two hemispheres. In this experiment, a task developed by Palmer (1980) was presented to unilateral brain-damaged patients and normal control subjects. The subjects were asked to indicate in which direction an equilateral triangle appeared to point either when it was presented individually or aligned within other equilateral triangles or circles. This task enables an analysis of the influence of a more global reference frame (i.e., the aligned triangles) on the perception of more local elements (i.e., a single triangle; see Palmer, 1980, for a discussion of this procedure as well as his theory on the role of reference frames in normal perception). The results of the experiment revealed that the LHD patients were influenced significantly *more* by the global alignment than the control subjects, whereas the RHD patients were influenced significantly *less* by the global alignment than the control subjects.

These findings suggest that differential processing of levels of hierarchical structure has a biological basis in the brain. Future research in this area should investigate the mechanisms underlying the manifestation of levels of visuospatial processes. For example, the question arises as to which stimulus parameters inherent in a hierarchically constructed stimulus elicit differential responses at different levels of structure. Differential responses may emerge because the perceptual system is sensitive to relative-size differences or spatial-frequency differences between the forms at different levels of hierarchical structure (Sergent, 1982).

There is currently an unresolved issue in cognitive psychology of whether response differences corresponding to global and local levels of a stimulus represent a sequential unitary process or independent modes of processing (Kimchi & Palmer, 1982; Robertson & Palmer, 1983). The finding that processing at more global or local levels was differentially affected by lesions in the right and left hemispheres argues for the presence of independent modes of processing rather than a unitary process (see Marr, 1982, and Kosslyn, this volume, for discussions on processing independence and separability in the brain).

The research discussed in this section demonstrates the advances that can be made in cognitive-neuropsychological investigations in characterizing both visuospatial processes and the selective breakdown of these processes following focal brain damage. Other areas in which specific processes of visuospatial functioning are being investigated using both normal subjects and patients with focal brain damage include studies on mental imagery (see Kosslyn, this volume) and hemispatial attention (Bisiach & Luzzatti, 1978; Heilman, 1979). An example of another area of study that has been investigated with normal subjects and could also be studied with brain-damaged patients is whether the mechanisms involved in imagery are equivalent to the mechanisms involved in perception (Neisser, 1976; Shepard, 1975). Support for this notion has been provided by experiments showing that normal subjects respond to imagined objects and perceived objects in the same way (see Finke, 1980 for a review). Brain-damaged patients who have perceptual deficits could also be studied to determine if their perception of objects and their ability to imagine objects are disrupted in the same way.

MEMORY

A number of the theoretical frameworks within which cognitive psychologists have experimentally studied memory have been applied to the study of the amnesic syndrome. In each of these theoretical frameworks, the existence of separate and somewhat independent memory structures or processes has been posited. In some cases the results of studies with amnesics have provided support for distinctions made in the normal memory literature and in other cases have suggested modifications of normal memory theories. The focus here is on anterograde amnesia, that is, the loss of the ability to remember events subsequent to the onset of the amnesia in the presence of relatively normal intellectual functioning. For empirical and theoretical reviews that cover the variations in etiology and behavioral expression among amnesic syndromes, the reader is referred to Cermak (1982), Hirst (1982), and Squire (1982b).

Earlier Frameworks

The first theoretical memory framework to be applied to the study of amnesia was the dual-store model. The distinction between a short-term memory (STM) store and a long-term memory (LTM) store was supported by the memory performance of Korsakoff's syndrome patients (Talland, 1965) and of the temporal lobectomized (bilateral) patient H. M.(Milner, 1970), who were impaired only on LTM tasks. However, many of the STM–LTM distinctions posited for normal memory have not withstood further experimental scrutiny (see reviews by Crowder, 1982; Wickelgren, 1973, 1975), and STM processing has been shown to be abnormal in some amnesics (e.g., Cermak & Butters, 1972; Cermak, Naus, & Reale, 1976).

The levels of processing framework (Craik & Lockhart, 1972) was presented as an alternative to the dual-store model and to structural models of memory in general (as exemplified by Atkinson & Shiffrin, 1968). The degree of semantic (associative) processing during the encoding stage was stressed as the major determinant of retention. Numerous studies with normal subjects in which level of initial processing was manipulated via orienting tasks showed superior retention after semantic as compared to nonsemantic processing (e.g., Craik & Tulving, 1975). The results of levels of processing studies with Korsakoff patients converged on the notion that their ability to encode semantic features was selectively impaired (Cermak, Reale, & Baker, 1978; Squire, 1982a; Wetzel & Squire, 1980). Impaired semantic processing has been demonstrated in amnesias of other etiologies as well (Wetzel & Squire, 1982).

Not long after the initial levels of processing studies with amnesics were published, the neuropsychological literature began to reflect the increasing trend in normal memory research toward a consideration of both encoding and retrieval processes in investigations of memory (e.g., Cermak, Uhly, & Reale, 1980; Winocur, Kinsbourne, & Moscovitch, 1981). Results of these studies have shown that it was overly simplistic to attribute the poor memory performance of these amnesics to a deficit in one particular stage of information processing. Rather, these patients seem to have difficulties with certain qualitative types of processing (e.g., semantic), and these difficulties may negatively affect memory processes from the time of learning through the time at which attempts are made to access previously learned information.

Semantic versus Episodic Memory

Independent of the dual-store and levels of processing frameworks, Tulving (1972) proposed a distinction between memories that are tied to a particular spatial–temporal context and memories that comprise one's knowledge about the world (linguistic knowledge, rules, facts, concepts, etc.). The former type of memory was termed episodic, the latter semantic. Although amnesics have severe impairments in learning and remembering lists of items and in remembering events that have occurred since amnesia onset, verbal skills and world knowledge seem to be well preserved. These observations have led to the proposal that episodic memory is selectively affected in amnesia, with semantic memory being spared (Kinsbourne & Wood, 1975, 1982; Schacter & Tulving, 1982a; Wood, Ebert, & Kinsbourne, 1982).[1]

---

[1]There is somewhat of a controversy at the present time, as to whether *retrograde* amnesia data support the semantic/episodic memory distinction. Zola–Morgan, Cohen, and Squire (1983) have reported that several types of amnesic patients can recall remote episodic memories to single word cues, with sufficient probing. They have argued that the distinction between semantic and episodic memory is not a useful one in amnesia research. In contrast, Cermak (1984) reports that his testing of Korsakoff patients for remote episodic memories revealed only "empty phrases" in response to each item and has argued in favor of the semantic/episodic memory distinction for explaining the pattern of memory deficits in amnesics.

Support for the preservation of semantic memory functions includes a report by Warrington and Weiskrantz (1982) that amnesics do not differ from controls in time taken to access orthographic knowledge in semantic memory (producing words from specified three-letter beginnings) or in the time required to access categorical knowledge in semantic memory (e.g., naming the superordinate category "animal" or "plant" for a given exemplar). Meudell, Mayes, and Neary (1980) have also shown normal reaction times on semantic memory tasks for amnesic patients. Further, Korsakoff's syndrome patients do not differ from controls in their ability to perform such semantic knowledge tasks as sentence completion or event sequencing (Weingartner, Grafman, Boutelle, Kaye, & Martin, 1983).

If episodic and semantic memory are actually separate components of memory functioning, it is conceivable that a neuropsychological syndrome could occur in which semantic memory functions are impaired but episodic memory functions are spared. Warrington (1975) has described three relevant cases (a follow-up study of one of these patients is reported in Coughlan and Warrington, 1981). These patients were selectively impaired on semantic memory tasks such as the matching of a spoken word to its pictorial representation, or the defining of words.

A Reformulation of the Episodic-Semantic Memory Distinction

Since the original distinction between episodic and semantic memory was proposed, evidence has been accumulating that indicates that amnesics can, in fact, acquire and retain skills such as mirror drawing (Milner, 1970), utilizing a mathematical rule for generating number sequences (Kinsbourne & Wood, 1975), and reading mirror-imaged words (Cohen & Squire, 1980). Preserved skill learning in amnesia is seen as a serious problem for the episodic-semantic dichotomy (Schacter & Tulving, 1982a, b). Episodic and semantic memories are based on propositional knowledge, whereas memories for skills or operational rules are comprised of procedural knowledge. Therefore, there does not appear to be any means by which memories for skills can be incorporated within the episodic-semantic framework.

According to Schacter and Tulving (1982b), the ability of amnesics to retain some of the factual content of learning experiences poses another problem for the original episodic-semantic memory distinction. An example of a dissociation between the factual and autobiographical content of an episode has been reported by Weiskrantz and Warrington (1979). Their amnesic subjects were trained in a classical conditioning paradigm using an eye-blink response and demonstrated retention of this conditioning after 24 hours. However, these subjects had no memory for the training sessions or the apparatus that had been used during training. Because the amnesics were not retaining the autobiographical features of episodes, they were not demonstrating episodic memory, at least not in the way it was originally defined by Tulving. In their reformulation of the episodic versus semantic memory framework, Schacter and Tulving (1982b) have proposed an additional distinction—between the *factual* content of an episode and *autobiographical* memory for that episode. The autobiographical features of the episodic memory tie the memory to a particular time, place, or other aspects of the personal context in which it was encoded. This issue, that autobiographical aspects of episodic memories are potentially separable from factual aspects of episodic memories, is just beginning to be explored by cognitive psychologists; one relevant series of studies is discussed in the next section.

Perceptual versus Autobiographical Recognition of Prior Episodes

The time required to identify a briefly presented word can be decreased by prior exposure to the to-be-identified material (e.g., Jacoby & Dallas, 1981; Murrell & Morton, 1974). This effect of prior exposure need not require the subjects' awareness. In contrast, a recognition decision (as to whether or not the item has been seen before) requires active participation and, therefore, awareness. Mandler (1980) has posited two forms of normal recognition memory: one that involves a judgment of familiarity without necessarily involving memory for the context in which the item occurred, and one that involves retrieval of the context in which the recognized item occurred (i.e., retrieval of autobiographical information as described in the previous section).

This distinction between two types of recognition memory has been pursued in an interesting series of studies with normals by Jacoby and Dallas (1981; see also Jacoby, 1982). Among those variables affecting both the identification of a briefly presented word (which Jacoby and Dallas refer to as perceptual recognition) and autobiographical recognition of a word (deciding whether or not the word was recently presented) was the number of times a word had been previously presented. In contrast, variables related to the extent of meaningful, effortful processing of the item at the time of study (e.g., answering orthographic, rhyme or meaning questions about the item) significantly affected autobiographical recognition memory in the expected direction (more meaningful processing leading to increased recognition accuracy) but had no effect on the item's later perceptual identification.

Jacoby (1982) has discussed the implications of these findings with normals for understanding memory dysfunction in amnesia. He has suggested that Korsakoff patients rely heavily on the relative ease with which items can be perceived in making a decision as to whether they have seen an item before. A dependency on ease of perceptual identification is consistent with the inordinately high false alarm rate on yes/no recognition memory tests seen with Korsakoff patients (e.g., Huppert & Piercy, 1976). All the items on the test look familiar, because the patients have seen them all before. In the absence of memory for the context in which the items were last seen, the recognition decision is based more often on perceptual factors alone than on perceptual and autobiographical factors combined. A dissociation between familiarity and auto-biographical recognition happens to all of us on occasion, e.g., knowing that we have met a person before, but not knowing where or when. Korsakoff patients (and perhaps other types of amnesics) may rely relatively more on the processing of physical features of to-be-remembered items because they are impaired in more elaborative, semantic types of processing; this would explain their tenden-cy to rely on ease of perceptual identification at the time of test.

The dissociation of autobiographical recognition from perceptual recognition posited by Jacoby is conceptually similar to the dissociation between the auto-biographical and factual content of memories for previous experiences, which Schacter and Tulving discussed as troublesome for the original definition of episodic memory. In each case, the claim is being made that the amnesics' memory trace for previous experiences is incomplete. And, in each case, the trace is incomplete because it is devoid of information concerning the time, place, or other circumstances of the original experience.

Automatic versus Effortful Memory Processes: A Framework for Integrating the Amnesia Data

In two very influential papers, Schneider and Shiffrin (1977) and Shiffrin and Schneider (1977) detailed a theory for controlled versus automatic information processing. A priori, these authors assumed that the momentary availability of attentional capacity is limited and that mental operations differ in the amount of attentional capacity that they require (Kahneman, 1973). They then stated that "automatic cognitive processes" are involuntary, require little or no attention, interfere minimally with concurrent cognitive processes, and may operate with-out awareness; in contrast, "controlled cognitive processes" (referred to as effortful processes here) were stated to be voluntary, require attentional capacity, interfere with other processes, and usually occur with awareness.

Hasher and Zacks (1979) have expanded the automatic-effortful framework for the purpose of incorporating a large range of memory phenomena within it. They have proposed that those aspects of events that are automatically encoded into memory include frequency of occurrence, spatial location, and temporal relation to other events. Hasher and Zacks report several experiments on frequen-cy of occurrence judgments in order to demonstrate the use of converging criteria for defining a particular memory operation as automatic or effortful. Frequency judgments were found not to be affected by age, depression, or intention to learn, which together were said to be indicative of the automaticity of frequency encod-ing. (See Zacks, Hasher, & Sanft, 1982 for further evidence that frequency is encoded automatically.)

Within the automatic-effortful framework, at least two explanations of the memory dysfunctions in amnesia are possible. It may be the case that all pro-cesses that are automatic in young and old normal subjects remain automatic, and therefore preserved, in amnesia. Or, it may be that some of the encoding processes that are automatic in normals become effortful in amnesics, and therefore subject to disruption. Huppert and Piercy (1978) have reported Korsakoff patients to be unable to make recency and frequency judgments for previously seen pictures (subjects had to decide whether a given picture was presented "yesterday" or "today" or "one" versus "three" times). The Korsakoff patients' judgments were a joint function of the two attributes, thus implicating overall trace strength as the basis of the judgments. More recently, Hirst and Volpe (1982) have demonstrated that amnesics of mixed etiology can have significantly impaired memory for the order of events that are nonetheless recognized at normal levels. This heterogenous population of amnesics has also been shown by Hirst and Volpe (1984a) to be more severely impaired as compared to control subjects on spatial location information than on recognition of the pictures for which spatial location was tested (the pictures were scenes from a walk along a city street that the subjects had made). Interestingly, these amnesics exhibited improved performance on spatial and order information tests in intentional as compared to incidental learning conditions, whereas the control subjects did equally well on these tests in the two learning conditions (Hirst & Volpe, 1984a,b). It would thus seem that the encoding of spatial and temporal information about an event, which is regarded as an automatic process for normals, does require effort for amnesics, and that the shifting of attention or effort to these features can improve performance.

Thus, the automatic-effortful processing distinction holds promise as a framework for integrating much of the extent data on memory dysfunctions in amnesia. Amnesics are impaired on LTM encoding and retrieval processes that require considerably more effort than the relatively spared STM encoding and retrieval processes. The incorporation of new information into episodic memory requires more effort than accessing information that is part of the permanent knowledge system (semantic memory), and we have seen that the episodic memory processes are more susceptible to dysfunction in the amnesic syndrome. Furthermore, the difficulty that amnesics have in encoding semantic features of items presented in an episodic list learning task could be attributed to failures in this more effortful type of encoding. In contrast, skill or procedure learning is often normal in amnesics, and these skills probably become automatic as the components are organized into "chunks." The Jacoby and Dallas (1981) studies with normals on autobiographical versus perceptual recognition memory have indicated that the perceptual identification of an item is more automatic than the recognition of that item as having been previously seen. An automatic type of perceptual recognition can account for the ability of amnesic patients to complete previously studied words from initial letters or fragments, even though they cannot recall these words (Weiskrantz & Warrington, 1970).

With regard to the nature of the episodic memory impairments, the encoding of both semantic and contextual features may require relatively more effort than the encoding of the more physical or item-based features of to be-remembered items in amnesia and, therefore, be more sensitive to disruption. Not only would this result in less information being incorporated into LTM, but, when information is encoded into LTM, the resulting memory representation may be so impoverished, i.e., devoid of autobiographical and semantic features, that it often cannot be accessed and/or retrieved on demand.

If a deficiency in the amount of effortful (i.e., controlled) processing during a memory task is a critical determinant of memory impairment in amnesia, parallels should be seen between memory performance of amnesics and memory performance of young normals when effortful processing is reduced for the normals. Graf, Mandler, and Haden (1982) have, in fact, reported a parallel of this type. In their study, separate groups of young normals were focused on either elaborative or nonelaborative characteristics of verbal items (the pleasantness or vowel properties of the words, respectively). The nonelaborative group was able to recall almost none of the items, whereas the elaborative group recalled almost one-third of the items. Both groups, however, were able to complete about one-third of the list words when given the initial three letters and asked to put down the first word that comes to mind, presumably because this task depends on automatic processes (which are not affected by the level of initial processing). In a similar vein, Tulving, Schacter, and Stark (1982) have demonstrated an independence of recognition memory for previously studied words from the ability to complete fragments of these words. The comparison of word completion to other more effortful forms of memory testing has been extended to several amnesic populations by Graf, Squire, and Mandler (1984). The results showed that amnesics perform as well as normals on word completion (regardless of orienting task) and are impaired on all explicit forms of episodic memory testing. Further studies of the conditions under which amnesics' memory performance is equal to that of normals as well as of the conditions under which normal memory performance simulates amnesics' memory performance will no doubt increase our understanding of the component processes by which memory is impaired in anterograde amnesia.

LANGUAGE

In its most basic formulation, linguistic competency is commonly broken down into three interacting components—phonological, syntactic, and semantic—with each component comprising a set of hierarchical rules. Each of these three general components has been found to be selectively disrupted in different types of aphasia in ways predicted by various linguistic theories.

Phonological Processing

The strongest evidence for a biological basis of a linguistic component that subserves phonological processing derives from the acquired syndrome of deep dyslexia (Coltheart, Patterson, & Marshall, 1980; Marshall & Newcombe,

1973). The patient with deep dyslexia is unable to read real or nonsense words by sounding them out phonetically. In the face of this loss in phonetic reading, however, the patient still is able to extract the meaning of some reading material (e.g., individual words). In addition, when reading errors are made, they tend to be *semantic* rather than phonemic in nature (e.g., "lunch" is read as "dinner"; see reports by Marshall & Newcombe, 1973; Nolan & Caramazza, 1982; Patterson, 1979; Shallice & Warrington, 1975). The significance of this syndrome is that it demonstrates that meaning can be accessed while bypassing phonological processing.

Caramazza and Berndt (1983) conducted a series of experiments on a patient who displayed many symptoms that are the opposite of those found in dyslexia, that is, the patient showed superior comprehension of written versus spoken words. Although able to analyze correctly the semantic aspects of words presented visually, this patient was unable to match pictured objects whose names rhyme or to match rhyming words. Caramazza and Berndt concluded that the patient's pattern of spared and impaired linguistic abilities implicated a central phonological deficit. This case study as well as those on deep dyslexia demonstrate that a relatively selective impairment in phonological processing can occur, a deficit that can primarily affect the processing of either written or oral linguistic stimuli.

Syntactic and Semantic Processing

A dissociation between the syntactic and semantic components of language is inherently suggested in the two classical types of aphasia first described by Broca and Wernicke. The "Boston group" (Geschwind, 1970; Goodglass, 1968, 1980; Goodglass & Kaplan, 1983; Zurif & Caramazza, 1976) has conducted extensive investigations documenting the aberrant syntactic and semantic structure in the speech of these two types of aphasia. The Broca's aphasic is able to generate open-class content words (i.e., substantive nouns, verbs, and adjectives) but telegraphically sequences them in the absence of the syntactic frame of the sentence. Closed-class function words (i.e., grammatical morphemes such as articles, prepositions, and quantifiers) are typically omitted. For example, when asked what had happened to him, one Broca's aphasic responded, "Blood . . . brain . . . September." The Wernicke's aphasic, in contrast, is typically able to generate long, syntactically complex sentences replete with grammatical morphemes, but in the absence of meaningful content. A typical sample of speech (Goodglass & Kaplan, 1983) of a Wernicke's aphasic is, "The kids aren't right here because they don't just say one here and one here—that's all right, although the fellow here is breakin' between the two of them, they're comin' around too" (p. 82).

Although most aphasiologists agree that Wernicke's aphasics suffer severe deficits in semantic processing, a controversy arose in neuropsychology regarding whether Broca's aphasia represents a "competency" deficit in syntactic processing or a "performance" deficit in speech articulation (see Zurif & Blumstein, 1978). Because verbal comprehension appears relatively intact in Broca's aphasia, several researchers posited intact linguistic knowledge in these patients, attributing their speech impairment to a problem in the motor coordination of the speech apparatus (Locke, Caplan, & Kellar, 1973; Weigl & Bierwisch, 1970). According to this view, the telegraphic speech of Broca's aphasics represents a compensatory strategy of economizing on impaired articulation by generating only the most essential words.

In a series of studies, Zurif, Caramazza, and their colleagues found convincing evidence for a syntactic competency deficit in Broca's aphasia. In one study, Zurif, Caramazza, and Myerson (1972) bypassed demands on the patients' articulation by presenting written sentences to the subjects and asking them to point to the words that "go best together." The clustering of the normal subjects reflected hierarchical syntactic organization of both function and content words, whereas the clustering of the Broca's aphasics mirrored their impaired spontaneous speech. These patients typically coupled only the content words together, failing either to include the grammatical function words or clustering them incorrectly (e.g., an article before a verb).

Other investigations by these researchers have shown that, even though Broca's aphasics often appear to have relatively intact verbal comprehension, their comprehension breaks down for those sentences that rely heavily on accurate syntactic processing. For instance, Caramazza and Zurif (1976) found that Broca's aphasics successfully comprehended sentences that could be deciphered using a "probable event" strategy (e.g., "the apple the boy is eating is red") but often failed to comprehend sentences that required accurate syntactic processing to link the final adjective to the correct antecedent noun (e.g., "The girl the boy is chasing is tall"). Collectively, these studies indicate that relatively selective impairment in the syntactic component of language does occur in Broca's aphasia, an impairment that is manifested in both verbal expression and comprehension.

A problem that is receiving increased attention in recent years concerns the "autonomy" of the proposed components of language. Pylyshyn (1983) has stated the problem for syntactic processing as: "Is there a part of the cognitive system that exclusively computes syntactic forms and performs its computations independent of other knowledge and beliefs about the world?" (p. 147). This issue is exceedingly complex because precise characterizations of syntax are continually changing (Chomsky, 1980). Zurif (1983) discussed this problem with regard to the open-class content word versus closed-class function word distinction, stating that this dichotomy does not unequivocally demarcate words with semantic content from words that serve a syntactic function. For example, one subset of closed-class words—prepositions—often carry semantic content and also serve as syntactic placeholders (e,g., locative prepositions). Friederici

(1982) has found, in fact, that Broca's aphasics, who are impaired in producing prepositions in general, are significantly more likely to produce prepositions that carry semantic content than prepositions that function more syntactically. This study demonstrates the importance of continually defining the boundaries between the proposed processes of language in investigating the selectivity with which these processes are disrupted following brain damage.

Studies in aphasia not only can provide a neuropsychological reality to the constructs of linguistics and psycholinguistics, but they can also suggest novel characterizations of normal language processing. For example, clues to the semantic organization of lexical items in normal cognition may derive from the selective breakdown of different semantic categories and types of stimuli following brain damage. As Goodglass (1980) states:

> In many instances, these impairments create dissociations that would not be anticipated from experience with normal language. For example, aphasics may be able to understand the spoken names of American cities and geographical features and to locate them on an outline map but fail totally to understand names of common body parts. They may read aloud words which denote objects but fail with the simplest grammatical words, as in the case of a patient who could read "hymn" but not "him." (p. 647)

Geschwind and Fusillo (1966) and Goodglass (1980) have reported differential impairment in the naming of objects, letters, numbers, actions, and colors across different types of aphasias.

Because the structure of language is discrete and readily observable and because brain injuries often arrest linguistic processes in relatively well-defined ways, investigations of aphasia have proven to be a fruitful avenue for exploring underlying processes of cognition. Examples of current trends in neurolinguistics include investigations on more elaborate component models of language production (e.g., Shallice, 1981), and on language impairment at the discourse level (e.g., Ulatowska, Doyel, Stern, Haynes, & North, 1983).

CONCLUSION: CAVEATS AND POTENTIAL

There is no question that, throughout the history of neuropsychology, inferences made from the study of brain-damaged patients regarding the nature of mental activity have often been overly speculative. In the late 1800s, the field of neuropsychology had the misfortune of being associated with phrenology—the field that strove for the rather ignoble goal of discovering mind–skull relationships. Even the early neurologists committed inferential errors of being too nebulous in their proposed mental constructs and too narrow in their neuroanatomical bench marks (e.g., "personal ego" was once localized in Brodmann's area 11; Kleist,

1934, cited in Luria, 1973). One can only sympathize with the caveats of the first antilocalizationists (e.g., Goldstein, 1939; Head, 1920), who bemoaned the narrowness with which general mental abilities were thought to be encapsulated within relatively small areas of grey matter. From the observation that general intellectual functions such as arithmetic could be impaired by focal lesions in diverse areas of the brain, the antilocalizationists were compelled to propose that intelligence was a unitary function represented throughout the brain in a global, equipotential manner.

This unitary conception of intelligence and its cortical organization was later challenged by Luria (1966, 1970, 1973), who was the first to propose a "neo-localization" theory of brain functions. Luria's theory is able to account for the presence of neuropsychological syndromes (e.g., the aphasias, acalculias) while overcoming the criticisms of early antilocalizationists such as Head and Goldstein. In Luria's model, a particular intellectual activity (e.g., arithmetic) is dependent on a multitude of underlying processes subserved by different functional systems of the brain. The ability to perform arithmetic operations can be, as the antilocalizationists observed, disrupted by focal lesions in many areas of the cortex. What the antilocalizationists failed to note is that the *nature* of the arithmetic deficit will be qualitatively different depending on the location and nature of the lesion (see also Kaplan, 1983). For example, a frontal lesion will not impair basic arithmetic facts but may disrupt more executive processes necessary for the organization of elementary arithmetic operations. A left-parietal lesion, in contrast, may arrest the ability to perform even the most basic arithmetic operations, because this area seems critical for spatial manipulation of symbols (Luria, 1966). In effect, Luria's model overcomes the criticisms of the antilocalizationists through an integration of the goals of cognitive psychology, that is, through investigations of the relationship between cognitive processes and cerebral regions. This approach becomes especially valuable when findings from investigations of both brain-damaged patients and normal subjects implicate the same cognitive processes.

Another caveat in generalizing from brain-damaged to normal cognition—one that continues to resist a comprehensive explanation from neuropsychologists—is the problem advanced by Gregory (1974) in an analogy to a radio: If a "howling" sound commences when a resistor is removed from a radio, that does not necessarily mean that the "howl inhibitor" has been identified and localized. This problem makes any interpretation regarding the organization of cognitive processes in the brain hazardous. Neuropsychologists attempt to address this problem, however, through compliance with Teuber's (1955) principle of double dissociation: A cognitive process can be correlated to a particular brain region only when that process is impaired following a lesion limited to that region and spared following a lesion to any other area of the brain (which results in deficits in other cognitive processes; see also Jones, 1983, for a recent reformulation of this principle). Compliance with this principle does not demonstrate that a cognitive process is somehow seated in a particular brain area, but it does isolate the brain area that plays a critical role for the execution of that process.

Recently, Hardyck (1983) has advanced another potential caveat in generalizing from brain-damage to normal cognition. In comparing studies that investigate hemispheric specialization in normal subjects (using visual half-field or dichotic listening procedures) versus patients with unilateral brain damage, Hardyck noted that cognitive functions do not seem so linked to one hemisphere or the other in normal subjects as they do in brain-damaged subjects. For example, investigations with brain-damage patients suggest that language is lateralized in the left hemisphere in approximately 95% of all cases, whereas studies with normal subjects frequently find a left-visual-field or left-ear advantage—putatively right hemisphere superiority—for processing of verbal material (Hardyck, 1983). Because of this discrepancy, Hardyck concluded that "generalizations from patient populations to normally functioning individuals seem inappropriate and frequently misleading, given the current state of knowledge about the flexibility of normal functioning in the performing of cognitive tasks" (p. 222).

This conclusion, we believe, is accurate, but only as it applies to the problem of how cognitive processes are *localized* in the brain. When the focus of inquiry centers on the *nature* of specific cognitive processes, then the question of how these processes are localized in the brain is not important. What becomes important is only the question of whether the same specific processes proposed in normal cognition can be selectively disrupted by brain lesions, regardless of the location of the patients' lesions. The caveat advanced by Hardyck (1983) poses an important problem, but only for neuropsychologists interested in charting mind–brain correlations and not for cognitive psychologists interested in charting the components of mind.

In light of these caveats, there is much to be gained from a greater interaction between researchers in cognitive psychology and neuropsychology. We have seen in this chapter that many of the constructs and experimental procedures developed in cognitive psychology have proven to be powerful tools for investigating the breakdown of cognitive processes following brain damage. In return, we have seen that many of these constructs have been found to have convergent validity from the study of the breakdown of specific cognitive processes following brain damage. We have also seen that various unsolved issues in cognitive psychology, for example, the question of independent modes of processing for different hierarchical levels of visual stimuli, have received illuminating data from studies with brain-damaged patients. Furthermore, neuropsychological investigations have called attention to distinctions between cognitive processes, for instance, Cohen and Squire's (1980) distinction between propositional and procedural learning, which have necessitated the reformulation of theories of normal cognition.

A relatively recent trend in cognitive psychology involves the computational analysis of more general cognitive processes into more specific, relatively independent, components (Kosslyn, this volume; Posner, Pea, & Volpe, 1982; Shallice, 1981). Cognitive neuropsychological investigations offer a unique methodology for component analyses of cognition: The differential breakdown of subprocesses of various cognition functions following focal brain damage can lead to characterizations of these functions not available in the study of normal functioning individuals (see Shallice, 1981 for a model of reading based on nine different syndromes of alexia). Through collaboration between cognitive psychologists and neuropsychologists, we can maximize our efforts to characterize the processes of cognition and their realization in the brain.

ACKNOWLEDGMENTS

We thank Laird Cermak, Nina Dronkers, Curtis Hardyck, Lynn Robertson, Gregory Shenaut, Gregory Simpson, and Edgar Zurif for their comments on an earlier draft of this chapter.

REFERENCES

Atkinson, R. C., & Shiffrin, R. M. (1968). Human memory: A proposed system and its control processes. In K. W. Spence & J. T. Spence (Eds.), *The psychology of learning and motivation* (Vol. 2). New York: Academic Press.

Bisiach, E., & Luzzatti, C. (1978). Unilateral neglect of representational space. *Cortex, 14,* 129–133.

Boring, E. G. (1950). *A history of experimental psychology.* New York: Apple–Century–Crofts.

Bradshaw, J. L., & Nettleton, N. C. (1981). The nature of hemispheric specialization. *The Behavioral and Brain Sciences, 4,* 51–91.

Caramazza, A., & Berndt, R. S. (1983). The selective impairment of phonological processing: A case report. *Brain and Language, 18,* 128–174.

Caramazza, A., & Zurif, E. B. (1976). Dissociation of algorithmic and heuristic processes in language comprehension. *Brain and Language, 3,* 572–582.

Cermak, L. S. (Ed.). (1982). *Human memory and amnesia.* Hillsdale, NJ: Lawrence Erlbaum Associates.

Cermak, L. S. (1984). The episodic-semantic distinction in amnesia. In L. R. Squire & N. Butters (Eds.), *The neuropsychology of memory.* New York: Guilford Press.

Cermak, L. S., & Butters, N. (1972). The role of interference and encoding in the short-term memory deficits of Korsakoff patients. *Neuropsychologia, 10,* 89–95.

Cermak, L. S., Naus, M. J., & Reale, L. (1976). Rehearsal and organizational strategies of alcoholic Korsakoff patients. *Brain and Language, 3,* 375–385.

Cermak, L. S., Reale, L., & Baker, E. (1978). Alcoholic Korsakoff patient's retrieval from semantic memory. *Brain and Language, 5,* 215–226.

Cermak, L. S., Uhly, B., & Reale, L. (1980). Encoding specificity in the alcoholic Korsakoff patient. *Brain and Language, 11,* 119–127.

Chomsky, N. (1980). *Rules and representations.* New York: Columbia University Press.

Cohen, N. J., & Squire, L. R. (1980). Preserved learning and retention of pattern-analyzing skill in amnesia: Dissociation of knowing how and knowing that. *Science, 210,* 207–210.

Coltheart, M., Patterson, K., & Marshall, J. C. (1980). *Deep dyslexia.* London: Routlege & Kegan Paul.

Coughlan, A. K., & Warrington, E. K. (1981). The impairment of verbal semantic memory: A single case study. *Journal of Neurology, Neurosurgery, and Psychiatry, 44,* 1079–1083.

Craik, F. I. M., & Lockhart, R. S. (1972). Levels of processing: A framework for memory research. *Journal of Verbal Learning and Verbal Behavior, 11,* 671–684.

Craik, F. I. M., & Tulving, E. (1975). Depth of processing and the retention of words in episodic memory. *Journal of Experimental Psychology: General, 104,* 268–294.

Crowder, R. G. (1982). The demise of short-term memory. *Acta Psychologia, 50,* 291–323.

Delis, D. C., Robertson, L. C., & Efron, R. (in press). Hemispheric specialization of memory for visual hierarchical stimuli. *Neuropsychologia.*.

Finke, R. A. (1980). Levels of equivalence in imagery and perception. *Psychological Review, 86,* 113–132.

Friederici, A. (1982). Syntactic and semantic processes in aphasic deficits: The availability of prepositions. *Brain and Language, 15,* 249–258.

Gazzaniga, M. S. (1970). *The bisected brain.* New York: Appleton–Century–Crofts.

Geschwind, N. (1970). The organization of language and the brain. *Science, 170,* 940–944.

Geschwind, N., & Fusillo, M. (1966). Color naming defects in association with alexia. *Neurology, 15,* 137–146.

Geschwind, N., & Kaplan, E. (1962). A human cerebral disconnection syndrome. *Neurology, 12,* 675–685.

Goldstein, K. (1939). *The organism: A holistic approach to biology, derived from pathological data in man.* New York: American Books.

Goodglass, H. (1968). Studies on the grammar of aphasics. In S. Rosenberg & J. Kaplin (Eds.), *Developments in applied psycholinguistic research.* New York: Macmillan.

Goodglass, H. (1980). Disorders of naming following brain injury. *American Scientist, 68,* 647–655.

Goodglass, H., & Kaplan, E. (1972). *The assessment of aphasia and related disorders.* Philadelphia: Lea & Febiger.

Goodglass, H., & Kaplan, E. (1983). *The assessment of aphasia and related disorders (rev. ed.).* Philadelphia: Lea & Febiger.

Graf, P., Mandler, G., & Haden, P. E. (1982). Simulating amnesic symptoms in normal subjects. *Science, 218,* 1243–1244.

Graf, P., Squire, L. R., & Mandler, G. (1984). The information that amnesic patients do not forget. *Journal of Experimental Psychology: Learning, Memory, and Cognition, 10,* 164–178.

Gregory, R. L. (1974). The brain as an engineering problem. In J. J. Rosen (Ed.), *Learning and memory.* New York: Macmillan.

Hardyck, C. (1983). Seeing each other's point of view: Visual perceptual lateralization. In J. B. Hellige (Ed.), *Cerebral hemispheric asymmetry.* New York: Praegar.

Hasher, L., & Zacks, R. T. (1979). Automatic and effortful processes in memory. *Journal of Experimental Psychology: General, 108,* 356–388.

Head, H. (1920). *Studies in neurology.* Cambridge: Oxford University Press.

Hécaen, H. (1962). Clinical symptomotology in right and left hemisphere lesions. In V. B. Mountcastle (Ed.), *Interhemispheric relations and cerebral dominance.* Baltimore: Johns Hopkins Press.

Hécaen, H., & Albert, M. L. (1978). *Human neuropsychology.* New York: Wiley.

Heilman, K. M. (1979). Neglect and related disorders. In K. M. Heilman & E. Valenstein (Eds.), *Clinical neuropsychology.* New York: Oxford University Press.

Hirst, W. (1982). The amnesic syndrome: Descriptions and explanations. *Psychological Bulletin, 91,* 435–460.

Hirst, W., & Volpe, B. T. (1982). Temporal order judgments with amnesia. *Brain and Cognition, 1.*

Hirst, W., & Volpe, B. T. (1984a). Automatic and effortful encoding in amnesia. In M. S. Gazzaniga (Ed.), *Handbook of cognitive neuroscience* (pp. 369–386). New York: Plenum Press.

Hirst, W., & Volpe, B. T. (1984b). Encoding of spatial relations with amnesia. *Neuropsychologia, 22,* 631–634.

Huppert, F. A., & Piercy, M. (1976). Recognition memory in amnesic patients: Effect of temporal context and familiarity of material. *Cortex, 12,* 3–20.

Huppert, F. A., & Piercy, M. (1978). The role of trace strength in recency and frequency judgements by amnesic and control subjects. *Quarterly Journal of Experimental Psychology, 30,* 347–354.

Jacoby, L. L. (1982). Knowing and remembering: Some parallels in the behavior of Korsakoff patients and normals. In L. S. Cermak (Ed.), *Human memory and amnesia.* Hillsdale, NJ: Lawrence Erlbaum Associates.

Jacoby, L. L., & Dallas, M. (1981). On the relationship between autobiographical memory and perceptual learning. *Journal of Experimental Psychology: General, 110,* 306–340.

James, W. (1890). *Principles of Psychology* (Vol. 1). New York: Holt, Rinehart, & Winston.

Jones, G. V. (1983). On double dissociation of function. *Neuropsychologia, 21,* 397–400.

Kahneman, D. (1973). *Attention and effort.* Englewood Cliffs, NJ: Prentice–Hall.

Kaplan, E. (1983). Achievement and process revisited. In S. Wapner & B. Kaplan (Eds.), *Toward a holistic development psychology.* Hillsdale, NJ: Lawrence Erlbaum Associates.

Kimchi, R., & Palmer, S. E. (1982). Form and texture in hierarchically constructed patterns. *Journal of Experimental Psychology: Human Perception and Performance, 8,* 521–535.

Kinchla, R. A., & Wolfe, J. M. (1979). The order of visual processing: "Top-down," "bottom-up," or "middle-out." *Perception and Psychophysics, 25,* 225–231.

Kinsbourne, M., & Wood, F. (1975). Short-term memory processes and the amnesic syndrome. In D. Deutsch & J. A. Deutsch (Eds.), *Short-term memory.* New York: Academic Press.

Kinsbourne, M., & Wood, F. (1982). Theoretical considerations regarding the episodic-semantic memory distinction. In L. S. Cermak (Ed.), *Human memory and amnesia.* Hillsdale, NJ: Lawrence Erlbaum Associates.

Lashley, K. S. (1937). Functional determinant of cerebral localization. *Archives of Neurology and Psychiatry, 38,* 371–378.

Levy–Agristi, J., & Sperry, R. W. (1968). Differential perceptual capacities in major and minor hemispheres. *Proceedings of the National Academy of Science, 61,* 1151.

Locke, S., Caplan, D., & Kellar, L. (1973). *A study in neurolinguistics.* Springfield, MA: Thomas.

Luria, A. R. (1966). *Higher cortical functions in man.* New York: Basic Books.

Luria, A. R. (1970). The functional organization of the brain. *Scientific American, 22,* 66–78.

Luria, A. R. (1973). *The working brain.* London: Penguin Press.

Luria, A. R. (1976). *Neuropsychology of memory.* Washington, DC: Winston.

Mandler, G. (1980). Recognizing: The judgment of previous occurrence. *Psychological Review, 87,* 252–271.

Marr, D. (1982). *Vision.* San Francisco: Freeman.

Marshall, J. C., & Newcombe, F. (1973). Patterns of paralexia. *Journal of Psycholinguistic Research, 2,* 175–199.

Meudell, P., Mayes, A., & Neary, D. (1980). Amnesia is not caused by cognitive slowness. *Cortex, 16,* 413–419.

Milner, B. (1966). Amnesia following operation on the temporal lobes. In C. W. M. Whitty & O. L. Zangwill (Eds.), *Amnesia.* London: Butterworths.

Milner, B. (1970). Memory and the medial temporal regions of the brain. In K. H. Pribram & D. E. Broadbent (Eds.), *Biology of memory.* New York: Academic Press.

Moscovitch, M. (1979). Information processing and the cerebral hemispheres. In M. S. Gazzaniga (Ed.), *Handbook of behavioral neurobiology* (Vol. 2). New York: Plenum Press.

Murrell, G. A., & Morton, J. (1974). Word recognition and morphemic structure. *Journal of Experimental Psychology, 102*, 962–968.

Navon, D. (1977). Forest before trees: The precedence of global features in visual perception. *Cognitive Psychology, 9*, 353–383.

Neisser, U. (1976). *Cognition and reality*. San Francisco: Freeman.

Nolan, K. A., & Caramazza, A. (1982). Modality-independent impairment in word processing in a deep dyslexic patient. *Brain and Language, 16*, 237–264.

Palmer, S. E. (1980). What makes triangles point: Local and global effects in configurations of ambiguous triangles. *Cognitive Psychology, 12*, 285–305.

Patterson, A.,& Zangwill, O. L. (1944). Disorders of visual space perception associated with lesions of the right cerebral hemisphere. *Brain, 67*, 331–358.

Patterson, K. (1979). What is right with 'deep' dyslexics? *Brain and Language, 8*, 111–129.

Posner, M. I. (1980). Orienting of attention. *Quarterly Journal of Experimental Psychology, 32*, 3–25.

Posner, M. I., & Cohen, Y. (1984). Components of visual orienting. In H. Bouma & D. Bowhuis (Eds.), *Attention and performance*. Hillsdale, NJ: Lawrence Erlbaum Associates.

Posner, M. I., Pea, R., & Volpe, B. (1982). Cognitive-neuroscience: Developments toward a science of synthesis. In J. Mehler, E. T. Walker, & M. Garrett (Eds.), *Perspectives on mental representation*. Hillsdale, NJ: Lawrence Erlbaum Associates.

Posner, M. I., Walker, J. A., Friedrich, F. J., & Rafal, R. D. (1984). Effects of parietal injury on covert orienting of visual attention. *Journal of Neuroscience*.

Pylyshyn, Z. (1983). Syntax as an autonomous component of language. In M. Studdert–Kennedy (Ed.), *Psychobiology of language*. Cambridge: MIT Press.

Robertson, L. C., & Delis, D. C. (1984). *Visuospatial processing in unilateral brain damage: A reference frame analysis*. Paper presented at the annual meeting of the International Neuropsychological Society, Houston.

Robertson, L. C., & Palmer, S. E. (1983). Holistic processes in the perception and transformation of disoriented figures. *Journal of Experimental Psychology: Human Perception and Performance, 9*, 203–214.

Schacter, D. L., & Tulving, E. (1982a). Amnesia and memory research. In L. S. Cermak (Ed.), *Human memory and amnesia*. Hillsdale, NJ: Lawrence Erlbaum Associates.

Schacter, D. L., & Tulving, E. (1982b). Memory, amnesia, and the episodic/semantic distinction. In R. L. Isaacson & N. E. Spear (Eds.), *The expression of knowledge. Neurobehavioral transformations of information into action*. New York: Plenum Press.

Schaff, A. (1973). *Language and cognition*. New York: McGraw–Hill.

Schneider, W., & Shiffrin, R. M. (1977). Controlled and automatic human information processing: I. Detection, search, and attention. *Psychological Review, 84*, 1–66.

Sergent, J. (1982). The cerebral balance of power: Confrontation or cooperation? *Journal of Experimental Psychology: Human perception and performance, 8*, 253–272.

Sergent, J., & Bindra, D. (1981). Differential hemispheric processing of faces: Methodological considerations and reinterpretation. *Psychological Bulletin, 89*, 541–554.

Shallice, T. (1981). Neurological impairment of cognitive processes. *British Medical Bulletin, 37*, 187–192.

Shallice, T., & Warrington, E. K. (1975). Word recognition in a phonemic dyslexic patient. *Quarterly Journal of Experimental Psychology, 27*, 187–199.

Shepard, R. N. (1975). Form, formation, and transformation of internal representations. In R. L. Solso (Ed.), *Information processing in cognition: The Loyola symposium*. Hillsdale, NJ: Lawrence Erlbaum Associates.

Shiffrin, R. M., & Schneider, W. (1977). Controlled and automatic human information processing: II. Perceptual learning, automatic attending, and a general theory. *Psychological Review, 84*, 127–190.

Sperry, R. W. (1964). The great cerebral commissure. *Scientific American, 210*, 42–52.

Squire, L. R. (1982a). Comparisons between forms of amnesia: Some deficits are unique to Korsakoff's syndrome. *Journal of Experimental Psychology: Learning, Memory, and Cognition, 8*, 560–571.

Squire, L. R. (1982b). The neuropsychology of human memory. *Annual Review of Neuroscience, 5*, 241–273.

Talland, G. A. (1965). *Deranged memory*. New York: Academic Press.

Teuber, H. L. (1955). Physiological psychology. In *Annual review of psychology* (Vol. 6). Palo Alto, CA: Annual Reviews.

Tulving, E. (1972). Episodic and semantic memory. In E. Tulving & W. Donaldson (Eds.), *Organization of memory* (pp. 381–403). New York: Academic Press.

Tulving, E., Schacter, D. L., & Stark, H. A. (1982). Priming effects in word-fragment completion are independent of recognition memory. *Journal of Experimental Psychology: Learning, Memory, and Cognition, 8*, 336–342.

Ulatowska, H. K., Doyel, A. W., Stern, R. F., Haynes, S. M., & North, A. J. (1983). Production of procedural discourse in aphasia. *Brain and Language, 18*, 315–341.

Warrington, E. K. (1975). The selective impairment of semantic memory. *Quarterly Journal of Experimental Psychology, 27*, 635–657.

Warrington, E., James, M., & Kinsbourne, M. (1966). Drawing disability in relation to laterality of cerebral lesion. *Brain, 89*, 53–82.

Warrington, E. K., & Weiskrantz, L. (1982). Amnesia: A disconnection syndrome? *Neuropsychologia, 20*, 233–248.

Weigl, E., & Bierwisch, M. (1970). Neuropsychology and linguistics: Types of common research. *Foundations of Language, 6*, 1–18.

Weingartner, H., Grafman, J., Boutelle, W., Kaye, W., & Martin, P. R. (1983). Forms of memory failure. *Science, 221*, 380–382.

Weiskrantz, L., & Warrington, E. K. (1970). Verbal learning and retention by amnesic patients using partial information. *Psychonomic Science, 20*, 210–211.

Weiskrantz, L., & Warrington, E. K. (1979). Conditioning in amnesic patients. *Neuropsychologia, 17*, 187–194.

Wetzel, C. D., & Squire, L. R. (1982). Cued recall in anterograde amnesia. *Brain and Language, 15*, 70–81.

Wetzel, C. D., & Squire, L. R. (1980). Encoding in anterograde amnesia. *Neuropsychologia, 18*, 177–184.

Wickelgren, W. A. (1973). The long and the short of memory. *Psychological Bulletin, 80*, 425–438.

Wickelgren, W. A. (1975). More on the long and short of memory. In D. Deutsch & J. A. Deutsch (Eds.), *Short-term memory* (pp. 65–72). New York: Academic Press.

Winocur, G., Kinsbourne, M., & Moscovitch, M. (1981). The effect of cuing on release from proactive interference in Korsakoff amnesic patients. *Journal of Experimental Psychology: Human Learning and Memory, 7*, 56–65.

Wood, F., Ebert, V., & Kinsbourne, M. (1982). The episodic-semantic memory distinction in memory and amnesia: Clinical and experimental observations. In L. S. Cermak (Ed.), *Human memory and amnesia*. Hillsdale, NJ: Lawrence Erlbaum Associates.

Zacks, R. T., Hasher, L., & Sanft, H. (1982). Automatic encoding of event frequency: Further findings. *Journal of Experimental Psychology, 8*, 106–116.

Zola-Morgan, S., Cohen, N. J., & Squire, L. R. (1983). Recall of remote episodic memory in amnesia. *Neuropsychologia, 21*, 487–500.

Zurif, E. B. (1983). Aspects of sentence processing in aphasia. In M. Studdert-Kennedy (Ed.), *Psychobiology of language*. Cambridge: MIT Press.

Zurif, E. B., & Blumstein, S. E. (1978). Language and the brain. In M. Halle, J. Bresnan, & G. A. Miller (Eds.), *Linguistic theory and psychological reality*. Cambridge: MIT Press.

Zurif, E. B., & Caramazza, A. (1976). Psycholinguistic structures in aphasia: Studies in syntax and semantics. In H. Whitaker & H. A. Whitaker (Eds.), *Studies in neurolinguistics* (Vol. 1). New York: Academic Press.

Zurif, E. B., Caramazza, A., & Myerson, R. (1972). Grammatical judgments of agrammatic aphasics. *Neuropsychologia, 10*.

12 Putting Cognitive Psychology to Work: Examples from Computer System Design

Louis M. Gomez
Susan T. Dumais
Bell Communications Research, Inc.

One legitimate measure of the maturity and usefulness of a scientific approach is the quality of its interaction with the world of practical problems; that is, the growth of a science is sometimes judged by the solutions it offers to "real" problems and by how readily it uses feedback from the "real" world to help shape its core research questions.

Psychology has had a long history of scientific concern for practical problems. Indeed, application plays a defining role in the fields of educational, industrial, clinical, and engineering psychology. Examples of the use of engineering or human factors psychology range from traditional applications in aircraft displays, warning systems, and workstation design to larger social issues in the design of residences and communities. By contrast, many of the recent research efforts in cognitive or information-processing psychology seem neither motivated by nor destined for applications. This appears to be the case despite the fact that many fundamental research questions and methodologies in cognitive psychology grew out of a search for solutions to practical problems (Broadbent, 1958; Chapanis, Garner, & Morgan, 1949; Fitts & Posner, 1967).

In the last few years, designers have turned to cognitive psychology and asked what it can contribute to the applied problem of designing more useful and usable computer systems. In this chapter we discuss cognitive psychology's response to this challenge. We do not give cognitive psychology a report card, however. An evaluation of this sort would be quite premature. Only 5 years ago the potential utility of cognitive science to the design of complex computer systems was largely unrecognized. Recently, however, there has been a growing awareness that the success or failure of a computer system (either in the marketplace or in the workplace) hinges on its human users. This is particularly evident with the popular emphasis on "user friendliness." Along with this emphasis has come a growing research and development interest in understanding and improving human productivity and performance in complex computer-based systems. This growth in interest can be documented by the increasing number of special journal issues (*International Journal of Man–Machine Studies*—Vol. 15[1], July 1981; *Computing Surveys*—Vol. 13[1], March 1981), books (Card, Moran, & Newell, 1983; Shneiderman, 1980; Smith & Green, 1980; Thomas & Schneider, 1984; etc.), and conferences (Human Factors in Computer Systems, Gaithersburg, March 15–17, 1982; CHI'83, Boston, Dec. 12–15, 1983; INTERACT'84, London, Sept. 4–7, 1984) devoted to better understanding the human–computer interface. Many of the researchers and designers involved in such endeavors were trained as cognitive psychologists and therefore use results and tools from cognitive psychology.

This meeting of cognitive psychology and computer technology is interesting and probably not accidental. Both disciplines are concerned with the processing of information. Cognitive psychology has for the past two decades been a developing discipline trying to understand the nature of the human intellect. The central approach of cognitive psychology has been to view people as general information-processing devices operating on rich internal knowledge structures. An important characteristic of the information-processing analysis is to trace the transformation of information through a sequence of mental operations. This cognitive or information-processing approach has discovered both specific *results* in human memory, perception, problem solving, and thought, as well as a set of research *methods* and tools to explore such issues. (See Lindsay & Norman, 1977 and Neisser, 1967 for more details.) We believe that the extension of this approach to the study of human–computer interaction is quite natural.

Recent advances in computer technology promise to extend man's intellectual capabilities. For example, the technology currently exists to give people access to a wealth of electronically stored information of all kinds. In one sense this technology is an aid that, in effect, extends the memories of its users. People's problem-solving abilities can also be augmented by providing new ways to organize and operate on information. For the promise of this new technology to be kept, computers will have to accommodate to the physical attributes and abilities of users, but, more importantly, they will also have to suit the way people think and process information; that is, in order to be maximally useful, computer systems must be designed to go beyond physical compatibility and on to *cognitive* compatibility.

In order to build computer systems that will successfully extend and complement the way people think and make decisions, we believe it is important to understand the abilities and liabilities that people bring to the interaction. For example, the design of an information retrieval system that allows its users to browse and categorize information would probably benefit from an understanding of how people query their own internal memories or other external memories (e.g. other people, libraries). There seem to be a number of areas like this where data and methods from cognitive psychology appear to be relevant, and some preliminary attempts have been made to see how they might be applied (see Allen, 1982; Miller & Thomas, 1977; Moran, 1981; and Ramsey & Atwood, 1979 for reviews). Nonetheless, there are numerous examples of poorly designed systems in which such considerations have apparently been ignored. When people use systems that are ill-suited to them the consequences can range from irritation, in the case of a text editor that is difficult to use (Landauer, Galotti, & Hartwell, 1983), to the disaster of poorly designed nuclear power plant controls as in the case of Three Mile Island (Kantowitz, 1977; Kemeny, 1979). Although it is easy to find examples of poorly designed interfaces, it is harder to arrive at a consensus about the roots of the problem and what the solutions should be. Even a cursory observation of the current computer industry suggests the need for an application of a science of human performance to improve system design.

In this chapter, we report on progress toward the application of data, concepts, and methods from *cognitive psychology* to the design of more humanly usable *computer systems*. Because, as noted earlier, directly relevant research has only been going on for a few years, not enough of the needed applied cognitive psychology exists yet for us to provide an account of notable successes and failures. However, we point to some pertinent data, methodologies, and theories from cognitive psychology and offer suggestions about changes that we believe will be required for significant progress. In addition, we point to examples of how the study of human–computer interaction as a content domain might suggest new areas for development in cognitive psychology. We begin by considering the more general relationship between applied and basic research in psychology.

Cognitive Psychology and Application: Past and Present

Psychological research in general has long been concerned with the practical application of its basic science. Cognitive psychology has had an interesting history in this regard. Although many of its methods and questions grew out of solutions to practical problems, application seems to play a less central role in cognitive psychology today.

The Past

Garner (1972) reviewed a number of research questions, of current interest to cognitive psychology, that were initially motivated by applied problems. Work on selective attention began as an attempt to help air traffic controllers sort out several simultaneously incoming messages (Broadbent, 1952; Webster & Thompson, 1954). Interest in vigilance, and in particular vigilance decrements, arose during World War II when soldiers were given long monitoring or watch-keeping assignments (Lindsley, 1944; Mackworth, 1944). Gibson's (1950) the-orizing about ecological optics was greatly influenced by his attempt to under-stand how aircraft pilots estimated distances in order to successfully land planes—the traditional depth cues failed to provide a satisfactory answer. Many topics of interest in speech perception and psychoacoustics can trace their roots to early work by Fletcher (1922) aimed at improving the quality and intel-ligibility of speech transmitted over telephone networks. Applied problems have also led to the development of new methodological tools. For example, the theory of signal detectability (TSD) was first developed in an engineering context where ideal sensing devices were required. Only later did Tanner and Swets (1954) extend and apply these ideas to human perceptual performance. Thus, real-world problems played an important role in defining several of the content areas and methods of experimental psychology during the 1950s–1970s.

Before considering the state of affairs today, we briefly examine the more general question of the relationship between basic and applied research. Kan-towitz (1982) has discussed four possible relationships between applied and basic research: (1) Basic research aids applied work but not vice versa; (2) applied research aids basic research but not vice versa; (3) the two are independent; and (4) the two mutually influence and aid each other. Although many people believe that the first view is (or should be) the norm, Garner (1972) has argued that this unidirectional flow is a myth—and a quite dangerous one: "The fable is that scientists acquire knowledge, that this knowledge goes into the public domain, and that when a problem solver needs some knowledge to solve his problem, he extracts if from the public domain, uttering words of gratitude as he does so, and solves his problem" (p. 942). Garner goes on to cite several important concepts and topics in human experimental psychology that, at least initially, were moti-vated by practical questions whose answers were unknown (see preceding dis-cussion). Chapanis (1971) has used similar evidence to take the argument one step further in suggesting that applied research is the appropriate starting point for basic research (relationship [2] aforementioned). He says: "it is my firm belief that the best basic work in psychology starts not with psychological theory but with the attempt to solve questions posed by the real world around us" (p. 950). Neither of these unidirectional extremes is probably the case. Relationship (3) has had few vocal supporters. But, Skinner (e.g., Skinner, 1950) is a notable exception and has been an influential proponent of the separate-but-equal view. Basically the argument is that applied research aimed at solving practical prob-lems and basic research aimed at developing and testing theories tackle different problems, and that interaction between the two is unnecessary. Finally, a number of authors (Garner, 1972; Kantowitz, 1982; Wright, 1978) have argued that basic and applied research can (and should) be carried out side-by-side to the mutual benefit of both. The quality of basic research is improved by contact with real-world problems, and applied psychologists must maintain contact with basic results and models in order to take advantage of new developments.

In some disciplines the coupling between fundamental research and applications is tight and fairly direct. Practical problems act as both a test bed for existing methods and theories and also as a stimulus for new developments. Operations research, applied mathematics, and statistics, for example, are disciplines that are tightly linked to mathematics. Problems in operations research, for example, are initially analyzed to see if they can be stated in terms of existing methods or solutions; if not, new mathematical developments may be required (Wagner, 1975). Psychoacoustics is another area where basic research findings about the auditory system can often be applied, more or less directly, to practical problems. Warning signals can be designed for unique acoustic environments using known detection data (Fidell, 1978). However, even in this domain, not all problems are equally amenable to such analyses—the design of top-quality concert and opera halls is still as much an art as a science (Beranek, 1962; Schroeder, 1980). In the area of computer hardware design, behavioral science research has had a rather direct impact. Standards for visual display terminal design, for example, are directly influenced by results from vision research (Krebs, Wolf, & Sandvig, 1978). Making accurate recommendations about correct levels of contrast, intensity, size, and many other aspects of visual displays would be much more difficult without results from fundamental research. Again, however, there are large gaps that must be filled for certain applications (for example, Christ, 1975).

The Present

Although rather tight couplings exist between research and its application in some areas, it is not possible to point to many clear examples of the direct application of research from cognitive psychology to the design of computer interfaces. This is somewhat surprising because, as we alluded to earlier, many of the topics of interest to and methods employed by cognitive psychologists appear to be extremely relevant to human–computer interaction (e.g., problem solving, categorization ability, human memory, stimulus–response compatibility, mental models, and knowledge representation). We consider a couple of examples in more detail, focusing on why existing knowledge was insufficient for design applications.

The topic of human memory has occupied a central place in human information-processing research and theory for several decades. During this period a good deal has been learned about the capabilities and fallibilities of human memory (see Baddeley, 1976; Crowder, 1976; Kintsch, 1977 for reviews). Computer interface design seems to be a fertile ground for applying or testing these theories. Computer systems often require users to retain sizable amounts of information about commands and procedures. One question for cognitive psychology is what, if anything, do the decades of human memory research have to say about how to build command sets and specify procedures that are manageable by humans?

The answer is: "Perhaps not as much as expected." Consider, as a more specific example, the application of research about paired associate learning to the problem of assigning names to text-editor commands. Tremendous amounts of data have been collected about the factors (e.g., number of items, presentation time, meaningfulness) that control the amount and quality of information people remember from paired associate lists. At first glance, the general paired associate task appears to be quite similar to that faced by people learning to use a command language. In the paired associate task, subjects learn to associate pairs of items; and in using a command language, users must pair a command name with a desired function. But, upon closer examination there are differences that make the direct application of results from standard memory paradigms to command language learning difficult. First, computer users are not really learning isolable pairs of words. The text-editor commands will be related not only to each other (so that similar operations are accomplished in similar ways, thus enabling generalizations, etc.), but also to the larger computing environment, of which the editor is but a small part. Perhaps then research on artificial language learning is more relevant to consider. But here too a practitioner trying to apply research results is faced with the second, and perhaps more important, problem, task demand differences. Much of the classic memory research studies isolated memory phenomena in controlled laboratory situations (and there are good reasons for doing this). However, when a computer user tries to recall the association between a command name and a computer procedure, remembering is not an isolable act. On the contrary, the user is immersed in a complex of subtasks that include not only memory, but also problem solving, making sense of a computer terminal's behavior, etc. As Landauer (1983) has pointed out, it is probably unrealistic to expect the effects found in standard memory laboratory situations to dominate and to be additive with the new difficulties encountered in tasks like command language learning. So, it is not as simple as one might have expected.

In a similar vein, people's ability to categorize natural and artificial stimuli is fundamental in managing information in the environment and has been the object of much research (Rosch & Lloyd, 1978; Smith & Medin, 1981). Among the more important and robust findings are that: (1) categories are "fuzzy" both in the sense that they overlap with one another and that items are only probabilistically contained in them; (2) there is a "basic" level of categorization at which it is most natural to divide the world into alternative categories—it is also argued that this basic level maximizes within-category similarity relative to between-category similarity; and (3) many natural categories are organized around prototypical exemplars (although there are a number of other ways in which categories can be defined and represented). The contents of many large computerized information systems are categorized to allow users access to the information (e.g., bibliographic systems and videotext or home information systems). Menu-based retrieval systems are the best (and most prevalent) example of categorization in automated information systems. In menu systems, users are presented with a list of category descriptions and must choose the category to which the item they are looking for belongs. The choices are typically arranged in a hierarchy of menus such that choices at one level lead to a refinement of the selected category. So, for example, one could divide psychology books into subcategories like: cognitive, clinical, social, developmental, physiological, statistics, animal learning, etc. In what way can the large body of knowledge about human categorization aid in the design of such information systems (Dumais & Landauer, 1984; Evans, 1982; Young & Hull, 1982, 1983)?

The following is intended to give the reader a flavor for the kinds of questions that arise when trying to apply existing knowledge about human categorization. First, for reasons of storage and search efficiency, many menu-based systems are (or are close to being) strictly nested hierarchical partitions of the information. A first suggestion might be to make these organizations more compatible with those that people appear to have—that is, to allow overlapping (fuzzy) categories with richer and more complex interrelations than hierarchical nesting. Assume that this can be done. The categorization results would suggest that the best categorization scheme is one that divides the information into basic level categories using prototypical examples to describe the categories. How can basic level categories be constructed? For a few simple domains (e.g., furniture, animals) the basic level categories are known, and for other domains one might try using multidimensional scaling or clustering techniques to find categories that satisfy the similarity criterion in (2) earlier. There are at least two problems. The first is a pragmatic one. How can the pair-wise similarity data that is needed be obtained when one is dealing with large domains like all the books in a university library? For 10,000 objects, for example, on the order of 100,000,000 (10,000 × 10,000) similarity measures must be collected. The second problem is that basic level categories are not universal. They vary over individuals of different expertise and across cultures and seem to be related to the attributes that an individual notices in objects. So, whose basic level categories should be used? Even if one could settle on some basic level categories, how should they be displayed and described? If there are more than a few dozen basic level categories, it may be difficult to display them all simultaneously, and it will certainly be tedious for users to scan through them. Perhaps it would be better to display fewer higher level superordinates, although individually they are somewhat more difficult for people to deal with. A designer needs to know the tradeoffs between displaying many good categories and fewer poorer ones. Finally, what happens if the data base changes somewhat? In real data bases, new items are being added and old items are being deleted all the time. Does the process of categorizing information start all over again when this happens? These, and many other, questions face practitioners who try to apply existing knowledge about human categorization. In spite of the fact that research about human categorization has pointed to several important considerations, its results are far from being a useful practical design tool.

These are but a few examples of the many questions where research about cognitive processes and mechanisms might be applied to the design of complex computer systems. Unfortunately, it has not been as directly relevant as one might have hoped in answering detailed design questions.

There are several reasons for the lack of direct applicability. One reason is time. The recognition of the relevance of cognitive psychology to interface design is recent. In fact, several new journals in the area are just beginning (e.g., *Human–Computer Interaction, Behaviour & Information Technology*). Over the next several years, applications of findings from information-processing research may find their way into software engineering. As an aside, we note that this is not necessarily an easy process. There is a growing concern and a vast literature about what has been called technology or knowledge transfer, which suggests that the flow of information from research to application is neither rapid nor terribly effective. In areas of rapid change, like computer software and hardware, time is especially critical if results from research are to be fully exploited in designing new systems (Abelson, 1980; Bikson, Quint, & Johnson, 1984).

A second reason why there are few examples of a direct coupling between cognitive psychology and computer system design may be an incompatibility between the answers provided by cognitive psychology and the answers needed by designers. There are at least two aspects to this. The first is that basic research is often aimed at understanding a very specific aspect of human cognition. But, naturally occurring cognitive processes are embedded in a continuous stream of mental activity. It may not be enough to know how individual components work—they have to be combined in order to design a working system. Consider a person sending electronic mail—he/she is composing sentences, recalling text-editor commands, and being interrupted by error messages or phone calls. The second aspect is essentially that of effectively communicating across disciplines. Results from cognitive psychology must be communicated not only to psychologists involved in system design, but also to engineers, computer scientists, etc. For example, although problem-solving research is, in a general way, relevant to computer programming, it may be difficult for a computer system designer to abstract relevant information in a usable form. How easy is it for someone interested in designing a programming language interface to use performance results from isomorphs of the Four Monsters Problem (Hayes & Simon, 1977)? This is not to say, of course, that the information and insights gained in this domain are not relevant to questions of programming—designers of programming languages would almost certainly be interested in how the statement of a problem influences its solution. It is to say, however, that the results and implications may be opaque to people other than researchers concerned with problem solving.

Despite these difficulties, there have been attempts by psychologists to abstract and generalize findings from basic research for designers. These often take the form of guidelines or checklists. Guidelines for screen design first appeared (e.g., Krebs et al., 1978), followed more recently by guidelines for dialogue design (e,g., Smith, 1982). The guidelines for dialogue design point to many useful "facts" (the short-term memory limit of 7 ± 2 items being the most popular) and relevant research from cognitive psychology. Such guidelines are certainly not irrelevant—at the very least they codify some of the important dimensions in interface design and point to general constraints on design. Without this knowledge, systems would probably be noticeably worse. Although guidelines they can be quite useful in avoiding grievous errors, and in sensitizing designers to issues that they may not have explicitly thought about before, they fall far short of being a science of design.

There are several reasons for this, many of which we have touched upon in the examples. First, guidelines, in and of themselves, do not carry enough information to be directly interpretable or applicable by designers. Recommendations at a very general level like: "know thy user" or "don't overuse color" are just too vague to be very useful in prescribing an appropriate design. Guidelines like these are valuable in drawing attention to relevant considerations, but they typically fail to provide methods for arriving at a solution. Second, more specific guidelines may be based on preliminary experimental evidence or only on armchair judgments and may therefore be inaccurate. This is especially true in relatively new areas of investigation like dialogue design. Finally, guidelines tend to be simple statements organized by some characterization of the important aspects of human–computer interaction (e.g., displays, user characteristics, tasks, etc.). This organization is not very effective in handling the wide range of tradeoffs and interactions among simple variables that can occur in complex tasks environments (for which computer systems are often being designed). Human performance is often significantly influenced by the task, domain and individuals under investigation. As Jenkins (1984) has concisely stated: "it depends." The usefulness of pictures in text, for example, depends on the kind of text, the kind of pictures, who the readers are as well as their goals in reading, and the criterial tasks. Thus, although guidelines serve some useful functions and may provide a starting point from which to incorporate knowledge about human cognition into system design, they are currently far from being *prescriptive*. Certainly, one cannot go from first principles to the design of even a simple computer system, say a text editor. (See also Barnard, 1983 and Williges, 1982 for discussions of the need to establish better means of acquiring, representing, and applying knowledge about user cognition and its consequences.)

So, despite the apparent overlap of problems in cognitive psychology and the needs of computer interface design, the two fields, for the most part, coexist in an independent rather than interdependent fashion. How might the coupling between the two disciplines become tighter—hopefully making the relationship more beneficial to both? We begin by looking at what cognitive psychology is starting to contribute to system design both in terms of specific results as well as more general methods for characterizing and studying human–computer interaction. Where applicable, we also mention some changes in cognitive psychology that can occur as a result of its contact with practitioners in computer interface design.

Cognitive Theory Meets Practical Problems

In the previous section, we suggested two reasons why cognitive psychology and computer interface design are not as closely linked as they might be. One reason is time. Only relatively recently have computer system designers acknowledged the importance of designing for end-users, and have cognitive psychologists become interested in the complexities of human cognition in computer environments. The second reason is an incompatibility in the answers provided by cognitive psychology and those needed by system designers. Not much can be done about the problem of time; but the compatibility problem is perhaps more tractable. One way in which to address the issue is to investigate problems of general interest to the psychological research community using content domains that are relevant to software design. Such efforts potentially yield several important types of results. First, the researcher learns valuable information about the specific domain of investigation. This may be of immediate practical value. It may also point to new variables in need of further systematic investigation (e.g., qualitatively different kinds of memory or problem-solving situations may be encountered in these new environments). Second, tools and concepts born in the applied domain may find their way into the analysis of more traditional problems from basic cognitive psychology. Finally, research done in domains of practical interest can be used to set bounds on the generalizability of theories or methods initially developed in other contexts. Sometimes existing theories and methods can successfully be extended; other times new developments will be needed. We now consider several examples of domains relevant to computer interface design that have served as a meeting ground for applied and basic cognitive psychology.

Content Relevant Domains

Skill Acquisition. Cognitive psychologists have for some time been interested in skill acquisition and expert performance. Many aspects of human–computer interaction, especially computer programming, require a good deal of training. Learning to program a computer or learning to use a text editor can be viewed in terms of acquiring a cognitive skill. As a result of enormous amounts of practice, experts acquire knowledge and/or strategies that lead to successful and efficient performance. One approach to the study of expertise has been to systematically characterize how experts and novices differ. The argument goes that if the knowledge of experts and novices can be made explicit, more effective training programs can be developed to speed the transition from one to the other.

One useful approach has been to look at characteristics of the memory representations that experts and novices have for skill-relevant information. For example, when chess players are asked to study and later report the positions of chess pieces from real games, experts recall more than novices. By virtue of their experience, experts apparently see certain patterns in the stimulus materials that allow them to process, store, and retrieve more information than less experienced observers. However, when the board pieces are randomly placed (i.e., not coherent parts of a chess game), expert performance does not differ from novice performance (Chase & Simon, 1973). Similar research techniques have been applied to the study of skilled performance in other domains including physics (Larkin, McDermott, Simon, & Simon, 1980), symbolic electronic drawings (Egan & Schwartz, 1979), and "go" (Reitman, 1976). The results from all these experiments have been quite consistent. Experts generally take advantage of definable structure in content material, but novices do not.

Similar techniques have recently been used to study skilled performance in the computer programming domain (Adelson, 1981; Jeffries, Turner, Polson, & Atwood, 1981; McKeithen, Reitman, Rueter, & Hirtle, 1981; Shneiderman, 1976). In general, the programming results point to differences between experts and novices that are similar to those found in other domains. For example, novices' memory protocols for lines of program code show clusters that are strongly influenced by syntactic properties of the programming language, whereas experts' memory protocols tend to cluster according to more abstract programming concepts. Results like these are promising because they suggest that acquiring complex computer-based skills is similar to skill acquisition in other, better studied, domains. Of course, how to apply results like these to the teaching of computer programming or the use of complex software systems remains an open question. The research in computer programming is not alone, however, in this regard. Although an important part of the motivation for studying the differences between expert and novice performance has been to apply the results to instructional design, this has seldom been realized. Research has tended to focus on characterizing expert performance and knowledge rather than on its acquisition or its application to training.[1] This work then has not gone far enough. A theory with a different emphasis is needed—it should focus on how a novice becomes an expert. In order for knowledge about expert–novice differences to be

---

[1]One exception is found in Larkin (1983). She began by characterizing the representations and strategies that expert and beginning physics students use in solving physics problems. Students use "naive" representations and means–end strategies, whereas experts appear to use "physical" representations and schemata to arrive at solutions. She then showed that instruction aimed at increasing students' ability to develop physical representations resulted in better problem-solving performance than instruction emphasizing a standard algebraic approach.

relevant to instructional design, a theory about the *acquisition of competence* is needed (see also Glaser, 1976). Research in the more applied domain of computer programming has pointed to what is missing in extant theories of expert–novice differences, and as we now discuss, it may provide hints as to a solution.

Perhaps the generalization of the expert–novice approach from earlier experimental domains to computer programming is not too surprising. After all, the methods were initially developed to understand behavior in relatively complex domains (physics, chess, etc.). There is little reason to believe that interacting with computers is qualitatively different from these other complex tasks. Unfortunately, as noted previously, although much effort has been expended in characterizing differences between experts and novices, it has had little impact on instruction or training practices. Computer programming is a skill that many believe is becoming more and more critical to acquire—not just for fledgling computer scientists, but for everyone. Consequently effective training methods are being sought. Perhaps the work on expert–novice differences in programming will be successfully extended to develop new instructional design methodologies. Already, some researchers (Ehrlich & Soloway, 1984) have begun to shift away from simply showing that experts have more and/or better organized knowledge about programming than novices. They have begun to explore methods for identifying the specific plans that experts use. The idea is to use these plans to teach programming, and as the basis for programming tutors and programming aids (see Rich, 1981 for a discussion of a programming environment organized around experts' plans). The programming example is interesting and important because it helped point out a weakness of the expert–novice research (namely its lack of emphasis on skill acquisition and training prescriptions) and, further, may have hints as to a possible solution.

As an aside, it is interesting to note that a very different approach to expertise exists both in cognitive theory and in computer practice. A number of researchers (Anzai & Simon, 1979 and Bransford, 1984, for example) have argued that a different tack should be followed in order to understand and take advantage of expertise. They question whether expertise can explicitly be taught by means of instruction. For example, can a new bicyclist be told how to maintain balance? Instead, they suggest that practical training or apprenticeship is the road to expertise. A good learning environment is one that enables or facilitates practical training. Although not stated in precisely these terms, similar principles underly the design of text editors where people "learn by doing" (Carroll & Carrithers, 1984; Carroll & Mack, 1984), the design of command or help systems tailored to the level of experience of users (Schneider, 1982), and the popular press descriptions of learning to use Apple's new personal computer, MacIntosh.

Individual Differences.   In addition to the utility of the expert–novice approach, other techniques used to study learning and skill acquisition have also been fruitful in the world of system design. Egan and Gomez and their colleagues (Egan & Gomez, in press; Gomez, Egan, & Bowers, in press) were interested in understanding the difficulty that some people seem to have in learning to use a text editor. They and others had informally observed that some people have no trouble learning to edit text with a computer, yet other people seem to try and try and never completely succeed. They reasoned that if they could understand the sources of these differences, it might be possible to suggest new editor designs or training regimens to allow more people to learn, or to learn more quickly.

In their work they made extensive use of the cognitive correlates and cognitive components approaches (Pelligrino & Glaser, 1979; Sternberg, 1977). Each of these approaches seeks to understand human performance by analyzing the differences between individuals along several measurable cognitive (e.g., verbal ability) and background (e.g., educational level) characteristics. The cognitive correlates approach tries to localize similarities and differences in the performance of high- and low-ability individuals to specific stages of information processing. Cognitive components, on the other hand, begins with a detailed task analysis and attempts to localize differences between people to specific task components. Egan and Gomez began by examining the learner characteristics associated with success in learning text editing. In initial work with a line-based editor, they found that older users and those who scored low on a standard test of spatial memory consistently made more errors and required more time to solve text-editing problems than younger users and those with higher spatial memory test scores. They further analyzed the text-editing task into three general components (finding, counting, and generating) and determined that the *age* effect was primarily due to the complex nature of the command generation sequence required by the text editor, and that the *spatial memory* effect was caused by the manner in which users searched for text items. One way to simplify the command sequence is to use function keys rather than commands to specify changes. A redesigned display editor, that employed function keys instead of a command language, did indeed significantly reduce the age effect (Egan & Gomez, in press).

This research is important with respect to the relationship between cognitive psychology and interface design for at least two reasons. First, the research was motivated not by an effort to build a better text editor, but rather by an interest in understanding factors that control learning in complex situations. Yet it provided potentially useful information for the design process. Second, this work points out the value of research in revealing counterintuitive explanations. Prior to this work it was fairly clear that display editors were better than line editors for a variety of text-editing tasks (Roberts, 1980). However, the source of this design success was not clear—although many designers argued that the advantage of full-screen editors was *clearly* due to the reduced demands they made on spatial memory (see Gomez, Egan, Wheeler, Sharma, & Gruchacz, 1983, for a more detailed discussion). As a result of this and other work (Roberts & Moran, 1983), it is becoming apparent that many full-sereen or display editors are superior not because of spatial features per se, but rather because they typically provide a simpler (less procedurally complex) command interface.

Knowledge Representation. Another area of investigation that is receiving considerable attention is the development of formal descriptions of people's internal representations of complex systems (Card, Moran, & Newell, 1980, 1983; Kieras & Polson, in press; Young, 1981). The goal of this work is to provide formalisms that will give system designers a language or a set of techniques to specify the procedures and knowledge a person needs in order to interact with a system. Card, Moran, & Newell (1983), for example, have developed what they call the GOMS (goals, operators, methods, and selection) model in order to quantitatively analyze and predict behavior. The model incorporates many concepts from Newell and Simon's (1972) general problem solver (including production systems as the language for describing behavior) but adds quantitative measures of the importance of various independent variables on performance. One simplification of the GOMS model at the "keystroke level" has been used to predict text-editing time (accurate to a standard error of 21% over a variety of tasks and systems). The power of this formalism lies in its ability to predict performance without requiring testing in actual situations. For example, benchmarks can be calculated for different proposed systems (as long as operations can be expressed in terms of comparable model parameters), and sensitivity analyses can be performed—that is, changes in predicted performance as a function of changes in model parameters can be examined. Thus the GOMS model and related analyses are another example where theories and modeling techniques from cognitive psychology have been useful in understanding some aspects of human–computer interaction, and in evaluating design alternatives. Furthermore, the practical goal of arriving at useful design approximations has suggested several extensions. The model is currently limited to describing the error-free aspects of expert behavior. It therefore needs to be extended to account for error data, and to describe more creative and less routine tasks, which are probably the norm in human–computer interaction. It is too early to tell whether or not these extensions will influence ongoing work in cognitive psychology, but it is hard to believe that they will not, because much of human cognition is error prone and occurs in novel problem-solving situations.

These examples are part of a growing body of research by cognitive psychologists done in the service of basic research, but in domains relevant to interface and software design. They illustrate cases where issues of importance in computer interface design were amenable to study using, for the most part, techniques or ideas that had been developed in cognitive psychology. The results of such efforts can be quite important to designers. They can also provide cognitive psychology with information about areas in need of further investigation or methods in need of development. Although such results are encouraging and point to the usefulness of studying content-relevant domains as a way to reduce the communication gap between applied and basic cognitive psychology, much of the promise of these efforts is still couched in terms of its future or potential utility. The work is still relatively long-term research, and these investigators are not trying to answer specific design questions. There are, however, a number of cognitive psychologists who are much more closely involved in day-to-day design decisions. We believe that the communications between applied and basic work can also be improved by looking at the decisions that these applied practitioners make, the information they use, and the information they are missing.

Cognitive Psychology in the Field

There are many cognitive psychologists now in the field making design decisions every day. We believe that important gaps in cognitive psychology can be revealed by examining their ability (and inability) to solve the practical problems they encounter. Such information can be used as data about the adequacy and completeness of the current theories, methods, and data of cognitive psychology. Interestingly (and somewhat surprisingly), when asked what knowledge and skills they bring to the system design process, cognitive psychologists often respond ''none.'' Since cognitive psychology tries to understand exactly those processes that people interacting with computers engage, we are puzzled about why practitioners feel they have so little to offer.

Perhaps the methods and tools that cognitive psychologists bring to bear are irrelevant. There are certainly some properties that limit the usefulness of traditional research techniques as tools in day-to-day system design, and these have been discussed by Skinner (1950) and Newell and Simon (1972), for example. Among the more salient problems are that: (1) experimental research takes a good deal of time to yield useful answers; (2) hypothesis testing may be less useful to a designer than the estimation of the size of an effect (especially in the context of other variables); (3) theories or models aimed at understanding ''how'' something works may be less useful for making design decisions than knowledge about ''when'' it works; and (4) limitations in time, money, and the necessity to conform to larger system design considerations often require that a good, although not necessarily optimal, design be found. (We note that these problems are not limited to the tools of cognitive psychology and apply, more generally, to the methods of experimental psychology. But, they are an important component of the feelings of frustration expressed by cognitive psychologists and deserve mention for that reason.)

Whereas the traditional methods of cognitive psychology may have limited utility in day-to-day design, the situation is probably not as gloomy as some make it out to be. A significant part of the methodological training of psychologists, independent of any particular substantive interest, is focused on designing materials, tasks, and apparatuses to get people to generate the kind of behavior they want to study. In many ways, the task of a system designer is to build devices that help elicit some set of behaviors, just the sort of thing psychologists do in the lab every day. In the context of designing computer systems, it may be that cognitive psychologists are particularly good at this because of the correspondence between the processes they study in the laboratory and those required to successfully interact with many current computer systems, but this is an open question. Nonetheless, these are useful design skills, although they might not be recognized as skills learned as a result of training in cognitive psychology.

A particularly interesting example of this kind of methodological innovation has been quite useful in computer system design. How can alternative interfaces be tested before the technology exists? Gould, Conti, and Hovanyecz (1983), Carbonell (1983), and Kelley (1983) have all used humans to simulate certain aspects of proposed computer systems that current technology could not create. For example, Gould et al. tested the usability of various "listening typewriters"—"devices" that recognized speech under different constraints and displayed it on a CRT. Because of limits in current speech recognition technology, humans served as the recognizers. In this way human performance trade offs between isolated and continuous speech, vocabulary size, etc. could be studied. Techniques like this allow psychologists to speed or direct system development by exploring the utility of yet to be realized technical developments. Perhaps some of these "simulation" tools will also be useful in studying more complex cognitive processes in the laboratory.

So, although traditional research tools may have limited applicability in system design, they are not irrelevant. Perhaps then the content of cognitive psychology is totally irrelevant. As we have alluded to earlier, we do not believe that this is the case. Many aspects of human–computer interaction involve exactly those facilities that cognitive psychologists are trying to understand. To some extent, we suspect that cognitive psychologists underestimate what they know. There is a large body of content-relevant knowledge that cognitive psychologists have, by virtue of their training, but may take for granted. They know innumerable details about human performance and its limits—short-term memory is limited, compatibility is important, experience changes peoples' perceptions and memories, etc.

In spite of this body of knowledge, there seems to be a genuine gap between what cognitive psychologists bring to the design situation and what they need to know. Why? First, we believe that although laboratory experiments study factors that are relevant to human–computer interaction, they do so in contexts that are too narrow. Complex interactions in the real world can often bury effects observed in the laboratory. For example, in designing computer command languages, several factors that are likely to affect learning can be enumerated—size of the command set, patterns of command usage, compatibility with natural language, consistency of argument order within the command set, etc. But, how will these factors combine, and, more importantly, how will they do so in the context of different tasks where other factors will tax memory, attention, etc.

(see Barnard, 1983)? Similarly, our ability to divide the world into categories is important and pervasive in the real world and has been extensively studied in the laboratory. But research has focused on a limited number of nice, neat categories. In information retrieval contexts, however, such categories may be the exception rather than the rule. Designers of computer information systems must decide how to present large, ill-defined, constantly changing, and hard-to-describe categories. We certainly do not want to argue that all the noise and complexities of the world should be brought into the laboratory. It is clearly necessary to abstract important variables and study them under more controlled conditions. But, we caution against letting the variables or methods for studying them take on lives of their own. It is under these circumstances that results tend to be incomplete when returned to the real world. Neisser (1976) has raised many of these issues before us. We, however, emphasize that concern with studying cognitive processes in complex situations need not preclude careful experimentation. But, this concern should shape the kinds of variables and situations studied so that extensions back to the complexities of the world around us are possible.

This problem of narrowness may be nothing more than the observation that the science of cognitive psychology is incomplete. Certainly there is some truth to this, but we also suspect that it reflects some weaknesses in cognitive psychology's current conceptualizations of cognition. First, cognitive psychology tends not to be prescriptive. There are many interesting and important facts, but how can they be applied? Consider as an example the robust and pervasive demonstration that experience can bias or change perception. It is nicely demonstrated in the inability of perceptually naive observers to see "hidden figures," and in the inability of more experienced viewers not to see them—that is, to return to the naive view. A similar bias is also pervasive in system design. It is clear that the end-users of a system will not view it in the same way as a designer who has been working on it for 5 years (Landauer, Dumais, Gomez, & Furnas, 1982). Although this is an interesting observation, a more relevant question, in practice, is what can be done about it. How can one prevent or compensate for these differences in viewpoints, so that the designer can better appreciate the new users' perspective and difficulties in learning? Similarly, although expert–novice differences are well documented in a number of domains, the question remains about how to progress from being a novice to an expert. Answers to this question will involve not only a characterization of experts and novices but also a better theoretical understanding of the processes involved in the transition. These are but two examples of gaps in cognitive psychology that are pointed out by trying to apply it. There are numerous others of these "how to" questions that current models largely ignore. They tend to focus on characterizations of static states, rather than on the situations or processes that lead to these states.[2]

---

[2]We hasten to point out that not all theories are subject to this criticism. Research by Schneider and his colleagues (Schneider, 1982; Schneider & Shiffrin, 1977, for example) on automatic and

Another problem related to the lack of prescription is the lack of practice that cognitive psychologists have in finding and applying relevant facts to real problems. Most textbooks are oriented toward teaching facts (and their associated theoretical accounts). Perhaps the issue of how practitioners go about solving problems is best addressed in applied textbooks. But here too, most books are but compendiums of details, and the problem of how to decompose a problem, find relevant information, and apply it are largely ignored. (Nice exceptions can be found in Card, Moran, & Newell, 1983, and Kantowitz & Sorkin, 1983.) Practice at analyzing applied problems would almost certainly sharpen task analysis and other skills that are useful in interface design. The problem of applying the results of psychological research is not limited to textbooks and is a more pervasive aspect of the field in general. Many results in cognitive psychology are discussed in terms of particular theories (or tests between alternative theories) and are therefore often not in a form that is useful to practitioners or to other researchers.

In order for researchers to fill some of these gaps, they must be aware of the difficulties that practitioners face. Practitioners must therefore provide feedback to basic researchers about the theoretical and empirical inadequacies of cognitive psychology for design purposes. In addition, we suggest that an inductive approach be taken. Cognitive psychologists in the field make numerous design decisions every day (some of which are certainly more successful than others). It would be instructive to collect and try to organize the results of specific experiments and design decisions. This would serve the useful practical function of preventing unnecessary repetitions of the same experiment or mistakes. But, more importantly, this inductive approach can complement basic research by providing a way to see where theoretical and empirical gaps exist.

Cognitive psychologists involved in the design process often feel that their training is largely irrelevant. We think that some gaps in cognitive psychology's current conceptions of cognition can be revealed by examining some of the reasons behind this. Some of the inadequacies of current cognitive theory that have been revealed by examining its difficulty in answering practical questions include the need to examine and model cognitive processes in more complex situations (or at least to worry about how to generalize and combine variables studied in the laboratory to more complex situations), be more prescriptive (i.e., to go beyond demonstrating that phenomena exist and on to describing ''how to'' achieve/avoid them, etc.), and practice applying existing facts and theories to practical problems. These, we believe, provide reasonable directions in which to take cognitive psychology. In order to make this possible, practitioners must provide feedback about gaps that exist, and about design successes and failures.

---

controlled processing is a good example of a more complete view. They began with a characterization of automatic and controlled processing, then described training conditions that enabled controlled processes to become automatic, and are now concerned with how this transition occurs in tasks more complicated than letter detection, where the distinction was originally demonstrated.

Summary

As we have just seen, cognitive psychology has already contributed some useful facts to system design (although they are often not in a readily usable form), and, just as important, it has contributed methods for eliciting desired behaviors and for designing and evaluating prototype systems. Continued contributions will have to take into account the complexities and parameters of relevant situations. We believe this is best done by studying content-relevant domains—as we have illustrated in the first part of this section. Such efforts have the added benefit that applied solutions to problems (e.g., programmer training or text-editor design) can provide new tools and problems for cognitive psychology.

Conclusions

We began this chapter by pointing out the potential that cognitive psychology has, both in terms of content and methods, for contributing to the design of more usable computer systems. Can cognitive psychology live up to this promise? And, can the interest in these more applied issues lead to new and exciting developments in cognitive psychology? Until recently, cognitive psychology and computer interface design existed as independent (rather than interdependent) disciplines. We have tried to document how the disciplines have begun to meet and have discussed what might be done to make this more than a nominal relationship.

One strategy, which has been successful in the past, is for "basic" researchers to think about more complex domains and real-world problems. This may be a first step in solving the communication gap between cognitive psychology and computer system design. We believe that the road to progress will involve becoming driven by problems from the world in addition to theories from journals. We have cited examples from computer programming, text-editor design, and knowledge representation in which practice and theory have *met,* by the choice of relevant domains. But there is still a long way to go before a meaningful relationship develops. New concepts and methods need to be developed for a variety of areas in human–computer interaction including theory-driven instruction and training, task analysis, and formalisms to specify the knowledge and procedures needed to interact with systems. The methods of psychology must also be extended beyond tools for recognizing poor designs, to tools for doing something about them. It is one thing to describe a task, structure, or process, and quite another to use this knowledge to *predict* the success of subsequent designs. Only by developing tools to propose successful and novel designs can cognitive psychology begin to anticipate computer technology rather than lag behind it.

By emphasizing the importance of studying domains relevant to interface design, we do not mean to say that all psychologists should abandon basic research efforts and rush out into the computer world ready to put out fires. There is certainly the need for theory and research whose primary goal is not immediate application. Such efforts are likely to form the basis for longer term applications, and, perhaps more importantly, they may lead to an understanding of underlying mechanisms and the development of powerful theories.

On the other hand, we do not wish to argue that the study of content-relevant domains should be an end in itself. Face validity should not be an excuse for sloppy or poorly motivated research, as it sometimes is. Many experiments aimed at evaluating particular design alternatives will be of limited generality and should be acknowledged as such. If an experiment comparing text editor A (a line editor) with text editor B (a screen editor) shows that editor B is easier to learn and faster to use, this does not mean that screen editors are superior to line editors. This methods problem (i.e., comparing instances of more general ideas, but not the ideas themselves) is fairly widespread in the human–computer interaction literature, without being appropriately acknowledged as a difficulty, as it has been in educational psychology, for example.

In addition to studying problems in relevant domains, another way to improve the coupling between theory and practice is to look at design decisions that are now being made in applied settings. There are a number of cognitive psychologists in the field who make design decisions every day. They conduct standard psychological experiments to evaluate particular design alternatives; and, in addition, they talk with and observe users, and they try various prototypes. Although such experiments and observations are intended to lead to fairly specific information about what works and what does not work, they can also provide valuable information and stimulation for basic research. Wright (1978) has argued that the information flow between applied and basic research should start with exactly these applied solutions to practical problems. Ideally, after having discovered a useful practical solution, the process then continues toward an explanation of why the solution was successful (thus enabling a refinement of the original solution), and so on in this cyclic fashion. Some aspects of the Roberts and Moran (1983) text-editor research described earlier in this chapter can be viewed in this way. There was an observation that screen-based editors were easier to learn and faster to use for a number of core tasks. Research was then undertaken to understand the reasons behind this effect. As it turns out, it was largely the simplicity of the command interface, and not spatiality per se, that accounted for the effect. The results of this research should be useful in refining the design of text editors, and hopefully also in designing other kinds of human–computer dialogues.

It is clear that cognitive psychology is a long way from providing methods or data for designing computer interfaces from first principles, if indeed this is an attainable or desirable goal. We have seen, however, that some tools and concepts from cognitive psychology have provided insights into the design of more usable computer systems. Not only are ideas from basic cognitive psychology proving useful in applied work, but, as we noted, cognitive psychology can be moved into new research areas by problems uncovered in trying to build more humanly usable computer systems. Experimental psychology has, in the past, gained a wealth of ideas from attempts to solve practical problems. Perhaps the information age and its attendant problems (particularly those in human–computer interaction) present another opportunity for tremendous growth and development in both basic and applied cognitive psychology.

ACKNOWLEDGMENTS

We thank a number of our colleagues for insightful comments and helpful discussions: Phil Barnard, Sharon Greene, Robert Kraut, Thomas Landauer, Carol Lochbaum, Lloyd Nakatani, Chris Riley, Lynn Robertson, and Ernst Rothkopf.

REFERENCES

Abelson, P. H. (1980). Scientific communication. *Science, 209*, 60–62.

Adelson, B. (1981). Problem solving and the development of abstract categories in programming languages. *Memory and Cognition, 9*, 422–433.

Allen, R. B. (1982). Cognitive factors in human interaction with computers. In A. Badre & B. Shneiderman (Eds.), *Directions in human/computer interaction.* Norwood, NJ: Ablex.

Anzai, Y., & Simon, H. A. (1979). The theory of learning by doing. *Psychological Review, 86(2)*, 124–140.

Baddeley, A. D. (1976). *The psychology of memory.* New York: Basic Books.

Barnard, P. J. (1983). Applying the products of research on interactive dialogues. In M. J. Elphick (Ed.), *Man–Machine Interaction: Proceedings of the Joint IBM/University of Newcastle Seminar.*

Beranek, L. L. (1962). *Music, acoustics & architecture.* New York: Wiley.

Bikson, T. K., Quint, B. E., & Johnson, L. L. (1984, March). *Scientific and technical information transfer: Issues and opinions.* The Rand Corporation (N-2131-NSF).

Bransford, J. D. (1984, August). *Microcomputers and the development of thinking and learning skills.* Paper presented at the Meeting of the American Psychological Association. Toronto, Canada.

Broadbent, D. E. (1952). Listening to one of two synchronous messages. *Journal of Experimental Psychology, 44*, 51–55.

Broadbent, D. E. (1958). *Perception and communication.* London: Pergamon Press.

Carbonell, J. G. (1983). Discourse pragmatics in task-oriented natural languages interfaces. In *Proceedings of 21st Annual Meeting of the Association for Computational Linguistics*, 164–168. Menlo Park, CA: Association for Computational Linguistics.

Card, S. K., Moran, T. P., & Newell, A. (1980). Computer text-editing: An information processing model of a routine cognitive skill. *Cognitive Psychology, 12*, 32–74.

Card, S. K., Moran, T. P., & Newell, A. (1983). *The psychology of human–computer interaction.* Hillsdale, NJ: Lawrence Erlbaum Associates.

Carroll, J. M., & Carrithers, C. (1984). Training wheels in a user interface. *Communications of the ACM, 27*(8) 800–806.

Carroll, J. M., & Mack, R. L. (1984). Learning to use a word processor: By doing, by thinking, and by knowing. In J. C. Thomas & M. Schneider (Eds.), *Human factors in computing systems.* Norwood, NJ: Ablex.

Chapanis, A. (1971). Prelude to 2001: Explorations in human communications. *American Psychologist, 26,* 946–961.

Chapanis, A., Garner, W. R., & Morgan, C. T. (1949). *Applied experimental psychology: Human factors in engineering design.* New York: Wiley.

Chase, W. G., & Simon, H. A. (1973). Perception in chess. *Cognitive Psychology, 4,* 55–81.

Christ, R. E. (1975). Review and analysis of color coding research for visual displays. *Human Factors, 17*(6), 542–570.

Crowder, R. G. (1976). *Principles of learning and memory.* Hillsdale, NJ: Lawrence Erlbaum Associates.

Dumais, S. T., & Landauer, T. K. (1984). Describing categories of objects for menu retrieval systems. *Behavioral Research Methods, Instrumentation, and Computers, 16*(2), 242–248.

Egan, D. E., & Gomez, L. M. (in press). Assaying, isolating, and accommodating individual differences in learning a complex skill. In R. Dillon (Ed.), *Individual differences in cognition,* (Vol. 2). New York: Academic Press.

Egan, D. E., & Schwartz, B. J. (1979). Chunking in recall of symbolic drawings. *Memory and Cognition, 7,* 149–158.

Ehrlich, K., & Soloway, E. (1984). In J. C. Thomas & M. L. Schneider (Eds.), *Human factors in computer systems.* Norwood, NJ: Ablex.

Evans, N. J. (1982). Human processing of natural categories. In *Proceedings of the ASIS Annual Meeting* (Vol. 19), 80–83.

Fidell, S. (1978). Effectiveness of audible warning signals for emergency vehicles. *Human Factors, 20,* 19–26.

Fitts, P. M., & Posner, M. I. (1967). *Human performance.* Belmont, CA: Brooks/Cole.

Fletcher, H. (1922). The nature of speech and its interpretations. *The Bell System Technical Journal, 1*(1), 129–144.

Garner, W. R. (1972). The acquisition and application of knowledge: A symbiotic relationship. *American Psychologist, 27,* 941–946.

Gibson, J. J. (1950). *The perception of the visual world.* Boston: Houghton–Mifflin.

Glaser, R. (1976). Cognitive psychology and instructional design. In D. Klahr (Ed.), *Cognition and instruction.* Hillsdale, NJ: Lawrence Erlbaum Associates.

Gomez, L. M., Egan, D. E., & Bowers, C. (in press). Learning to use a text editor: Some learner characteristics that predict success. *Human-computer interaction.*

Gomez, L. M., Egan, D. E., Wheeler, E. A., Sharma, D. K., & Gruchacz, A. M. (1983). How interface design determines who has difficulty learning to use a text editor. In *Proceedings of CHI'83: Human Factors in Computing Systems* (176–181). New York: Association for Computing Machinery.

Gould, J. D., Conti, J., & Hovanyecz, T. (1983). Composing letters with a simulated listening typewriter. *Communications of the ACM, 26*(4), 295–308.

Hayes, J. R., & Simon, H. A. (1977). Psychological differences among problem isomorphs. In N. J. Castellan, Jr., D. B. Pisoni, & G. R. Potts (Eds.), *Cognitive theory* (Vol. 2). Hillsdale, NJ: Lawrence Erlbaum Associates.

Jeffries, R., Turner, A. A., Polson, P. G., & Atwood, M. E. (1981). The processes involved in designing software. In J. R. Anderson (Ed.), *Cognitive skills and their acquisition.* Hillsdale, NJ: Lawrence Erlbaum Associates.

Jenkins, J. J. (1984, August). *Contextualism, cognition, and instruction.* Paper presented at the Meeting of the American Psychological Association, Toronto, Canada.

Kantowitz, B. H. (1977). Ergonomics and the design of nuclear power plant control complexes. In T. O. Kvalseth (Ed.), *Arbedsplass og miljobruk av ergonomiske data.* Trondheim, Norway: Tapir.

Kantowitz, B. H. (1982). Interfacing human information processing and engineering psychology. In W. C. Howell & E. A. Fleishman (Eds.), *Human performance and productivity* (Vol. 2): *Information processing and decision making*. Hillsdale, NJ: Lawrence Erlbaum Associates.

Kantowitz, B. H., & Sorkin, R. D. (1983). *Human factors: Understanding people-system relationships*. New York: Wiley.

Kelley, J. F. (1983). *Natural language and computers: Six empirical steps for writing an easy-to-use computer application*. Unpublished doctoral dissertation, The Johns Hopkins University.

Kemeny, J. G. (1979, October). *The accident at Three Mile Island*. Report of the President's Commission.

Kieras, D. E., & Polson, P. G. (in press). An approach to the formal analysis of user complexity. *International Journal of Man–Machine Studies*.

Kintsch, W. (1977). *Memory and cognition*. New York: Wiley.

Krebs, M. J., Wolf, J. D., & Sandvig, J. H. (1978). *Color display design guide* (Report ONR-CR213-136-2F).

Landauer, T. K. (1983, November). *Naming and paired associate learning*. Paper presented at the meeting of the Society for Computers in Psychology, San Diego.

Landauer, T. K., Dumais, S. T., Gomez, L. M., & Furnas, G. W. (1982). Human factors in data access. *The Bell System Technical Journal, 61*(9), 2487–2509.

Landauer, T. K., Galotti, K. M., & Hartwell, S. H. (1983). Natural command names and initial learning: A study of text-editing terms. *Communications of the ACM, 26*(7), 495–503.

Larkin, J. H. (1983). The role of problem representation in physics. In D. Gentner & A. L. Stevens (Eds.), *Mental models*. Hillsdale, NJ: Lawrence Erlbaum Associates.

Larkin, J. H., McDermott, J., Simon, D. P., & Simon, H. A. (1980). Models of competence in solving physics problems. *Cognitive Science, 4*, 317–345.

Lindsay, P. H., & Norman, D. A. (1977). *Human information processing: An introduction to psychology* (2nd ed.). New York: Academic Press.

Lindsley, D. B. (1944). *Radar operator "fatigue": The effects of length and repetition of operating periods on efficiency of performance*. Office of Scientific Research and Development (Report No. 33334), Washington, DC.

Mackworth, N. H. (1944). *Notes on the Clock Test—A new approach to the study of prolonged perception to find the optimum length of watch for radar operators*. Air Force Ministry, F.P.R.C. (Report No. 586), London.

McKeithen, K., Reitman, J. S., Reuter, H., & Hirtle, S. C. (1981). Knowledge organization and skill differences in computer programmers. *Cognitive Psychology, 13*, 307–325.

Miller, L. A., & Thomas, J. C. (1977). Behavioral issues in the use of interactive systems. *International Journal of Man–Machine Studies, 9*, 509–536.

Moran, T. P. (1981, March). Special issue: The psychology of human–computer interaction. *Computing Surveys, 13*.

Neisser, U. (1967). *Cognitive psychology*. New York: Appleton–Century–Crofts.

Neisser, U. (1976). *Cognition and reality*. San Francisco: W. H. Freeman.

Newell, A., & Simon, H. A. (1972). *Human problem solving*. Englewood Cliffs, NJ: Prentice–Hall.

Pellegrino, J. W., & Glaser, R. (1979). Cognitive correlates and components in the analysis of individual differences. *Intelligence, 3*, 187–214.

Ramsey, H. R., & Atwood, M. E. (1979). *Human factors in computer systems: A review of the literature*. Englewood, CO: Science Applications, Inc., (Tech. Rep. SAI-79-111-DEN, NTIS AD A075679).

Reitman, J. S. (1976). Skilled perception in go: Deducing memory structures from inter-response times. *Cognitive Psychology, 8*, 336–356.

Rich, C. (1981, August). A formal representation for plans in the Programmer's Apprentice. In *Proceeding of the Seventh International Joint Conference on Artificial Intelligence*, Vancouver.

Roberts, T. L. (1980). *Evaluation of computer text editors.* Unpublished doctoral dissertation, Stanford University.

Roberts, T. L., & Moran, T. P. (1983). The evaluation of text editors: Methodological and empirical results. *Communications of the ACM, 26*(4), 265–283.

Rosch, E., & Lloyd, B. B. (Eds.). (1978). *Cognition and categorization.* Hillsdale, NJ: Lawrence Erlbaum Associates.

Schroeder, M. R. (1980, October). Toward better acoustics for concert halls. *Physics Today.*

Schneider, M. L. (1982). Models for the design of static software user assistance. In A. Badre & B. Shneiderman (Eds.), *Directions in human/computer interaction.* Norwood, NJ: Ablex.

Schneider, W. (1982, April). *Automatic/control processing concepts and their implications for the training of skills.* University of Illinois, Human Attention Research Laboratory (Tech. Rep. 8101).

Schneider, W., & Shiffrin, R. M. (1977). Controlled and automatic human information processing: I. Detection, search, and attention. *Psychological Review, 84,* 1–66.

Shneiderman, B. (1976). Exploratory experiments in programmer behavior. *International Journal of Computer and Information Sciences, 5,* 123–143.

Shneiderman, B. (1980). *Software psychology: Human factors in computer and informations systems.* Cambridge, MA: Winthrop.

Skinner, B. F. (1950). Are theories of learning necessary? *Psychological Review, 57,* 193–216.

Smith, E. E., & Medin, D. L. (1981). *Concepts and categories.* Cambridge, MA: Harvard University Press.

Smith, H. T., & Green, T. R. G. (Eds.). (1980). *Human interaction with computers.* London: Academic Press.

Smith, S. L. (1982). *User-system interface design for computer-based information systems* (Tech. Rep. No. ESD-TR-82-132), The Mitre Corporation.

Sternberg, R. J. (1977). *Intelligence, information processing, and analogical reasoning: The componential analysis of human abilities.* Hillsdale, NJ: Lawrence Erlbaum Associates.

Tanner, W. P. Jr., & Swets, J. A. (1954). A decision-making theory of visual perception. *Psychological Review, 61,* 401–409.

Thomas, J. C., & Schneider, M. L. (Eds.). (1984). *Human factors in computer systems.* Norwood, NJ: Ablex.

Wagner, H. M. (1975). *Principles of operations research with applications to managerial decisions* (2ne ed.) Englewood Cliffs, NJ: Prentice-Hall.

Webster, J. C., & Thompson, P. O. (1954). Responding to both of two overlapping messages. *Journal of the Acoustical Society of America, 26,* 396–402.

Williges, R. C. (1982). Applying the information processing approach to human/computer interaction. In W. C. Howell & E. A. Fleishman, (Eds.), *Human performance and productivity (Vol. 2): Information processing and decision making.* Hillsdale, NJ: Lawrence Erlbaum Associates.

Wright, P. (1978). Feeding the information eaters: Suggestions for integrating pure and applied research on language comprehension. *Instructional Science, 7,* 249–312.

Young, R. M. (1981). The machine inside the machine: User's models of pocket calculators. *International Journal of Man-Machine Studies, 15,* 51–86.

Young, R. M., & Hull, A. (1982). Cognitive aspects of the selection of view data options by casual users. In M. B. Williams (Ed.), *Proceedings of the 6th International Conference on Computer Communications* (571–576). New York: North–Holland.

Young, R. M., & Hull, A. (1983, September). Categorisation structures in hierarchical menus. In *Proceedings of the 10th International Symposium on Human Factors in Telecommunications* (111–118). Helsinki.

13 A Coordination of Differences: Behaviorism, Mentalism, and the Foundations of Psychology

Roger Schnaitter
Illinois Wesleyan University

Psychology is a conceptually diverse discipline, prone to disputes and controversy. On the contemporary scene, a major tension exists between behaviorism and cognitive psychology. Historians and philosophers of psychology have proposed a variety of means for understanding this and other disputes, and the present chapter joins this task. It is in two parts. Part I begins by briefly reviewing, and finding inadequate, several standard approaches to the analysis of theoretical diversity and conflict. It concludes by developing an alternative perspective on the conceptual foundations of psychology. Part II considers behaviorism and cognitivism specifically. Working from the conceptual scheme of the first part of the chapter, a case is made for the complementarity (though certainly not for the equivalence) of cognitive and behavioral psychology.

I. THE CONFLICT BETWEEN COGNITIVISM AND BEHAVIORISM

For anyone who has attended to matters of psychological metatheory over the last 25 years, it is no news that behaviorism has been in a prolonged confrontation with that version of mentalism called cognitivism (or cognitive psychology). Sigmund Koch, who is neither cognitivist nor behaviorist, said near the end of the 1963 Rice University symposium on "Behaviorism and Phenomenology" (Wann, 1974) that: "I would be happy to say what we have been hearing could be characterized as the death rattle of behaviorism, but this would be a rather more dignified statement than I should like to sponsor, because death is, at least, a dignified process" (p. 162). And if it was the death rattle of behaviorism Koch

291

sensed two decades ago, then any number of commentators have been busy hammering nails in the coffin (Chomsky, 1959, Dennett, 1978a, Mishler, 1975, Scriven, 1957, Wann, 1964, and Wheeler, 1973 provide a reasonable cross-section of this extensive literature). The corpse, however, will not lie down. Although it is probably true that mentalism has assumed the position of estab-lished orthodoxy throughout most of academic psychology today, large numbers of psychologists, educators, and mental health professionals continue to advance the cause of behaviorism with vigor. Thus mentalism and behaviorism are coex-isting, however uneasily, for the moment.

Neither behaviorists nor mentalists seem ready to reconcile with any form of coexistence, however. Most arguments in the dispute are based on a Kuhnian view of science, either explicitly or implicitly (Kuhn, 1962). Segal and Lachman (1972) argued, for example, that neobehaviorism constituted a dominant para-digm in psychology during the three decades from 1930 to 1960. During the decade of the 1960s, the paradigm broke down due to developments external to psychology in fields such as information theory, computer science, and lin-guistics, and due to failures of the paradigm to provide an adequate analysis of many significant phenomena. The failure of associationism to account for serial order and syntactic relationships was central. Coincident with the decline of neobehaviorism a new interest in the higher mental processes emerged, and Segal and Lachman consequently saw cognitive psychology assuming the role of a new paradigm.

As historical narrative there is much to be said for such a story, but its implication that behaviorism has been tried and found lacking would be strongly resisted by a radical behaviorist such as Skinner. He would argue, instead, that mentalism has always dominated psychology, and that the prevailing neo-behaviorism of the middle third of the century maintained many of the traditional tenets of mentalism. Associationism, as a case in point, clearly originated in mentalistic doctrine, not in behaviorism. The radical behaviorist is as ready to say "good riddance" to neobehaviorism as is the cognitivist; but cognitivism is, to the radical behaviorist, just a resurgence of the mentalistic paradigm that has dominated modern thought since Descartes. An authentically behavioristic posi-tion has never achieved paradigmatic status in the field of psychology, so there hardly can have been a revolution against it. What Skinner still works to achieve is the *first* behavioristic scientific revolution through which behaviorism will indeed come to serve as the dominant paradigm of the profession.

Unsatisfactory approaches to understanding theoretical diversity

Whereas both behaviorists and mentalists, then, can turn the Kuhnian analysis to their purposes, the consequences of such a move have not been completely fortunate. The allure of the paradigmatic view is strong, as it seems to promise the inevitable elimination of disagreeable theories from the field. As mature sciences *do* have dominant paradigms, according to Kuhn, it can be concluded that for psychology to be respectable it *ought* to have such a paradigm. To the extent that the work of different groups of psychologists does not naturally coalesce into some facsimile of paradigmatic harmony, however, the stage is set for moral conflict. All manner of extrascientific flummery then comes to the fore, one consequence being that tasteless ad hominem now runs through much of the behaviorism/mentalism debate (though certainly not in Segal and Lachman's thoughtful paper). As I believe a simplistic version of the succession of prevailing paradigms is the wrong model for the nature of psychological inquiry, this state of affairs is quite disheartening. Herewith an attempt is made to develop a more satisfactory scheme through which to understand the relationship between radical behaviorism and contemporary mentalism as framework theories, as well as the relationships of each to humanistic and phenomenological psychology on the one hand and to biopsychology on the other.

Certainly a number of alternatives to the Kuhnian analysis have already been developed by historians of psychology. Robert Watson (1967) proposed that psychology is preparadigmatic in the Kuhnian sense and better understood as adopting various sets of "prescriptions," of which Watson proposed 18 contrasting pairs. In a formal sense at least, this analysis sets the stage for 2^{18} distinct theoretical positions! Surely, there must be more parsimony to psychology than that. Perhaps the most standard treatment of distinctly different psychological orientations is via the notion of a "school," the usual candidates being structuralism, functionalism, behaviorism, psychoanalysis, and Gestalt psychology. The age of schools ran out by 1930 or so, however, and whereas the schools did tend to separate along significant lines, they were more a product of historical circumstance than of conceptual necessity. The updated suggestion that there are now three "forces" in psychology—behaviorism, psychoanalysis, and humanistic psychology—is useless in that it simply fails to recognize cognitive psychology at all. Koch (1976) has proposed that psychology consists of a free-ranging set of search cells:

> the psychological studies represent an assemblage of specialized language communities, research groups, or, if you will, cliques, claques, application groups, action groups, interest groups, and the like. I will call such associations of inquirers pursuing roughly common problems from a common point of view, and thus sharing a specialized language, *search cells.* (pp. 542–3)

However accurate as sociology, such a notion is entirely too undisciplined to lend any conceptual clarity to problems of psychological metatheory. It is time to strike off in some other direction.

A foundational conceptual distinction

What is needed is a useful *conceptual* distinction. Just such a distinction for dividing mentalism and behaviorism is readily at hand, for mentalism is that position that employs mentalistic concepts, whereas behaviorism is a position even defined at times by its rejection of such concepts. Mentalistic concepts permeate ordinary English language, as well as much professional psychological language. Intuitions on distinguishing mentalistic from nonmentalistic concepts are probably quite accurate: Hopes, desires, wishes, beliefs, thoughts, ideas, dreams, and feelings are all mentalistic, whereas action potentials, reaction times, and response rates are not. However, a more explicit demarcation is desirable.

Intentionality. It is now typical to develop the distinction between mentalistic and nonmentalistic concepts through the notion of "intentionality," as introduced to modern thought by Franz Brentano (1874; quoted in Chisholm, 1967):

> Every mental phenomenon is characterized by what the scholastics of the Middle Ages called the intentional [and also mental] inexistence of an object, and what we would call, although not in entirely unambiguous terms, the reference to a content, a direction upon an object [by which we are not to understand a reality . . .), or an immanent objectivity. Each one includes something as an object within itself, although not always in the same way. In presentation something is presented, in judgment something is affirmed or denied, in love [something] loved, in hate [something] is hated, in desire something is desired, etc. This intentional inexistence is exclusively characteristic of mental phenomena. No physical phenomenon manifests anything similar. Consequently, we can define mental phenomena by saying that they are such phenomena as include an object intentionally within themselves. (p. 201)

Mental concepts are those concepts referring to mental phenomena, and mental phenomena, it is often claimed, are just those phenomena that include an object intentionally within themselves, or are "intentional" for short. This is not completely true, as counterexamples can be given. Pains are mental phenomena, and although feelings of pain may be caused by some external irritant or condition of the body, pains are neither about such conditions, nor are such conditions objects within pains. Moods or emotions appear sometimes to be intentional in Brentano's sense, sometimes not. Usually one's happiness is about some thing or state of affairs, but some days one is recklessly happy about nothing at all; and although anxiety is often directed upon some dire exigency, it may also be free floating. Nonetheless, intentionality characterizes a great many of the referents of mental concepts, and it usefully demarcates most mental phenomena from nonmental phenomena.[1]

---

[1] In point of fact, it is notoriously difficult to state a rule or procedure for distinguishing the mental from the nonmental in a way that corresponds to the bounds of our intuitions. Rorty (1979, Chapter 1) gives a particularly pessimistic account of these difficulties. For those unacquainted with these issues who want a maximum payoff for a minimum effort, I suggest careful reading of the aforemen-

If intentionality is not quite the perfect mark of the mental, other possible candidates are less so. "Consciousness," for example, will not do. Whereas many mental concepts refer to conscious acts or events (e.g., feelings, thoughts, dreams, images), other mental concepts do not refer to acts or events that are directly experienced or available to consciousness. At least since Freud, much of the motivational activity of the mind has been assumed to function at an unconscious level. By the same token, the information-processing mechanisms proposed in contemporary cognitive psychology are neither part of consciousness nor accessible to introspective scrutiny. Furthermore, various contents of mind that may become conscious are not conscious at all times. It is often said that "beliefs" are just such a case. Freud's preconscious contains memories not presently conscious but capable of becoming so; and in contemporary cognitive psychology, the long-term memory store is not open to awareness, whereas transfer of contents to the short-term store for processing may bring them into awareness. Although mentalists often focus on phenomena outside of consciousness, radical behaviorists do acknowledge conscious phenomena. Skinner (1974) takes introspectable events to be meaningful objects of behavioral interpretation: "Radical behaviorism . . . restores introspection . . . [But] this does not mean that what are felt or introspectively observed are the causes of behavior," etc. (p. 16–7). So Skinner questions not the reality of introspectable phenomena but their causal role, and consciousness fails to demarcate mentalistic from behavioral concerns.

Not only does reference to consciousness fail to sunder the mental from the rest of nature, even the apparent truism that mental concepts refer to states or processes of the mind, where mind is taken to be some sort of cloudy essence pervading the brain, fails to hold as a demarcation. Whereas longings and pains and beliefs might be matters of internal states alone, one's duties, obligations, and responsibilities cannot simply be matters of internal states. Instead, these concepts refer to outward relationships holding between a person and a social context. That such relationships do not necessarily implicate mind as an internal organ can be seen in the fact that we attribute these relational properties to social groups and entities such as corporations, as well as to people. But whereas a corporation may have a responsibility of a certain sort to its employees or to its customers, it does not have pains, dreams, or memories, and the related internal

---

tioned chapter by Rorty, as well as papers by Davidson (1970), Dennett (1978b), and Searle (1979). Several philosophers, but most notably Roderick Chisholm and W. V. O. Quine, brought attention during the 1950s to certain logical peculiarities of concepts and statements referring to intentional phenomena (Chisholm, 1957; Quine, 1960). Concepts displaying these peculiarities are called *intensional*. Intensionality ranges over several concepts having no clear relationship to psychological concerns, however (i.e., modal operators such as "necessarily"), and it continues to be a matter of some controversy as to just what relevance intensionality has to mentalism (e.g., Searle, 1983). So the logicogrammatical features characterizing intensionality are not pursued here, although it is worth remembering that, as a rule, mental idioms about intentional phenomena are intensional.

mental apparatus. To again use antimentalistic objections as further evidence for what constitutes mentalism, Skinner objects to explanatory use of intentional concepts like duty and responsibility on grounds indistinguishable from his objections to concepts like memories, ideas, and perceptions (e.g., Skinner, 1974, p. 186, and elsewhere).

Mental concepts are sometimes given a functional interpretation, but as both intentional and nonintentional concepts can be functional, mental and nonmental concepts cannot be distinguished through functionalism. A functional interpretation of pain might be that pain is any state whose function is to motivate withdrawal from events producing that state; or a functional interpretation of belief might be that belief is any state whose function is to represent propositions held to be true, or some such (see, e.g., Block, 1980). But a doorstop, functionally defined, is any device whose function is to prevent a door from swinging shut, and a class of operant behavior is the set of all behaviors whose functional effect is the production of a reinforcing consequence of a given sort.

Although intentional phenomena are by their nature relational (consisting of a relationship between a phenomenon and its intentional object), not all relational phenomena are intentional. Confusion can arise due to this assymetry. A magnet's attraction is *for* iron filings, and the mirror's reflection is *of* light waves, for example, and that seems to approximate Brentano's requirement for the intentional, yet magnetic attraction and the like are not mental phenomena. Brentano's use of the expression "intentional inexistence" is sometimes incorrectly taken to mean that intentional objects do not exist, whereas its meaning is actually that the intentional objects exist within mental phenomena. Intentional objects, however, may be nonexistent in a material sense. I may desire a late evening rendezvous with Nastassja Kinski, for example, and although Nastassja exists the rendezvous as a material reality surely does not; or I may believe in the existence of the Loch Ness monster even though such a creature in all probability does not exist. A magnet, however, cannot attract nonexistent iron filings (even though the magnetic force may be present without attracting anything), and a mirror cannot reflect a nonexistent image. Hence, attraction as an attribute of magnets and reflection as an attribute of mirrors are not intentional even though at first they appear to meet Brentano's original criterion.

At this point the concept of intentionality might begin to rub one's ontology the wrong way, and efforts have been made to refine Brentano's initial insight so that it is not necessary to grant existential status, even as abstract objects, to fictional objects of intentional states. Searle (1983), for example, suggests that an intentional state consists of a "representative content in a certain psychological mode," where the content is understood to be a representation of the conditions of satisfaction for the intentional state. If Bill believes in the existence of unicorns, then Bill stands in the mode of believing relative to the conditions expressed in the proposition "unicorns exist." The external *object* of the belief, as distinct from its representational *content*, is unicorns proper, which, so far as we know, do not exist. It is a simple contingent matter whether or not the object or condition represented in some intentional state exists or does not. The content as a representation does not hinge in any way on the existence of the external object, as fictional objects are representable quite as well as real ones. The important relationship on which intentional states depend, therefore, is that from some psychological mode of an agent to a representation. Searle further asserts that this relationship is purely logical in character, meaning that a special ontological category of thing in the brain of believing beings occupied by representations is not called for. So, Searle concludes, intentionality doesn't raise any special ontological puzzles, at least not of the sort that have traditionally been considered in mind–brain controversies. (There are, of course, other philosophical views on intentionality.)

Willard Day (1980) has argued that the behavioristic concept of the operant is intentional in Brentano's sense: "This is because what amounts to an intentional object is automatically brought into play in the specification of reinforcing consequences necessary for the identification of any operant class. The intentional object for an operant class consists of its reinforcing consequences" (p. 217). If Day is saying that what behaviorists speak of as operant behavior is the kind of thing to which intentional descriptions can be applied, he is surely right; but if he means to say that the concept of the operant is itself an intentional concept, then the demarcation between mentalism and behaviorism for which I have argued has failed. The second interpretation seems dubious, however. To begin with, it is necessary to get straight the fact that the intentional idioms need to be expressed as states or acts of an agent: It is a *person* who believes, desires, remembers, and so forth. In contrast, the "agent" of behavior, according to Skinner, is not the organism whose body may move in the performance of any given act but the environmental circumstances of which that act is a function. Consequently, the prefix of sentences about operants concerns functional properties of the environment. With that clarification, it is quite apparent that sentences of the form, "Attention from his mother reinforced Billy's tantrum," or "Destruction of the Zaxxon attackers reinforced Edna's play on the video game," fail to have any instances where the object of the putatively intentional verb is materially nonexistent; or, by Searle's account, it is equally apparent that such sentences do not specify a representative content in a psychological mode of any sort. Simply put, "reinforce" is not a propositional attitude verb. As "reinforcer" and "operant" are symmetrical and codefined relational concepts (see Schnaitter, 1978), then even though the operant has no satisfactory verb form the argument against the intentional character of the reinforcement concept would seem to work equally well against the intentional character of the operant concept.

Agency.   Radical behaviorism does not conceive of the person as an agent, to whom causal powers are assigned. Instead, causality is a function of environmental variables. In contrast, mental phenomena *are* normally taken to be causally efficacious. Attributing beliefs and desires is senseless if the believing and desiring being has no capacity to act in accordance with its beliefs in order to achieve its desires. And whereas biopsychology would part with behaviorism by locating causal processes within the individual, such processes consist of physical, extensional phenomena, not of mental, intentional phenomena.

The notion of an agent, then, seems to be deeply intertwined with intentionality and the mental. Theodore Mischel (1976) has made the following comments along this line, which effectively extend the distinction as developed to this point:

> we must start by recognizing that there are two very different points of view which we can take toward human behavior, that neither of these points of view can be rejected, and that an adequate conceptualization of human behavior must have room for both. One point of view is that of theoretical sciences like physics. Whatever else we may want to say of persons, they surely are material organizations, and as such, the laws of physics, chemistry, etc. must apply to them; whatever else we may want to say of human actions, they are, at least if we are talking of overt actions, events in space and time and so presumably caused by other events in space and time. So actions can . . . be viewed as physical phenomena whose explanation must be found in other physical phenomena in the brain and nervous system. The possibility of a neurophysiological explanation for all human behaviors is implicit in the point of view adopted by sciences like physics.
>
> A very different, but equally indispensable, point of view is that of the agent who is faced with choices, deliberates, makes decisions, and tries to act accordingly. . . . human beings can have a *conception* of what it is they want and what they should do in order to get what they want, and . . . their conceptions—the meaning which situations and behaviors have for them in virtue of the way they construe them—can make a difference to their actions. Rational beings have a faculty of taking a rule of reason for the motive of an action [Kant, 1788, p. 151], they have the capacity to formulate plans, policies, or rules, and they can follow these rules— they have the power to act from the mere conception of a rule. . . .
>
> Seen in this way, the claim that people are agents is not a Cartesian claim about the role played by introspectable inner states as causal antecedents of outer bodily movements, but is the claim that we have the power to act according to our conceptions, so that what we do depends, at least in part, on the way we understand our situation. We cannot eliminate the notion that we are agents because it is central to our conception of what it is to be a person who can engage in practical life. But I can also look at myself from a purely external point of view, as an object in nature, and that my behavior must then be seen as caused by other events in nature is central to our conception of physical science. (pp. 145–6)

The distinction just drawn, developed from Kant, has been expressed widely both by philosophers and psychologists. The particular value Mischel's remarks have in the present context is to emphasize that adoption of an agent's or an observer's point of view puts one in either of two wholly distinct conceptual stances toward the subject matter of psychology. This is a big, fundamental kind of difference. From one point of view human behavior consists of actions of an agent that follow from modes through which the agent stands in relation to intentional objects (or to propositional representations, if Searle is right); but from another point of view, human behavior is made up of events of the same sort as other naturally occurring events, and it is caused by the same kind of causes as serve in the rest of nature. Nothing could be more fundamental to the foundations of psychology than adoption of one or the other of these points of view, or conceptual stances.

Here it only remains to adopt the most useful names for the distinction developed in the preceding discussion. Consider the following pairs of possibilities:

A	*B*
intentional	nonintentional
intensional	extensional
agent's point of view	observer's point of view
nonphysical	physical
immaterial	material
subjective	objective
supernaturalistic	naturalistic
personal	organismal

In each of these pairs something seems a bit off on one side or the other. I like "intentional" from list *A,* but I do not want to call position *B* a "non" something, any more than I want to call myself a non-Frenchman, or a non-woman, or non-dead. I like "naturalistic" from list *B* but don't want to suggest that there is anything supernatural about mentalism, properly conceived. My solution is to note that intentional and agency concepts have had their origin in common sense, no matter how remote from folk psychology current cognitive science examplars may be; hence, any conceptual framework built on concepts with these properties can be considered a commonsense foundational approach. By contrast, anything else is a "fresh-start" approach.

A foundational explanatory distinction

The distinction between commonsense and fresh-start conceptual foundations, whereas essential to the distinction between mentalism and behaviorism, is not sufficient. More separates them. Or to put it another way, even within a commonsense conceptual stance, important distinctions need to be made; and within the fresh-start conceptual stance, additional distinctions need to be made. For example, whereas phenomenological and existential and humanistic psychology are deeply and fundamentally intentional in perspective, these psychological positions focusing on the nature and quality of the immediate experience of the agent need to be distinguished from the approach of contemporary cognitive psychology that focuses on the nature and functioning of mechanisms underlying the phenomenology of the agent. And the behaviorism of Skinner, which invokes no causal or explanatory variables outside the level at which behavior and the environment appear to interact, must be distinguished from the various neo-behaviorisms that posit intervening mechanisms between behavior and environment, and from biopsychology, which turns directly to the physiological substrates of behavior for its explanations of psychological phenomena. What is needed is a second distinction, independent of the basic conceptual divide discussed so far, which captures these further differences in theoretical orientation.

This further distinction I will call *presentationalism* versus *representationalism*. The distinction is similar to though not as sharply drawn as that made in philosophy between phenomenalism on the one hand and indirect, or representative, or scientific, realism on the other (Sellars, 1963; Smart, 1963). A presentationalist position is the view that phenomena, just as presented or encountered as one considers them, constitute a level of reality that needs to be addressed and understood in its own right, at its own level. A representationalist position, by contrast, holds that immediately given phenomena are representative of events or processes taking place at some other level or in some other dimensional system, and it is at this deeper level that the truly important realities of nature are found. If it is inescapable that one observes only what is presented, then the issue of presentationalism versus representationalism more directly concerns the *interpretation* of what is presented, or the *understanding* of its meaning, or its *explanation*. Indeed, Hempel (1966) characterizes scientific theory in wholly representational terms:

> Theories are usually introduced when previous study of a class of phenomena has revealed a system of uniformities . . . Theories then seek to explain those regularities and, generally, to afford a deeper and more accurate understanding of the phenomena in question. To this end, a theory construes those phenomena as manifestations of entities and processes that lie behind or beneath them, as it were. (p. 70)

A representational stance toward the understanding and explanation of phenomena is typical of most modern science, although the phenomenalistic version of presentationalism continues to be influential in modern physics. The presentational stance had its finest hour in nineteenth-century physical science, where it was most forcefully advocated in the phenomenalism of Ernst Mach. An interesting illustration of presentational argumentation can be seen in the following quotation from Mach's book on *Conservation of Energy* (in Blackmore, 1972):

> We say, now, that water *consists* of oxygen and hydrogen, but this oxygen and this hydrogen are merely thoughts or names which, on the sight of water, we keep ready, to describe phenomena which are not present but which will appear again whenever, as we say, we decompose water. (p. 85)

The quotation from Mach is especially pertinent because it is mirrored in the equally presentationalist attitude of Skinner. Skinner talking about mentalism sounds remarkably like Mach talking about the chemistry of water. Consider the following example from Skinner (1977):

> Let us suppose that a young girl saw a picture yesterday and when asked to describe it today, does so. What has happened? A traditional answer would run something like this: when she saw the picture yesterday the girl formed a copy in her mind (which, in fact, was really all she saw). She encoded it in a suitable form and stored it in her memory, where it remained until today. When asked to describe the picture today, she searched her memory, retrieved the encoded copy, and converted it into something like the original picture, which she then looked at and described . . . But do we do anything of the sort in our minds? . . . Where is behavior when an organism is not behaving? Where at the present moment, and in what form, is the behavior I exhibit when I am listening to music, eating my dinner, talking with a friend, taking an early morning walk, or scratching an itch? [Just as Mach might say, rhetorically, where is the oxygen in water when it drowns a swimmer, the hydrogen when it quenches a flame?] The observed facts are simple enough: I have acquired a repertoire of behavior, parts of which I display upon appropriate occasions. The metaphor of storage and retrieval goes well beyond these facts. (pp. 6–7)

Clearly, presentationalism reads better today as psychology than it does as chemistry.

Mentalistic positions such as psychoanalysis and cognitive psychology are representational in their approach to explanation. The information-processing approach to cognitive psychology might be taken as canonical for representational approaches in psychology, in that observable psychological phenomena are taken to be the outcome, product, or manifestation of information-processing mechanisms and processes that underlie them. Neobehaviorist theories, in which underlying mechanisms (described extensionally) are proposed as explanations for overt phenomena, are representational as well. Biopsychology uses the underlying molecular level of physiological processes to account for phenomena observable at the molar behavioral level. Skinner's radical behaviorism, as illustrated in the preceding quotation, is tenaciously presentational. And the trio of phenomenological, existential, and humanistic psychology shares this commitment to presentationalism.

A coordination of foundational distinctions in psychology

The commonsense/fresh-start distinction in conceptual foundations and the presentational/representational distinction in explanatory stance appear to be independent, and thus a simple matrix can be constructed in which the two dimensions are orthogonal. Such a matrix is proposed in Fig. 13.1. The four cells

		CONCEPTUAL FOUNDATIONS	
		Common-sense	Fresh-start
EXPLANATORY FOUNDATIONS	Presentational	Phenomenological, Existential, and Humanistic psychol.	Radical behaviorism Psychophysics
	Representational	Cognitive psychol. Psychoanalysis	Neobehaviorism Biopsychology

FIG. 13.1. The relationship between conceptual and explanatory foundations in psychological metatheory.

of the matrix specify four distinct possibilities for the construction of psychological theory, although the form of such theories remains in other ways unconstrained by the features of this analysis. Consequently, a variety of theories can occupy the cells of the matrix, and several candidates are proposed in the figure.

It should be immediately obvious that neither do all the theoretical positions of psychology fall neatly into the cells of this matrix, nor do all positions of the same generic "family" fall into the same cell. For example, humanistic psychology, although predominantly presentational, is characterized by one centrally significant representational concept, the idea of some sort of motivational force for psychological growth and wholeness. Radical behaviorism and methodological behaviorism, often considered to be slight variants on the same basic theme, are in fact as distinct from each other as are phenomenological and cognitive psychology, according to this scheme. And a position such as James Gibson's approach to perception, usually considered to be a cognitive theory, might conceivably be placed in the same general position as Skinner's behaviorism, at least in certain important respects. Some of these relationships have already come to the attention of others, e.g., Gibson's views have begun to receive attention in behavioristic journals (Rakover, 1983; Wilcox & Katz, 1981). Whereas the distinctions of the matrix are descriptive, it is at least interesting to speculate on what theoretical realignments might occur were this formal analysis to carry prescriptive force.

The foregoing analysis can be taken as a case for the possibility of psychological theory developed from the stance defined by each of the four cells of the matrix. It does not argue for the adequacy or inadequacy of any of the resulting theories. Arguments about the inadequacy of various kinds of theory are available in abundance elsewhere, and much of this argumentation is undoubtedly on the mark. Though detailed evaluation of such arguments is not on the agenda of this chapter, it *is* worth noting that such arguments are usually taken by their advocates to establish the wholesale inadequacy of their objects. But having a certain fondness for the scheme developed to this point, I am inclined to defend the legitimacy of *all* approaches defined in Fig. 13.1, at least as approaches to some subset of matters deserving psychological inquiry. In particular, it seems to me that something rather like behaviorism, and something rather like cognitivism, may eventually evolve to fit felicitously one with the other. For that, the remainder of this chapter attempts to build a case.

II. GETTING FROM FOLK PSYCHOLOGY TO PSYCHOLOGICAL SCIENCE

As noted earlier, intentional language is the normal means through which we talk about ourselves and each other. As we use the intentional to explain human action (e.g., "She did *x* because she knew it would outrage, and that, for her, is pleasure," or "He did *y* because he believed it would serve to gain him the approval of his peers which he so abjectly desired," or whatever) it is natural to seek an explanation for the intentional itself. If beliefs and desires are offered as the explanation for behavior, then what is the explanation of the beliefs and desires? The intentional, however, appears to lead inescapably into a regress. Davidson (1970) makes the point as follows:

> Suppose we try to say, not using any mental concepts, what it is for a man to believe there is life on Mars. One line we could take is this: when a certain sound is produced in the man's presence ["Is there life on Mars?"] he produces another ["Yes"]. But of course this shows he believes there is life on Mars only if he understands English, his production of the sound was intentional, and was a response to the sounds as meaning something in English; and so on. For each discovered deficiency, we add a new proviso. Yet no matter how we patch and fit the non-mental conditions, we always find the need for an additional condition [provided he *notices, understands,* etc.] that is mental in character. (p. 113)

Our naive psychology begins with the intentional idioms of ordinary language, and by this account we can't get beyond them. If this is absolutely so, then the prospect for any kind of psychological science seems doomed. Yet various ways out of this dilemma have been proposed. Two related approaches attempt to establish some manner in which the intentional is coordinated with the brain and its functions; a third approach is to establish the manner in which the intentional is coordinated with performance in the external world.

1. The Intentional in Direct Relation to the Brain.   One proposal is that the phenomena denoted in the intentional idioms of folk psychology stand in some sort of *direct* relationship to the physical structure and operation of the brain. All plausible psychological investigation is accomplished, according to this scheme, by philosophical analysis of folk psychology on the one hand, and by physiological investigation of the brain on the other. Whereas this approach makes physiological investigation of psychological problems plausible, it eliminates the need for any kind of a scientific psychology, if not making such a prospect completely incoherent. Searle (1983) seems to hold this view:

> mental states are both *caused by* the operations of the brain and *realized* in the structure of the brain (and the rest of the central nervous system). Once the possibility of mental and physical phenomena standing in both these relations is understood we have removed at least one major obstacle to seeing how mental states which are caused by brain states can also cause further brain states and mental states.
>
> But this model of 'caused by' and 'realized in' only raises the next question, how can Intentionality function causally? Granted that Intentional states can themselves be caused by and realized in the structure of the brain, how can Intentionality itself have any causal efficacy? When I raise my arm my intention in action causes my arm to go up. This is a case of a mental event causing a physical event. But, one might ask, how could such a thing occur? My arm going up is caused entirely by a series of neuron firings. We do not know where in the brain these firings originate, but they go at some point through the motor cortex and control a series of arm muscles which contract when the appropriate neurons fire. Now what has any mental event got to do with all of this? As with our previous questions, I want to answer this one by appealing to different levels of description of a substance, where the phenomena at each of the different levels function causally. (p. 265, p. 268)

If I read Searle correctly, he sees only *two* relevant levels of description: the intentional and the physical (i.e., neurophysiological). As I argue in point 2 to follow that cognitive psychology is concerned with a level of description *between* the two levels invoked by Searle, this view appears to be inhospitable to cognitive psychology.

Oddly enough, Skinner's view parallels Searle's in this important respect, except that Skinner would claim intentional descriptions themselves are defective and ought to be replaced by behavioral descriptions. The kinds of causal relations described as environment-behavior regularities then are realized in the physical organism in some currently unknown way, directly, without some additional intervening level of specification. For example, according to Skinner (1974):

> A person is changed by the contingencies of reinforcement under which he behaves; he does not store the contingencies. In particular, he does not store copies of the stimuli which have played a part in the contingencies. There are no 'iconic representations' in his mind; there are no 'data structures stored in his memory'; he has no 'cognitive map' of the world in which he has lived. He has simply been changed in such a way that stimuli now control particular kinds of perceptual behavior. (p. 84)

Similar remarks can be found repeatedly through Skinner's writings. But that is, to a degree, getting ahead of our story.

2. The Design of Intentional Systems.   If it is not the case that *nothing* stands between intentions and the brain, then it must be the case that *something* stands between intentions and the brain. That something is the *mind* according to the most popular current view, but for such an answer to be at all informative it is necessary to develop a satisfactory analysis of what the mind consists of, and how it relates on the one hand to intentions, and on the other to the brain.

Daniel Dennett, in his interesting book, *Brainstorms* (1978a), particularly in the essay, "Intentional systems," distinguishes among three stances that can be taken toward a complex system for the purpose of predicting its behavior. Such systems include humans and other organisms, to be sure, but are not necessarily restricted to them. The three stances, which by implication are the only ones leading to meaningful understanding of these complex systems, are identified as the "intentional stance," the "design stance," and the "physical stance." The intentional stance toward a complex system is just the stance one takes when ascribing to that system any of the intentional expressions of ordinary language, whereas the physical stance is directed at determining the actual physical states and processes of the mechanisms underlying intentionality. The design stance stands intermediate between these two concerns, however, and thus provides an answer to what it is that exists between the intentionality of human behavior on the one hand and the brain on the other.

The goal of the design stance is specification of the design of a mechanism (e.g., the brain) capable of delivering a given type of (intentional) performance. Designs are articulated in terms of functions, or in terms of component parts that serve functional roles. Contemporary cognitive psychology, under this interpretation, is in the business of "mind design" (Haugeland, 1981), and the information-processing model of mental functioning is the dominant model on which designs are based. One important consequence of the information-processing model, the computer metaphor, and explicit adoption of the design stance by scientific mentalism is a resolution of the Cartesian or dualistic problems that have plagued mentalistic theory in the past. The analysis of a system provided by a design is abstract, but it is not dualistic in the sense of postulating a kind of substance existing outside the natural world. Consequently, antidualist arguments against contemporary scientific mentalism seem to be beside the point.

Cognitive psychology, as the devising of design specifications for the functioning of the brain, seems to me to be a quest whose a priori plausibility is overwhelming. Who could possibly claim that the central nervous system as the mechanism underlying psychological phenomena is a designless system—a system undifferentiated in its parts and in the coordination of those parts? If there is a design to such a system, as there surely must be, then the search for it is a worthy endeavor.

Cognitive psychology is a kind of theoretical engineering, then. A fundamental difference between the design stance of the standard sort of engineer and that of the cognitive psychologist must be noted, however. Whereas a computer designer, or the designer of any other device for that matter, works up a design that provides a plan for the construction of a physical device, the cognitive scientist is presented with an immensely complex preexisting physical system that presumably operates on the principle of some unknown design, and through study of the performance of that system, attempts to reconstruct the design. The task is not without its hazards. A reputed text in cognitive psychology by John Anderson (1980) includes the following comments in the introductory chapter.

> The task of the cognitive psychologist is a highly inferential one. The cognitive psychologist must proceed from observations of the behavior of humans performing intellectual tasks to conclusions about the abstract mechanisms underlying the behavior. Developing a theory in cognitive psychology is much like developing a model for the working of the engine of a strange new vehicle by driving the vehicle, being unable to open it up to inspect the engine itself. (p. 12)
>
> It is well understood from automata theory . . . that many different mechanisms can generate the same external behavior. (p. 17)

The seriousness of these problems is hard to determine. One might think that the test of time and experience will sort out the issue most effectively, although some have attempted to evaluate through argument alone the possibility of success for the cognitive program (e.g., Haugeland, 1978). Fodor (1983) has made a case that the cognitive psychology of the forseeable future will find success in the analysis of what he calls ''input systems'' but for various reasons is fated to failure in analysis of ''central systems,'' those systems including much of the traditional subject matter of mentalistic theory, such as long-term memory and problem solving. On the other hand, neurobiologists are in the process of developing designs with a bottom-up strategy (see, e.g., Shepherd, 1983, for countless examples), as distinct from the top-down strategy of cognitivism, with success that is hard for even the most diehard skeptic of mind designing to deny. So arguments against cognitivism might be most convincing if they are directed at a top-down-only constraint, or at limitations of the information-processing/computational model, rather than at the very idea of design.

3. The Performance of Intentional Systems. So much for strategies of explicating intentionality by moving into the brain and its design features. Dennett assumes that is the only direction to move from the intentional stance, but there he is wrong. One can move out into the world, as well. Suppose one sees a chicken cross the road. Of course, one can attribute to it beliefs and desires (that is, intentionality; see Dennett, 1983, for a serious proposal of the efficacy of talking about animals with ordinary intentional concepts) and attempt to account for its behavior in that manner. But if attributing beliefs and desires to the chicken is unsatisfactory because it leaves unexplained the working of the beliefs and desires themselves, a psychologist is not limited to postulating designs for a believing/desiring/road-crossing mechanism. One can, for instance, attempt to map out the kinds of conditions whereby a chicken comes to believe it is desirable to cross the road. What does the environment have to be like for the chicken to believe this (perhaps there has to be food across the road), and what does the chicken have to do in that environment to believe it (perhaps the chicken has to see the food across the road), and what must the chicken have done in past situations so that the present environment is sufficient to induce the belief (perhaps it has to have had certain kinds of experience with successfully crossing the road to eat food)? Similarly, one can raise questions about the chicken's desire— what causes a desire leading to road crossing, and what satisfies it, and how much is required to satisfy it? Dealing with this kind of question naturally gives rise to further questions: What will the chicken do if there is food on *both* sides of the road, and what will it do if the quantities of food differ? Here, intentional stance intuitions lose their way entirely, and psychologists who have been interested in such questions have found that the mentalistic vocabulary of the intentional stance hinders more than helps. A good name for the position just characterized is the *performance stance,* and it is the stance taken by radical behaviorism.

To spell out this tactic somewhat more formally, consider Wittgenstein's (1953) conundrum, "When I raise my arm what is left over if I subtract the fact that my arm goes up?" (para. 621). What is left over, or more properly, what further needs to be said, depends on whether or not one is stretching to relieve a cramp, emphasizing a philosophical point, casting a vote, obtaining a book from a high shelf, and so on indefinitely. To the behaviorist, careful individuation of these cases requires detailed specification of three further considerations: (1) the nature of the antecedent (pre-arm-raising) environmental context and its functional relation to behavior; (2) the nature of environmental conditions contingently consequential to arm raising and their functional relations to behavior; (3) and a range of extraepisodic historical circumstances to which the episodic functional relations can be traced causally. If one raises one's arm to reach for a book, for instance, then the important antecedent context is the presence of the shelf of books; and the important consequential condition is the presence of the book in one's grasp. Extraepisodic factors include having placed the book on the shelf previously, or having seen it there, or something equivalently responsible for the shelf being where one directs one's reach for the particular book in question; and conditions that have established the contingent consequence as the kind of event that can functionally individuate the associated class of antecedent consequence-producing movements, such as having just been asked, "Do you have a copy of James' *Principles* I could look at?"

I have quite knowingly continued to use intentional terms in these further specifications, anticipating that a criticism along the lines of Davidson's remarks is unavoidable. Here is the best answer I can give. Concerning operant experimental research, Dennett (1978a) says "Skinner's experimental design is supposed to eliminate the intentional, but it merely masks it" (p. 15), an assessment whose chief virtue is that of being precisely dead wrong. The intentionality of behavior, in Brentano's sense of its directedness, is just what operant behaviorism is about. The experimental design of the operant conditioning chamber is meant to peel the intentionality of overt action back to its barest bones to expose its most vital ingredients, a purpose quite the opposite of masking it. Pressing a lever is little different from that venerable example of raising one's arm, after all, though it might convincingly be claimed that 50 years of almost exclusive attention to such a case is about enough. What in fact Dennett is getting at in his criticism is that the richness, the complexity, the subtlety, the nuances of meaning in full-blown human intentionality are eliminated in the operant conditioning chamber. Proust could not have written much of a novel from the point of view of the laboratory rat, one imagines. The simplification is a matter of standard scientific practice, however, and has nothing to do with the nature of behaviorism as such. One could address the same charge, with equal justification, to the cognitive scientist's reaction-time apparatus. The real issue dividing cognitivism and behaviorism concerns the most effective *concepts* to deploy in *describing* and *analyzing* the complex features of human and animal functioning naively marked off by intentional concepts, not to endorse or deny the presence of these features.

The behaviorist, then, is interested in many of the *same* phenomena as the mentalist. Furthermore, being just as much a member of the community of ordinary-language speakers as is the mentalist, he is conversant in ordinary-language mentalistic talk. For the purposes of behavior analysis, however, he attempts a description in terms of the mode of interaction of behavior and environment. In doing so, he does not first describe these phenomena in intentional/mentalistic language and then formulate some logical translation into behavioral language. That is logical behaviorism, a position that at times has mistakenly been conflated with radical behaviorism. For example, Fodor (1968) states: "the propositions that enunciate the radical behaviorist's reductions of mental to behavioral predicates are supposed to be analytic" (p. 155; but it is possible that Fodor does not have Skinner in mind here). Rather than "reducing" mental to behavioral predicates, the radical behaviorist simply proposes a new way of talking about behavior, including the phenomena ordinarily described mentalistically. The adequacy of such behavior talk then can be evaluated in its own right, not in terms of the analyticity of purported reduction sentences (see Day, 1977).

The behaviorist attempts to move directly from psychological phenomena to talk about these phenomena in terms of the manner in which the subject is relating to and has related to the world. In doing so, the concepts used are pretty much about the world, and not much about the psychology of the inner being. It is, of course, entirely possible that some important features of intentional phenomena fall through the cracks of the worldly language of the behaviorist. I would never hazard to claim that all worth telling about intentional phenomena can be told in the language of behaviorism (though perhaps Skinner would make this claim), because all that is needed to justify behaviorism is to establish that a good deal of very interesting stuff can be found out that way, stuff that tends not to be found out any other way.

The complementarity of design and performance

It should be clear that the design stance and the performance stance are after different kinds of analysis, but not analyses that necessarily conflict with one another. The development of mental designs has tended to follow what Fodor (1983) calls the "divide and conquer" strategy (p. 1): Because the complexity of human functioning is so great, it is likely to be most effective to approach the mind as a set of separate subunits each of which can be studied relatively independently. Consequently, cognitive psychology is often broken down into study of such subunits of mind as perception, memory, language, and thought. The integration of cognitive models into a comprehensive theory of mind is still in the future; the most comprehensive box-and-arrow models still leave the organism as a processor of inputs, not the performer of actions (see Fig. 13.2-A).

Behaviorism, on the other hand, takes an extreme molar view of the functioning of the organism as a whole. As such, the functional subunits mediating behavior-environment interactions are collapsed into an undifferentiated interaction. The behaviorist focuses his or her analytical eye on the organism-environment interface where, it turns out, many complex things happen as well. If, by Anderson's (1980) metaphor, cognitive psychology is "like developing a model for the working of the engine of a strange new vehicle, being unable to open it up to inspect the engine itself" (p. 12), then behaviorism is much like developing a driver's manual for such a vehicle, the manual directed at the driver who is inclined to leave tinkering under the hood strictly to professionals. (And a good practicing behaviorist, an *applied* behaviorist, is one who can win at Indianapolis in such a vehicle.) Although behaviorists are not particularly keen on box-and-arrow models, to the extent that they are used they tend to look like Fig. 13.2-B. The organism box is empty in the behaviorist model, not because its contents are deemed unimportant, but because they are taken to be the subject of another discipline (neurophysiology, primarily). About that, of course, the cognitivist who wants to fill the box with a mental design disagrees. But the behaviorist can be effectively agnostic vis-a-vis the program of the cognitivist. So no conflict necessarily exists between the two models in Fig. 13.2; they seem to offer the possibility of fitting together quite nicely. It is even possible that some day cognitivists will get to the point of proposing designs capable of generating the kind of performance in which behaviorists are interested.

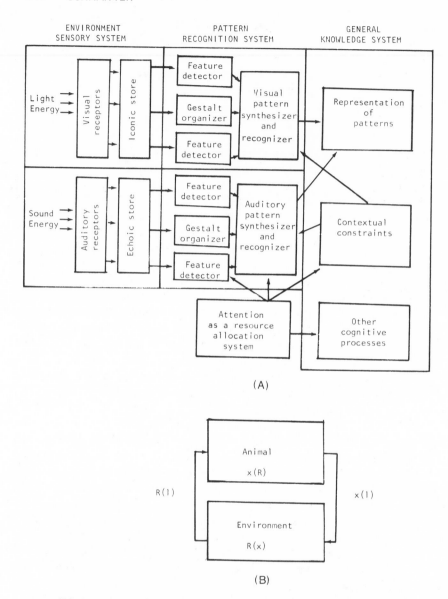

(A)

(B)

FIG. 13.2. (A) An information flow diagram indicating the processing of information from initial input to the "general-knowledge system." (From Anderson 1980, p. 57) (B) A depiction of feedback and control functions indicating the effects of behavior on the environment and the effects of the environmental changes produced by behavior on subsequent behavior. (From Staddon, 1980, p. 104)

Cognitive psychologists are interested in developing and evaluating the designs for mechanisms that are capable of performing certain sorts of tasks. The dominant position in contemporary cognitive psychology conceives these tasks to be the processing of information, although the design stance and the goals of scientific mentalism are not necessarily constrained to this approach. Behaviorists, on the other hand, are interested in developing analyses of the relationships between context and performance, between environment and behavior. One approach is directed at the computational processes of the internal mechanism that delivers an observable performance; the other approach is directed at the pattern of adaptation that emerges in the interaction between the activity of a subject organism and its environment. The concerns are different, but not antagonistic.

Some limitations of pure performance and design approaches

Indeed, it can be argued that a *complete* psychology requires both behaviorism and mentalism, as each encounters limitations. Consider behaviorism first. Behaviorism by its very nature cannot succeed in a functional analysis of any feature of performance that is a function of environmentally independent properties of the internal mechanisms generating the behavior. There are two kinds of illustrative case, one in which behavior is invariant regardless of environmental change, the other where behavior is changeable within the limits of the controllable constancy of the environment (including the historical environment). To illustrate the first case with a relatively trivial but quite clear-cut example, Premack (1965) has suggested that rats lick a drinking tube at an invariant rate of seven licks per second. Whereas the molar relationship between the occurrence of bouts of licking and environmental circumstances can be analyzed from the performance stance, to the extent that licking consists of the turning on and off of an internal "licking motor" that runs at invariant speed, the molecular features of lick rate will be resistant to anything but narrative description from the performance stance.

In the second kind of case, behavior needs to vary unpredictably within the confines of constant environmental conditions. This is a softer boundary condition than the first case, because ad hoc and hypothetical variations in environments, particularly historical environments that are inaccessible, can always be postulated to account for observed differences. The most frequently encountered example is the novelty of expression in human language. Skinner's (1957) functional categories of verbal behavior seem to work best at the most molar level (roughly, suggesting *what* it is that gives someone something to say, and *when* it is that someone will say it) and at a quite molecular level (suggesting plausible processes behind oddities like accidentally saying "Minnesnowta" during a Minneapolis blizzard). But it really is entirely hopeless for this analysis of verbal behavior to predict anything worthwhile about the detailed semantic and syntactic structure that will show itself to a simple, standardized condition like the request, "Say aloud whatever comes into your mind right now."

Complements of these two limitations also apply to mentalism. In the first case mental state is constant between instances whereas environmental conditions vary, with consequent variation in behavior. In the second case, mental state varies between instances whereas environment remains constant, with a resulting constancy in behavior. A simple sort of illustration of the first case can be seen in noting that what any given behavior "counts as" is often dependent on external circumstances rather than internal states. Smith may be as much intent on winning the 100-meter dash today as tomorrow, but today someone is faster, whereas tomorrow's race is populated with duffers. Smith loses today but wins tomorrow, even though her mental state is invariant across races. In the second case, suppose that Jones stammers whenever he has to report to his boss. But over the weekend he has read a book on the power of positive thinking and enters Monday's meeting having resolutely made up his mind not to stammer. Yet he stammers anyway. Although this latter example has been developed from the point of view of presentational rather than representational mentalism, equivalent limiting cases can be developed for representational mentalism as well. For more extended analysis, see Schnaitter (1984).

Whereas much of the continuing tension between behaviorism and mentalism arises in skirmishes and boundary disputes over the sort of case outlined previously, the contrast as well as ultimate complementarity of approaches becomes most clear in examining the treatment of phenomena equally within the pale of each. Comprehension of ambiguous sentences is such a case. Much has been made by psycholinguists of "They are flying planes," "They are cooking apples," and the like. Each of these sentences has at least two obvious and distinct meanings, but the meanings cannot be differentially assigned on the basis of terminal strings alone. The strategy of mentalism is to make the assignment on the basis of the means whereby a putative linguistic mechanism might generate equivalent terminal strings from distinctly different initial material (i.e., from different deep structures). Comprehension might then engage such a mechanism in reverse, as it were, via a sort of hypothesis test. Behaviorists, in contrast, find it derelict to discuss meanings of sentences, ambiguous or not, outside their contexts of origin. If an ambiguous sentence has been contrived by a linguist (as have been most textbook examples of ambiguity), then it is "constructed" verbal behavior, on a par with "This sentence is false" and other verbal parlor tricks. The behaviorist's attitude is that such contrivances have about as much relevance to understanding language as lithographs by Escher do to understanding the geometry of the natural world. But if it is a natural language utterance, then the ambiguity will usually turn out to be an artifact of extracting it from its (disambiguating) natural context. If one has just asked Uncle Sid, "What are little Becky and Auntie Maude doing this afternoon?," then the word "They" that initiates the response "They are flying planes" is taken to mean "little Becky and Auntie Maude" before any of the rest of the utterance is heard, and ambiguity never arises. Any interpretation other than "little Becky and Auntie Maude" would be anomalous given the practices of normal, nonpathological discourse.

The point of such an illustration is to contrast the modes of understanding offered by mentalism and behaviorism, without claiming the superiority of one mode or the other. Even though context may disambiguate natural occurrences of utterances that, in isolation, appear ambiguous, an underlying linguistic mechanism is just as surely required of verbal creatures in the behaviorist's world as in the mentalist's; and though only an organism with a functioning linguistic parser will comprehend, it is likely that such a parser is responsive to much more that people see and hear than the purified and impoverished word strings admitted as input within the usual linguistic account. Whatever they are and however they work, the internal mechanisms required for language comprehension must be complex. Much of the apparent mystery of their operation, however, might be evaporated by a more forthright treatment of the contribution of the external context within which utterances understood in ordinary discourse normally occur.

Concluding remarks

The eventual relationship between mentalism and behaviorism might be illuminated by considering a parallel in another discipline. I am told by my colleagues in biology that during the 1950s, when molecular biology was in first bloom and the possibility of unraveling the biochemistry of all cellular processes was beginning to be realized at an ever-accelerating rate, environmental biology fell completely out of fashion. Departments of biology stopped making appointments in that subfield, and those already on board were seen as an embarrassment. After all, how could any thoroughly modern biologist maintain professional self-respect when a colleague was known to frolic over a meadow mapping foraging patterns of honey bees? One simply wanted to disown such tomfoolery. Of course, that attitude has changed today. Environmental biology is again a respected part of the professional biological community along with molecular biology and other specialities, and no one feels the worse for it. It is clear today that both environmental biology and molecular biology address significant disciplinary concerns, and that the problems of each are not well addressed by the methods and concepts of the other. The resource allocation of a plant is determined by studying the relationship between environmental factors such as light, water, and nutrient availability, and responses of the plant in the allocation of its finite energy resources to foliage, flowering, and seed sets. Any attempt to determine these relationships by studying DNA structures would be foolhardy. I think this analogy between biology and psychology—between environmental biology and the performance stance of behaviorism on the one hand and molecular biology and the design stance of mentalism on the other—has considerable merit. Indeed, behaviorists seem increasingly sensitive to parallels between their concerns and those of evolutionary biology (e.g., Skinner, 1981; Staddon, 1980), and Dennett has commented on the parallel between cognitive psychology and molecular biology (Dennett, 1978a, pp. 102–104). Perhaps, in another decade or two, behaviorism and mentalism can also come to see themselves as working on different but complementary aspects of our complex and fascinating field.

ACKNOWLEDGMENTS

Preparation of this chapter was made possible through the generosity of Illinois Wesleyan University in providing me with a sabbatical leave, and through the hospitality of New York University during that leave. The analysis offered here was developed over a number of years in teaching a course titled "Contemporary Psychology in Perspective," and I have benefited from the interaction with a number of my students. A preliminary version of this chapter was presented at Temple University in December, 1983.

REFERENCES

Anderson, J. R. (1980). *Cognitive psychology and its implications*. San Francisco: W. H. Freeman.
Blackmore, J. T. (1972). *Ernst Mach*. Los Angeles: University of California Press.
Block, N. (Ed.). (1980). *Readings in philosophy of psychology* (Vol. 1). Cambridge, MA: Harvard University Press.
Brentano, F. (1874). *Psychologie vom empirischen Standpunkt*. Vienna.
Chisholm, R. M. (1957). *Perceiving*. Ithaca, NY: Cornell University Press.
Chisholm, R. M. (1967). Intentionality. In P. Edwards (Ed.), *The encyclopedia of philosophy* (Vol. 4). New York: Crowell–Collier & Macmillan.
Chomsky, N. (1959). Review of Skinner's "Verbal Behavior." *Language, 35*, 26–58.
Davidson, D. (1970). Mental events. In L. Foster & J. W. Swanson (Eds.), *Experience and theory*. Amherst: University of Massachusetts Press.
Day, W. F., Jr. (1977). On Skinner's treatment of the first-person, third-person psychological sentence distinction. *Behaviorism, 5*, 33–37.
Day, W. F., Jr. (1980). The historical antecedents of contemporary behaviorism. In R. W. Rieber & K. Salzinger (Eds.), *Psychology: Theoretical-historical perspectives*. New York: Academic Press.
Dennett, D. C. (1978a). *Brainstorms*. Montgomery, VT: Bradford Books.
Dennett, D. C. (1978b). Current issues in the philosophy of mind. *American Philosophical Quarterly, 15*(4), 249–261.
Dennett, D. C. (1983). Intentional systems in cognitive ethology: The "Panglossian paradigm" defended. *The Behavioral and Brain Sciences, 6*, 343–390.
Fodor, J. A. (1968). *Psychological explanation*. New York: Random House.
Fodor, J. A. (1983). *Modularity of mind*. Cambridge: Massachusetts Institute of Technology Press.
Haugeland, J. (1978). The nature and plausibility of cognitivism. *The Behavioral and Brain Sciences, 1*, 215–226.

Haugeland, J. (Ed.). (1981). *Mind design.* Montgomery, VT: Bradford Books.

Hempel, C. G. (1966). *Philosophy of natural science.* Englewood Cliffs, NJ: Prentice–Hall.

Kant, I. (1909). Critical examination of practical reason. In T. K. Abbott (Trans.), *Critique of practical reason and other works.* New York: Longmans. (Originally published, 1788)

Koch, S. (1976). Language communities, search cells, and the psychological studies. In J. K. Cole & W. J. Arnold (Eds.), *Nebraska Symposium on Motivation* (Vol. 23). Lincoln: University of Nebraska Press.

Kuhn, T. S. (1962). *The structure of scientific revolutions.* Chicago: University of Chicago Press.

Mischel, T. (1976). Psychological explanations and their vicissitudes. In J. K. Cole & W. J. Arnold (Eds.), *Nebraska Symposium on Motivation* (Vol. 23). Lincoln: University of Nebraska Press.

Mishler, E. G. (1975). Skinnerism: Materialism minus the dialectic. *Journal for the Theory of Social Behavior, 6,* 21–47.

Premack, D. (1965). Reinforcement theory. In D. Levine (Ed.), *Nebraska Symposium on Motivation* (Vol. 13). Lincoln: University of Nebraska Press.

Quine, W. (1960). *Word and object.* Cambridge: Massachusetts Institute of Technology Press.

Rachlin, H., & Burkhard, B. (1978). The temporal triangle: Response substitution in instrumental conditioning. *Psychological Review, 85* (1), 22–47.

Rakover, S. S. (1983). In defense of memory viewed as stored mental representation. *Behaviorism, 11,* 53–62.

Rorty, R. (1979). *Philosophy and the mirror of nature.* Princeton, NJ: Princeton University Press.

Schnaitter, R. (1978). Circularity, trans-situationality, and the law of effect. *The Psychological Record, 28,* 353–362.

Schnaitter, R. (1984). Behavior as a function of internal states and external circumstances. In *Symposium on Analysis and Integration of Behavioral Units.* St. Paul, MN.

Scriven, M. (1957). A study of radical behaviorism. In H. Feigl & M. Scriven (Eds.), *Minnesota studies in the philosophy of science* (Vol. 1). Minneapolis: University of Minnesota Press.

Searle, J. (1979). What is an intentional state? *Mind, 138,* 74–92.

Searle, J. R. (1983). *Intentionality.* New York: Cambridge University Press.

Segal, E. M., & Lachman, R. (1972). Complex behavior on high mental process: Is there a paradigm shift? *American Psychologist, 27*(1), 46–55.

Sellars, W. (1963). *Science, perception, and reality.* New York: Routledge & Kegan Paul.

Shepherd, G. M. (1983). *Neurobiology.* New York: Oxford University Press.

Skinner, B. F. (1938). *The behavior of organisms.* New York: Appleton-Century-Crofts.

Skinner, B. F. (1957). *Verbal behavior.* New York: Appleton-Century-Crofts.

Skinner, B. F. (1974). *About behaviorism.* New York: Knopf.

Skinner, B. F. (1977). Why I am not a cognitive psychologist. *Behaviorism, 5*(2), 1–10.

Skinner, B. F. (1981). Selection by consequences. *Science, 213* (4507), 501–504.

Smart, J. J. C. (1963). *Philosophy, and scientific realism.* New York: Routledge & Kegan Paul.

Staddon, J. E. R. (Ed.). (1980). *Limits to action: The allocation of individual behavior.* New York: Academic Press.

Wann, T. W. (Ed.). (1964). *Behaviorism and phenomenology.* Chicago: University of Chicago Press.

Watson, R. I. (1967). Psychology: A prescriptive science. *American Psychologist, 22*(6), 435–443.

Wheeler, H. (Ed.). (1973). *Beyond the punitive society.* San Francisco: W. H. Freeman.

Wilcox, S., & Katz, S. (1981). A direct realistic alternative to the traditional conception of memory. *Behaviorism, 9,* 227–239.

Wittgenstein, L. (1953). *Philosophical investigations.* New York: Macmillan.

Author Index

Numbers in *italics* denote pages with complete bibliographic information.

A

Abelson, P. H., 274, *287*
Adelson, B., 277, *287*
Albert, M. L., 244, *262*
Allen, R. B., 269, *287*
Allport, F. H., 14, *32*
Amsterdam, B. K., 101, 103, *106*
Anderson, J. R., 23, *32*, 49, 51, 70, *74, 75,*
  99, *106*, 228, 229, *241*, 306, 309, 310, *314*
Anderson, R. C., 28, *32*
Anson, R., 202, 206, 207, 208, 209, *220, 221*
Anzai, Y., 278, *287*
Arieti, S., 98, *106*
Aristotle, *2, 3*
Ashby, F. G., 54, 55, *77*
Atkinson, R. C., 48, *74*, 250, *261*
Attneave, F., 21, 22, *32*, 84, 90, 165, 167,
  184
Atwood, M. E., 269, 277, *288, 289*
Ausbel, D. P., 28, *32*
Austin, G. A., *32*, 97, *106*

B

Baddeley, A. D., 49, *74*, 271, *287*
Baer, D. M., 93, 97, *107*
Baker, E., 250, *261*
Balda, R. P., 131, 132, *133, 135*

Banks, W., 172, 173, *184, 187*
Barker, R. G., 137, *155*
Barnard, P. J., 275, *287*
Barrett, J., 238, *241*
Bath, K., 97, *107*
Battig, W. F., 29, *32*
Baxley, N., 94, *106*
Beck, J., 159, *184*
Benary, W., 199, 209, 210, *219*
Benson, S. B., 102, *108*
Benton, A., 232, *241*
Beranek, L. L., 271, *287*
Berlo, D. K., 22, *32*
Berndt, R. S., 256, *261*
Bever, T. G., 111, 124, *135*
Bierwisch, M., 257, *265*
Bikson, T. K., 274, *287*
Bindra, D., 246, *264*
Bingham, G., 137, *156*
Bisiach, E., 237, *241*, 249, *261*
Bitterman, M. E., 128, *133*
Blackman, D. E., 116, 123, 133, *134*
Blackmore, J. T., 300, *314*
Block, N., 72, *74*, 246, *314*
Blough, D., 100, *106*
Blumstein, S. E., 257, *266*
Bobrow, D. G., 55, 56, *74, 76*
Bolles, R. C., 115, *134*

317

Subject Index

A

abstraction, 80
Administrative Behavior, 26
affordances, 147–148, 153
agency, 297–299
agnosia, 231
algorithm, 68, 225, 228
ambient optic array, 141–144
ambiguous sentences, 312
amnesia, 249–254
amodal completion, 214
analogue-propositional imagery debate, 229
analytic/holistic distinction, criticisms of, 246–247
animals, *also see* pigeons
　learning, 111
　memory, 118–128
　self-awareness, 124–127
　temporal sensitivity, 123
　why study, 127–128
aphasia, 243, *see* Broca's, Wernicke's
applied behaviorist, 309
applied psychology, 267, 270
Aristotle, 2, 3, 148
artificial intelligence, 224
　strong, 68, 71–73
　weak, 68–69
assimilation effect, 193
association, 79, 173, 232
associationism, 6, 292

Aquinas, St. Thomas, 4
attentional deficits, 245
auditory cortex, 240
Augustine, St., 4
autobiographical memory, 251–252
automatic chaining, 102
awareness, 90

B

behavior, 81, 85, 102, 113, 126, 305, 310–311
　adaptive function, 131
　novel, 93–98
　operant, 83, 297, 308
　repertoires, 95, 96
　rule-governed, 87
　units of, 93
　variation in, 95
Behavioral & Information Technology, 274
behaviorism, 14, 28, 42, 60–65, 91, 244, 291–303, 311
　logical 308
　methodological, 60–62, 115, 302
　neo, 61, 292, 301
　purposive, 62
　radical, 60–62, 72, 112, 114, 116–118, 122, 126, 297–298, 300–303
　theoretical, 60
　Watsonian, 13, 60, 113

linguistic fallacy, 7
localization, 244, 258–260
Locke, John, 6
logic, 10, 11
Luria, A. R., 259

M

Mach, E., 300
mapping theories, 44–47, 66
Marr, D., 178, 226–227
matching to sample, 119, 121
maze behavior, 120
meaning, 17
memory, 85–86, 91, 118–129, 152, 154, 248,
    249, 269, 271, 306
  autobiographical, 251–252
  effortful, 253–255
  perception, 148
  representations, 277
  scanning, 122
  semantic vs. episodic, 250–251
  spatial, 131–132
  visual, 236
mental
  apparatus, 88
  concept, 7, 294–297, 303
  events, 40, 60–61, 67, 71, 223
  processes, 72
  rotation, 229
  vs. nonmental, 294–297
  surrogates, 85
mentalism, 291–292, 305, 311, *also see*
    cognitivism
menu-based retrieval system, 273
method, 99, 117
methodological behaviorism, *see* behaviorism
Mill, J. S., 6–7, 8
Miller, G. A., 21
mind, 18, 41, 44, 69–72, 81, 84, 99, 295,
    305
  blindness, 231–232
  body, 3, 38, 55–57, 70, 294–297
  measures, 98–110
  theories of, 62, 309
mirrors, 102–104, 124–127
modular design, 224
Molière, 88–89
mood, 294
Moore, T. V., 16
motivation, 212

N

NMR (nuclear magnetic resonance), 231
Nativism, 5, 161–162
naming, 258
natural selection, 129
necessity, 3, 8
Necker cube, 168
neolocalization, 259
neurological deficits, 230, *also see* brain
    damage
neuropsychological
  data, 229, 231, 234, 239
  explanation, 298
  laboratories, 244
neuropsychology, 230–233
  history of, 243–245
  limitations of, 233
Newell, A., 20, 24
novelty, 93–98

O

occluding edges, 145–146
ontology, 1
operant behavior, 83, 297, 308
operant chamber, 308
optical structure, 144
ordinary language philosophy, 29
organism-environment interface, 309
organization, 173–174, 213

P

PET (positron emission tomography), 231, 240
paired associate learning, 272
Palmer, S. E., 166
parietal-lobe brain damage, 234, 246
parsimony, 101
parts and wholes, 169, 173, 246–249
pattern perception, 168
Pavlov, I., 80
perceiving, 144, 148
perception, 138, 142, 148, 154, 161, 170,
    191, 205, 219
  cognition, 138, 151–155, 189–191
  direct, 65–66
Perception and Cognition, 23
perceptional rationalization, 208
percepts, 4, 9–11, 150, 217
perceptual
  completion, 213
  grain, 170–172